DISRUPTING DIGNITY

D1529131

LGBTQ POLITICS

General Editors: Susan Burgess and Heath Fogg Davis

Disrupting Dignity: Rethinking Power and Progress in LGBTQ Lives
Stephen M. Engel and Timothy S. Lyle

Disrupting Dignity

Rethinking Power and Progress in LGBTQ Lives

Stephen M. Engel and Timothy S. Lyle

NEW YORK UNIVERSITY PRESS

New York

NEW YORK UNIVERSITY PRESS
New York
www.nyupress.org

References to Internet websites (URLs) were accurate at the time of writing. Neither the author nor New York University Press is responsible for URLs that may have expired or changed since the manuscript was prepared.

Library of Congress Cataloging-in-Publication Data

Names: Engel, Stephen M., author. | Lyle, Timothy S., author.
Title: Disrupting dignity : rethinking power and progress in LGBTQ lives / Stephen M.
    Engel and Timothy S. Lyle.
Description: New York : NYU Press, 2021. | Series: LGBTQ politics | Includes bibliographi-
    cal references and index.
Identifiers: LCCN 2020049521 | ISBN 9781479852031 (hardback) | ISBN 9781479899869
    (paperback) | ISBN 9781479833740 (ebook) | ISBN 9781479836161 (ebook other)
Subjects: LCSH: Sexual minorities—United States—History. | Sexual minorities—United
    States—Social conditions. | Gay rights—United States—History. | Dignity.
Classification: LCC HQ76.25 .E54 2021 | DDC 306.760973—dc23
LC record available at https://lccn.loc.gov/2020049521

New York University Press books are printed on acid-free paper, and their binding materials are chosen for strength and durability. We strive to use environmentally responsible suppliers and materials to the greatest extent possible in publishing our books.

Manufactured in the United States of America

10 9 8 7 6 5 4 3 2 1

Also available as an ebook

CONTENTS

Introduction

On November 14, 2019, the New York City Council transferred jurisdiction over Hart Island from the Department of Correction to the
Department of Parks and Recreation. It also passed legislation requiring the Department of Transportation to construct plans to increase
public access to the island.[1] Parts of Hart Island have functioned as
a public cemetery, a final resting place for many unknown, indigent, or
unclaimed individuals since the late nineteenth century. In the 1980s, the
bodies of many who died from AIDS were interred there in mass graves.
Because so much was unknown about the disease in the early years
of the epidemic, these bodies were buried apart from others, segregated
to the southern part of the island. Aside from a marker for the first
child to die from AIDS in New York City, visitors will find no
gravestones—no way to know who is buried there, when they were born,
and when they passed on.[2] As Council Speaker Corey Johnson tweeted
after this legislation passed, the city council offered AIDS victims "a
more respectful, more dignified resting place" than they were provided
when they died.[3]

By centering dignity in the rationale for and as a consequence of
the council's actions, Johnson's tweet illustrates how these policies may
function as restitution, as an attempt to restore the dignity once denied
to many gay, transgender, and queer people in the 1980s. They work
perhaps as a public acknowledgment of wrongdoing, of apology, and of
making amends. Furthermore, Johnson's tweet compels us to ask what
exactly dignity connotes, how it may be acknowledged, how and to
what end it might be denied, whether it can be restored and by whom,
and what purpose the bestowal and acknowledgment of dignity serves.

Denials of dignity and later attempts at restitution are not only evident in policy actions but also apparent in jurisprudence. For example,
when the United States Supreme Court ruled in 2003 that same-sex intimacy between two consenting adults could not be criminalized without

running afoul of the Constitution, one legal observer characterized the ruling to be "as close as the Court would ever get to an apology to gay and lesbian Americans for the wrong, and for the harm, it had done to them."[4] That decision—*Lawrence v. Texas*—emphasized an individual's dignity to choose how to express intimacy in connection with another.[5] A decade later, in *United States v. Windsor*, the Court would affirm the dignity of same-sex loving couples by declaring unconstitutional the federal refusal to acknowledge their state-sanctioned marriages.[6] In 2015, the Court would go further, ruling in *Obergefell v. Hodges* that no state government could deny the dignity of a same-sex couple by refusing to grant or recognize their marriage.[7]

Even when LGBTQ+ rights advocates did not see victory in the Supreme Court's 2018 ruling in *Masterpiece Cakeshop v. Colorado Civil Rights Commission*, which involved the denial of commercial services to a same-sex couple—a seeming affront to what the Court had previously called their "equal dignity"—the decision nevertheless rhetorically affirmed the dignity of gays and lesbians.[8] Justice Anthony Kennedy, who spoke for the majority in every pro-gay Supreme Court ruling while he served on the Court, noted in *Masterpiece* that "our society has come to the recognition that gay persons and gay couples cannot be treated as social outcasts or as inferior in dignity and worth."[9]

While the New York City Council's actions connect dignity with some conception of respect and the Supreme Court's rulings have linked dignity with a concept of worth or individual agency, a recent piece of queer popular culture tethers dignity to visibility and recognition. In June 2019, Netflix released the miniseries *Tales of the City*.[10] The show drew inspiration from a set of novels by Armistead Maupin that details the lives of Mary Ann Singleton, Michael Tolliver, and the other residents of 28 Barbary Lane, all of which transpire under the eye of their trans matriarch and landlord, Anna Madrigal. Set primarily in San Francisco of the 1970s and 1980s, earlier televised versions were produced by PBS and Showtime.[11] However, this most recent Netflix adaptation, timed to premiere during the fiftieth anniversary celebrations of the Stonewall riots of 1969, was set in the present day.

While the plot—like that of many of Maupin's novels—revolved around mysteries with Dickensian twists, this Netflix version also illustrated how much racism, sexism, and anti-transgender bias persist within the LGBTQ+ communities despite advances made. In an exemplary scene, the twentysomething African American boyfriend (Ben) of the fiftysomething central character (Michael) is chided by older cisgender gay white men when he calls attention to the importance of not using derogatory terms like *tranny* for members of our community. Ben asserts, "What you call someone is important. It is about dignity. It is about visibility. I think we owe that to people."[12] The statement moves beyond an important claim about transgender inclusion and even beyond a critical narrative device to highlight intergenerational conflict, especially as the older men, in response, bristle and point to their own struggles with discrimination during the AIDS crisis of the 1980s and 1990s—before Ben may have even been born. The statement also critically captures a theme of the series—namely, that dignity comes from being *seen*, from being recognized by others as having value. In the final episode, Michael emphasizes this idea when he reflects on what Anna has always provided him: "Once you feel seen like Anna Madrigal makes you feel seen, you don't want to leave."[13]

In these examples drawn from public policy, law, and pop cultural representation, dignity has numerous meanings or synonyms. Regardless of whether dignity connotes respect, worth, agency, or recognition, we can say that within the cultural, political, and legal imagination, dignity is having a moment. The word pervades our discourse, and in particular, it has become a discursive and jurisprudential basis to advocate for LGBTQ+ rights. With this in mind, we offer some vital questions: How has the word been invoked? Who has done so and to what end? How has the term been embraced or treated with skepticism by those within LGBTQ+ communities? Should the recognition of LGBTQ+ peoples as dignified be a cause for celebration or, ironically, a cause for concern? Put differently, does the recognition of the dignity of LGBTQ+ individuals expand the boundaries of equality and foster inclusion, or does it mark and maintain new boundaries of respectability, delimiting who has value and who remains unvalued?

We start with a seemingly simple question, which does not have an easy answer: What is dignity? We contend, first, that the word does not have a stable meaning, and we do not attempt to provide it with one; instead, we explore how the word is deployed by different authorities in different ways at different times so that its meanings are highly contextual.[14] Second, because *dignity* is a term deployed by political, cultural, and social authorities, such as politicians, judges, and creators of culture, we posit that wielding this term is an exercise of power. That is to say, to name something or someone as having dignity or as being dignified serves to exclude or to mark a boundary. Furthermore, it is the power to provide the content of what constitutes dignity and, perhaps more importantly, to naturalize or normalize a particular definition such that alternatives are rendered illegible at best or dangerous at worst.[15]

To describe and assess this power to deploy dignity, we survey how the term is brandished by state and cultural authorities across three distinct domains: public health, popular culture, and law. We have selected these domains for two reasons. First, within each, normative boundaries of appropriateness are set, enacted, and made public; consequently, political institutions and media representation can often reify status quo power imbalances and inequity.[16] Second, within each, these boundaries can also be contested; in other words, under certain conditions, these domains can function as venues of social change just as much as they can bolster existing circumstances.[17] We seek to discover some of those conditions, and we highlight them in the conclusion of this book.

Our reflections and analysis build on the work of political, historical, and sociological scholars who have shown how our identities are shaped through recognition.[18] As Iris Marion Young reminds us, we are always constituted by and through the gaze of others—particularly through that of dominant authorities.[19] As such, our examination of dignity focuses on a particular set of questions: How does recognition—by judges, policymakers, cultural creators—that LGBTQ+ persons are dignified constitute boundary making? How does being included within the category of "dignified" affect our notions of equality? And what is lost in our inclusion?

Insofar as there is any common theme among dignity's invocations and deployments, we see that the term is often tethered to a sense of individual self-worth and to a subsequent requirement of others to show respect for an individual's agency and choices. Political theorist Martha Nussbaum, for example, has contended that dignity and respect form "a concept-family to be jointly elucidated."[20] But even *respect* is a slippery term. We may think of respect in a context of freedom of choice such that to have dignity is to have one's choices respected. The Supreme Court connected dignity to this sort of autonomy when it upheld access to abortion in *Planned Parenthood v. Casey*: "These matters, involving the most intimate and personal choices a person may make in a lifetime, choices central to personal dignity and autonomy, are central to the liberty protected by the Fourteenth Amendment."[21] Justice Kennedy quoted this passage when he later ruled criminalization of consensual same-sex intimacy to be unconstitutional in *Lawrence*: "It suffices for us to acknowledge that adults may choose to enter upon this relationship in the confines of their homes and their own private lives and still retain their dignity as free persons. . . . The liberty protected by the Constitution allows homosexual persons the right to make this choice."[22] In this sense, dignity captures a domain of rights that is inviolable, that must be respected even if others disapprove.

Used in this way, dignity seems to be pre-political or, as the Declaration of Independence suggests, to have an "inalienable" quality.[23] A similar conception follows from the 1948 Universal Declaration of Human Rights, which speaks of the "inherent dignity" of "all members of the human family."[24] That document, which is so foundational to dignity clauses found in post–World War II constitutions that now contribute to dignity being a "most fashionable concept in modern constitutional discourse," was written, in part, as an acknowledgment of how dignity, which is inherent in all, can be so violently denied by others.[25] For legal scholar Bernadette Atuahene, such dignity taking stems from the "failure to recognize an individual or group's humanity" and infantilizes any person or class of persons; it is a "restriction of an individual's or group's autonomy based on the failure to recognize and respect their full capacity to reason."[26] While we might normatively aspire to a notion of dignity as inherent to ourselves, given the reality of such takings, we must nevertheless contend with how dignity is conditioned upon certain treatment by others. Furthermore, for dignity to be actualized, certain prerequisite needs must be met, often through government action.

Given this requirement, some scholars have argued not only that dignity is used to connote a requirement of respect that follows from an *inherent* value but also that it carries with it more exclusionary potential because it seems premised upon *external* recognition. For example,

Yuvraj Joshi nuances Nussbaum's connection between dignity and respect by contrasting the conception of dignity offered in *Casey* and *Lawrence* with the Court's distinct invocation of the term in its marriage equality decisions: *United States v. Windsor* and *Obergefell v. Hodges*. When describing New York's decision to recognize same-sex marriages in *Windsor*, Justice Kennedy writes, "The State's decision to give this class of persons the right to marry conferred upon them a dignity and status of immense import."[27] The Court considered the federal government's refusal to recognize these marriages to be an "injury and indignity."[28] Similarly, in *Obergefell*, Kennedy wrote that one of the questions at issue was "whether Tennessee can deny to one who has served this Nation the basic dignity of recognizing his New York marriage."[29] The Court characterized petitioners as "ask[ing] for equal dignity in the eyes of the law" and held that "the Constitution grants them that right."[30] In these rulings, dignity does not acquire meaning through its connection to respect for an individual's autonomy to choose how to live. Instead, powerful others bestow dignity on a particular act that they value.

In this sense, dignity operates as a form of recognition—an external validation of an individual's decision to behave in a *particular* way. Dignity is not so much a guarantee of individual choice; it is a conferral of status for engaging in behavior that is deemed worthy. Here, dignity has "connotations of an aspirational standard one should live up to, or not sink below. . . . When used in this sense, the synonym of 'dignity' is 'noble' and its antonym, 'base.' It implies, as well, that its bearer, a person having dignity, lives up to the standard. . . . She thus achieves a kind of (appraisal) self-respect and avoids what would elicit her own contempt."[31] To consider same-sex marriage as equal to cross-sex marriage is to recognize that same-sex couples maintain certain standards, that their relationship is and should be valued because it conforms to particular norms.

As Joshi describes the term, dignity may mean *respect* (as in *Lawrence* or *Casey*), or it may signify *respectability* (as in *Windsor* or *Obergefell*): "Dignity as respect appeals to a person's freedom to make personal and intimate choices without interference. . . . By contrast, dignity as respectability appeals to the social acceptability and worthiness of the personal choices being made and those making them."[32] We build on this distinction by highlighting how dignity functions across three domains of our lives as LGBTQ+ persons. We argue that to be seen by others as respectable—to be recognized as dignified—LGBTQ+ persons must exercise certain forms of responsibility and restraint, especially in their forms of sociality. We further contend that these actions not only align with heteronormative ways of being and interacting in the world but also privilege privacy, individualism, and a notion of universalism that centers whiteness and cisgender norms.

Ultimately, we see both tension and opportunity in the many uses of dignity. Within the multiple ways the term may be invoked resides both its strategic political, cultural, and legal value to governing regulatory and cultural authorities and its seductive allure or the desire and demand to be recognized as having dignity. As legal scholar Erin Daly has said of dignity, "Its appeal lies in its very amorphousness. Its core meaning . . . is tiny, but universally appealing. Beyond that, it seems to mean whatever its beholder would like to see in it."[33] Across the coming chapters, we trace how political, cultural, and legal authorities deploy dignity in ways that expose the term's potential for exclusion and harm. In other words, we showcase the term's potential for rhetorical violence when it is deployed by authorities, even as we acknowledge and probe when and why members of LGBTQ+ communities often seek to invoke and be defined by the parameters of dignity.

Furthermore, since dignity is deployed as an individual quality as well as an aspirational universal value, it is useful to the aims of neoliberal governance. Neoliberalism stands for the idea "that human well-being can best be advanced by liberating individual entrepreneurial freedoms and skills within an institutional framework characterized by strong private property rights, free markets, and free trade."[34] Building on this definition offered by David Harvey, Matthew Hindman contends that neoliberalism "combines classical liberalism's embrace of public austerity, private enterprise, and entrepreneurship with the demand that government actively and aggressively promote free market principles and an individualistic ethic."[35] Neoliberalism posits a coercive role for the state in protecting property but rejects a strong role in other rights domains. With regard to human rights, neoliberalism "relegates such concepts to the level of the individual [thereby] removing structural or institutional perspectives."[36] Racial or gender inequality, for example, is conceptualized as a consequence of personal failings and individual choices instead of as a result of entrenched structural inequities.[37]

Importantly, neoliberalism's emphasis on individual choice can depoliticize citizens. As Hindman argues, citizens learn to "mobilize not as members of groups fighting to share power over the collective direction of the nation; rather, they mobilize as private actors who disavow public or collective power in favor of privacy rights, state noninterference, and a respect for diversity of interests."[38] In practice, this might mean that a claim to equal treatment does not require any acknowledgment of difference or recognition of long-standing histories of discrimination and political powerlessness. Instead, discrimination can be conceptualized as "the negation of everyday citizens who—despite being gay—are [otherwise] living normal lives."[39] In other words, discrimination can be cast as the denial of some universal quality, and the category of difference on which any biased act is taken is rendered unimportant, unvalued, and unseen. Neoliberalism promotes equality to mean sameness. As such, it aligns with a definition of dignity as respectability. Dignity, then, can be deployed to promote a neoliberal conception of appropriate political action and expectations.

Finally, it is critically important to note that governing authorities code promiscuity, non-monogamy, sex without romance, and sex beyond private spaces—practices long associated with queer politics and identities—as undignified. Unfortunately, these norms are also often embraced by some within LGBTQ+ communities in the political strategies that prioritize inclusion without disruption. This inclusion among and within what is considered normatively respectable constitutes dignity's allure and seductive possibilities. Indeed, respectability can become a survival tactic of an otherwise often despised class of persons. As Brittney Cooper has written in the context of African American history, "Initially, respectability politics was a survival strategy but an imminently reasonable one for nineteenth- and early twentieth-century Blacks. . . . Showing these Black people how to present a respectable image became a key strategy in securing their survival in hostile and violent conditions."[40] Conforming to dominant norms, even if doing so sacrifices alternative values, beliefs, and ways of being, is a strategy to survive within a society that operates with distinct, and often hegemonic, values. Speaking to that loss, Cooper argues, "The problem with all provisional strategies, particularly when they begin to work for the exceptional few, is that they rise to the level of ideology. Soon, Black folks began to blame other Black people for bringing the race down. . . . Taken to its extreme form, respectability politics will net you Black people who don't love Black people."[41]

Building on Cooper's insight, one of our aims is to trace how dignity, when it conveys respectability, is not only deployed by political and cultural governing authorities but also adopted by some within the LGBTQ+ communities. This dynamic often occurs when the community is under assault—for example, during the early years of the HIV/AIDS crisis in the 1980s and 1990s or when states and the federal government were actively seeking to limit or ban relationship recognition in the 1990s and 2000s. Indeed, dignity deployed to mean respectability can be a political strategy employed by some within LGBTQ+ communities. This strategy, while often achieving short-term gains, can sow discord within these communities. We labor to understand how and why this particular meaning proves seductive and when, how, and to what effect that seduction may be resisted.

To summarize, in this book, we explore how—in the areas of public health politics, film and television representation, and gay, lesbian, and bisexual rights Supreme Court jurisprudence[42]—multiple governing authorities have undermined notions of community, public responsibility, and long-standing historical and structural forms of inequality and replaced them with a neoliberal discourse of individual rights and individual responsibilities.[43] While we explore examples of a queer penchant for resistance and a corresponding valorization of difference in each domain, we also note how and why such resistance has its limits. To be seen and named as dignified is to be marked as behaving in ways that correspond to neoliberal principles and aspirations of individual responsibility. Put differently, neoliberal principles are communicated through the contemporary rhetorical deployment of dignity in policy, popular culture, and law. Once dignity can be seen through this neoliberal lens and understood to function as a neoliberal tool—once normative dignity is understood as neoliberal dignity—then its capacity to reinforce boundaries, even as it tears down some walls, and its potential to offer equality to some while failing to provide equity for others become evident and its limits exposed.

Our Skepticism of a Legal Conception of Dignity

Dignity, as a constitutional right or legal value, is far more developed in international law and in constitutional traditions from Europe and South Africa than in those of the United States.[44] Specifically, the US Constitution does not contain an explicit dignity clause. Even where dignity has some textual grounding, scholars do not find consensus on what the word means or what outcomes it guarantees. While Erin Daly contends "that the right to dignity has content and boundaries. It means *something*, but not everything," she also acknowledges that there is "no agreed-on working definition of dignity that courts invoke, nor are there customs and usages of the trade that cabin discretion or direct when a court should or should not invoke or vindicate dignity rights."[45] Because dignity has no "concrete meaning or consistent way of being defined," some scholars have argued against employing it as a standard.[46] Ronald Dworkin has called the term "debased by flabby overuse."[47] Others have called it undefinable,[48] overly flexible,[49] or lacking in substantive content.[50] One scholar understands dignity as "an empty formula without precise content" and, therefore, a "conversation stopper."[51] Another called it "universally attractive" because it is "comprehensively vague."[52] As Aharon Barak cautions, "Dignity can be seen as a Trojan horse that will lead to severe limitations of human rights . . . [because] the use of the concept grants judges the power to do with it as they please."[53] Indeed, US Supreme Court justices—liberal and conservative alike—have increasingly used the term as a foundation for rights recognition.[54] In this context, it is imperative to understand how and why authorities have deployed the term.

Despite its fashionable invocation across the spectrum of justices' ideological positions, dignity has no consistent definition in US constitutional tradition. As Daly notes, "American constitutional jurisprudence is always something of an outlier, and no less with respect to human dignity . . . uniquely in the world, the U.S. Supreme Court has always been much more comfortable attaching dignity to inanimate things, such as states and courts and contracts, than to human beings."[55] Even so, dignity has been invoked to expound upon the requirements of the First,[56] Fourth,[57] Fifth,[58] Sixth,[59] Eighth,[60] Ninth,[61] Fourteenth,[62] and Fifteenth Amendments[63] and on issues ranging from free expression, regulation of search and seizure, and voting rights to contraception, abortion, and the death penalty. In recent years, dignity has been consistently invoked in the Supreme Court's decisions vindicating gay, lesbian, and bisexual equality.[64] Indeed, one legal scholar pointed to Justice Kennedy's rulings in *Lawrence*, *Windsor*, and *Obergefell* as building a foundation for a "doctrine of equal dignity."[65]

Because dignity may be conferred through marriage—as Kennedy posits in *Obergefell*—and because marriage is a status conferred by the state, dignity's value is contingent upon how those with power choose to recognize it. As Michael Warner argues when he warns against "speak[ing] of inclusion as if it were synonymous with equality and freedom," the expansion of marriage as open to individuals with same-sex attraction is not only an expansion of rights but also an expansion of state power to construct, define, and limit its citizenry in ever-changing ways.[66] Since the late nineteenth century, civil marriage has been a tool through which the state defines who counts as a valued member of the political community.[67]

The boundaries of neoliberal dignity are sharply exposed in the marriage equality context, where dignity's meaning is constructed through verisimilitude to a heteronormative ideal.[68] That ideal, at its most extreme, compels the abandonment of context—of community, of history—that might function as the alternative for a queerer notion of what dignity might capture, value, or mean. In her poignant critique of the marriage equality movement and its successes, queer activist Urvashi Vaid contends that while the achieved recognition "deliver[s] meaningful rights, tangible benefits, access, recognition, and social respect for those who participate in the institution," it nevertheless "fails for the reasons that formal legal equality as an end goal fails—it does not deliver justice, transform family or culture, nor expand queer freedom for all." To position marriage as the summit of LGBTQ+ rights aspirations "reduce[s] justice to access, liberation to liberalism, same sex to same old sex. Equality in this narrative is little more than a straight people's club to which queers most willing to conform have gained admission."[69] If marriage is the route to dignity, then dignity depends on sameness and legibility to the straight majority. Again, as Warner reminds us, "even though people think that marriage gives them validation, legitimacy, and recognition, they somehow think it does so without invalidating, delegitimizing, or stigmatizing other relations, needs, and desires."[70] Our aim is to lay bare that stigmatization, invalidation, and delegitimation.

Because dignity can function as a tool of boundary making, we seek to interrogate deeply the potential consequences of the Court's recognition of gays and lesbians as having dignity.[71] This turn to dignity as a legal marker of gay and lesbian status is often celebrated as progress.[72] Nevertheless, we question whether it is singularly positive.[73] Its potential for harm emanates from its plasticity. Because dignity resides at the level of the individual and also aspires to be a universal good, it holds within it a power to sever the individual from historical, communal, and cultural contexts that offer meaning and value. In short, as dignity aspires to a universal value—the claim that, fundamentally, all persons have some inviolable dignity—it often reinforces dominant conceptions of value, especially neoliberal values that center individualism, privacy, and responsibility.

Our contention is that political, cultural, and legal authorities often deploy dignity to harness this quality of universal appeal, even as the term can promote restricted ways—heteronormative and neoliberal ways—of being and acting in the world. Indeed, the universal and aspirational qualities of the term obfuscate the deeply political work of prioritization and naturalization that it produces. If dignity operates as a hegemonic concept to universalize a particular set of norms and values—to make those norms and values appear natural, commonsensical, or hardly the political and social constructs that they, in fact, are—then the term commits a certain kind of violence. It shreds communal ties, renders persons invisible, and requires an abandonment of alternative ways of being. By reaching for normative universality, the empirical contingency of the concept—when, where, by whom, and to what effect the term is deployed—can be hidden and ignored. Consequently, we expose dignity's limits, harms, and exclusions, but we also turn to queerer values and possibilities.

Queering Dignity: Doing Not Being

Dignity is a disciplining force, and in this way, it can be used to des-ignate normative success or failure—to delineate between acceptable and unacceptable. To be called undignified is to bear all the markers of being undisciplined and, indeed, disruptive. To be undignified is to be branded as irresponsible, childish, infantile, and even dangerous to the broader public.[74] Insofar as dignity can be deployed by state and cultural authorities to mean or to require respectability or alignment with majoritarian norms, queer ways of being, knowing, and acting in the world challenge this meaning.

While *queer* is often used conversationally or even politically as a stable identity category, we align ourselves with the major current of queer theory that understands and uses *queer* differently.[75] By *queer*, we mean a slippery signifier that does resistance work—that resists the very idea of stable identity categories or stable meaning in the broader social order more generally. Summarizing queer theory's most com-mon refrains about the "meaning" of queer, Calvin Thomas offers the following:

> For "queer" is less of an identity than a *critique* of identity . . . a site of permanent becoming.[76] "Queerness" involves the open mesh of possi-bilities, gaps, overlaps, dissonances and resonances, lapses and excesses of meaning where the constituent elements of anyone's gender, of anyone's sexuality aren't made (or *can't* be made) to signify monolithically.[77] For "queer," writes David Halperin, "is by definition *whatever* is at odds with the normal, the legitimate, the dominant. *There is nothing in particular to which it refers*. It is an identity without an essence."[78] "Queerness," writes Lee Edelman, "can never define an identity; it can only ever disturb one. . . ."[79] There is no kingdom of the queer.[80]

Reinforcing Thomas's reading of queer theory, Nikki Sullivan reminds us of Halperin's important distinction: "Queer is a positionality rather than an identity in the humanist sense."[81] While Thomas and Sulli-van both realize that strategic claims to "queer" as an identity function politically—often as an umbrella term to communicate an array of identities within LGBTQ+ communities—they remain clear that theoretical queerness resists this identitarian impulse.

With these ideas in mind, we might do better to think of *queer* as a doing, and importantly, as a doing that can fuck with dignity's generative work to bolster the agenda of the state and to split LGBTQ+ communities into factions that either succeed or fail. Sullivan continues to read queer theory's major contributions to the *being* queer versus *doing* queerly debate by offering the following:

> One way of avoiding the problems associated with the notion of queer as an identity—albeit a non-essential, provisional, and fragmented one—is, as Janet R. Jakobsen suggests, to "complete the Foucauldian move from human being to human doing."[82] What Jakobsen means by this is that it may be more productive to think of queer as a verb (a set of actions). This seems to be the position taken by Michael Warner who says that queer is not just a resistance to the norm, but more importantly, consists of protesting against "the idea[l] of normal behavior."[83] Queer, in this sense, comes to be understood as a deconstructive practice that is not undertaken by an already constituted subject, and does not, in turn, furnish that subject with a nameable identity.[84]

Sullivan's rendering of this debate in queer theory provides a convincing argument for thinking of *queer* not just as an unstable or a shifting identity but, instead, as a *doing* that takes as its central goal the acts of contestation and deconstruction. For Sullivan and the battery of queer theorists with whom she thinks, *queer* is a verb that can produce serious consequences and that can offer rich possibilities for rethinking dignity—as a doing at which we might succeed or fail.

Furthermore, once we conceptualize *queer* as a kind of doing, we might then consider how doing queerly might be more aptly described as a failing: failing to measure up, failing to restrain, failing to comply, failing to produce, and failing to mean (that is, in an orderly and legible fashion). Jack Halberstam, in *The Queer Art of Failure*, makes a compelling detour into the alternative world constructed by animated films to theorize (lowly, of course) about alternatives and queer failure.[85] Halberstam's understanding of queer failure provides important theoretical valances to our exploration of dignity, particularly for thinking about dignity's deployments and their concomitant demand for certain kinds of "success" and for assessing how queer alternatives to dignity's deployments signal certain kinds of "failure," or at least, failures to align with a neoliberal norm.

As Halberstam argues, "Under certain circumstances failing, losing, forgetting, unmaking, undoing, unbecoming, not knowing may in fact offer more creative, more cooperative, more surprising ways of being in the world. Failing is something queers do and have always done exceptionally well."[86] He further posits that "academics, activists, artists, and cartoon characters have long been on a quest to articulate an alternative vision of life, love, and labor and to put such a vision into practice," but these alternatives regularly require that we get lost—as it were—and fail to walk prescribed lines in thought and in body.[87] In short, failure means refusing to practice endorsed modes of thinking and doing and being to see what else comes into view when one detours non-normatively.[88] More than that, though, the relentless pursuit of alternatives that Halberstam concerns himself with requires that we fundamentally undo or unbecome, which also necessitates a contestation of our socialization. This includes, but is not limited to, a resounding "no" to rehearsed grand narratives of being, doing, and thinking offered by parents, school systems, churches, and the law.

For Halberstam, failing (and failing spectacularly queerly) necessitates undoing the work of the state. Building on the work of James C. Scott, Halberstam highlights that "the demand by the state for legibility through the imposition of methods of standardization and uniformity," and for Scott, "'legibility is a condition of manipulation.'"[89] This state-seeing importantly demands an abandonment of other ways of knowing and being and questioning: "For Scott, to 'see like the state' means to accept the order of things and to internalize them; it means that we begin to deploy and think with the logic of superiority of orderliness and that we erase and indeed sacrifice other, more local practices of knowledge, practices moreover that may be less efficient, may yield less marketable results, but may also, in the long term, be more sustaining."[90] In Halberstam's estimation, then, much is at stake in failing, for failing brings other possibilities into view, ones that could be more sustaining.

Indeed, as he notes, "We may in fact want to think about how to see *unlike* a state; we may want new rationale for knowledge production, different aesthetic standards for ordering or disordering space, other modes of political engagement than those conjured by the liberal imagination."[91] But if we want to resist the normalizing and/or naturalizing thrusts of the state—the "commonsense" traps that are neither coincidental nor politically neutral—then "we have to untrain ourselves so that we can read the struggles and debates back into questions that seem settled and resolved."[92] To be sure, if queers fail well, then there is potential to open up that which has seemingly been closed as settled business and to welcome a proliferation of new possibilities. Indeed, failure can pay important dividends for the unsettled, wayward queer wanderer: that which has been restricted by meaning-making mandates has the opportunity to return to excess—to the mess that so-called meaning-making "cleaned up" and "ordered."[93]

For Halberstam, if we dare to fail—if we trade in legibility and being taken seriously for illegibility and frivolity—perhaps we can "flesh out alternatives . . . in terms of how to live, how to think about time and space, how to inhabit space with others, and how to spend time separate from the logic of work."[94] This embrace of failure has the potential to reconnect us to those left behind by more conventional narratives of success and failure that separate the non-compliant from the compliant or the "correctly" oriented from the curious wanderer. In his estimation, "in losing we will find another way of making meaning in which . . . no one gets left behind."[95]

If queering is doing, if failing queerly is rife with rebellious potential, and if dignity is conceptualized as a normative set of neoliberal requirements and eligibilities constructed and deployed by governing authorities, then to fail at dignity could be a deeply subversive and constructive act. Because dignity achieves its work by establishing parameters of what is acceptable and who is worthy, its strikes us as urgent to reflect on how thinking queerly about dignity could give us something rather than take something away. If Halberstam is right to suggest that the state achieves its work by ignoring, eliding, or even demonizing unruly forms of knowing with those that are coded as normal or natural or necessary, then failing at the state's work—failing at dignity—might involve spotlighting or reconsidering or resuscitating queer knowledges that have been paved over or abandoned to reach for dignity. Without doubt, queer doing threatens the power of (hetero)normative ideas about the world:

ideas about how we should use public and private spaces and what bodies can and should do—when, with whom, and for what purposes—to further the aims of the state and other institutional authorities who labor alongside the state. Queer logics of space, time, and contact are so antithetical to hetero norms that active engagement with them brings to light how contemporary state actions that invest LGBTQ+ persons with dignity rely on their refusal.

Queer notions of space challenge the supposedly neat, tidy boundaries that separate "public" from "private," and they spotlight the problematic politics of taking up public space.[96] Indeed, in a context in which sexual intimacy is criminalized and the open acknowledgment of desire and longing is culturally denigrated, the liberal legal logics of privacy as they emerged in the mid- to late twentieth century seemed inapplicable. For example, in chapter 1, we reconsider the gay bathhouse as a dynamic institution of queer kinship and community-building at the height of the HIV/AIDS crisis, and through this example, we explore how public space becomes the safe location for intimacy, how darkness and anonymity provide security, and how personal nakedness offers the public foundation for community. In short, heteronormative ideas about safety and order in public or in private hardly seemed relevant to the queer experience.

Time can also be reformulated in queer ways. Time orders space, behavior, and bodies. Moreover, constructions and deployments of temporality structure narratives about productivity and responsibility—ones that ensure bodies, thoughts, and behaviors align with the goals of the state and with capitalistic functionality. In short, to behave in ways that transgress the norms of time and that challenge the order of relationship, marriage, reproduction, and family is to risk being dismissed as irresponsible, childish, infantile, and even undignified. Thus practicing a kind of queer futurity—what Lee Edelman describes as "no future"—is to probe, resist, and offer alternatives for how we understand time, particularly in ways that do not support normative projects.[97] As a result, unruly queers suggest a configuration of time that does not rely on heteronormative standards of relationship that may privilege marriage, monogamy, children, and so on.[98] Rather than take refuge in a seemingly stable fantasy of the future, queer ways of being may embrace an abandonment of order—of the promise of a tomorrow. While this approach

to life is often mischaracterized as immature, irresponsible, or even narcissistic by governing and cultural authorities, we consider how queer
temporality can amplify the possibility of an alternative relationship to
"progress" or even a divergent relationship to constructions of time—
how we calculate it, fill it, and ultimately measure its productive use.[99]

The entire construction of community, of belonging, and of contact,
which occurs within the bounds of space and time, can be queered in
ways that threaten heteronormative standards. Governing authorities
dismiss these challenges by denying the dignity of the individuals and
communities who practice them. Casual sex, public sex, and polyamorous relationships all transgress normative sociality because they refuse
to observe propriety. Without expectations of monogamous commitment or without the promise of interaction beyond immediate moments
of pleasure and mutual exchange, these ways of being with one another
reveal an alternative value system that reconceptualizes how bodies can
and should interact.[100]

Queering time, space, and relationship brings into focus the boundaries that dignity's deployments erect through public policy, cultural
representations, and legal recognition of the LGBTQ+ subject. Indeed,
failing to engage with queer approaches to living obscures the limits of
contemporary efforts to invest LGBTQ+ individuals and communities
with dignity. Queer logics of kinship—the exploration of new and distinct ways of interpersonal connection—can remain denied and denigrated. Too often the governing authorities in our policy, cultural, and
legal domains premise dignity on the state's reinforcement of heteronormative, and often private, couplings. When they do, they deny the
history and value of more radical ways of being, revealing the limits
of dignity.

Dignity's Seduction versus Transgression and Resistance

Even as dignity's boundaries have expanded and dignity has become
more capacious and inclusive, troubling exclusions remain. In particular,
some within LGBTQ+ communities have been recognized as dignified or have been invested with dignity by aligning their behaviors and
relationships with those of the heterosexual majority. As the political
and cultural authorities as well as some within the community denigrate

the value of queer life and its inherent position of difference, dignity's demands for sameness often prevail as the foundation for establishing the value of LGBTQ+ life. Even so, a queer penchant for difference never fully dissipates. Instead of a pure adoption of sameness, contemporary LGBTQ+ practices and representations reveal a dynamic tension between dignity's seductive rhetoric of homogenization and efforts to reclaim a historical potential for transgression and a celebration of difference. This tension creates one possible pathway to understand who we have been and who we might become.

To travel that path, this book is divided into three parts; each part focuses on a particular domain in which authorities deploy dignity and in which LGBTQ+ community members promote and/or contest the meanings, mechanisms, and parameters of that deployment. Each part is composed of two chapters so that the dynamic tension described above comes through the pairings. Part 1 focuses on the politics of public health policy. Chapter 1 discusses how authorities in San Francisco and New York City pursued the closure of gay bathhouses during the HIV/AIDS crisis. We begin here for two reasons. First, within this particular episode of queer history, the rhetoric of dignity proves to be at its most seductive. During the early years of the HIV/AIDS crisis—a vulnerable time of uncertainty and increasing death tolls—state authorities explicitly dehumanized, infantilized, and abandoned gay men, creating a narrative of blame for supposedly undignified behavior.[101] These authorities issued an ultimatum to gay men: be dignified or suffer death. Death became the consequence of an undignified choice. To illustrate this state position, chapter 1 discusses how bathhouse closures were part of a larger anti-gay and anti-HIV politico-cultural discourse that denied the dignity of men who have sex with other men. In other words, the state began to do intentional generative work to dehumanize and infantilize queer communities, which was work that reached beyond the long-standing criminalization of same-sex intimacy. At this critical moment, the state compelled these communities to abandon transgressive kinship practices, to reform their intimacies, and to "behave" if they were to be protected by whatever public health policies state officials might develop. By deploying a notion of dignity as tethered to certain kinds of sexual behavior, state officials offered a way out of a perceived death sentence but only on the condition of abandoning commitments to queer particularity and communal ethos. The state's characterizations of queer space and practice, many of which were adopted by community members themselves, fractured a community already decimated by disease and fostered a narrative of culpability. By illustrating how the state deployed dignity to do generative political work in the midst of a public health crisis—to consolidate the power of heteronormative logics—we reveal the limits of dignity as a central route through which queer folks can ever hope to achieve liberation specific to queer experience.

Second, we begin in the early years of HIV/AIDS because the crisis is causally connected to one of the primary mechanisms through which state and cultural authorities have come to recognize the dignity of LGBTQ+ people—namely, marriage, which is discussed in chapters 5 and 6. HIV/AIDS exposed the legal precariousness of same-sex couples. As historian George Chauncey details, "The early battles to protect the rights of people with AIDS and their partners nonetheless had an enduring impact on many gay people's thinking by abruptly confronting them with the legal inequality of their relationships."[102] We begin our book at this moment because it provides a historical and conceptual foundation for how our book ends, with an assessment of the jurisprudence of marriage recognition, which is deeply embedded in dignity claims.

In chapter 2, in the context of the transformation of HIV into a chronic, manageable condition rather than a "death sentence"—at least for those who can access and respond to available medication—we identify contemporary circumstances that may provide some potential to reclaim queer alternatives.[103] Specifically, we explore three possibilities: (1) the social interactions encouraged in contemporary bathhouses and by geolocative social media apps, (2) the sexual possibilities afforded by the development of HIV/AIDS prevention strategies like pre-exposure prophylaxis (PrEP) and treatment as prevention (TasP), and (3) the subcultures of intentional HIV transmission. By utilizing the provocative theoretical frameworks offered by Samuel Delany and Tim Dean, we examine the extent to which each has potential to invigorate queer contact and kinship and, by contrast, have been absorbed into and transformed by normative deployments of dignity.[104]

Part 2 explores distinct visions of dignity in popular culture, particularly representations of what we call neoliberal restraint and what we see as disruptive challenges to neoliberal dignity.[105] In chapter 3, we closely read the 2018 film *Love, Simon* and contrast it with its source material, Becky Albertalli's young adult novel *Simon vs. the Homo Sapiens Agenda*.[106] We selected these texts because *Love, Simon* was the first film produced by a major Hollywood studio that focused on a gay teenager, grossed over sixty million dollars worldwide, and was considered so popular that it has produced the spin-off television series *Love, Victor* that premiered in the summer of 2020.[107] Because this film marketed itself as a project of radical inclusion and a contestation of heteronormativity, *Love, Simon* deserves sustained critical analysis.[108] The comparative reading of the film with its original source material in the young adult novel makes clear not only how much dignity has become an anchoring theme in representations of LGBTQ+ life but also how the term's meaning commonly emerges as a recurrent claim that LGBTQ+ people are "just like you" or just like the straight majority. Sexuality is reduced to a de-historicized, insignificant, and highly personal individualistic trait. Within this narrative, the exclusionary force of dignity becomes immediately evident, for it is always privileging certain raced, classed, and gendered ways of living that conform to heteronormative and neoliberal assumptions.

In chapter 4, we turn to representations that transgress these boundaries of normatively appropriate sexuality, identity, and relationships. As the standard bearers of representation have diversified, we see a pivot toward celebrating difference on its own terms without the invocation of dignity, or at least without the invocation of dignity to achieve equality through sameness. In particular, with the increasing inclusion of trans persons and queers of color in the writing room, a politics and discourse of respectability becomes less relevant and even subject to critique. Our primary illustration of these ideas comes through a close reading of the FX series *Pose*.[109] We focus on this groundbreaking television series not only because it centers a cast of transgender people of color and thereby deliberately transgresses the normative representation of cisgender white gay men but also because it defies industry norms by deliberately centering the voices and perspectives of transgender women of color who serve as writers, producers, and directors of particular episodes. The series has received multiple awards and has garnered critical and popular acclaim across its two seasons (with a third one in production).[110] Our reading points to practices that might be pursued to expose underlying inequalities and to make clear why dignity conceptualized as respectability is both so troubling and so seductive.

In Part 3, we trace the development of dignity within the US Supreme Court's rulings on gay, lesbian, and bisexual rights and marriage recognition. Decisions that have decriminalized same-sex intimacy and recognized marriage equality rest on a foundation of dignity, and their reasoning has been lauded as holistic and principled.[111] Yet because these decisions conceptualize dignity as an individual characteristic as well as a universal good, they render unnecessary any deep engagement with the context, history, structure, and systems of inequality. In chapter 5, we analyze the existing jurisprudential line from *Lawrence* to *Obergefell* to build a multifaceted critique of dignity, and we suggest that the Court's deployment of dignity proves problematic—especially so in the hands of an ascendant conservative legal movement.

Since the Supreme Court majority's conception of dignity proves so troubling, chapter 6 turns to evaluating alternatives. We begin with an assessment of Justice Clarence Thomas's dissent in *Obergefell*, the only opinion that offers a substantive response to the majority's deployment of dignity. Thomas conceives of dignity not only as an inherent individual quality but also as beyond the state's reach either to protect or to denigrate. This construction of dignity can be easily read as part of a broader political project to promote the neoliberal aspirations of a limited state hardly accountable to citizens' claims to equitable treatment. Since Thomas's alternative proves problematic, we survey legal theories that underlie plural marriage, exploring if they can provide alternative constructions of dignity. Tellingly, though, the formal recognition sought by plural marriage advocates often perpetuates the limits of dignity that follow from an aspiration to respectability. Finally, we suggest that dignity may fruitfully stand as an anti-stigma principle, and we illustrate how such a principle can find constitutional footing in the Thirteenth Amendment through original and contemporary understandings of that amendment. Despite its potential, we remain unconvinced that our reading would be pursued, especially since doing so requires recognizing how much our dominant interpretations of the Thirteenth and Fourteenth Amendments are saturated with racism.

Our conclusion points to actions that might be taken to expose dignity's limits and to reconceptualize dignity as a principle that challenges stigma. Our fundamental question motivating this book is not "If not dignity, then what?" We are not searching for an alternative term. Any possible replacements—humanity, personhood, autonomy, choice—can be subjected to similar criticisms of definitional malleability and exclusionary potential. Instead, we ask the following: "In a context where we can now conceptualize dignity's limits, what policies, practices, and commitments follow?" We provide a framework of principles through which to address this question, and we also hope that the work of this book—our examination of biases in public health, our contrasting of cultural representations, and our interpretation of how and why the Thirteenth Amendment is a strong proscription against stigmatization—illustrates the actions that could emerge from our critique.

Each chapter answers its guiding questions by referencing and analyzing a variety of source materials: documentary film, fiction, movies, television shows, policy statements, judicial rulings, websites, and social media apps. We draw on political and legal scholarship on dignity, queer theory, Black queer studies, cultural studies, and LGBTQ+ histories. While our book is built on these disciplinary foundations, we work to bridge them to contribute to each of these fields. We offer reflections that can only come through this disciplinary promiscuity. By describing and assessing the deployment of and the chase for dignity across distinct domains and by employing methodologies common to multiple disciplines, we hope to provide more compelling insights than would be possible from the perspective of a single discipline.

We have structured our book as only one possible way to read it. Its organization emphasizes the dialectical dynamic of authoritative deployments of dignity and attempts at resistance by some within LGBTQ+ communities. However, our observations and themes transgress the boundaries created through this particular organizational format. For example, across the chapters, the dichotomous requirement of restraint versus the celebration of excess repeatedly comes to the fore. Such excess is illustrated by the critical kinship practices that occurred within the bathhouses before municipal authorities shuttered them as discussed in chapter 1. It is exemplified in the subcultural practices of sex without condoms as described in chapter 2. It is a key characteristic of narrative time and focus in *Pose* as explored in chapter 4. Finally, it is evident in the messiness of suspect class analysis, which requires engagement with history and particularity and thereby resists the tidiness of seemingly universal principles of suspect classification as outlined in chapter 5.

Another anchoring theme that emerges across the chapters is the importance of listening to and empowering communities to speak for themselves on their own terms. If state and cultural authorities often deploy dignity only to mean respectability, then dignity refuses the value of particular ways of being, and it denigrates any self-understanding of individuals and communities that could prove transgressive. By surveying narratives that offer a community's self-descriptions and values—for example, Dennis Cooper's *The Sluts* (discussed in chapter 2) and *Pose* (discussed in chapter 4)—we can expose the limits created when dignity is deployed to include some, but only some, within the LGBTQ+ communities.

Finally, throughout much of this book, we utilize the acronym LGBTQ+ to promote an inclusive understanding of the various communities to which we hope to speak. Nevertheless, at particular moments, our reflections focus on particular communities for accuracy and specificity. For example, our discussion of bathhouse closures in chapter 1 highlights actions by individuals who mostly identified as cisgender gay men. Similarly, our analysis of how contemporary bathhouses in chapter 2 present their businesses to potential customers explores how gay cisgender masculine boundaries are promoted. By contrast, our analysis of geolocative apps indicates how certain apps cater to lesbian, bisexual, and transgender individuals, seeking to decolonize dating and intimacy in ways that transgress racial and gender boundaries. Our exploration of popular culture, in chapters 3 and 4, focuses on how some films reinforce white gay cisgender masculine experience as normative, while other representations have unsettled that normativity by focusing explicitly on the lives of transgender people of color. And our discussion of Supreme Court jurisprudence in chapters 5 and 6 deliberately drops the LGBTQ+ acronym for the phrase "gay, lesbian, and bisexual," as the Supreme Court had not, until June 2020, issued a ruling that explicitly addressed discrimination against transgender individuals.[112]

A Polyvocal Way Forward

While we bring attention to how dignity is deployed by political, legal, and cultural authorities, we do not discount the progress made—for example, increased visibility (but always of a certain kind), decriminalization (but compelled closeting at first), and marriage equality (but the privileging of certain relationships that can be public and thus dignified through recognition by others).[113] Furthermore, we understand the desire to be recognized as having dignity. That such recognition has been refused for so long is a fundamental harm that should require not only apology but also, perhaps, reparation. Without doubt, we are aware of dignity's seductive allure. Nevertheless, we remain cautious of treating dignity as an unalloyed good. Our aim is to reveal that dignity—as it has been deployed in the United States to consolidate and amplify heteronormative and neoliberal logics—comes with costs for certain bodies and for particular alternative ways of worldmaking.

Communal efforts to reclaim what our chase for dignity has forced us to abandon showcase how the logic of dignity reverberates in—or even infiltrates—our best efforts at resistance. We find much to celebrate in each of these efforts at repair, yet none remain unstained by the exclusionary limits of dignity. Indeed, instead of inclusion and equity, dignity's required individualization and concomitant claim to universality—that we are or can become just like you—has severed us from the potential of queer worldmaking, a possibility that has always threatened the power of political, legal, and market authorities. By exploring what we have lost and by identifying the limits of any attempts to recover through transgression, we question whether dignity can ever be a sufficient value to define and recognize the worth of our queer selves and communities. At its most dangerous, dignity can become a poisonous signifier that obliterates the inherent value of difference. By queering dignity—by failing to do normative neoliberal work—we reveal how dignity can be reconceptualized and what we can *gain* in the process. And ultimately, when we gain an anti-stigma principle, we come closer to a more dynamic, contextual, and polyvocal way forward.

PART I

Dignity's Disciplining Power

The Politics of Public Health from AIDS to PrEP

1

Fucking with Dignity

Bathhouse Closures and the State's Degradation of Queer Kinship during the Early AIDS Crisis

As an entry into understanding how dignity can be deployed as a disciplining and boundary-making tool, this chapter explores how dignity operated during a particular episode of HIV/AIDS history: in the name of public health, municipal authorities in San Francisco and New York City pursued the closure of gay bathhouses in 1984 and 1985, respectively. During this vulnerable time of uncertainty and increasing death tolls, many individuals in positions of power explicitly created a narrative of blame for supposedly undignified sexual behavior. State authorities issued an ultimatum to gay men: be dignified or suffer death. In other words, the state did intentional generative work to degrade, infantilize, and dehumanize gay men in ways that reached beyond the long-standing criminalization of same-sex intimacy.[1] The state compelled gay men to abandon what we see as transgressive kinship practices, to reform their intimacies, and to, in short, "behave," if they were to be protected by whatever public health policies officials might enact.[2] By deploying a notion of dignity as tethered to practices defined as restrained and responsible sexual behavior, these officials offered a way out of a death sentence, but only on the condition of abandoning commitments to queer logics and a queer communal ethos.

We acknowledge that the history of bathhouse closures in San Francisco, New York City, and other cities across the United States is territory well-trod by academics and journalists alike.[3] We also recognize that *dignity* was not a term explicitly invoked at the time to defend or challenge closure policy. Indeed, battles were often framed around either responsibility or promiscuity and the potentially liberating politics thereof. But by treating dignity as a lens through which to view this particular episode of public health politics and queer history, we can demonstrate the rhetorical harm that authoritative deployments of dignity do to the queer worldmaking that happens in gay male sexual spaces like bathhouses. While bathhouses could initially be conceptualized as spaces in which gay men could flout convention—places where expectations of dignity could be challenged or ignored—municipal and state authorities could now politicize a public health crisis to promote conformity to narrower notions of acceptable behavior. With blame placed upon gay men, any political resistance to normative dignity could be castigated as infantile, irresponsible, and harmful to themselves and their community.

This chapter does not contend that the bathhouses should not have been shut down. Instead, we expose how the debate about closures and the policies that followed reveal the ways that dignity can be a tool to define, regulate, and recognize whom and what the state values. We also use the bathhouse policy debate in New York City and San Francisco to illustrate and make quite concrete how the state can deploy dignity in order to discipline and exclude.

The dominant historical narrative that justified the closings, which has been promoted by historians and public officials alike, has been ostensibly epidemiological: bathhouses were sites of unsafe sex, and unsafe sex is linked to the transmission of HIV. Therefore, these institutions needed to be closed to promote public health.[4] By centering dignity as the operative concept, we challenge this narrative. Even as gay bathhouses had always been subjected to state harassment under the guise of public morals regulation, this moral panic took on new urgency during the early years of the HIV crisis.[5] Often public officials' first response to the crisis was to invade community institutions considered sites of the problem and to blame gay men for their behavior at the same time that they underspent on HIV education, prevention, and resources.[6] Indeed, state policies revealed a deep desire to lay accountability for the crisis on gay men, who had long been considered threats to the state, and to position the state as offering the solution.[7]

By engaging queer logics that reject the exclusionary state-deployed notion of dignity, we argue that the bathhouse closings deprived gay men of spaces they understood as integral to their own safety, identity, and community—all of which was invisible to or disregarded by the state. We first detail how the bathhouse functioned as a symbol of gay visibility, pride, and freedom deeply connected with the post-Stonewall gay liberationist ethos of the 1970s. Public sex within the bathhouse challenged narrower notions of dignity that privileged romantic heterosexuality, privacy, and monogamy. Furthermore, the function of public sex—to be watched, applauded, and celebrated by others in community and in intimacy with someone of the same sex when such acts were despised, pathologized, and criminalized—helped develop the bathhouse as a site where community, connection, and kinship could be fostered. These public commercial establishments provided safety and anonymity at a time when oppressive regimes of homosexual criminalization reigned and when daily life was replete with aggression toward gay men. As such, they fostered the potential for intimacy that transgressed the liberal jurisprudential doctrine of constitutional privacy and individual rights as it took shape beginning in the 1960s, which relied on heteronormative boundaries between private and public space.

Second, we describe how, as the HIV/AIDS crisis began to decimate gay male communities in San Francisco and New York City, many gay men worked to retain the bathhouses because of their symbolic and communal value. In particular, they created systems of education and self-regulation that differentiated among various forms of sexual practice rather than entirely shuttering a site critical to queer identities. Their work took place in the midst of a broader public debate that, perhaps too simplistically, pitted a public health imperative against the liberal logic of individual private sexual freedom. Importantly, the public health narrative bolstered a state-sponsored understanding of dignity—one that misunderstood queer aims only as a libertarian impulse to have sex without consequences and then cast that limited conception as fundamentally selfish, irresponsible, and a threat to the broader public. This binary construction of public health safety versus selfish and irresponsible sex refused to acknowledge how bathhouses fostered queer community and kinship. It also failed to recognize how gay men had worked for years prior to the public debate to develop more nuanced approaches to the crisis that might maintain these vital community institutions and achieve larger public health gains.

Third, we review actions taken by municipal governing officials in New York City and San Francisco that precipitated the closure of most bathhouses. Few bathhouses were unable to sustain themselves under newly imposed state guidelines, which obliterated the queer logics that defined them in the first place. All things considered, the state's public health approach was predicated on a neoliberal and heteronormative logic of privacy and intimacy that privileged a narrow set of relationships and practices. What becomes clear through our analysis is that the state deployed dignity during a crisis to do generative political work: to consolidate the power of heteronormative logics that queers had already fucked with well before the onset of HIV/AIDS.[8]

The Queer Logics of the Bathhouse

To entertain any notion that closures damaged the gay community and psyche, we must resist the urge to pathologize public, anonymous, casual sex or the spaces in which these activities take place. As Tim Dean reminds us, while "it would be a mistake to idealize gay sex institutions as utopian spaces liberated from the conflicts that permeate the world outside their walls," we can still posit "that institutions sponsoring such play should not be considered automatically as pathological spaces." Indeed, the erotic play that was encouraged within these establishments is, for Dean, a sign as well as a tool of "psychic health."[9]

According to historian Allen Bérubé, bathhouses constituted complex public sites for gathering during a time when gay men experienced extraordinary limits to meet this need. For Bérubé, "the baths seemed to offer an alternative to sex in the parks, and there was additional safety in numbers." Despite their public, commercial character, these spaces "created the first urban zone of privacy, as well as safety, for gay men."[10] The baths were dynamic spaces that were very much a part of a vibrant, safe, and prideful gay male sexual culture. Because they provided safety, democratic camaraderie, and mutually understood and valued sexual pleasure free of stigmatization—particularly when homosexuality was criminalized—they contributed immensely to the development of emotional empowerment and community-building.

Many urban centers in the United States had well-known Russian or Turkish baths or other health resorts by the nineteenth century. While these institutions were not established for men to discover same-sex sexual encounters, Bérubé notes that by the turn of the twentieth century, some became known as "favorite spots" where such behavior was not discouraged.[11] Publicly known gay bathhouses sprang up by the 1920s, and Bérubé highlights how they encouraged a prideful gay male identity; men would go to gay bathhouses rather than furtively searching for same-sex encounters in establishments not intended for this activity:

> When the bathhouses emerged in the 1920's and 1930's, they offered homosexual men a new option: they could meet and have sex in a gay bathhouse, in addition to having sex with "normal" men in a public bath-house. Many men who came out before there were any gay bathhouses looked down on having sex with other gay men. . . . It was a later genera-tion of gay men who, partly by using the openly gay bathhouses, learned to enjoy having sex with and loving other gay men. At a time when no one was saying "gay is good," the creation of an institution in which gay men were encouraged to appreciate each other was a major step toward gay pride. Since then, several generations of gay men—partly because of opportunities provided them by gay bathhouses and, later, gay bars—have learned to prefer sexual partners who are also gay. The bathhouses, thus, are partly responsible for this major change in the sexual behavior and self-acceptance of gay men.[12]

Historian George Chauncey echoes this idea; because baths were sites that encouraged "overt expressions of homosexual interest," they pro-vided space for men to socialize as *identifiably* gay men.[13] For Chauncey, bathhouses, even more than bars, were a "starting point" for a distinct gay identity and subculture; baths functioned as a "very large closet" within which "a gay world was built."[14] By the mid-twentieth century, especially during World War II, when San Francisco and New York City were sites of soldier embarkation for the European and Pacific fronts, the baths were an important resource for enlisted men seeking safe same-sex sexual encounters: "They offered a safe and private place at a time when hotel rooms downtown were impossible to find . . . [and] were also a useful alternative to the gay bars that began to open in San Francisco during the war, because many of the bars were declared 'off-limits' to military personnel."[15] Bérubé makes the communal value of baths clear: "For the gay community, gay bathhouses represent a major success in a century-long struggle to overcome isolation and develop a sense of community and pride in their sexuality, to gain their right to sexual privacy, to win their right to associate with each other in public, and to create 'safety zones' where gay men could be sexual and affectionate with each other with a minimal threat of violence, blackmail, loss of employment, arrest, imprisonment, and humiliation."[16]

Throughout the 1950s and 1960s, gay bathhouses proliferated in San Francisco and New York City even as their increased visibility triggered more raids by police forces.[17] The gay bathhouse assumed even more symbolic value in the context of the 1970s post-Stonewall era of gay liberation, particularly as queer sex acts themselves were increasingly characterized as an expression of liberation from heteronormative constraints. Queer theorist Ira Tattelman notes how choosing nonnormative sex while being watched, and affirmed, by other men was liberating:

> For many, gay liberation was primarily about sexual expression. Gay men used this freedom to develop erotic environments that celebrated communal sex options. These spaces offered new social structures, pleasure practices and changing definitions. To make a sexual choice in front of others, who by their presence were involved contingently and applauded the ability to make these kinds of decisions, became an impetus for self-sufficiency, a redefinition of who the gay man is and what he can do. Sex between men (especially in safe environments) created opportunities for resistance, strategic positions from which to construct the "meaning" of one's existence.[18]

Sex in the bathhouse became integrally interwoven with the expression of gay identity, gay pride, and gay resistance to years of heterosexual oppression. That one's desired sexual practice could be acted upon in a safe place, and that it could be done with the watchful and approving support of other gay men, was an ennobling experience. It was surely a root of queer kinship.

Beyond this emotional impact, by the 1970s, baths provided an array of activities, thereby attesting to their growing role in defining gay cultural practice and functioning as community institutions. For example, the Continental Baths on Manhattan's Upper West Side offered a dance floor, a Saturday-night cabaret, and a pool. The Liberty Baths and the Barracks in San Francisco invited local artists to decorate the walls with murals. Bathhouses even scheduled movie nights to screen campy cult classics. The Continental Baths featured entertainers like Bette Midler and Barry Manilow. These establishments also hosted benefits for the Gay Activists Alliance provided onsite testing for sexually transmitted infections, and encouraged voter registration. For example, the St. Marks Baths in New York City worked with the League of Women Voters to register gay men to vote in the 1984 election.[19] As Dianne Chisolm describes, the modern gay bathhouse offered "cafés, bars, lounges, game rooms, disco dance floors, cabarets and seasonal holiday parties" and provided spaces for "work, residence, business and leisure under one roof."[20] Overall, the baths were not merely sites for furtive, anonymous sex. They were important sites of community development and kinship formation that included multiple ways for gay and queer men to interact beyond the carnal encounter.

The debate over whether bathhouses should remain open, which characterized HIV policy discussions in San Francisco in 1984 and in New York City in 1985, failed to acknowledge the role the baths played in community development. To understand the functions and benefits of these institutions and to assess why they were viewed as threatening by broader heteronormative publics, we must recognize how these institutions and the activities that occurred within them adopted specific queer logics of time/space, contact, intimacy, and kinship/belonging.[21] These queer understandings ruptured conventional orientations that bolster heteronormative logics of order, stability, and safety.[22] Consequently, institutions that nourished oppositional queer logics had to be surveilled, critiqued, and eliminated for state authority to persist.

Whether our critical eye turns to the architecture, actions among bodies, or activities housed in these spaces, what becomes clear is that the bathhouses served as what queer theorist Michael Warner calls a counterpublic.[23] Counterpublics are alternative spaces that probe and resist normativity to offer subordinated communities different possibilities and divergent logics. They act as vital sites of contestation, possibility, and reformulation.[24] This queer counterpublic of the bathhouse assumed vast importance during a fraught era for gay men and their fight to reclaim and nourish open, safe, and healthy expressions of sexuality; build like-minded collectives; and assert a stake in conceptualizations and deployments of public space.

A close examination of these counterpublics reveals how their patrons reconfigured what it means to inhabit public space or perform "acceptable" public behavior. Simply put, as the men who populated the bathhouses wrestled for their right to space and exhibited their determination to fuck boldly, they challenged the supposedly tidy boundaries separating "public" and "private," and they spotlighted the problematic politics of taking up public space. Instead of hiding in the throes of sexual repression or attempting sexual expression in spaces that they considered unsafe or—at worst—unavailable (like a "home"), they opted to venture into public and to seek refuge in the bodies and conversations of their like-minded peers.[25] Where public space became the safe location for intimacy, where darkness and anonymity provided security, and where personal nakedness provided the public foundation for community, the legal logic of heterosexual sexual privacy behind the bedroom door hardly seemed relevant to queer experience.

Within the bathhouses, interactions defied normative dictations of intimate connection because they challenged social propriety; in other words, bathhouse patrons could engage with one another's bodies without formal introductions, without the imperative to follow social protocol, without the expectation of monogamous commitment, and even without the promise of a protracted interaction beyond those immediate moments of pleasure and mutual exchange.[26] In so doing, they demonstrated a divergent value system that rethinks how people negotiate what can happen in and through available physical space and how bodies can and should interact.

To borrow from writer and social theorist Samuel R. Delany, these men engaged "in thinking through the problem of where people—with their bodily, material, sexual, and emotional needs—might discover (or even work to set up) varied and welcoming harbors."[27] As they developed welcoming harbors in bathhouses, they discovered substantial alternatives to heteronormative relationship building and kinship formation in order to experience a cultural belonging perhaps not available elsewhere. Providing a firsthand account of his experience as a queer patron and his analysis as a theorist, Delany explains the possibilities of these sites of gay male contact. He details how they offer ethically sound democratic exchange. As Delany notes, "A glib wisdom holds that people like this just don't want relationships. They have 'problems with intimacy.' But the salient fact is: These *were* relationships. . . . Intimacy for most of us is a condition that endures, however often repeated, for minutes or for hours. And these all had their many intimate hours."[28] He describes these connections in more detail:

> Most were affable but brief. . . . More than half were single encounters. But some lasted over weeks; others for months; still others went on a couple of years. And enough endured a decade or more to give them their own flavor, form, and characteristic aspects. *You learned something about these people (though not necessarily their name, or where they lived, or what their job or income was); and they learned something about you.* The relationships were not (necessarily) consecutive. They braided. They interwove. They were simultaneous. . . . They were not the central relationships of my life. They made that central relationship richer, however, by relieving it of many anxieties.[29]

In his account and analysis of public sex locales, Delany unpacks how these institutions showed a need for recognizable and accessible physical space, redefined what relationships can and should be, and explored the meaning of ethical engagement with otherness.

Indeed, many interactions within the bathhouse were not centered on the immediacy of orgasm; they were not merely places for a quick way to get off. For example, Richard Tewksbury describes the pleasures of being in community with multiple like-minded men, moving among them, engaging in contact with them, but not necessarily reaching the point of sexual release quickly with any one of them: "Men may move from partner to partner relatively quickly. Most sexual contacts and interactions in a communal, semi-public area do not result in ejaculation. Rather many men will engage in sexual contact with numerous men sequentially, seemingly seeking a range of diverse and varying sexual contacts rather than one (or several) long interactions."[30] Echoing this, sociologists Adam Isaiah Green, Mike Follert, Kathy Osterlund, and Jamie Paquin contend that "the bathhouse no longer has the orgasm as its telos."[31] Rather, patrons could imagine the bathhouse as having more complex meanings and purposes associated with interaction and community.

Because he is chiefly interested in how and why people come together and what happens when they do or do not, Delany delineates between the ideas of contact and networking—with the former being a more organic, accidental interclass interaction with potential and the latter being a calculated, ordered, and even stifled system of communication that supports divisions (class-based, racial, gendered, and so on) among folks. Illustrating Delany's contention, Michael Rumaker, from his first-hand perspective at the Everard Baths in Manhattan, reflects on how social norms around nakedness potentially produced a sense of safety and camaraderie:

> Here, we were our naked selves, anonymous, wearing only our bodies, with no other identity than our bare skins, without estrangements of class or money or position, or false distinctions of any kind, not even names if we chose none. Myself, the other naked men here, were the bare root of hunger and desire, our prime need to be held, touched and touching, feeling, if only momentarily, the warmth and affectionate response of another sensuous human. Here, was the possibility to be nourished and enlivened in the blood—heat and heartbeat of others, regardless of who or what we were. Nurturing others we nurture ourselves.[32]

Delany privileges interclass contact as a more ethically sound, democratic form of engagement with otherness. He argues, "Given the mode of capitalism under which we live, life is at its most rewarding, productive, and pleasant when large numbers of people understand, appreciate, and seek out *interclass contact and communication* conducted in a mode of good will."[33]

Additionally, since the interactions do not demand or even regularly offer a future or a life commitment, they reformulate configurations of time in crucially queer ways. Without question, constructions of and narratives about temporality are in constant thrall with social, political, and economic structures, for time operates as the mechanism by which we order space, behavior, and bodies. Moreover, constructions and deployments of temporality structure narratives about productivity and responsibility—ones that ensure bodies, thoughts, and behaviors align with the goals of the state and capitalism. In short, time is serious business. But because patrons of public sex institutions often adopt and practice a kind of queer futurity—what Lee Edelman describes as "no future"—they probe, resist, and offer alternatives for how we understand the usage of time, particularly in ways that do not support normative projects.[34] Instead, these patrons suggest alternative configurations of time that do not rely on reproductive logics and heteronormative productivity standards—children, marriage, and so on. Rather than taking refuge in a stable fantasy of the "future," people who frequented public sex institutions like the baths had the tendency to (or at least the potential to) abandon order or the promise of a tomorrow. While this embrace is often mischaracterized as immature, irresponsible, or even narcissistic (or undignified), we might instead consider how these queer temporal decisions can amplify the possibility of an alternative relationship to "progress" or a divergent relationship to constructions of time itself—how we calculate it, fill it, and measure its productive usage.

Seeking contact with radical otherness—in public space—in nonnormative time is a fundamentally queer endeavor because it subverts normative discourses that delimit where bodies can go, when, and what they can accomplish. Put differently, queer practice resists the disciplining demands that normative conceptions of dignity as deployed by state officials require. The normative thrust that governs bodies in time and space is particularly powerful when a non-normative use of the body threatens to undermine social, political, and economic structures that are firmly intact but that rely on the compliance of bodies to maintain "order."

Adopting a queer logic of contact, Delany contends, "is vital to the material politics as well as to the vision of a democratic city."[35] Moreover, he suggests that contact "fights the networking notion that the only 'safe' friends we can ever have must be met through school, work, or preselected special interest groups: from gyms and health clubs to reading groups and volunteer work."[36] For Delany, contact is usually attacked and misrepresented as dangerous or irresponsible or undesirable precisely because it threatens to rupture and potentially dissolve the barriers that hegemonic structures police so steadfastly to order bodies, actions, and discourses. In short, this contact is undignified in the eyes of the state.

The state constructs a conservative discourse of safety in the guise of public health to discourage such queer understandings of contact with others.[37] Interestingly, though, Delany highlights that "if *every* sexual encounter involves bringing someone back to your house, the general sexual activity in a city becomes anxiety-filled, class-bound, and choosy. This is precisely *why* [public sex institutions] are necessary for a relaxed and friendly sexual atmosphere in a democratic metropolis."[38] Without these subversive spaces as sanctuaries for connecting in, through, and across difference, Delany and other patrons of these counterpublics find themselves asking difficult questions about when, where, and how to achieve the contact that they deeply value and need. Because of its very conceptualization as an oppositional logic, this contact is not valued or offered in heteronormative publics—and certainly not characterized as dignified.

During a complicated era in which gay men were already accultur-ated to distrust and suspect one another, the state's decisions to limit or close the physical spaces upon which contact depends left gay men with a fundamental lack. Dean similarly concludes that "the loss of this gay institution—along with the opportunities for inter-class contact and erotic sociability that it sponsored—marks a moment in gay history characterized by a bid for respectability at the expense of non-middle-class persons and values."[39] Delany stresses that this loss cannot be mended by "freedom" discourses, such as the civil libertarian argument for sexual privacy and freedom, which spoke to the emerging juridi-cal notions of constitutional sexual privacy rights and which many gay bathhouse advocates proffered to counter the public health narrative. Because "social contact is of paramount importance in the specific pur-suit of gay sexuality," he is not interested in the "freedom" to "be" gay without any of the existing gay institutions or without other institutions that can take up and fulfill like functions.[40] He details his opposition more firmly by noting a harrowing truth: "Such 'freedom' means noth-ing. Many gay institutions—clubs, bars of several persuasions, baths, tea-room sex, gay porn movie houses . . . have grown up outside the knowledge of much of the straight world. . . . The freedom to 'be' 'gay' without the freedom to choose to partake of these institutions is just as meaningless as the freedom to 'be' Jewish, when, say, any given Jewish ritual, text, or cultural practice is outlawed."[41]

Often gay liberation, as it developed in the wake of the Stonewall riots and flourished over the 1970s, is singularly associated with sexual liber-tarianism.[42] While the bathhouses are associated with sexual liberty, to consider them by this singular dimension promotes an impoverished notion of the liberationist ethos, for it "panders to popular misconceptions about LGBT history, which take a teleological—one might say mythic—view of the 1970s as a debauched period that had to conclude with the HIV/AIDS epidemic."[43] Focusing on an understanding of liberation that protects only individual sexual freedom also misses what AIDS activist Richard Berkowitz called for in 1983 when he urged gay men to take "responsibility for [our] own health and the health of [our] community" on their own terms.[44] To recover a more robust conception of liberation that is grounded in oppositional queer logics—like the ones espoused in the baths—we move past the dichotomous construction of the bathhouse closure debate of public health versus personal sexual freedom. Rather, we examine this historical episode through a queer lens that centers the state's exclusionary deployment and conferral of dignity.

Community Mobilization to Save the Bathhouse amid the Crisis

Histories of the early HIV/AIDS crisis often detail how many LGBTQ+ people mobilized to understand, educate, and prevent disease transmission when governing authorities at the municipal, state, and federal levels ignored the spreading epidemic. Many of these histories describe LGBTQ+ communities as divided between libertarians and public health advocates, reinforcing the simplistic narrative that refuses to consider the communal value of the bathhouse. Randy Shilts's *And the Band Played On* is illustrative. Shilts characterizes early AIDS activists (such as playwright and novelist Larry Kramer or Michael Callen and Richard Berkowitz, who drafted the first safer sex manual, "How to Sex in an Epidemic: One Approach") as rejecting the sexual libertarianism associated with gay liberation and advocating shuttering the baths instead. Shilts writes of Kramer, "Larry Kramer was growing more militant in this stance . . . [to] tell people that, if they wanted to survive, they should just stop having sex."[45]

A common narrative that positions public health against sexual freedom might start with Callen and Berkowitz's publication of "Two Gay Men Declare War on Promiscuity" in a November 1982 edition of the *New York Native* as representative of the former position. The essay begins by calling gay men to account for their promiscuity and by suggesting that this behavior is the root cause of the HIV/AIDS crisis: "Those of us who have lived a life of excessive promiscuity on the urban gay circuit of bathhouses, backrooms, balconies, sex clubs, meat racks, and tea rooms know who we are. We could continue to deny overwhelming evidence that the present health crisis is a direct result of the unprecedented promiscuity that has occurred since Stonewall, but such denial is killing us. Denial will continue to kill us until we begin the difficult task of changing the ways in which we have sex."[46] Importantly, however, another reading could suggest that altering "the ways in which we have sex" need not require closing the baths. To claim that this consequence necessarily follows would require grappling with how, at the time of writing, Callen and Berkowitz held to the then reigning theory of the disease—namely, the multifactorial theory. The theory posited that "there is no mutant virus"; instead, through promiscuity, gay men have "overloaded our immune systems with common viruses and other sexually transmitted infections." Their understanding of the theory further suggested that "our lifestyle has created the present epidemic of AIDS." What followed was their suggestion that the "obvious and immediate solution to the present crisis is the end of urban gay male promiscuity as we know it today."[47] And insofar as bathhouses enabled that promiscuity, it would seem that they had to be closed by state officials or boycotted and thus forced, by lack of business and profitability, to shut down.

This was certainly the position taken by Kramer and Shilts. For example, in a blistering attack against the Committee for the Freedom of Choice, which took a libertarian approach to sexual freedom, Kramer dismissed efforts to defend the baths. He wrote, "I wish you guys had better things to do with your time than devote it to stuff like this. There are some among us who think the baths should be closed. It is not a civil rights issue, it is a contagion issue—and we look like assholes defending this right. . . . How many of us have to die before you stop defending our right to fuck ourselves to death?"[48] Kramer's rejection of sexual liberty, his full embrace of the public health narrative, and his characterization of gay men as simply wanting "to fuck ourselves to death" capture all the markers of the state's own deployment of dignity, of its boundary making that degraded gay men as unable to behave within bounds of appropriateness.

Kramer may be thought of as advocating that gay men adopt the romantic, relational, and sexual norms of heterosexual society, of what constituted dignified behavior. In his novel *Faggots*, Kramer voiced these ideas through his protagonist Fred Lemish: "I'm tired of being a New York City–Fire Island faggot, I'm tired of using my body as a faceless thing to lure another faceless thing. I want to love a person!, I want to go out and live in that world with that Person, a Person who loves me, we shouldn't *have* to be faithful, we should *want* to be faithful."[49] Embedded within this passage is not only a clear longing for monogamy but also a valuing or prioritizing of a certain heteronormative romantic ideal.

By contrast, Charles Jurrist, a prominent critic for the *New York Daily News*, is often considered to occupy the libertarian position in the debate. In the issue of the *Native* that followed Callen and Berkowitz's published call to end promiscuity, Jurrist wrote "In Defense of Promiscuity." He accused his fellow AIDS activists of "unleashing . . . hysteria within our community" and offering a narrow understanding of sexuality that undermined liberationist identity. In the years after Stonewall, open sexuality permitted if not embraced "the stereotypical sexual marauder, the man who visits the Mineshaft [bathhouse] and at least one bathhouse every week and picks up a few men at the bars as well." Callen and Berkowitz (and one could add Kramer), according to Jurrist, declared war on this man, shaming him, and thereby shaming all of the political and cultural imperatives and achievements of the first post-Stonewall generation: "They are not merely calling on us to forego that type of orgiastic unselectivity. They seem to be saying that anything other than monogamy or sex restricted to two or three ongoing, tightly controlled relationships constitutes promiscuity and ought to be avoided."[50] For Jurrist, Callen and Berkowitz shamed the transgressive possibilities gay men invented as queer alternatives.

We read Callen and Berkowitz differently precisely because they were concerned with how gay men might fuck one another without dying. Indeed, we understand Kramer and Callen/Berkowitz as making different arguments; they were not shaming gay men for their undignified practice. While Kramer may embrace monogamy as the dignified route forward, Callen and Berkowitz clearly did not. In their essay, they stated, "We are not suggesting legislating an end to promiscuity. Ultimately, it may be more important to let people die in the pursuit of their own happiness than to limit personal freedom by regulating risk."[51] Callen and Berkowitz advocated education and information over simple bans and closure: "The tradition of allowing an individual the right to choose his own slow death (through cigarettes, alcohol, and other means) is firmly established in this country; but there is also another American tradition represented by the Federal Trade Commission and the Food and Drug Administration which warns people clearly about the risks of certain products and behaviors."[52] Aware of the history of government raids of bars and baths, Callen and Berkowitz favored community-led regulation over government imposition: "It would be preferable to avoid further governmental interventions. . . . [Instead,] the gay community must take responsibility of providing its members with clear and unequivocal warnings about the health risks of promiscuity."[53] In short, their call was less for monogamy than it was for a community-based response to the crisis.

Heeding this call, gay community organizations such as the Gay Men's Health Crisis (GMHC) began to produce educational materials that did not advocate bathhouse closure but that recommended safer sex practices within the baths. By late 1983, AIDS activists in New York City, including Berkowitz, Callen, Keith Lawrence, Joseph Sonnabend, and Roger Erlow, among others, created the Committee on Safer Sex. That committee established the Subcommittee on Bars and Baths, the meeting notes of which indicate efforts to design community-based regulation of the baths. Highlighting the fear of government intervention, the notes emphasize that all actions to regulate the baths and attempts to educate for safer sex must be seen as a gay community initiative. Otherwise, what "would be seen as govt [sic] intervention" would mean "political death" of this group. Instead, it had to be clear that this initiative was about "gays helping gays."[54]

In a memo dated January 14, 1984, the Committee on Safer Sex enumerated six items for community education: (1) a bathhouse poster with pamphlets and phone numbers, (2) the same poster for "bookstores" and bars, (3) subway posters with the phone number of the subcommittee, (4) posters for public places such as post offices, (5) public service announcements on television and radio, and (6) other pamphlets that would lay out answers to basic questions like "What is the immune system?" and provide a glossary of AIDS terms. The committee emphasized that "pamphlets provided with [the] poster will describe healthy low-risk sexual practices, give appropriate phone numbers, etc." The memo also indicated that the committee was seeking funding from the New York City health department, suggesting an early effort to partner with public health officials. The proposed mock-up for the poster embraced sex positivity. In bold letters, it proclaimed, "SEX IS WONDERFUL!" then below, it warned, "BUT DON'T LET AIDS KILL YOU!" It then provided a set of high-risk activities to be avoided: "DON'T RIM, DON'T LET HIM COME IN YOUR ASS. MAKE SURE YOU DON'T COME IN HIS. DON'T COME IN HIS MOUTH, AND DON'T LET HIM COME IN YOURS."[55] This phrasing reaffirmed the relational aspects of sexual encounters; it refuted the sexual libertarianism of *individual* pleasure and reminded the reader that we must take care of one another in community.

The proposed mock-up became a GMHC poster that reminded its viewer, "Great Sex Is *Healthy* Sex." Across the top, the poster read, "Great Sex! Don't Let AIDS Stop It." It included warnings against high-risk activities, promoted low-risk acts by noting that "Jacking off is hot and safe," and added that "Affection is our best protection."[56] The final poster also dropped the threatening language that AIDS will kill you and instead acknowledged the danger of AIDS while reminding viewers to embrace a healthy sexuality.

By late February 1984, the Subcommittee on Bars and Baths of the Committee on Safer Sex recommended a sequence of outreach efforts, beginning with working with the Community Council of Lesbian and Gay Organizations, then coordinating with the Greater Gotham Business Council, and then hosting a meeting with bar and bathhouse owners and managers. The committee would partner with gay media, including the *Advocate*, the *New York Native*, and *NYC Gay News*. The outreach, they said, "would update them on our current efforts and intentions, to reiterate our invitation to participate in our efforts and meetings, and to seek their support in whatever ways they deem appropriate."[57] In short, gay men led an effort to educate one another about high-risk and low-risk sexual activities, emphasizing that particular acts—not the location of those acts—were to be avoided.

Community activists came together in December 1984 (again, before the public debate over bathhouses began in earnest in New York City) to establish the Coalition for Sexual Responsibility (CSR).

This group was established by "gay men interested in engaging establishments where on-site sex occurred in AIDS education/prevention efforts. . . . The members of the coalition represented a wide spectrum of views . . . ranging from closing all establishments with on-premise sexual activity [to] making minor changes in how these businesses operated."[58] In an interim report released in October 1985, the CSR listed its objectives as "encouraging commercial establishments whose primary purpose is to permit high risk sexual activities to occur on their premises to provide an environment where safer sex is encouraged and promoted" and "encouraging these same establishments to help educate the community about AIDS and safer sex."[59] The report defined these establishments to include gay bathhouses, gay bars with "back rooms," gay movie houses, and some gay bookstores where on-site sex occurred. Importantly, not listed among the CSR's objectives was advocacy for full closure. In fact, one of the CSR's members, Dr. Stephen Caiazza, resigned because he contended that the bathhouses should be closed, whereas the CSR sought to address prevention of unsafe activities within these establishments and to promote distribution of safer sex information.[60]

The CSR drafted nineteen recommendations that focused on educational, hygienic, and structural recommendations for the bathhouses. The group then invited bathhouse owners and managers to a meeting on February 11, 1985, which was facilitated by the directors of Lambda Legal Defense and the National Gay Task Force. The CSR noted in its interim report that it promoted community self-regulation under the assumption that "if the government decided to regulate (including closure) the baths . . . [, then] restaurants and other places frequented by gays where no on-premise sex occurs could become vulnerable to government regulation."[61] The committee also sought to enlist the direct participation of the bathhouses out of a fear that if they "failed to comply with [the CSR's] modest recommendations then they would be inviting government intervention by their action."[62] Without question, the CSR aimed to avoid direct government intervention, in part because government action had long been associated with repression of gay sexuality and a refusal to recognize gay sexuality as valuable or responsible.

After receiving written consent from ten New York City bathhouses—Ansonia Baths, Barracks, Beacon Baths, Broadway Arms, East Side Sauna, Everard Baths, Mt. Morris Baths, Northern Men's Sauna, St. Marks Baths, and Wall Street Sauna—the CSR organized a set of three inspections of the bathhouses that would be conducted by volunteers throughout 1985. These volunteers would enter the bathhouses armed with a clipboard and "Inspection Sheet" of the CSR's thirteen items and evaluate whether bathhouse owners were complying with them. This list included the following:

1. Framed Safe Sex Posters were displayed in prominent, well-lit places.
2. Safe sex information in written form (the brochure) is directly offered to each patron upon admission.
3. Management has set aside a separate community space/table where questions can be answered and literature distributed.
4. Management has made available and encourages the exchange of pre-printed cards so that sexual partners can exchange names and addresses.
5. The premises were clean. It appeared that management had regularly cleaned premises with Clorox (or similar substance) every 6 hours or more often.
6. The water in hottubs & swimming pools appeared clear and clean. It appeared that management had used appropriate levels of chlorine in hottubs/swimming pools.
7. Management had made available water-based lubricant in appropriate containers, e.g. pump tops or small disposable packets.
8. Management exchanged all soiled towels and sheets free of charge.
9. Management provided liquid soap rather than bars.
10. Management provided, free of charge, each patron upon admission with a medically approved condom.
11. There were no glory holes.
12. The lights had been turned up.
13. There were no slings or bathtubs.[63]

The archived typewritten inspection sheets are covered with handwritten comments like "More than half the soap dispensers were empty!" and "Room had come [sic] stains on wall + door." All of these checklists noted that safe-sex posters were "not framed."[64]

On June 4, 1985, the CSR distributed letters to owners indicating "poor results and requesting that they take immediate remedial action."

The committee then convened a meeting with seven of the ten owners on June 13, which was followed by a letter to all bathhouses that urged "full compliance as soon as possible." A second round of inspections occurred in June and July, which revealed that "while the results were somewhat better with some of the establishments there were still no establishments in full compliance."[65] The CSR also faced some resistance to the inspection regime; the Barracks, for instance, refused to participate after the first inspection. The CSR then partnered with GMHC, and GMHC worked with the bathhouses to arrange on-site tables where GMHC members could distribute safer sex pamphlets to patrons.

The second round of inspections saw modest improvements in compliance. The third round, which took place in October, again saw improvements but noted only "full compliance in two of the ten bathhouses in the city." The report concluded by noting that city and state authorities were considering direct actions against the bathhouses and lamented that community efforts had fallen short. It did note that a majority of the NY AIDS Institute Advisory Board members (discussed further in the next section) advocated for the CSR's inspection regime to be adopted by city and state officials rather than endorsed shuttering the bathhouses; indeed, the New York City AIDS Education Coordinator referred to the CSR's approach as "noteworthy" and as representing "the cutting edge of community education on AIDS." But even the CSR concluded by noting, "The response from the bathhouses has been, for the most part, irresponsible and disappointing."[66]

We detail this evidence of how LGBTQ+ communities developed methods to regulate bathhouse usage and to educate community members about HIV to reveal how proactive some within the community were in trying to save the bathhouse as an important community institution. Furthermore, with this retelling of the history, we have highlighted how some within the community voiced, internalized, and even previewed what the state would offer as the solution to the crisis: be dignified by not being queer. To be queer was to tempt death.

Advocates of bathhouse regulation offered a different vision. Early on and quite contrary to the government action described in the next section, they distinguished between low- and high-risk sexual activities, recognizing that this approach would be far more effective than banning the baths that were so critical to gay identity and community. The comprehensive regimes of inspection innovatively developed by community members, even as they were endorsed by some officials, were often disregarded by authorities. Instead, elected officials, in the debates that raged in San Francisco and New York City, dehumanized gay men and painted them as depraved, oversexed animals incapable of responding to the crisis. In other words, the debates and the state-directed closures that followed did substantial cultural and political work to render gay men culpable for their own community's sudden and relentless demise.

Diseasing Queer Sex: The Moralizing Public Health Narrative

The debate over whether the bathhouses should remain open is often said to have begun in San Francisco and to have dominated that city's public AIDS discourse during 1984. This debate culminated with Dr. Mervyn Silverman, the city's director of the Department of Public Health, calling for closure on October 9, 1984. Indeed, it was reported that New York City officials were stunned by San Francisco's actions. These officials were quoted as suggesting that such action either violated privacy rights or would simply fail to achieve the stated objective of curbing the spread of HIV.[67] In 1985, this debate defined New York City's public discussion of HIV and AIDS policy. While this two-stage chronology is generally accurate, a closer review of primary source materials indicates that New York City officials considered whether and how they might target the bathhouses for closure well before the debate gripped San Francisco. Public officials had repeatedly targeted bathhouses as nuisances, especially given the goals of urban renewal. Additionally, how the public health narrative developed over time in each city reveals striking parallels. First, both cities' leading health officials initially opposed the closures only to adopt the opposite position by year's end. Second, both cities adopted policies that failed to distinguish between low- and high-risk sexual acts, thereby defining all queer sex as diseased; that defined the bathhouses only as sites of disease; and that defined all queer sex in these baths as inherently threatening to public health. Third, officials in both cities characterized bathhouse clientele as irrational and suicidal. Finally, the cities' monitoring regimes challenged the very queer logics of anonymity that made these bathhouses safe spaces for sex, identity, and community in the 1980s.

During the early years of the epidemic, when it was unclear how the disease was transmitted and before the viral agent was discovered, the dominant theory of infection held that HIV/AIDS was caused by multiple infections.[68] If HIV was caused by having a lot of sex, then sites that enabled such behavior contributed to the spread of disease. Consequently, it is hardly surprising that the New York State Commissioner of Public Health, David Axelrod, asked the state's general counsel, Peter J. Millock, to investigate if and how bathhouses might be closed. Millock replied in a memo dated July 25, 1983: "The reported multiplicity of sexual contact, especially among strangers in bathhouses patronized by homosexuals, suggests that closing them will significantly reduce the risk of exposure of homosexual and bisexual males to AIDS. This discussion, therefore, describes the statutory, regulatory, judicial or administrative powers possessed by or available to the following agencies or officials to effect a closing of such facilities, to wit, (1) the City of New York; (2) the Governor; (3) the State Commissioner of Health; and, (4) the District Attorney." The memo notes that because Article 165 of the New York City Health Code both "requires a bathing establishment to be maintained in a clean, sanitary and safe condition" and "requires a person with sore or inflamed eyes, nasal or ear discharge or other bodily infection to be excluded from the bathing establishment," then "patron conduct, the consequences of which, if permitted to continue unabated or unchecked, are likely to result in sexually transmissible diseases or new cases of AIDS, would seem to fall within the power of the health official to suspend or to revoke the permit of an offending bathing establishment, on the grounds of endangerment of life, health or safety." Alternatively, the baths could be closed under the administrative legal definition of "public nuisance" as "whatever is dangerous to human life or detrimental to human health." Therefore, bathhouses, "which, by their use, may be the breeding grounds of venereal disease, herpes and now AIDS, which are spread to members of the public who are not bathhouse patrons, are within the definition of common law nuisances. In any event, they are nuisances under the specific statutory definition because they are dangerous to human life or detrimental to health." The governor under New York public health law could "direct the State

Health Commissioner to conduct examinations concerning nuisances," and the governor could then act on that report by ordering such nuisances "to be changed, abated, or removed (Public Health Law, Section 1301(2))." Furthermore, public health law also empowered the state commissioner to direct a local board of health to investigate whether such a nuisance existed, and "the Commissioner, in effect, would still have such directory power over the New York City Board of Health under his power to exercise general supervision of all local boards of health and health officials."[69]

While no immediate public action in New York City followed from this memo, the memo nevertheless defines bathhouses as breeding grounds of disease and, therefore, as something that the state should not countenance as a site of normatively dignified behavior. Given that the space and behavior within it were understood as unworthy, the memo reveals no impulse to distinguish between high- and low-risk sexual activity, a distinction already discussed in the New York City gay press.[70] Indeed, while the memo offered the rationale for what would follow in New York in 1985, the *public* debate over closure sparked first in San Francisco.

The San Francisco debates were triggered when gay activist and *San Francisco Chronicle* reporter Randy Shilts wrote an article published on February 4, 1984, which quoted a local gay physician, Marcus Conant, who asked indirectly about the baths: "What are we going to do about compulsively promiscuous men?" In that article, Shilts quotes San Francisco supervisor Harry Britt: "Sexual activity in places like baths or sex clubs should no longer be associated with pleasure—it should be associated with death."[71] The statement foreshadows the state's death ultimatum—behave or die—in stark language.

A month later, Larry Littlejohn, the former president of the San Francisco gay-rights organization Society for Individual Rights, announced that he would seek over seven thousand signatures for a ballot initiative so that "sexual activities among patrons of public bathhouses should be prohibited."[72] Littlejohn had privately corresponded with Mervyn Silverman, director of the San Francisco Department of Public Health (DPH). In that conversation, Silverman wrote that it was "inappropriate and in fact illegal for [him] to close down all bathhouses and other such places," and he also noted that such action would "insult the intelligence of many of [the] citizens and it would be an invasion of their privacy." Instead, Silverman initially advocated that the DPH should work with the baths and other gay organizations "to educate the public, both gay and straight" about how the disease was spread.[73] However, by the end of 1984, Silverman not only endorsed shutting down the bathhouses but also "disregarded findings available in mid-1984 that attendance at San Francisco's baths was not correlated with AIDS risk."[74] In fact, in April 1984, scientists announced they had discovered the viral agent that caused AIDS, what would be named HIV in 1986.[75] As such, the rationale for closure grounded in a multiple infections theory was undercut. Nevertheless, Silverman pressed forward with the ban, and on April 9, 1984, he announced, "All sexual activity between individuals [is to] be eliminated in public facilities in San Francisco where the transmission of AIDS is likely to occur."[76]

Within two months of this announcement, four bathhouses in San Francisco—the Liberty Baths, the Catacombs, the Caldron, and the Sutro Baths—closed their doors. By late May, a *San Francisco Examiner* article revealed that Mayor Diane Feinstein had ordered on-duty plainclothes police officers to pose as bathhouse patrons to gather information about the sexual activities inside. Responding to accusations of privacy violations, Feinstein gave voice to the death ultimatum: "My concern with this has nothing to do with anything I may or may not think about morality. It has to do with life versus death."[77] On June 11, Feinstein asked the Board of Supervisors to pass an ordinance to transfer regulatory control from the San Francisco police to the Department of Public Health, which would strengthen Silverman's authority to complete the ban, but given growing criticism of Feinstein, the board took no action besides announcing a forty-five-day delay in deciding if it would transfer authority from the SFPD to the DPH.[78]

Indeed, city officials were at cross purposes. In August, the city's Human Rights Commission unanimously adopted a resolution opposing any regulation of "private consensual sexual activity in any bathhouse or sex establishment, absent a showing that it is a necessary and essential measure supported by clear and convincing medical and epidemiological evidence." Attesting to the growing awareness of the viral agent theory and calling for a more nuanced strategy than a blanket ban, the commission noted, "Health professionals cite types of sexual behavior, and not location, as the causative factors in the transmission of AIDS."[79]

As if responding to the commission and following the advice of the City Attorney's Office that closures would be more sustainable if they were based on evidence of unsafe sex acts occurring within the baths, in late September, Silverman hired four private investigators to document the activities within six bathhouses, four sex clubs, two adult bookstores, and two adult theaters.[80] According to historian Ronald Bayer, the reports "achieved the desired impact. Whatever the actual tabulations of safe, unsafe, and possibly safe acts observed might have revealed, the descriptions portrayed the existence of activity that would serve to shock the sensibilities of the conventional and disturb those concerned with the transmission of a deadly disease."[81] On October 9, 1984, Silverman ordered the closure of fourteen baths:

> Today I have ordered the closure of fourteen commercial establishments that promote and profit from the spread of AIDS—a sexually transmitted disease. . . . These businesses have been inspected on a number of occasions and demonstrate a blatant disregard for the health of their patrons and of the community. When activities are proven to be dangerous to the public and continue to take place in commercial settings, the health department has a duty to intercede and halt the operation of such businesses. Make no mistake about it: These fourteen establishments are not fostering gay liberation. They are fostering disease and death.[82]

The statement captures how, for Silverman, the baths were commercial enterprises only, and their role in fostering community (to say nothing of their potential for health education) went unacknowledged. Baths were sites of death; their clientele was either to be rescued by the state or culpable in the spread of disease and irresponsible for neglecting their own health and that of others. In short, Silverman's statement characterized bathhouse patrons as undignified. The bathhouses were nothing more than dens of disease and undignified behavior that hardly merited recognition, much less protection, by the state. All queer sex was threatening.

Silverman's ban was stopped by a preliminary injunction from Judge Roy Wonder, who ruled that the baths could remain open "as long as they contained no private rooms operated without a hotel license, and removed the doors of their rooms, booths, and video cubicles. The businesses were also to employ at least one monitor for an average of every twenty patrons, who would circulate every ten minutes, watching for 'high-risk sexual behavior' as the phrase was defined by the AIDS Foundation, and expelling patrons who engaged in it."[83] Wonder's injunction provided more nuance than Silverman's ban, and it shifted the emphasis from location to particular sex acts as the appropriate public health concern. Nevertheless, the proposed regime of surveillance smacks of infantilization; it assumes gay men to be incapable of altering their behavior unless compelled by the watchful eye of the state.

Additionally, the parameters of surveillance would undermine the spatial logics of desire and anonymity that were valued and important. Prior to state intervention, architecture within the baths was intricate, creating opportunities to live out tropes of gay male pornographic fantasy, including glory holes, mazes, prison cells, and trailers, each recalling other sites of public sex, such as toilets, parks, truck stops, and prisons. As queer theorist John Lindell explains, the operating logic of the bathhouse was "the notion of drift [that] is essential to the experience of a sex club, where fluidity facilitates passing into an aimless 'let's see what happens' state of mind . . . [where] one browses, in search of something vaguely determined."[84] This experience was no longer possible in a context of bright lights and monitors imposed by the state.

When the public debate in San Francisco had seemingly reached its conclusion, it was just beginning in New York City. Just as in San Francisco, New York City officials were initially not in favor of a ban. Mayor Ed Koch opposed closing the baths, but he considered the possibility of regulation.[85] David Sencer, the New York City health commissioner, was wholly opposed to banning the bathhouses. According to the *New York Times*, "Dr. Sencer maintains that closing bathhouses will have little if any impact on the control of AIDS and could even be counterproductive."[86]

A variety of physicians who played critical roles in treating people with AIDS and in developing AIDS policy in New York City, including Sonnabend, Lawrence Mass, Alvin Friedman-Kien, Roger W. Enlow, and Stephen Caiazza, opposed blanket bathhouse bans. In 1982, operating under the multiple infection understanding, Enlow advised gay men through the Gay Men's Health Crisis newsletter to "limit the number of sexual partners whose good health is not certainly known to [them]. For many, this will mean fewer sexual partners."[87] In an interview in the *Native*, Friedman-Kien expressed skepticism about whether closure would actually curb the spread of the disease. Closure made little sense, "not unless it could be shown that there were a specific communicable disease being spread from a specific location *because* of that location. The frequent sexual exposures that may take place at some baths or bars with back rooms are unquestionably a factor in venereal transmission. But the location itself is not the issue."[88]

In 1985, the GMHC voiced opposition to closure; the organization's rationale invoked the privacy right that had developed in constitutional jurisprudence since the 1960s: "We oppose any governmental closure or attempts by anyone to police individual behavior. . . . Proprietors of these places have a responsibility to provide AIDS information, condoms, and adequate lighting. And we agreed that any establishment which does not, should be boycotted by the community."[89] The GMHC maintained that the community was responsible enough to self-regulate; it refuted the ongoing criticisms implicit in governing officials' and others' advocacy for a blanket ban that characterized gay men as simply incapable of responsible behavior.

In February 1985, the New York State Department of Health established the Bathhouse Subcommittee to consider whether the state should take any action. This subcommittee included Dr. Stephen Caiazza; Michael Callen; GMHC member Robert Lee Cecchi; Richard Failla, a New York State judge; Dr. Jeff Laurence; Dr. Mathilde Krim, chair of the AIDS Medical Foundation; and David Leven, who would chair the committee.[90] The subcommittee released its findings in June 1985. It, like the San Francisco Human Rights Commission, opposed closure. According to the subcommittee, "State closure of the bathhouses is simply a means of controlling and regulating consensual sexual relations between gay men, and there is not currently a compelling need so great to justify government interference of this magnitude."[91] Furthermore, the subcommittee was concerned with a slippery slope: if the bathhouses were shut down, "then, perhaps, few obstacles would exist to further regulation of such relations in other locations, perhaps even in private homes."[92] Nevertheless, the subcommittee did recommend that the bathhouse owners should post safer sex information, maintain hygienic conditions, provide condoms, and ensure adequate lighting.

In fact, in an April 1985 memo outlining the subcommittee's likely recommendations, the subcommittee adopted the full nineteen recommendations put forward by the Coalition for Sexual Responsibility (CSR), which we discussed in the previous section. The state agency essentially coopted the community's efforts at self-regulation. According to David Leven, author of this memo, "This statement is almost identical to the draft proposal of the Coalition for Sexual Responsibility, except that the language is suggestive rather than mandatory. The [CSR] statement simply makes recommendations. It does not *require* anything."[93] Leven maintained that the community efforts had failed and that "the bathhouses . . . [had] not voluntarily taken reasonable steps which might lead to a decrease in the spread of AIDS."[94] Note that this assessment contradicts the findings of the community-organized CSR: the CSR inspections found increasing compliance over time, even though full compliance never happened. Consequently, Leven contended, "The time has come to strongly recommend responsible government action."[95]

New York governor Mario Cuomo, who at first steered clear of this debate, began to recommend regulation of the bathhouses in line with ideas proposed by the subcommittee, especially since the candidates challenging his reelection advocated full closure of the bathhouses.[96] Cuomo's position shifted when, in late October, state health commissioner David Axelrod informed the governor, "I have concluded that establishments which allow, promote and/or encourage sexual contacts that produce blood to blood or semen to blood contact are a serious menace to the public's health and must be prohibited."[97] A day later, the New York State Public Health Council approved an emergency addition to the state Sanitary Code. One new section, 24-2.2 stated, "No establishment shall make facilities available for the purpose of sexual activities where anal intercourse, vaginal intercourse or fellatio take place. Such facilities shall constitute a threat to the public health." Section 24-2.3 provided that "the State Health Commissioner, local health officers and local boards of health may close any such facilities or establishments as constituting a public nuisance."[98]

Similar to Silverman's blanket ban in San Francisco, section 24-2.2 employs a circular logic by defining the baths as a public health threat and by empowering public officials to close down all public health threats. Officials provided no acknowledgment that these institutions could be anything other than a threat or that the activities within could accomplish anything other than disease transmission. Furthermore, the provision, like the San Francisco ban, makes no distinction between high and low risk. For example, condom usage is not mentioned, and oral sex, despite its lower risk, is banned along with anal sex. The emergency measure, then, ignored the recommendations of the Bathhouse Subcommittee of the state's AIDS Advisory Council.

Mayor Koch was caught unawares by the implementation of the emergency measure, and he initially opposed it as executive overreach that the courts would strike down: "What is the sense in our doing something that is going to be thrown out of court?" he asked. "What would it look like if we take action and close a bathhouse and two days later a court opens it up? Then we look like jerks."[99] Nevertheless, later that day, Koch complied with the new guidelines. The mayor's resolve to keep the bathhouses open and regulated had been weakened, reportedly under a threat that Axelrod would send in state inspectors if the city did not surveil the bathhouses on its own.[100] The threat severely undermined Koch's authority and reputation in an election year.

Bathhouse owners did attempt to comply with the new Sanitary Code directive. For example, Bruce Mailman, the owner of the New St. Marks Baths, provided condoms and safer sex information, and he required patrons to sign a pledge indicating they had read and would comply with the state's guidelines banning oral and anal sex.[101] Nevertheless, Mailman publicly opposed the state's emergency sanitation measure, writing in a *New York Times* editorial that closure served no public health purpose. He argued that unsafe sex would simply occur elsewhere, that the state violated the constitutional privacy rights of his clientele, and that the policy focused on location (on bathhouses) rather than on a nuanced regulation of sex acts themselves. He noted that the policy "fails to distinguish between safe and unsafe sex, the amendment takes us a step backward in the highly successful educational effort that we and other responsible establishments have undertaken." Finally, he castigated Axelrod: "What he's doing isn't medical. It's political. He's using the office of the health department as a political forum."[102]

Mailman's editorial was published a month after the New York State Supreme Court issued the first order to close a bathhouse called the Mineshaft.[103] Under section 24-2, inspectors visited the bathhouse, and they subsequently reported witnessing anal intercourse, even though they also reported seeing condoms distributed. They also reported hearing whips being used (which is hardly surprising because this particular establishment catered to men interested in bondage/discipline and sadomasochism). Koch responded to the report by degrading queer sex: "It's tough stuff to read. It must be horrific, horrendous in its actuality to witness."[104] Then, on November 7, 1985, when the injunction to close the Mineshaft was issued, Koch gave a press conference where he described gay men at the baths as "suicidal": "[The court order] brings to the consciousness of those who have a predilection to engage in this suicidal behavior how ridiculous it is. Maybe it will deter them as well. We don't know. But we're going to do the best we can."[105] Koch's remarks display an "ick factor" that is the foundation for the degradation that marks the state's boundary making when denying dignity.[106]

Less than two weeks later, the New York City Council passed Resolution 1685A, which directed Commissioner Sencer to "close down bathhouses and other public heterosexual and homosexual establishments which make facilities available for certain high risk practices . . . known to contribute to the spread of AIDS."[107] Since the resolution reiterated what section 24-2 already provided, it had no immediate effect other than putting Sencer, who continued to oppose closure, in an untenable position. On December 4, 1985, Sencer announced his resignation, effective on January 3, 1986.[108] Two days after this announcement, the New York State Supreme Court closed the St. Marks Baths.[109] The closure order came one day after the St. Marks proprietor, Mailman, published his criticism of the emergency sanitation measure.

The closure was based on inspections, which occurred between November 2 and December 4, 1985, and detailed banned activities taking place. The *New York Native* challenged the evidence as circumstantial and subjective, highlighting that one inspector admitted, "I could not observe any activity as the door was closed" and that there were "several used condoms on the floor."[110] On December 16, signaling his complete reversal on the issue, Mayor Koch—much as San Francisco's Silverman had done—advocated closure: "We are monitoring institutions which, we believe, are allowing unsafe health practices to continue."[111] On January 6, 1986, just over a year since the public debate began, the city issued a request for an injunction to close the St. Marks Baths for up to a year.[112] Despite repeated appeals, many of which were premised on the claim that the state policy violated individual privacy rights, the St. Marks Baths never reopened.[113] Affirming the state's complete lack of comprehension of queer logics developed in the context of the bathhouse and public sex, the New York Supreme Court ruling against the St. Marks Baths refuted the privacy claim by relying on the traditional heteronormative conception of the private sphere: "It is by no means clear that defendant's rights will, in actuality, be adversely affected in a constitutionally recognized sense by closure of St. Mark's. The privacy protection of sexual activity conducted in a private home does not extend to commercial establishments simply because they provide an opportunity for intimate behavior or sexual release."[114] Dignified sexual behavior was private sex in the home; if gay men were to be dignified, they must behave only within the confines of heteronormative limits of sex, intimacy, and romance and reject any queer logics of space, time, and kinship.

Just over a year later, with the Mineshaft, the St. Marks Baths, and the Everard Baths all closed, Commissioner Axelrod declared, "Today, many of the baths openly encourage safe-sex practices. And based on our observations, dangerous sexual activities are no longer being encouraged and, in fact, are not occurring. We believe the remaining bathhouses have acted very responsibly."[115] In other words, the sexual activities that occurred within the bathhouse could be characterized by practices associated with restraint, maturity, or, indeed, dignity. Actions taken by the state had disciplined the undignified and thereby fostered behaviors far more worthy of respectability as conceptualized within the dominant public health narrative.

By 1987, four bathhouses were still operating, but none were in violation of sanitation measure 24-2. All had posted signage advertising safer sex practices, hosted workshops and showed films on such practices, and distributed condoms. Axelrod's claim that the bathhouses acted responsibly only after the state action tellingly ignores that many of these bathhouses were operating with the same safer sex measures in place via the community regulation that preceded state action. Furthermore, the success that the New York State Health Commissioner had achieved was not remarkably different from what the community's efforts accomplished in 1984; to be sure, the community efforts had recognized these same four bathhouses as complying with safer sex measures at the time of their own inspections.

Gay men, in their attempts to respond to the HIV crisis with little to no support from public authorities, developed methods of regulating bathhouse usage. Such innovation was disregarded by authorities who refused to acknowledge the dynamic community-building aspects of these physical spaces. Instead, these authorities saw bathhouses as diseased locales in which nothing productive or dignified could occur, and they often refused to accept scientific advice to distinguish between sex acts and locations. When we compare the community's strategies with the state's directives, it becomes clear that both achieved similar results without equal authority or credit and that each had different goals. Instead of approaching the bathhouses with an ethos of care and attention to the logic that shaped the spaces, state authorities flattened the dimensions of bathhouse culture. In so doing, they ignored intracommunal efforts that preceded state-directed ones and—ultimately—painted gay men as depraved, oversexed animals incapable of responding to the crisis. Therefore, public health policies reveal themselves as just one more iteration of the state's long-standing assault on queer bodies and spaces and of its commitment to eradicating troubling queer counterpublics. In short, the state's actions make clear how state authorities construct the boundaries of dignity to decide who is valued and on what terms.

Conclusion

We began this book at a critical moment in HIV/AIDS history to make clear what dignity can do. It can function as a device deployed to create boundaries and delimit who and what is valued. More specifically, the public health policies pursued in San Francisco and New York City culminated in eliminating queer community institutions. In this chapter, we argued that the state issued a death ultimatum during a public health crisis: die or behave. The state's characterizations of queer space and practice fostered and perpetuated a narrative of culpability, positioning death as the consequence of undignified choices. To live, gay communities were compelled to reject and abandon queer practices for more dignified behavior. If gay men were to be recognized as having anything like dignity that the broader public could or should value, they could no longer embrace any sense of time, kinship, or desire that transgressed heteronormative notions of romance, intimacy, and privacy. Dignified behavior was offered by the state—and by some within the community itself—as the solution to the health crisis.

This chapter has laid the foundation for understanding the state's capacity to confer dignity and the processes by which it can do so. We have contended that such a conferral of dignity has come at a substantial cost. Precisely because dignity is defined and deployed by the state, it operates with an exclusionary logic. The public health context in which the public officials demanded so-called dignified behavior has now substantially changed. In the next chapter, we examine if that altered context has influenced contemporary queer attempts to expose and transgress dignity's limits or if those actions have absorbed and worked within those limits.

2

Do You Swallow?

Possibilities for Queer Transgression in New Contexts

In 2014, the National Black Gay Men's Advocacy Coalition collaborated with the National Minority AIDS Council to release a short video titled "Do You Swallow"? It featured men discussing their use of medication to prevent HIV—namely, either pre-exposure prophylaxis (PrEP), which is taken daily to lower the risk of infection, or post-exposure prophylaxis (PeP), which is taken soon after possible exposure to the virus. But when asked whether they swallowed, the men giggled and demurred because the question carries specific meaning in queer vernacular.[1] The public health campaign plays with the question's original meaning: Do you swallow cum when sucking dick?

This video transforms an intimate act often framed as dangerous to bodily integrity into an act that promotes individual well-being and, by extension, public health. Swallowing also carries meaning as a metaphor. It moves us toward an understanding of sexual intimacy as welcoming to the stranger, to the other, to risk.[2] Swallowing semen is communing with another. By contrast, to spit out cum denies the other. To spit is to preserve the integrity of the self and to expel the other; it is a process of abjection.[3] In this campaign, swallowing is emptied of its capacity to breed queer kinship. An intimate act with subversive potential to embrace risk and to build community is harnessed by the pharmaceutical industry and the state's public health apparatus to promote respectable sexuality: safe, restrained, individualized, and dignified.

The dynamics at play in placing acts of queer kinship into the service of public health and thereby evacuating their potential for resistance or transgression—if only at the level of metaphor—foreground the questions that motivate this chapter. In a context in which HIV/AIDS is a manageable chronic condition, what practices inspire and nurture queer kinship?[4] How have these practices resisted or, as the question

"Do you swallow?" illustrates, been transformed to promote the state's deployment of dignity? We identify three practices to explore: (1) promoting contemporary bathhouses and geolocative social media apps, such as Grindr, to patrons and users for same-sex sex and intimacy; (2) taking PrEP or maintaining viral suppression through treatment as prevention (TasP) to engage in what some have called sex "without fear"; and (3) participating in subcultures of intentional HIV transmission.[5] We consider which of these actions promotes stratified, safe, controlled, and dignified interactions that maintain dominant hierarchical norms and further the work of the state. We also examine which efforts, by contrast, challenge what the state seeks to delimit, control, and banish from public sight. Our assessment is informed by Samuel Delany's distinction between networking and contact in *Times Square Red, Times Square Blue* and by Tim Dean's arguments about contemporary cruising in a digital age and "stranger sociality" in *Unlimited Intimacy*.[6] Through these concepts, we illustrate how the generative work done by dignity inflects certain contemporary efforts to reassert queer alternatives, while others resist its seductive promises.

This chapter proceeds in four parts. The first section examines contemporary bathhouses; the second section explores geolocative social media apps promoted to LGBTQ+ communities, which have been called "digital bathhouses."[7] Whereas in chapter 1 we discussed how bathhouses illustrated Michael Warner's concept of counterpublics, we now document how bathhouses and geolocative apps represent themselves to potential customers in an altered context.[8] In other words, we focus our attention on how these spaces and services are structured and marketed and on how they communicate what customers should expect and what is expected of them. We evaluate the myriad ways some bathhouses and apps have absorbed and advanced a particular idea of dignity, while others have attempted to contest it. We find that conceptualizations of dignity, which invoke privacy, monogamy, productivity, responsibility, and safety and seek to restrain queer excess, often, although not exclusively, have come to characterize those spaces, both physical and digital, that might otherwise serve as counterpublics.

The third section discusses PrEP and TasP, which, by lowering the risk of HIV transmission, could enable sexual practices often shunned in the 1980s, 1990s, and early 2000s to flourish. The implications of an

HIV diagnosis have changed; in September 2017, the Centers for Disease Control and Prevention (CDC) declared as much: "Across three different studies, including thousands of couples and many thousand acts of sex without a condom or pre-exposure prophylaxis (PrEP), no HIV transmissions to an HIV-negative partner were observed when the HIV-positive person was virally suppressed. This means that people who take ART [anti-retroviral treatment] daily as prescribed and achieve and maintain an undetectable viral load have effectively no risk of sexually transmitting the virus to an HIV-negative partner."[9] If HIV has become manageable, at least when treatment is accessible, then the state's death ultimatum (defined in the previous chapter) loses the power it once had. PrEP and TasP could inspire an ethic of radical openness that Dean, in particular, celebrates. Queer sex may be tolerated but only under certain conditions of surveillance: be on PrEP or maintain undetectability. In short, the boundaries of who counts as a "good gay," as a dignified gay, and how that status can be attained and maintained have been altered, but the logic of dignity's hierarchies persist.[10] Being on PrEP or maintaining undetectability becomes a marker of responsibility and dignity. Importantly, though, access to PrEP or TasP, given current strictures of the pharmaceutical and healthcare industries in the United States, and thus access to being deemed dignified by state authority, remains raced and classed. When we consider access limitations with the consequent implications for what constitutes dignified behavior, we see how PrEP and TasP have been absorbed into the state's deployment of dignity. Less evident is whether these medications can provide a pathway for a systemic reimagining of dignity and an effective challenge to its limits.

The fourth section explores the subculture of intentional HIV transmission, often called "gift giving and bug chasing," to do some of this reimagining. The barebacking, or condomless sex between men, associated with this subculture may have already established ethics and values that resist the deployments of dignity that bolster state power over queer bodies and practices. Because this subculture has been stigmatized and criminalized, its defiant logics and practices have fallen out of view. Additionally, the availability of PrEP and the reality of TasP alter the meanings that come with barebacking. Nevertheless, we maintain that this subculture offers lessons that map pathways of resistance. We do not argue that being on PrEP or becoming undetectable are bad developments. However, since access is intertwined with structural racism and capitalist imperatives of the state and private industry, we worry about their exclusionary potential. Consequently, we uncover how the subculture's ethics of contact and care—an openness to the stranger, which the state has deemed undignified—serve as models that expose the limits of the state's construction of dignity and counter its exclusionary power.

Access to and knowledge about these subcultures of intentional transmission are limited to outsiders, as they are premised on explicit defiance of public health norms.[11] Therefore, this section turns to representations of these cultures in documentary film and fiction. We examine Louise Hogarth's documentary *The Gift* and Dennis Cooper's novel *The Sluts* to think about these subcultures.[12] We are guided by Leora Lev's assertion that "a truly progressive politics respects the spectrum of the social-sexual epistemologies and practices, *on its own terms*, in life as well as in aesthetic explorations of eroticism and passion."[13] Rather than claim that one representation is right and one is wrong, by reading them side by side, we expose the ideological work done by each. What becomes clear in this comparison is that the former reinforces dignity as conceptualized and deployed by the state, whereas the latter empowers queer communities to claim agency and conceptualize their own autonomy beyond the limits of dignity.

Frequent Fucker Rewards: Cruising the Contemporary Bathhouse

In chapter 1, we characterized the bathhouse as a community institution animated by queer logics. In so doing, we revealed how state and municipal authorities that advocated shuttering these spaces in the midst of the HIV/AIDS crisis had little knowledge of—or purposefully ignored—the queer worldmaking principles that shaped them. Under the auspices of public health, these spaces were eliminated or intensely modified. That bathhouses remain open today would seem to testify to their staying power as sites that challenge values of privacy, individualism, and romantic intimacy that define neoliberal heteronormativity.

We challenge this interpretation by uncovering how particular conceptions of dignity influence these sites. Through textual analysis of websites advertising bathhouses—the bathhouse's self-descriptions, visual imagery of the spaces, and pricing information on access and membership—we demonstrate that bathhouses do not necessarily constitute a queer counterpublic. Instead, our exploration reveals how they pay some homage to queer logics of the past while also revealing how they have been influenced by a notion of neoliberal dignity that relies on privacy, restraint, safety, and individualism.

In his account of public sex institutions, Delany theorizes about their community value and explains why the demolition of—or intense modification to—them produces dire consequences for the most marginalized. His analysis distinguishes between contact and networking. The former functions as an unpredictable encounter saturated with possibility for pleasure, defying the boundaries that divide us along race, class, gender, and geographical lines. Delany collapses all sorts of contact among strangers within democratic pleasure:

> Contact is the conversation that starts in the line at the grocery counter with the person behind you while the clerk is changing the paper roll in the cash register. It is the pleasantries exchanged with a neighbor who has brought her chair out to take some air on the stoop. It is the discussion that begins with the person next to you at the bar. It can be the conversation that starts with any number of semiofficials or service persons—mailman, policeman, librarian, store clerk or counter person. As well, it can be two men watching each other masturbating together in adjacent urinals of a public john—an encounter that, later, may or may not become a conversation. Very importantly, contact is also the intercourse—physical and conversational—that blooms in and as "casual sex" in public restrooms, public parks, singles bars, and sex clubs.[14]

Because contact at bathhouses and sex clubs does not impose the same kind of order that one might find in a school, church, or workplace, Delany contends that it is rife with potential for interclass communication. As he explains, "Given the mode of capitalism under which we live, life is at its most rewarding, productive, and pleasant when large numbers of people understand, appreciate, and seek out *interclass contact and communication* conducted in a mode of good will."[15] Due to its potential for engagement with otherness, contact is charged with possibility and risk. Delany argues, "A discourse that promotes, values, and facilitates such contact is vital to the material politics as well as to the vision of a democratic city. Contact fights the networking notion that the only 'safe' friends we can ever have must be met through school, work, or preselected special interest groups: from gyms and health clubs to reading groups and volunteer work."[16] Public space that foregrounds contact could be a refuge of difference, which is particularly valuable for the most marginalized of queer people.

Delany's networking, by contrast, is a privatized form of interaction that necessitates grouping along and within ready-made categories of difference. When people enter into networking situations or navigate institutions shaped by networking, they are often in thrall with people of similar racial backgrounds, economic classes, professional arenas, belief systems, political affiliations, or even geographic locations. Because of its demand for sameness, networking is a "safer" option than contact. Consequently, for Delany, "there is a conservative, stabilizing discourse already in place that sees interclass contact as the source of pretty much everything dangerous, unsafe, or undesirable in the life of the country right now—from AIDS and 'perversion' in all its forms, to the failures of education and neighborhood decay, to homelessness and urban violence."[17] The political, legal, and moral intervention, as well as the "violent reconfiguration of [the city's] landscape" that took place through the elimination of public sex institutions in the late 1980s and early 1990s, according to Delany, privileged networking as the norm that should shape public interaction.[18] Using conservative deployments of notions of danger and safety—through the lens of public health or real estate zoning / crime rates—networking supplants contact as an animating feature of public engagement with others.

While contact and networking differ, Delany avoids constructing them as a stable binary: "The opposition between contact and networking may be provisionally useful for locating those elements between the two that do, indeed, contrast. But we must not let that opposition sediment onto some absolute, transcendent, or ontological level that it cannot command."[19] The distinction highlights how each contributes to different outcomes. These are fundamentally different forms of sociality. As Delany notes, "The benefits of networking are real and can look—especially from the outside—quite glamorous. But . . . such benefits are fundamentally misunderstood. More and more people are depending on networking to provide benefits that are far more likely to occur in contact situations."[20] More specifically, Delany worries that networks are saturated by both competition and a density of need. As he explains, "Briefly, what makes networking different from contact is that, in networking situations, the fundamentally competitive relationship between the people gathering in the networking group is far higher than it is in the general population among which contact occurs."[21] He contends that networking falls short because "the amount of need present in the networking situation is too high for the comparatively few individuals in a position to supply [the need] . . . in any equitable manner."[22] Networking can prove unfulfilling, especially as the primary form of social interaction.

A singular reliance on networking may produce dire consequences to democratic intercourse. Delany proclaims that "we need contact," for without it, we cannot grasp why, despite attaining material improvements, we still feel unsatisfied: "We are in a period of economic growth. . . . But most of us are asking, Why, then, isn't my life more pleasant? The answer is that 'pleasantness' is controlled by small business diversity and social contact; and in a democratic society that values social movement, social opportunity, and class flexibility, interclass contact is the most rewarding, productive, and thus privileged kind of contact."[23] Delany explains what can mitigate potential loneliness or emptiness: "Venues must be designed to allow these multiple interactions to occur easily, with a minimum of danger, comfortably, and conveniently."[24] The structures, design, and policies of access to a space can regulate the kinds of behaviors and interactions that may occur within it.

Dean extends Delany's foundational ideas to the act of cruising to theorize about ethical engagement with otherness. He distinguishes among different approaches to cruising to showcase how that act can embrace the values of Delany's contact or maintain values associated with networking. Cruising informed by contact offers a form of stranger sociality that Dean celebrates: "Cruising entails a remarkably hospitable disposition towards strangers" because "cruising exemplifies a distinctive ethic of openness to alterity."[25] It functions as an "intimate encounter with the other that does not attempt to eliminate otherness."[26]

Cruising constrained by networking, however, encourages "privatized forms of sociability" that maintain boundaries.[27]

In our exploration of contemporary bathhouses and social networking apps, we use Delany's and Dean's insights to study structure and design as well as to explore the kinds of behaviors they may encourage. We ask how these venues and their policies promote a particular kind of sociality that is welcoming or hostile to the stranger. Ultimately, as we survey spaces of gathering for queer communities today, we consider whether they render more likely the democratic exchange afforded by contact and stranger sociality or facilitate the more limited and "safer" interactions associated with networking. Furthermore, we contend that networking behaviors are likely to be coded as more dignified than contact. Contact encourages communication across differences; networking reifies those differences and reinforces boundaries and hierarchies of race, class, health, and masculinity. Ultimately, networking is coded and understood as dignified insofar as contact is tarnished as irresponsible and unsafe.

To uncover the values and behaviors that bathhouses promote to their potential customers, we built a database of contemporary bathhouses that cater to men who have sex with men. We included all listings under the categories "sauna and cruising" and "sex clubs" on the gay travel site Misterbandb.com and cross-referenced those with facilities listed on gaybathhouse.org. We confirmed which bathhouses maintained active websites and were open for business as of June 2019. This process generated a database of fifty-two bathhouses in the United States. Six companies maintained multiple bathhouses in locations throughout the United States—The Clubs,[28] Flex Spas,[29] Midtowne Spa,[30] Steamworks Baths,[31] Roman Holiday Health Clubs,[32] and Westside/Eastside Club[33]—and thirty bathhouses were independent. The former we refer to as the "corporatized bathhouse."[34] We explored bathhouse websites by adopting the role of a potential customer, navigating their pages and viewing photos of the physical spaces.[35] We gathered information to assess how bathhouses promote their services, policies, and pricing. We then grappled with how the textual and visual presentation of a space for sexual interaction constitutes and condones the types of cruising that might occur within them.[36] Our examination focuses on how the descriptions and presentations of the bathhouse reflect, constitute, and prioritize the kinds of cruising that can and, indeed, should—at least according to the digital marketing presented on the bathhouse websites—take place within them.

Networking and Contact within the Corporate Bathhouse

The corporate bathhouse is most likely to encourage networking behaviors almost by definition. As Delany reminds us, "Big business is anti-contact in the same way that it is anti-small business," and these particular bathhouses are structured as big business.[37] From their websites and policies of access, we uncover four ways in which networked sociality is prioritized: (1) their sites maintain a slick tourism aesthetic, (2) the text and imagery emphasize a particular hypermasculinity, (3) the bathhouses promote theme nights focused on specific identities (bears, jocks, etc.), and (4) the bathhouses' pricing structure defines access to and limits engagement within the bathhouses. However, at least two elements—opportunities to maintain anonymity and to participate in CumUnion parties—nod toward promoting an ethic of contact.[38]

First, the homepages of Midtowne Spa's three locations in Denver, Los Angeles, and Van Nuys and of The Clubs' seven locations in Columbus, Dallas, Fort Lauderdale, Houston, Indianapolis, Miami, Orlando, and St. Louis show their respective cityscapes. The image is stock photography that emphasizes locations and themes most associated with the city (the St. Louis Arch, the iconic Reunion Tower in Dallas, or the oceanfront of Miami) that could appear on any city's tourism agency's site or the city's Chamber of Commerce site.[39] In this way, the corporate bathhouses offer a rebranded image of the pre-HIV-era "diseased" bathhouses, which were lambasted as eyesores and lowered property values. The bathhouse is now repositioned as a clean, safe, modern, and nondescript space. The imagery acts as a sanitized projection of urbanity of which the bathhouse is part—respectable for the visitor. Such a rebranding works to communicate values and expectations for the clientele it welcomes.

Delany's discussion of the recent redevelopment and Disneyfication of Times Square helps unpack how these images operate. As he posits, the decisions that occur at the level of spatial design and management are shaped by the aspirations and anxieties of the middle-class tourist, particularly those who have absorbed a conservative discourse that associates the city with danger, sexual excess, and moral corruption. He writes, "The New Times Square is envisioned as predominantly a middle-class area for entertainment, to which the working classes are welcome to come along, observe, and take part in, if they can pay and are willing to blend in."[40] With these stock photos and rebranding, these bathhouses not only make clear who will be welcomed within these spaces but also provide guidance on what kinds of behaviors will be appropriate. Finally, this self-representation comports with broader imperatives of urban redevelopment and thereby wards off the threat of the bathhouse being stigmatized as a space of difference in which undignified behavior abounds. Again, Delany reminds us how institutions can use design, architecture, and visual presentation to promote particular forms of sociality over others: "Any social form (or, indeed, architectural form) that shies us away from contact and contact-like situations and favors networking or relatively more network-like situations is likely to be approved."[41] In short, the new bathhouse is designed for pre-selected groups of individuals and begins to promote its exclusionary networking logic on the homepage.

Second, the characteristics of the pre-selected groups sought are apparent once we study the website text. An aesthetic of cisgender hypermasculinity is prominent. The Steamworks Chicago homepage describes the bathhouse as "a private men's gym, sauna, bathhouse for men 18 years and older . . . you know, men looking for other men."[42] The language of "you know" winks to shared values; if potential patrons do not so identify, then Steamworks may not be for them. Similarly, Midtowne Spa describes itself as a "Place for Men" and that its goal is "to provide a safe, clean, and friendly place where men can meet and enjoy each other's company."[43] And The Clubs' website caters to "gay and bisexual men" and aims to "provide a place for men to meet in a safe, healthy and fun environment."[44] Masculinity remains the priority.

Images reinforce this welcomed masculinity. The homepages of Midtowne Spa feature muscled men paired with cityscapes. The Denver site has a young bearded white man with pronounced abdominal muscles.[45] The Los Angeles site depicts a young white man with large pecs and facial scruff.[46] An image further down on the Midtowne Spa homepage, and thus deprioritized in the visual field, offers modest alternatives to this ideal. It presents four men, one of whom can be read as Black. One is less muscled; all have some facial hair.[47] The Clubs' homepage contains an image of a young muscled white male posed with hands resting behind his head to emphasize his biceps, pecs, and armpits.[48] The Club Dallas page references masculinity by having a muscled man don a cowboy hat.[49] The Club Houston page features an image of a shirtless man wearing a dog tag.[50]

Even Steamworks's career page reinforces a masculine ideal with a nod toward military tropes: "We are always looking for a few good men to join the team at Steamworks."[51] Steamworks even takes its prioritization of masculinity to a hormonal level. When describing the music pumped through its sound system, Steamworks tells its customers that "house DJs produce our exclusive testosterone fueled sounds live in our clubs across North America."[52] Their recruitment text also sets clear parameters: "We are looking for DJs who want to play music that makes men want to fuck. Dark. Primal. Heated. This isn't music to dance to this is music to fuck to. No divas, no anthems and no top 40 pop. . . . We want a DJ who understands our club and the unique sex charged masculine atmosphere of the Steamworks experience."[53]

Third, bathhouses' theme nights illustrate the boundaries of networking. Recall that Delany is attentive to how networking constructs "pre-selected special interest groups." Theme nights can serve a filtering function. These nights ensure that patrons will not have to interact too much with customers of different ages and physical identities, such that sameness offers safety. Steamworks Seattle, Berkeley, and Chicago offer a weekly "Twink Night" or "Boyz Night" geared to attract patrons under the age of twenty-five. They promote "Bears, the Baths, and Beyond," which caters to "hot hunky men," as well as "Bear Hump," which is a "Monthly Mid-Week Gathering of Furry Men." They host "Daddy Issues," which encourages customers to "Work Yours Out," an invitation to Daddies and those who lust after them.[54]

Finally, the safety of networking is evident in the bathhouses' pricing structures. Patrons can select from different options based on their spending capacity. The lowest price for entry offers a shorter membership and use of only lockers. More expensive memberships allow for more time in the bathhouse as well as the option to reserve a private or particular room. For instance, Steamworks offers standard rooms or rooms with sexual accessories (like a sling).[55] Those with more money can have drastically different (and perhaps more private) experiences.

Steamworks also provides a VIP option, which dictates where bodies can go, when they can go there, and—potentially—with whom those bodies can interact. This option furthers the logic of networking insofar as it specifically enables a patron to avoid others. VIP members have an "exclusive VIP check-in window or head of the line/next in privileges," "top priority for room availability and selection," and even a "'No card present' option for card-less check-in and a card-free wallet."[56] From their entry to their exit, VIPs can separate themselves from others in the space. With this price stratification, Steamworks permits—or even encourages and profits from—exclusionary thinking. Since conservative rhetoric employs classist thinking to create narratives of safety and danger along economic lines, the VIP option would seem to provide a route for patrons with means to separate themselves from lower classes, which often intersect with race, to enable racial segregation and reify existing logics of white supremacy.

Additionally, some bathhouses offer discounts to attract customers. Incentivizing customer loyalty and repeat visits, Steamworks has a "Frequent Fuckers" rewards program through which customers earn points for future discounts. Other discounts cater to students and active military members.[57] Through these programs, the bathhouse prioritizes young, masculine, and successful customers (as education may be a marker of success or striving for success).

While these elements privilege networked cruising, some examples of text and images nod to an ethics of openness associated with Delany's contact and Dean's stranger sociality. For example, photographs of Steamworks Berkeley's club depict a clientele that is racially diverse. The potential for transgressing racial categories is suggested, even as it is impossible to know if these men occupy different class positions. The Berkeley site also attends to physical access by showing a man in a wheelchair.[58] However, this image may merely indicate compliance with accessibility law rather than an openness to contact with otherness, such as disability.[59]

Furthermore, Delany's contact and Dean's stranger sociality value anonymous interactions, particularly since such interactions involve risk. Contact associates strangeness with openness and pleasure. Potentially speaking to this desire, some bathhouses maintain theme nights, such as Lights Out at Steamworks Chicago or Anonymous Mondays at Steamworks Seattle. At the Seattle site, the event is described as follows: "Anonymous Mondays / The Club Goes Dark Every Monday 4 pm— 4 am / No Lights—No Names / Anonymous No Membership Entry Available."[60] Midtowne Denver advertises a similar Mask Night in which patrons can wear masks over their faces.[61]

Nevertheless, bathhouse policies limit anonymity. At Steamworks Chicago, even for Lights Out, customers must pay a membership fee, which includes a photograph for the membership card. On its FAQ page, Midtowne Spa writes, "We are sorry but we need your real name when you visit our clubs. This is the reason we need a valid photo I.D. You can be assured of complete privacy. We do not give out information to anyone about our members." Midtowne further justifies this policy: "This is for your protection as well as ours."[62] The Clubs also do not permit anonymity. On their FAQ page, the company states, "In order to comply with city ordinances for private clubs we cannot allow our customers to purchase memberships without identifying themselves."[63]

Despite these policies, pricing structures indicate that some degree of anonymity can be purchased through options like Steamworks Seattle's "Anonymous Entry" and Steamworks Berkeley's "Enter on the DL" program.[64] Ironically, although a membership plan is not required at the Seattle location, patrons seeking anonymity pay *more* for one visit than others pay for a thirty-day membership. A thirty-day membership is six dollars plus any rental fees (lockers, rooms, etc.); anonymous entry requires a thirteen-dollar upfront cost plus any rental fees.[65] At Steamworks Berkeley, the "Enter on the DL" offers anonymity if patrons pay a ten-dollar entry fee, which is three dollars more than a regular thirty-day membership. Furthermore, the "Enter on the DL" program invokes racialized language that references exclusionary boundaries that we seek to foreground. Indeed, "on the DL" is code for "on the Down Low," which refers to having non-normative sex secretly. Unfortunately, this DL language also promotes a faulty public health narrative, one that allegedly explains the disproportionate rates of HIV/AIDS cases in Black communities, especially among heterosexual Black women. Popularized in 2004 by author and activist J. L. King, the DL narrative smacks of racist public health arguments that attempt to factionalize Black communities into victims and victimizers.[66] This debunked myth-based epidemiology prioritizes an individuals-and-incidents approach, which blames individual Black people and/or isolated incidents for health disparities while ignoring the violence of institutionalized racism.[67]

By adopting this language and surrounding it with the visual inclusion of Black and Brown bodies on its website (importantly, the Berkeley club is the only Steamworks location with Black and Brown bodies occupying a primary place in its visual field), Steamworks demonstrates an awareness of a culturally specific need for Black and Brown bodies to remain anonymous. Because race cannot be separated from economic class, their decision to signal toward this specific need and then to charge more money for it becomes politically questionable at best and racially exploitative at worst. This "Enter on the DL" program prioritizes a logic of networking because it produces active barriers for customers at the intersection of race and class.

The anonymous options in Steamworks Seattle and Berkeley reveal an economic penalty for customers who prefer anonymity. Moreover, particular economic resources are required to practice something that resembles the contact that Delany and Dean value as a productive, pleasurable, democratic, and an ethical form of engagement. Importantly, we must recognize how what appears to be contact—risky, anonymous, and full of potential for stranger sociality—is not because it is commodified and exoticized. It is staged and performed in a networked space. The allure of risk associated with contact is essentially available for a price, for those who can afford it, but such behavior is less likely to be the kind of contact that Delany advocates because it relies on resources for access and limits interclass interaction. Ultimately, the pricing structures promote networking over contact as a way to cruise within Steamworks's walls. The most democratic of interactions is stratified, constrained, and undermined by economic class.

The final nod to contact and stranger sociality legible on these sites is the hosting of CumUnion parties. According to the CumUnion website, these parties promote sexual behaviors fueled by choice—ones that may include opportunities for intentional transmission of HIV:

Our mission is to provide a PRO-CHOICE, judgement-free [sic] environment for gay and bi men to meet where each individual can feel comfortable enough to act without fear of rejection or humiliation. By providing such an environment, we hope to help guys get off of their computers, cell phones and tablets (the normal means of "gay cruising" these days) and bring them together, in person, for some fun. As a pro-choice party, we encourage our members and guests to communicate openly and honestly with their play partners about their needs, thus allowing each individual to make their own decisions regarding what play behaviors are acceptable for themselves, what activities they wish to participate in, and what actions they wish to take to protect themselves from HIV and other STDs. At CumUnion, all men can fuck equally![68]

The language of choice describes respect for autonomy to express sexuality free from the moralizing associated with public health policies.[69] Furthermore, the New York City page on the CumUnion site advertises a sex party aimed at transgressing racial boundaries. Named MilkChocolateNYC.com, this party describes itself as "New York City's host of hot, interracial gay men's sex parties serving dark chocolate, tasty caramel and creamy white flavas of HOT MILK!"[70] This phrase "flavas of HOT MILK" could reference cum-swapping activities that would seem to transgress public health recommendations for safer sex. Ironically, the very activity that CumUnion promotes as foundational to kinship and connection has become an instrument to promote public health. As evident in the "Do You Swallow" PrEP campaign, public health authorities have linked swallowing to taking PrEP and TasP and transformed the act into an indicator of responsible and dignified behavior.

Networking and Contact at the Independent Bathhouse

The visual and textual emphases of these corporatized bathhouses' sites—their focus on masculinity, promotion of theme nights, stratified pricing structures and discount incentives for active military and students, and the cost penalty levied on customers who seek to maintain some anonymity—promote networking as the preferred mode of interaction. One might imagine that independent bathhouses are more open to the interactions and ethics that Delany and Dean advocate because they are local institutions unattached to national (and, in Steamworks's case, international) companies. Therefore, they may not be as driven to present themselves in such sleek ways that conform to normative tropes of masculinity or market logics that prioritize consistency of experience. While some independent bathhouses share with corporatized bathhouses a valorization of conventional masculinity and younger men—evident in their hosting of theme nights catering toward young customers and bears, as well as in their pricing discounts for students, military, firefighters, and police—they also showcase some distinctions that advance our assessment of how networking and contact shape these institutions.

Independent bathhouse websites maintain some text and imagery that differ from the corporate model. Often displaying an early-era website aesthetic and format (which may reflect that the larger companies have more resources to invest in website development), independent institutions like Eros in San Francisco, The Zone and Slammer in Los Angeles, and 321 Slammer in Fort Lauderdale characterize themselves in divergent ways that inform our analysis. For example, the Eros launch page has a warning indicating that it contains explicit language and content of a gay sexual nature and requires visitors to confirm age appropriateness, which sets a different tone. Similarly, the launch pages of The Zone, Slammer, and 321 Slammer contain direct sexual language and images to characterize their spaces in specific ways. All of these identify themselves as sex clubs rather than gyms, saunas, or spas. More specifically, The Zone calls itself a "private playground for men" and describes itself accordingly: "The most popular sex club for men in Southern California, THE ZONE offers two huge floors of mazes, private booths, BJ bullpens, and stalls, along with a TV lounge and patio for relaxation." Additionally, the Slammer Club has "Get Off" as part of its branding—coupled with alternating photos of unblurred cocks and asses in jockstraps with phrasing like "Behind every good hole" and "He's waiting for you." Finally, 321 Slammer opens with the image of the phrase "Come Play" in bright-red font, operating as a marquee to signal what patrons should expect.[71] This small sampling of self-presentations from independent facilities reveals a stark contrast from the language of relaxation, working out, and playing that animates the corporate bathhouses—like Steamworks's "Relax, work out and play."[72] While the introductory language of the corporatized bathhouses foregrounds safe, comfortable, and clean as descriptors, independent clubs like The Slammer and 321 Slammer spotlight glory holes, slings, and fucking.

Independent baths also provide different visual depictions of their spaces. Unlike the stock images of luxury skylines or a city's primary tourist attraction, independent bathhouse sites contain fewer images and do not seem preoccupied with presenting a sleek aesthetic. The images tend to be straightforward, showcase explicitly sexual spaces/equipment, and are less centered on airbrushed models. Indeed, these photos contain very few people, if any. They emphasize a functional view of how patrons might use the space to cruise; images of glory holes, slings, and fuck benches abound, while images that highlight porn models, holiday decor, and coffeemakers with various flavor pods remain sparse, if not missing all together.[73]

Economic access shapes independent bathhouses as much as corporatized ones. They, too, provide different membership options and discounts to particular groups. Nevertheless, many independent bathhouses lack VIP options, so patrons cannot pay for elite experiences. Fort Lauderdale's 321 Slammer tells its customers that "rooms are not assigned, but are available on a first-come basis and do not have beds or linens."[74] Interestingly, this information appears under the heading "Who We Are," suggesting that this democratic approach is part of their ethos. Compared to Steamworks's VIP option, 321 Slammer's description as first-come-first-serve suggests a resistance to economic stratification and its attendant networking logic.

Options for payment with cash or credit card signal that some spaces may provide the interclass contact that Delany and Dean consider to be more ethically sound (as credit access is class stratified). The Slammer, 321 Slammer, and Eros do not accept credit cards; they require cash and provide on-site ATMs.[75] Because currency options communicate information about access, the choice to take only cash could be an effort to reduce the importance of class and increase access. Taken together, these pricing and payment specifics might reveal that particular independent spaces are less saddled by the corporate prioritization of networking and are more invested in the interclass contact that Delany and Dean lament as fading from public sex spaces.[76]

Eros in San Francisco sets itself apart as the most likely counterpublic space that fosters cruising as contact and stranger sociality. It refers to itself as sex positive and has images of men who are not muscled. It seems less saturated with demands for hypermasculinity. Unlike the corporate language found on the websites for companies like Steamworks, Eros makes explicit that the institution is part of a larger queer community. Instead of using bounded phrases like "communities in which we do business," as found on the Steamworks site, Eros uses "Our Community" and invokes we/ours/us language in their messaging about partnerships beyond the club.[77] Similarly, instead of centering self-promotional articles about their company's participation in large marketing events like International Mr. Leather (IML), Market Days, and Pride—as Steamworks does—Eros includes articles from the queer press (like the *Bay Area Reporter*) and thus highlights news that is specific to the community and free of economic motivations. In this community section, Eros centers information about the recent death of a community icon and provides a history of their contributions and information about how to pay respect to their legacy.[78]

Our review of contemporary bathhouses illustrates how corporatized sites privilege a networking logic. Within these spaces, clientele may engage in the more transgressive forms of intercommunal connection akin to contact or stranger sociality, but our assessment is that the spaces are structured to maintain, encourage, and strengthen the limits of networking. By establishing particular policies and practices; promoting theme nights; highlighting a hypermasculine, cisgender aesthetic; and creating a hierarchical pricing structure, a logic of customization becomes their structuring force. For Delany, these policies, practices, and presentations of desirability all work together to constitute "the material and economic forces that work . . . to suppress contact in the name of 'giving people what they want.'"[79] Delany expresses skepticism about customization and furthers his contention that the benefits of networking are often misunderstood. People in networking situations often think they are getting exactly what they want, exactly what they came for, and then leave that very space with a feeling of lack, of not having accomplished that goal. This is primarily because they are asking institutions structured by networking logics to do the work that contact is more likely to do. As Delany suggests, "Networking situations start by gathering a population all with the same or relatively similar needs. While this concentration creates a social field that promotes the rapid spread of information among the members *about* those needs, the relatively high concentration of need itself militates against those needs being materially met within the networking situation."[80] If a space of sociality is "customized" to meet an ostensibly targeted need, the architects of that space have already envisioned who will occupy it and what work will be done there; in other words, the work of exclusion has already happened at the level of design. When people fill that space according to that logic of customization, they likely rob themselves of the potential to get what they want. They can even prevent themselves from discovering new possibilities, possibilities more likely to occur in spaces encouraging contact across difference.

Some independent bathhouses, by contrast, maintain elements more aligned with contact and stranger sociality. However, they also contain elements infected with the markers of safety, normativity, and exclusivity associated with networking. Our evaluation of what kind of cruising a particular bathhouse prioritizes and encourages is especially important if we consider Ira Tattelman's assessment of the educative function of the bathhouse. According to Tattelman, "When you left, you took those things you had learned from participating in the bathhouse, by communicating with your body, back out into the world."[81] If the bathhouse serves this purpose—if it educates its clientele about how to live and be and interact in the world—then insofar as it promotes networking, it reinforces sameness under the guise of safety as well as a preference for exclusion and boundaries even while bolstering a narrative of inclusion and access. By contrast, if bathhouses encourage contact, they promote a set of values more likely to produce stronger bonds of queer kinship; values of sociality, pleasure, and difference; and the democratic belonging that Dean and Delany celebrate. These spaces also imagine themselves as being an integral part of a community rather than selling customized services to that community.

The Digital Bathhouse: Swiping through the Apps

Perhaps more common today than cruising in the bathhouse is swiping via a smartphone through geolocative social media apps.[82] These apps have been pejoratively referred to as "digital bathhouses," in part to invoke an earlier pre-HIV era in which the bathhouse was linked to the alleged dangers associated with anonymous sex or sex outside of normative privatized romance and, more pointedly, to disease and death as discussed in chapter 1. The characterization itself is indicative of how often normative public health policies are unaware of or explicitly counter to the ethical aspirations of contact and stranger sociality.

Dean is critical of these web-based technologies. He contends that they promote the privacy, security, and confines associated with networking and links these values to neoliberal economic aspirations: "What troubles me about online cruising is that it contributes to the accelerating privatization of public life that began in earnest during the first decades of the AIDS epidemic, under the Reagan administration."[83] His assessment was based on internet sites, such as Gay.com and Manhunt.net (technologies that preceded smartphone applications). Because engaging with these sites tethered a user to their computer, their use often, but not always, required staying at home. By contrast, mobile technology has enabled a cruising culture to move beyond the home once more. The technology would seem to place a bathhouse in one's hand, on one's phone.

Some scholars have suggested that the apps have resuscitated a cruising culture associated with the bathhouses of the pre-HIV era, with the caveat that linguistics and other signaling have changed in this new technologically mediated context.[84] Importantly, such cruising is still subject to Dean's critique of privatization, especially when the app "is primarily used to facilitate sex in private spaces such as the home."[85] Furthermore, the apps allow for the performance of respectability because respectability is associated with privacy and the home. As Jodi Ahlm notes, the apps can foster the possibility of "respectable promiscuity," which we suggest may share some of the qualities of Delany's networking.[86] That one can be respectably promiscuous—if their sexual behavior averts risk and takes place privately—stretches the boundaries of dignity but does not question its foundational logics of restraint, individualism, privacy, and safety.

We wondered whether and how apps encourage networking and its associated notions of respectable promiscuity. As such, we paid attention to the apps' design, architecture, and presentation of information to the user. We built a database of apps by searching the Apple App Store for geolocative apps marketed to LGBTQ+ individuals and those interested in same-sex intimacy or sexual encounters. Our search parameters yielded thirty-two apps.[87] Some have been explored extensively in public health, sociology, and digital and computational studies scholarship.[88] While our database is a snapshot of apps that existed at a particular moment, we also recognize the need to grapple with how apps came to the market at different times. Newer apps aim to attract customers not yet captured and fill a niche not yet met.[89] As apps have proliferated, they have created ways to cater to specific desires. The capitalist market logic thereby may prioritize networking or seeking others most like oneself.

The apps we discuss are widely seen as hookup apps designed to facilitate immediate connection. While some disavow this characterization—Hinge describes itself as "DESIGNED TO BE DELETED," suggesting that its purpose is to introduce people interested in long-term, normative (dignified) relationships—the majority of the apps we discuss feature design parameters that could be used to expedite access to sexual play.[90] This use is often not easily acknowledged by users, suggesting that such play is not dignified. As Ahlm notes, many users attest that these apps have multiple functions, allowing users to engage in casual conversations, build friendships, or take a first step toward more traditional romantic dating: "The paradox is that everyone seems to know that there are users with varying intentions, and that the intentions of any one user varies by day or even hour, yet the reputation exists and is culturally salient. The fact that Grindr can, and often is, used to find casual, semi-anonymous sex contaminates any use of the app with the stigma of promiscuity."[91] That users (and apps) disavow this stigma shows how pervasive dignity is in defining respectable behavior. Indeed, we find that the most popular apps reflect and reinforce networking and illustrate the limits of normative neoliberal dignity as respectability. Nevertheless, we also note that some less-utilized apps emphasize building a diverse and inclusive community. Still, others have design features that embrace the risk associated with contact.

Grindr and Scruff: Looking to Network

Grindr, which describes itself as the "world's largest social networking app for gay, bi, trans, and queer people" and boasts millions of daily users, is emblematic of this format.[92] The image of the grid interface on its website's homepage illustrates what a user would see. As of June 2019, when a user logs into Grindr, across the top of their screen is a row of five images of users who are "fresh faces" or new users. Below this are larger thumbnails arranged in a three-by-four rectangular grid. A green dot in the lower left corner indicates who is currently online. Across the bottom of the screen are icons, including a star that allows a user to "favorite" a given profile and access it later; the Grindr logo of a mask, which reopens the grid; a rocket ship, which allows the user to explore profiles in a location different from one's own; and a speech bubble, which enables the user to see previous conversations or chats with users.

The image of the interface on Grindr's website homepage includes thumbnails of a diverse collection of users. Of the seventeen images, nine can be read as people of color—Black, Latinx, Asian. At least one presents as a woman who might be trans. Interestingly, no thumbnail is blank: while Grindr permits profiles without photos, it clearly suggests that users should provide a photo—even if that photo maintains a degree of anonymity (e.g., only shows a torso).[93]

Grindr also provides guidelines for photos that users may upload. These rules seem to prevent overtly sexual use of the app, providing evidence of Ahlm's notion of respectable promiscuity. The app does not permit nudity, images of sex toys, underwear shots, hints of genitals, or graphic emojis depicting sex acts. The overt sexuality of the bathhouse—if we maintain the metaphor of these apps as digital bathhouses—seems very much restrained.[94]

Out of all of Grindr's features, two of the most pertinent ones for our study are the filter function and the explore feature (symbolized by the aforementioned rocket ship). In the June 2019 version, users can filter other users based on "type." Doing so alters the content of their cruising grid. Choosing from a range of options, such as height, age, ethnicity, and body type, users can eliminate certain profiles from their grid. For example, a user could customize their options to see only people who are under 5'11", under 180 pounds, under twenty-five, white, and toned and prefer to be the receptive partner (bottom). This feature, which is accessible only with a paid membership, negates the possibility of unpredictable, interclass contact; it fosters a supposedly safer, controlled, and stratified form of networking that maintains rigid boundaries. In this way, the filter option offered with a paid Grindr subscription resembles the VIP membership benefits at a corporate bathhouse. Similarly, the explore function allows users to search for other geographic locations (still filtering if they prefer). For example, if a user in New York City was planning a vacation to Paris, they could combine the "type" filter with the explore function to schedule their ideal interactions before they even arrive. Taken together, these two pay-only functions take the logic of networking to its fullest potential: even when one is outside the familiar locale of their neighborhood spaces, they can strategize to ensure a desired result.

In late June 2019, Grindr introduced a new subscription option called Unlimited, which provides more options to target one's search. By paying forty dollars per month, a user could access the profiles of other users who had viewed them, search incognito to remain untracked, unsend previous messages and photos to limit or end connections with others, and avoid restrictions to the size of their grid. Grindr advertises the new subscription model with language that captures the trappings of economic success and elitism: "Your weekend is booked: you've got dinner with clients in an hour, drinks with friends after, and a flight to Hong Kong in the morning." It privileges the neoliberal and capitalist logics of being busy, overscheduled, and efficient with time. Interactions are scheduled without the possibility of the unexpected: "When it comes to your Grinding, every minute counts, and you can't afford to waste time—or have your clients see you in the grid during dessert."[95] The last clause suggests how much use of the app is shaped by assumptions of transgression and indignity.

These filtering and "unlimited" options would seem contrary to the aspirations featuring all sorts of different people, as described by Grindr founder Joel Simkhai: "The word Grindr comes from a coffee grinder. We're mixing people up together, a bit of a social stew. It is a little bit rough—not to mix, but to grind." Despite this emphasis on creating an inclusive community, Simkhai invokes boundary-making language when explaining the dominant color choice of yellow across the app's interface: "Our design, logo, colouring—we wanted something a little bit tougher, rough. It's also very masculine. It's a masculine word, sound. We wanted something that wasn't necessarily about being gay." Simkhai also problematically racializes sociality, particularly sociality that can be linked with sexual intimacy. When explaining the origins of Grindr's mask logo, Simkhai states, "We looked at this notion of meeting people and the idea is very much a basic human need to relax and to socialize. I went back to primitive tribal arts in Africa and Polynesia. One of the things I saw was [*sic*] these primal masks. It brings us back to basics, primal needs. Socialization is the basis of humanity."[96] Interestingly, while amplifying the need for socialization and describing it as a widespread human need, which would seem like a nod to Delany's arguments about the value of contact across identity boundaries, the structural architecture of the app and its defining features promote a logic of networking that actually reinforces boundaries. Furthermore, Simkhai's characterization of his brand and its invocation of African and Polynesian cultures does not engage ethically with otherness to strive toward democratic exchange; rather, Simkhai's remarks and the iconography of Grindr itself fall victim to a familiar tendency to appropriate, commodify, and exoticize otherness (and non-Western sexuality in particular). Finally, his remarks neglect to contextualize, historicize, and reckon with Western power and its impact on the bodies, practices, places, and narratives of African and Polynesian cultures, even as he profits from that inequitable global power dynamic.

Scruff, another geolocative app, which maintains a community of over fifteen million users, has an interface similar to Grindr's. Its tag line, "The guys you like are here," is vague, but the visual imagery on its website gives a sense of who those guys are: many sport facial hair and tattoos. As such, it caters to a narrower user base than Grindr.[97] In his study of the app, Yoel Roth notes that "the Scruff guy" embraces normative notions of masculinity.[98] Since Roth's analysis, Scruff has expanded its range of self-identifiers and appears more inclusive. While many options still connote bear cultures of older, hairy, larger, muscled, traditionally masculine men (Bear, Jock, Daddy, Muscle, Chub, Chaser, Guy Next Door, Otter, Leather, and Military), others go beyond these boundaries but are common identifiers among gay and bi men (Poz, Discreet, Geek, Queer, Bisexual, College, Transgender, Drag, and Twink).

Like users of other apps, a Scruff user can tap a thumbnail image to reveal a more extensive user profile, which can include multiple images of the user (more with a paid subscription) as well as numerous ways to interact. The user can indicate if they are interested or not interested in another user. They can take notes about another user for later use; this option might be valuable for remembering users' names if multiple users are engaged at once, remembering what sexual acts they prefer, or recording notes on their health status. A user can tap on a star, which will place a profile among the user's "favorites." A user can also tap an icon of a bear claw, which is called a "woof" and signals that the user considers a person attractive. Scruff also enables users to maintain a private collection of photos, which can be unlocked for particular users. Unlike Grindr, Scruff permits images of a more sexual nature.

Scruff allows a user to engage with multiple grids, with options expanding when a user purchases a subscription. As of June 2019, beyond the grid that contains users nearby, Scruff offered a "Global Grid" showing fifteen images of users farther away. Scrolling below this grid reveals another grid of fifteen "New Guys" who recently joined and are nearby. Scrolling further reveals a grid that highlights the dominant metric of value on Scruff—the woof—and shows fifteen of the "Most Woof'd (New Guys)." Finally, users can construct their own grids structured by location and desired traits. The search function allows a user without a subscription to locate users by profile name, location, descriptor (e.g., Bear, Geek, Daddy, Muscle), and a sexual activity. A paid subscription extends these logics of networking by enabling a user to narrow their search on the basis of relationship status, ethnicity, and preferred sexual practices.[99] Ultimately, a paid subscription on Grindr or Scruff provides a level of customization that enables the user to avoid contact with difference. Alternatively, they offer access to difference, but they do so to exoticize, eroticize, and ultimately fetishize that otherness rather than welcome the stranger.

Grindr's and Scruff's design and structure prioritize networking. The subscription options further discourage the possibilities and pleasures of contact. Similar to the policies, practices, and presentations of the corporate bathhouse, the levels of subscriptions available to the app user provide greater customization capabilities. Through their architecture, specifically the user's capacity to construct their grid, Grindr and Scruff reinforce sameness under the guise of safety.

More Than Networking: Attempts to Build Community and Inclusion in Some Apps

Hornet describes itself as "the home of the gay community," and it boasts twenty-five million users worldwide.[100] It maintains various features that aspire to build community and inform users of LGBTQ+ history. These aims mark Hornet as distinct from Grindr and Scruff because it has features that seem to advance Delany's and Dean's most democratic ambitions.

Unlike Grindr, where logging on leads the user to their cruising grid, logging onto Hornet, as of June 2019, leads to a home screen that has a "feed" similar to Facebook or Instagram. Here users can share images, and other users can "like" or leave a comment about them. Across the bottom of the screen are five icons. Reading from left to right, the first icon is a house that returns users to the home screen / feed. The next icon is an arrow that presents the grid of users. Users without a subscription can scroll down to see up to seventy-two users. Emphasizing community interaction (and not just private chats), Hornet's center icon is a plus sign within a circle. Tapping it allows the user to post a "Moment" to the feed so that the entire Hornet community can see what the user wants to share. The next icon is a speech bubble that holds all the chats the user has previously engaged in and shows who wants to speak with the user. The final icon opens the user's profile and enables editing. The profile, similar to other apps, allows the user to post a headline to pique the interest of other users and provides an area to describe oneself in one's own terms in 128 characters or fewer. It then provides a list of characteristics for the user to choose from and to select whether they are publicly visible. These include the user's age, ethnicity, height, weight, role, relationship, and HIV status.

Finally, and somewhat unique among apps, Hornet maintains a section called "Stories," which features information about queer culture, history, and politics, such as stories about the corporatization of Pride, Disney characters that exude stereotypically gay qualities, queer trivia, and icons of gay history.[101] The app also invites users to submit their own articles for publication. By providing users with this information, Hornet promotes an ethic of kinship, a historical connection, and a connection to LGBTQ+ community. Its structure, design, and content reach beyond the limits of networking.

As Grindr faces criticism for contributing to a monolithic and exclusionary notion of what is attractive,[102] other apps market themselves in the App Store with explicit language to emphasize diversity and inclusion and foster community-building. For example, Jack'd promotes itself as "the most diverse and authentic app for gay, bi, and curious guys to connect, chat, share, and meet." While Grindr attracts mostly men or those seeking men, the app HER may have developed in response, explicitly restricting its users, as advertised on the App Store, to those who identify as "lesbian, bi, and queer people." Similarly, Scissr "is designed by queer womxn for queer womxn to create a community for lesbians, bisexuals, nonbinary folks, and other queer womxn desiring to increase their connections with other amazing queer individuals."

Thurst goes further not only to welcome a broader community of users but also to redefine connection and love. The app opposes the cisgender and homonormative presentations of many apps by defining itself as "a dating app for queer people." It characterizes most apps as "trans-exclusive or not safe enough for marginalized members of the queer community." Consequently, Thurst "hopes to reshape and change the way we view all gender, sexuality, and how we share and express love. . . . Thurst is decolonizing dating through broadening the idea of who deserves love and how love can be given and received online." Thurst announces that it is for "Queer People of All Genders," and unlike most apps, it serves "LGBTQIA+ folks" and just gay, bi, or curious men. Its progressive politics are evident in its community guidelines: "We have no tolerance for racism, sexism, transphobia, ableism, xenophobia, fatmisia, kink-shaming, body-shaming, and discriminatory or violent beliefs, practices, or imagery, which include but are not limited to bullying, harassment, stalking, doxxing, abuse, threats, or implying harm."[103]

Apps such as Hornet, HER, and Thurst describe themselves in ways that transgress the boundaries of networking. They discuss constructing community by embracing difference, and they avoid valorizing the masculine. They do not code safety as sameness to the extent that Grindr and Scruff do. Some apps, such as Hornet, include features that connect users with history and politics, which creates potential for community-building. Even though they may not perpetuate networking logics, they do not fully embrace the tenets of contact, especially behaviors associated with stranger sociality, risk, and immediate and fleeting pleasures.

Apps, Anonymity, and Contact

While some of the most popular apps emphasize logics of restraint that are emblematic of Ahlm's "respectable promiscuity," less-popular apps unabashedly focus on facilitating sexual connection, often anonymously. Insofar as apps perform this function, their purpose may align more with Delany's contact. Squirt, for example, is focused on facilitating quick connection for sexual pleasure: "Whether you're at home or traveling abroad, Squirt.org is the best place to meet guys who are serious about hooking up and finding hot and horny hookups in just a few clicks." Squirt confronts the critique that these apps only promote privatized cruising by showing how users "can browse profiles of local guys" and "view cruising spots nearby."[104]

FAWN perhaps embraces the moniker of "digital bathhouse" most expansively by fostering encounters that are meant to be "RANDOM. ANONYMOUS. GAY." Its marketing language on the App Store explicitly positions itself against the dignified use of the more mainstream apps: "FAWN connects you with like-minded guys online in real time and you decide the rest. No need to scroll the endless user feeds on dating apps and social networks, no need to swipe left or right, no need to wait for hours for the partner's reply. FAWN is nothing like this—hop onboard and start chatting right away. FAWN is 100% private and anonymous. On FAWN you're assigned a random profile picture and a nickname—nobody will know your real name, see your photo or find your whereabouts unless you decide to share it yourselves." PURE goes further to maintain anonymity by deleting chats after one hour. The aim is anonymous sex. The app refuses to aspire to respectable and dignified relationships. As described on the App Store. "Pure is when you're looking for an after-dark adventure, not a relationship. It's quick, direct, and discreet. With Pure your private life stays private. No social media links. We provide end-to-end encryption and automatically delete your chats." Insofar as PURE prioritizes fleeting encounters and anonymity, it may be the app that best facilitates Delany's contact and Dean's stranger sociality.

Offering a succinct conclusion about whether and how the apps foster queer kinship is complicated because many of these apps have distinct aims (to say nothing of how users can interface with them to accomplish their own objectives). Nevertheless, some patterns do emerge. Insofar as all mobile apps require a smartphone or a tablet, they restrict access along economic lines. While all offer some access without a paid subscription, having the resources to purchase a subscription does expand a user's options. As such, their price stratification is reminiscent of the bathhouses' VIP options. Second, Grindr would seem most likely to foster networking. While the company promotes a multicultural collection of users that suggests the potential to interact with others outside one's own race, gender, and class, the app's guidelines absorb the strictures of dignity. If Ahlm contended that Grindr users often discussed their use in ways that suggested "respectable promiscuity," we contend that Grindr's architecture and textual self-representation foster "respectable promiscuity" and thereby reinforce normative dignity and its consequent limits. Third, some apps like Hornet foster community interaction, intracommunal knowledge development, and information sharing, offering access to queer community. Fourth, less-popular apps seem the most resistant to normative notions of dignity as respectability. Squirt, FAWN, and PURE stand out because they explicitly offer and value anonymity. They have the most potential to facilitate contact, but some remain vulnerable to critiques of privatization.

If we imagine contact and networking not as a binary but as a spectrum of behaviors and values, we can then place these apps at different positions on that spectrum. Delany might potentially support this construction. As he notes, "We must analyze both, so that we can see that elements in each have clear and definite hierarchical relations with elements in the other, as well as other elements that are shared. Only this sort of vigilant approach will produce a clear idea of what to expect (and not to expect) from one and the other, as well as some clear knowledge of why we should not try to displace one *with* the other and ask one to fulfill the other's job."[105] The point is not to privilege contact over networking but to understand their differing objectives and distinct logics and to realize that networking can be associated with the dignified underpinnings of the respectable promiscuity associated with and marketed by certain apps.

Sex without Fear? PrEP, U=U, and the Potential for Queer Community

Within LGBTQ+ communities, the HIV/AIDS crisis spawned intense divisions that centered on the causes, strategies, and very existence of the infectious microbe and instilled a deep distrust and/or fear of one another. In the decades since the early years of panic and confusion—after the emergence of highly active anti-retroviral therapy (HAART) in the mid-1990s—fear and distrust still loom large. While shifting medical realities rendered clear the efficacy of treatment and while side effects lessened for a large number of HIV-infected people, the trauma lingered and sustained factions within LGBTQ+ communities. While some always interacted across serostatus lines, many remained invested in the demarcation between HIV-negative and -positive.[106] As medical technologies changed and conversations about viral load (VL) became more common, *undetectable* found its way into social-sexual vocabularies by the early 2010s. Although not endorsed by the Centers for Disease Control and Prevention (CDC) or the National Institutes of Health (NIH) until later, some specialists in HIV care began to share information on how undetectable viral loads reduced the risk of transmission.[107]

One means to assert control and perform responsibility arrived in 2012. On July 16, 2012, the Food and Drug Administration (FDA) issued a press release discussing its approval of Truvada as PrEP. The drug has proven at least 90 percent effective in preventing infection.[108] As the FDA made clear, "Truvada [is] the first drug approved to reduce the risk of HIV infection in uninfected individuals who are at high risk of HIV infection and who may engage in sexual activity with HIV-infected partners. Truvada, taken daily, is to be used for pre-exposure prophylaxis (PrEP) in combination with safer sex practices to reduce the risk of sexually-acquired HIV infection in adults at high risk."[109] Although the announcement was not immediately endorsed by all members of LGBTQ+ communities or all members of the medical profession, the adoption of PrEP for prevention has increased over time.[110]

Five years after the FDA announced PrEP, the meaning and implications of HIV infection had once again changed. In September 2017, the CDC issued a letter agreeing with what hundreds of organizations had already stated: achieving an undetectable viral load meant that an HIV-positive individual could not transmit the virus to a sex partner. This spawned the slogan "undetectable equals untransmittable," or "U=U." Public health officials now argue that HIV-positive individuals who maintain undetectable status through effective anti-retroviral therapy (or TasP) can no longer transmit the virus.[111]

TasP and PrEP alter the landscape of queer sexual health. In this new context, we consider critical questions and implications for practices and values associated with queer kinship. How do TasP and PrEP change the state's deployment of what can and should be thought of as dignified or sexually responsible behavior? How has the CDC discursively constructed viral suppression and undetectability as the dignified way to be an HIV-positive person or argued that PrEP usage is the responsible choice for the HIV-negative individual? By attending to the limits of access to these medications—which correspond to long-standing economic class, racial, and gender-identity biases, vulnerability to biopower or continuous medical surveillance, HIV criminalization and reform, and intracommunal arguments and value systems—it becomes clear just how much advocacy of both PrEP and U=U have absorbed normative notions of dignity as restraint, self-control, responsibility, and safety.

Gilead Sciences Inc., the manufacturer of Truvada, is quintessential "big pharma," with over eleven thousand employees spread over six continents and annual revenues well into the billions of dollars.[112] With a strategic partnership, the state oversees regulations dictating PrEP usage, and large drug companies assign high price tags—inspiring hard questions about access and its relationship to broader exclusionary boundaries that structure life for various queer people. Specifically, to gain access to Truvada in the United States—to protect oneself and perhaps discover sexual pleasure without the specter of HIV—an individual must participate in a privatized and regulated healthcare industry. For example, in New York, an individual may access PrEP even if they receive Medicaid support, and Medicaid will cover the costs of doctor visits, the prescription, and the associated lab work. However, if an individual holds private insurance, that insurance company need not cover these costs.[113] Gilead does offer a co-pay coupon card, which covers up to $7,200 per year of costs associated with Truvada for individuals who do not have government-provided insurance.[114] Nevertheless, the cost in the United States can amount to $24,000 per year.[115] Moreover, the drug costs up to 350 percent more than generic options in other countries.[116] Even if one can find state-sponsored relief or benefit from big pharma payment options, activists highlight that navigating these corporatized and state-directed structures often produces gaps in care and requires that an individual remain vigilant in their pursuit of care.[117]

This critique, of course, only considers access through the lens of cost. Scholars who study how racism, homophobia, and transphobia affect access to healthcare often cite culturally competent messaging, geographic location and physical access to care, and particular versions of stigma (both in medical care and within patients' communities) as additional barriers that disproportionately impact people who reside at the intersections of marginalized communities.[118] Those most at risk for HIV infection—Black and Brown bodies, trans bodies, low-income bodies, sex workers' bodies—remain the most excluded from PrEP's benefits. The systemic inequities that permeate institutions make clear which bodies matter and which do not. The very logics that produce the disproportionate HIV-infection rates for marginalized communities also produce the disparities in prevention and care in those very same communities.

In addition to presenting problems with access and yielding high profits for various medical establishments, PrEP and TasP also serve a biopolitical function to insert the state into the sexual lives of queer people.[119] The deployment of PrEP and TasP, particularly as medical advances have transformed HIV into a chronic disease, can potentially supply governing authorities with reams of data about queer sexual behavior.[120] And due to the decrease of community-based, culturally specific, anonymous testing sites, both strategies offer a unique opportunity to monitor and police sexual behavior. For example, to acquire a prescription for PrEP, individuals must seek the counsel of their physician, a potentially complicated process when such a conversation is enshrouded in the stigmatizations of HIV/AIDS, so-called promiscuity, and queer sexualities more broadly. The same is true for individuals who use TasP. When seeking TasP or PrEP, individuals are subjected to potentially invasive conversations as physicians ask a battery of questions about their sexual practices. If they get a prescription, they are monitored throughout the year and become primary sources for data collection. These individuals may be the fortunate ones. Given the long-standing history of confusing politics for healthcare practice, doctors often have refused to prescribe PrEP because they understand it as a "party drug" that encourages reckless, hedonistic abandon among queer communities.[121] Without medical mandates and with the vestiges of "promiscuity debates" ever-present, queer people participate in a system replete with surveillance and policing.

If individuals lack an insurance policy with an amenable prescription drug plan, they can appeal to patient-assistance programs or to research efforts for help. These individuals are subjected to additional scrutiny and testing. They might procure Truvada temporarily if they offer their bodies for sample collection and detail their behavior for data acquisition.[122] In short, the most vulnerable of bodies must offer the most to the state to benefit healthcare developments.

The medical surveillance emblematic of biopower also connotes a lack of trust, which is evident in the CDC's early resistance to acknowledge that U=U, on the one hand, and in caregivers' contemporaneous refusal to share U=U information with patients, on the other.[123] Back in 2008, Swiss researchers released evidence that HIV-positive individuals who attained viral suppression to the point of undetectability could not transmit HIV.[124] By 2011, other academic medical journals were reporting similar findings, but the CDC did not endorse these findings until years later, in late 2017.[125] Commenting on this delay, HIV/AIDS advocate Naina Khanna notes "a confusing schism: people living with HIV (PLHIV) were simultaneously sexually radioactive while we were mathematically modeled as benign. The data was good enough to shift public health priorities but advancing human dignity of PLHIV was not a priority."[126] She also explains the lack of trust between providers and patients: "Reluctance from medical providers and public health officials to share information about viral suppression rests on a complex set of stigmas, but boils down to one basic idea: people with HIV can't be trusted. We can't be trusted to take our medications, to care about and protect others, and to tell our providers the truth about our sexual and medical decisions."[127] This lack of trust is also evident in how medical surveillance need not rely on subjective self-reporting. As Dean argues, "Sexual surveillance can now bypass subjectivity altogether by going directly inside the body to elicit information."[128]

This lack of trust exemplifies a normative position that an HIV-positive status is somehow always undignified, that it carries with it all the assumptions of excess and irresponsibility that normatively define indignity. Once again, this exclusionary logic, highlighted in chapter 1's discussion of how public health officials often defined gay men, is on display: some medical professionals assume that HIV-positive individuals are incapable of acting responsibly or managing their own care. The seeming fear is that if HIV-positive individuals are told that they are undetectable and that U=U, then they will pose a risk to others. The implication is that they need to be controlled, and one way to do so is to withhold information. The underlying logics of dignity as restraint and responsibility are evident.

Once the CDC did endorse U=U in 2017, the parameters of dignity shifted. And this occurrence illustrates just how much dignity, because the word itself is an empty vessel that can be filled with multiple meanings, can be a floating signifier—always available to maintain normative power. In 2018, the CDC released a public health campaign, HIV Treatment Works, which included twenty-five posters and videos, banners, and cards. All carried a clear neoliberal message of personal agency and ownership; treatment was defined as taking control and asserting personal responsibility. For example, one poster presents Aaron, who proclaims, "This is my disease. It's in my body and I need to know everything I can to fight it. . . . Three years ago, when I met my partner Phil, I told him I was HIV-positive in our first conversation. He said, 'That's OK. There are lots of ways to protect ourselves.' Phil takes PrEP and I take my meds every day. In this relationship, HIV ends with me."[129] Treatment exemplifies that ownership and responsibility. The campaign stresses how undetectability facilitates normative ways of living—romantic intimacy—once considered foreclosed: "You know what, HIV? There are many things I still want to accomplish and you are not going to stop me"; "HIV: This is not the end. It's just the start of a new way of life"; "HIV, it took time, but by learning to get you in control—my life knows no bounds."[130] While we do not deny the importance of such life-affirming messages, we do draw attention to how the CDC's campaign links undetectability to responsibility, restraint, and control; those actions will lead to benefits that the "irresponsible" among us cannot access.

Inequities of access—through the state's biopolitical power or the inequities of racism and classism that structure healthcare provision—are exacerbated by efforts to criminalize HIV status.[131] Because of disproportionate infection rates and access to care—as well as the criminalization of Blackness in the United States—HIV criminalization perpetuates violence against Black and Brown bodies.[132] And ironically, more recent efforts at HIV criminalization reform may only reify this inequity, not ameliorate it.[133] That HIV status could be criminalized is an obvious marker of indignity, and as such, attempts at reform would seem to be evidence of reducing this stigma. But where viral suppression has been used as a justification for legal reform, critical debate has emerged; undetectability can be an indicator of innocence, whereas failure to suppress the virus can be a marker of guilt.[134] This is a problematic possibility, since racial disparities also exist in maintaining undetectable levels of the virus: about twice as many white HIV-positive men have achieved this status as Black HIV-positive men.[135] Under the guise of reform, historical patterns of criminalization along raced and classed lines can persist.[136]

In addition to viral load being used in the criminal justice system, the popularization of the term *undetectable* also affects socio-sexual cultures. Because contemporary conversations do not traffic in the nuances of risk reduction, a byproduct of amplifying information about "undetectability" is the creation of more divisions among HIV-positive people. Instead of educating people about the details of risk reduction—a conversation that would necessarily differentiate between viral suppression and "undetectable" and would also feature dialogue about how the virus is and is not spread irrespective of undetectability—the message is distilled down to a digestible sound bite: undetectable = untransmittable. Ironically, the work performed to dismantle stigma runs the risk of reproducing stigmatizing logics and behaviors; the stigma just moves in different directions. Because "undetectable" is code for concepts like healthy, responsible, productive, and safe, HIV-positive people who cannot achieve undetectable levels (because of either a lack of access to care, treatment challenges, or otherwise) can be seen as less attractive. They are often characterized as unhealthy, irresponsible, unsafe, or worse.[137]

We are in the era of a third HIV status—at least rhetorically. "Undetectable" is cleansing the supposed stain of HIV-positive. Rather than saying, "I'm HIV-positive with an undetectable viral load," people say, "I'm undetectable." The phrasing moves from additional information about one's viral load to an identity—one that separates them (elevates them, one might say) from others in their HIV-positive community. The term *undetectable* itself is a biomedical construction that relies on specifics of current technology and viral measuring strategies. To be sure, the viral load that constituted "undetectability" a few years ago was higher than what qualifies for that designation today. Does this mean that the risk of infection was higher then? Not necessarily. Not necessarily. Rather, the medical technology has gotten better. But at the level of social interactions and sexual negotiations, these nuances are lost. Undetectability is reductively translated as "safe to fuck and/or date," while not achieving this status could produce negative consequences for social and sexual desirability. In elevating the undetectable viral load without providing more context about what *undetectability* actually means, we run the risk of fracturing an already-marginalized community instead of providing better risk-reduction methods. In so doing, boundary making persists.

Finally, the adoption of PrEP also raises interesting intracommunal tensions that produce boundaries. Harkening back to the promiscuity debates of the early HIV/AIDS crisis, the FDA announcement of PrEP ignited anti-PrEP and pro-PrEP arguments within queer communities. The anti-PrEP perspective is perhaps rendered most clearly through the critiques made by David Duran in his now-notorious "Truvada Whore" opinion piece in the *Huffington Post*, through Larry Kramer's moralizing, and through Michael Weinstein's proclamation that Truvada is nothing more than a "party drug."[138] In this early period of PrEP's short history, Duran, Kramer, and Weinstein maintained that the medication would give queer folks a license to fuck without condoms and thereby curb progress against the virus. Others understood this argument as saturated with sex-shaming impulses, anti-choice rhetoric, and/or anti-science backlash.

Pro-PrEP arguments varied in these initial years of PrEP's existence. Some proponents viewed PrEP as a valuable tool within a broader repertoire of risk-reduction strategies—as a medication to be used with condoms, for example.[139] Others repurposed the derogatory "Truvada Whore" as a moniker of pride and sex positivity, which embraced sexual excesses once derogated. Reacting to Duran and Weinstein, Adam Zeboski and Jake Sobo argued that PrEP could empower queer communities by enabling sex "without fear."[140] Indeed, some pornography eroticizes Truvada because it enables sexual practices once disparaged.[141]

As PrEP usage has become more common and as messaging about the prevention strategy has been promoted by state public health policy and private pharmaceutical interests, the conversations have evolved, and community members have updated their positions. Duran and Kramer, for instance, redirected their views and acknowledged the historical baggage that fueled their initial responses.[142] As state authorities accelerated their embrace of PrEP by 2017, pro-PrEP arguments solidified around the idea of safer sex. Because state and medical authorities could not endorse the initial pro-PrEP argument that considered the medication a tool that enabled transgressive sexual behaviors among queers, the argument that PrEP was a tool of safer sex became dominant. But more so, that particular pro-PrEP position was amplified by attaching the medicine to a discourse of safety and responsibility; taking PrEP emerged as a marker of responsible behavior.[143] While some may still use PrEP more defiantly, the widespread subversive potential for liberated sexual practices unmediated by the strictures of public health has been absorbed and defanged. This is precisely because public health discourse connects PrEP to responsibility. In an ironic twist, individuals who do not use PrEP can now be more easily marked by community members, state authorities, and medical providers as not up-to-date, as being irresponsible with their health and the health of others, or as prudish. What this new position makes clear is a dehistoricized understanding of this debate and a misunderstanding of access to health as an equitable process. Indeed, if we codify those on PrEP as safe, responsible, good—dignified—and if we recognize that both risk of infection and access remain divided among race, gender, and class lines, we reinforce the exclusionary boundaries drawn by the state and by economic structures in our communities.

Similar to the earliest years of the crisis and the discourses surrounding bathhouse closures, the state continues to police the behaviors and bodies of queer people. If PrEP and U=U represent efforts by the state to care for those bodies most at risk, we must ask hard questions to explore how exclusionary logics—ones diametrically opposed in public sex institutions like the baths and to democratic exchange loaded with interclass contact and risk—persist within this care model. Unquestionably, PrEP and TasP have liberating potential for queer sexual practice. This potential, however, is tempered by its relationship to capitalistic enterprises, to the state's efforts to police unruly bodies, and to the broader politics of healthcare in the United States. All these mechanisms of control seek to separate us based on the logic of networking rather than foster the kind of togetherness pregnant with potential based on the logic of contact.[144]

Just as state authorities refused to consider the queer logics expressed in the bathhouses or to recognize that gay men themselves were already doing public health work intracommunally, they now ignore queer worldmaking practices when they offer PrEP and TasP for a liberated future. While these state-sanctioned efforts ostensibly confer dignity to long-denigrated citizens by providing care, they fail to engage with the harm done to queer communities during this period—they fail to engage with what *exactly* was lost and what needs to be mended. PrEP and TasP may be conceived as insidious attempts to normalize, surveil, and police LGBTQ+ individuals who utilize these medications. Like the faulty deployment of the public health narrative during the HIV/AIDS crisis to achieve long-desired goals to obliterate queer spaces, contemporary public health narratives about PrEP and TasP advance exclusionary logics and practices.

Intentional HIV Transmission: Resisting Dignity's Demands

The subculture of bareback sex, particularly the practice associated with the intentional transmission of HIV, responded to the virus not with fear but with creativity, exploring how kinship could be built through the virus rather than understanding viral status as yet another division within the community. This subcultural practice took shape before PrEP or U=U emerged, and it may hold within it insights on how to confront and resist the boundary making and subsequent problematic exclusions that follow from some public health approaches that equate TasP and PrEP with responsibility and dignified behavior.

Through Louise Hogarth's documentary film *The Gift* and Dennis Cooper's novel *The Sluts*, we explore how gay men have creatively integrated the presence of the infectious microbe into their erotic lives as a fetishistic practice intensely charged with conflict and filled with meanings that defy the imposition of normative public health recommendations. Commonly referred to as "bug chasing" and "gift giving," the practice of deliberate HIV infection is a complex subcultural phenomenon. We turn to these cultural representations because of the limits of sociological studies on this topic. Furthermore, genres themselves—documentary and fiction—allow us to interrogate how ideological power can be deployed to reinforce norms or how we might imagine alternatives to current deployments of dignity that may prove difficult to realize.

Although whispers about the subculture of "bug chasing" or "gift giving" have been present in isolated communal circles since the early to mid-1990s, knowledge about its specifics has been largely shrouded in secrecy. Because powerful societal rewards and/or punishments proliferate for governing our bodies in particular ways rather than others—to behave with restraint is to be viewed as dignified—abandonment of condoms and fetishization of an infectious microbe remain submerged in and concealed from the normative dictations of proper bodily control. Consequently, deliberate HIV infection as an erotic practice remains characterized by coded discourse, selective inclusion, partial visibility, and silence.

Given the challenges of learning about this subculture, we turn to the messages that can be gleaned from *The Sluts* as compared to those offered in *The Gift*. Critical discussions about deliberate HIV infection from literary studies, cultural studies, and critical theory—which are few and far between—remain focused almost entirely on Hogarth's documentary and Gregory Freeman's sensationalist article in *Rolling Stone* magazine. Therefore, Cooper's alternative perspective can help identify the particular ideological work done by Hogarth.[145]

The Gift debuted in 2003. Beginning in the independent film circuit, quickly spreading to college campuses, and later becoming a staple on Netflix, the film itself went viral. It traces the subcultural practice of intentional HIV transmission through the voices of those who have sought infection, through the perspectives of people who host conversion parties, through a variety of voices from the medical establishment, and through a chorus of the previously infected (though not intentionally infected) AIDS generation. Hogarth employs the seductive power of a confessional paradigm that promises her spectators a chance to indulge in conventional logics about non-normative sexual expressions, gay male sexual communities, and a politics of blame.

Hogarth's film falls victim to an ill-developed practice of sociological gazing, which is a normative gaze that is as pleasurable as it is ethically insidious and misleading. This gaze functions like the municipal authorities discussed in chapter 1—namely, to present an ultimatum to behave in a dignified manner or die.[146] Hogarth structures a conservative argument that does little to shed light on the complexities of motivations to abandon condoms deliberately. Rather, she delivers a reductive cause-and-effect narrative and provides a perverse, touristic spectacle for heteronormative majorities to confirm their prior assumptions of alleged queer excess and the indignity of queer sexuality. Any potential for alternative understandings drowns in a sea of club music, flashing graphics, and statistics that detail carnal excesses.

Cooper's *The Sluts*, published one year after *The Gift* premiered, provides a different perspective on the eroticizing of HIV. Narrated through sex ads, message boards, and transcribed voice messages, *The Sluts* brings together castration play, necrophilia fantasies, consensual snuff scenes, bug chasing, intense S/M role-play, and more[147] in what the *Village Voice* lauds as "this will sound strange—the most enjoyable of Dennis Cooper's novels to date."[148]

Showcasing his knowledge of and participation in sexual subcultures, Cooper provides a platform on which the subculture can speak on its *own* terms. Unlike Hogarth's interviewees, Cooper's characters remain in the mediums in which the majority of these practices are negotiated (instead of being unearthed and deployed as lonely ethnographic subjects), participate in their likeminded sexual communities (instead of being isolated and alienated), refuse the confessional paradigm that pathologizes their erotic decisions (instead of apologizing and rehabilitating), and showcase some of the complicated motivations for engaging in such practices in the first place. In short, Cooper explores the subculture in its complexity.

Hogarth's ideological aspirations to deny gay men of dignity parallel the impulses that triggered the bathhouse closures. By contrast, Cooper provides a vehicle for the subculture to speak on its own terms and creates the possibility to reclaim dignity beyond the moralism of an oppressive state. When each work is read alongside Dean's theories of barebacking and his claim that sharing seropositive semen is loaded with meaning, Hogarth's celebration of restraint and Cooper's embrace of excess come into full view. Proffering a less common perspective in the midst of a global HIV/AIDS pandemic, Dean dared to ask dangerous questions about the deliberate abandonment of condoms and the sharing of semen (infected or not). In so doing, Dean challenges mainstream health norms and probes openness to radical alterity.

Strikingly influenced by Gayle Rubin's foundational "Thinking Sex," Dean adopts a principle of "benign sexual variation" to study a subculture subjected to stigma and swift judgment and misunderstanding.[149] Often centering his own participation in the subculture and his astute understanding of queer practices, Dean argues, "New, apparently unintelligible behavior such as the organized sharing of infected semen requires not a rush to judgment but a careful suspension of judgment, before certain actions may become remotely transparent."[150]

Contrary to assessments of the barebacker as hedonistic, irresponsible, and pathological, Dean offers a new template to understand these transgressive acts. This template is animated by notions of establishing queer kinship, democratically engaging with otherness, embracing risk, and challenging mainstream health norms and definitions of what constitutes a life worth living. Establishing baseline rationales, Dean highlights defining features of the subculture: "embracing risk as a test of masculinity, counter-phobically reinterpreting the pathogen as desirable, diminishing fear of HIV/AIDS, increasing doubts about HIV as the cause of AIDS, eliminating anxiety by purposefully arranging seroconversion, and resisting mainstream health norms." In this way, "HIV thus is pictured as a source of life rather than of death."[151]

Once sharing infected semen becomes a model of kinship and creativity, Dean can muse about how gay men engage in their own kind of breeding or reproduction: "The virus may be considered a particular form of memory, one that offers an effective way of maintaining certain relations with the dead."[152] He contends that "through HIV [one's DNA], it is possible to imagine establishing an intimate corporeal relation with somebody one has never met or, indeed, could never meet—someone historically, geographically, or socially distant from oneself."[153] In his estimation, one's openness to otherness—one's willingness to embrace intimacy without prophylaxis or serosorting—involves an undoing of the artificiality that promises a self that is free from *the other*. In other words, "to the extent that unprotected sex represents a disposition of openness to the other, it may be regarded as ethically exemplary."[154] Arguing from a psychoanalytic perspective, Dean offers a provocative argument that is counterintuitive (or radically opposed to the governing principles of normative socialization that define dignified behavior) and seductive. If Dean's theories hold, Hogarth's narrative can be contrasted with Cooper's *The Sluts* to reveal how the former deploys dignity to construct conservative boundaries of "responsible" behavior and to define which bodies are valuable, while the latter attempts to reclaim the dignity of queer kinship by asserting agency in an oppressive state.[155]

In *The Gift*, Hogarth derogates, desexualizes, and disempowers HIV-positive bodies, presenting them as fundamentally dangerous, and she consequently glorifies the HIV-negative body. From the openings of the film, Hogarth uses James Higginson's 2001 photograph called *Gun-Cock*. This image operates as a powerful symbol of both terror and impending "danger." As the cryptic music heightens, the camera zooms in on the deathly phallic instrument to make a clear statement about the dangers of sex. More specifically, though, the film focuses on the dangers of the sexualized HIV-positive body and of empowering the HIV-positive subject. Her film suggests that HIV-positive subjects have been *too* empowered or that in an effort to encourage HIV-positive people, prevention circles and medical professionals have created fraudulent realities that have an adverse effect on controlling the spread of the virus.

Since the early years of the crisis, persons living with AIDS (PWAs) have expressed a strong desire for self-empowerment and self-definition. We might read these efforts as a way to reclaim dignity in the face of state and private authorities that continuously have assaulted gay and queer men as irresponsible, childish, and dangerous. During the National

Lesbian and Gay Health Conference in 1983 in Denver, Colorado, PWAs met and drafted a manifesto that listed guidelines for PWAs and everyone else. Referred to as "The Denver Principles," this document, created under the informal leadership of AIDS activist Bobbi Campbell with input from Michael Callen, Richard Berkowitz, Gar Traynor, and more, served as a formal write-up that gave PWAs a space to communicate how they expected to treat themselves and how they expected to be treated by others.[156] "The Denver Principles" have since become a reference point for those from a variety of fields who engage people infected with the virus. Chief among these principles is the desire to avoid victimhood, combat blame, protect the emotional health of those afflicted, and present affirmative representations of people with HIV. In short, the principles help people *live with* rather than die from HIV/AIDS.

Contrary to the guidance of "The Denver Principles," Hogarth suggests that the empowerment of the HIV-positive subject is the problem. In a lucid moment in the film, Walt Odets (a psychiatrist) works with Doug (the guilt-ridden confessor) and Jim (a moralizing HIV-positive voice) to form Hogarth's ideological triumvirate. With this, she uses a simulated question-and-answer structure to present a neat sound bite to viewers. Odets embodies the voice of the positive individual when he asks, "Are you implying [as an HIV-negative man or as an HIV-negative society] that there is something wrong with me?" He then reassumes his HIV-negative subject position when he answers, "Yes, the answer is [that] there is."[157] Odets's definitive "Yes, there is something wrong with you" reverberates throughout the film. By examining how "gift givers" are portrayed, how certain stories about HIV-positive subjects are told, and how Hogarth cannot imagine an affirmative future for an HIV-positive body, viewers see how Hogarth assuages fears of the empowered, sexualized (and threatening) HIV-positive individual—ignoring "The Denver Principles" to derogate, desexualize, and disempower PWAs.

In a drama-filled, sensationalized moment in the film, Doug recounts for audiences one of his first conversations with a "gift giver." From his firsthand account, viewers witness Doug having a difficult time trying to share his experience. He pauses, awkwardly laughs, offers embarrassed smiles, and delivers all the proper hindsight bias. Temporally speaking, Doug travels back to his uninfected days to tell a story about an older sexual top who seduced him into welcoming infected semen. As if read-ing from a script, Doug explains that the older HIV-positive top wanted to control him, rob him of his innocence, and destroy his health perma-nently. HIV-positive men are presented as so bitter about their infections that they spend their lives spreading their infected DNA to unsuspect-ing HIV-negative people. Regardless of how "The Denver Principles" recommend avoiding scapegoating HIV-positive people or engaging in blame, Hogarth's selected and edited subjects follow her script: they work to derogate the "infectious" "Poz" subject and to reduce him to an angry, unethical agent of infection.[158]

Ultimately, *The Gift* elides the complexities of HIV disclosure, stigma, and HIV criminalization to present a reductive characterization of the positive subject as a sex fiend with murderous intentions. Again, the parallels to the messaging from municipal authorities during the bath-house controversies are apparent. The potential for a dynamic conversa-tion about HIV disclosure and its impact on infection rates succumbs to the easier and more familiar logic of blame. Consequently, ideas about consent or kinship go unexplored as a potential motivation that mer-its investigation, for such considerations might be too transgressive for the film.

Hogarth also centers narratives about HIV infection that frame her positive subjects as weak, dependent victims. Since Hogarth aims to control what people do with their bodies, she taps into the "fear of HIV/ AIDS" that she regrets is losing its influence. In her estimation, the only narratives that involve HIV-positive lives must be saturated with vic-timhood. As the members of the "AIDS generation" share their stories, they focus on issues of social and familial rejection, loves lost, and hor-rific bodily deterioration. Jim, in particular, embodies the idea that the HIV-positive subject will die—perhaps indirectly—of HIV infection and will die lonely. This is the fate he deserves, at least according to him. Supporting this logic, Hogarth does not include any information about their love lives, careers, hobbies, or sex lives. This older generation operates in a domestic, safe setting—providing narratives of disempow-ered victimhood and sadness. They do not exhibit active sexuality, press transgressive buttons, or threaten Hogarth's objectives. As her ideologi-cal mouthpieces from the "inside," they appear as non-threatening, pal-atable subjects who are deteriorating toward their inevitable deaths.

Continuing his role as a mouthpiece for Hogarth's rhetoric from the "inside," Jim makes clear statements about who should be telling their stories and who should be guiding the rest of us forward in the fight against AIDS. During one of his many diatribes, Jim contends, "We need to elevate these people who are HIV-negative. They are the ones who need to be talking. They are the ones who need to be glamorized."[159] Interestingly, what Jim encourages is what already exists culturally. The HIV-negative body is already glamorized. From Jim's (and, by extension, Hogarth's) perspective, the people who are HIV-negative need to be "spotlighted" in conversations about HIV/AIDS, they need to be at the center of prevention work, they need to populate the posters and prevention literature, and they need to be teaching everyone else their secret.

In earlier parts of the film, Jim admits to not knowing any gay male in his later thirties or early forties who has remained uninfected. But by the end of the narrative, Jim presents this elusive figure to his co-interviewees: Deej, a thirty-seven-year-old Black gay male, is HIV-negative and joins the other men to tell his story and discuss how he managed a fate for which they are ineligible. Hogarth's inclusion of Deej as an HIV-negative man is significant, especially since young Black gay men constitute a disproportionate number of HIV infections.[160]

Hogarth wants Deej to perform possibility. She wants his presence to signal that remaining negative is possible, and she does this work because she thinks (perhaps wrongly) that one of the main reasons individuals pursue HIV infection as an erotic practice is because they do not believe that remaining HIV-negative is possible. In a film ostensibly about exploring the subcultural practice of deliberate HIV infection as an erotic practice, Hogarth's curative impulses take over: all the "bug chasers" disappear, the "gift givers" never emerge directly, and every HIV-positive body is left to die. Additionally, viewers cannot find a single mention of an HIV-positive support group or an affirmative HIV-positive existence in *The Gift*; rather, Deej is the enshrined figure to be protected—the body that matters—the life worth living.

If glorifying the HIV-negative body does not provide enough confirmation of what constitutes the dignified subject, Hogarth also praises the heterosexual community while she blames gay men for HIV/AIDS. She also confirms conventional logics about gay male sexual culture.

This is clearest when Hogarth features one of Odets's main contentions: "Heterosexuals have done better prevention for gay men than gay men have done."[161] For the viewer familiar with the history of HIV/AIDS, Odets's commentary is mind-blowing, as he ignores the grassroots foundation of the safe(r) sex movement, which we traced in chapter 1.[162] When considering the totality of the film's rhetorical thrusts, though, Odets's commentary makes sense as further support for Hogarth's theses. Contrary to the heterosexual community, Hogarth depicts the gay community as a group of irresponsible degenerates, as being the reason the epidemic continues, as people who have a perverse death wish, and as individuals who have a deficient understanding of HIV/AIDS. Instead of speaking to participants of the sexual subculture who make calculated decisions about their health, relationships, and pleasures, she presents gay men (particularly those who choose to participate in "chasing" or "giving") as unrestrained, ignorant, and irresponsible. In a word, they are undignified.

Hogarth also sensationalizes gay men's sexual culture to confirm entrenched assumptions about sexual excess. Gay men are contrasted with heteronormative monogamy, maturity, responsibility, and productivity, which her film values as the way to live. Hogarth's commentary on barebacking and deliberate HIV infection as an erotic practice supports her dismissal of gay men and her engagement in a politics of blame. Without ever delving deeply into the subcultural erotic practice(s) with which she is so preoccupied, she reduces gay men to flawed images. She remains wrapped up in Doug's apologetic admission: "I had *a lot* of promiscuous, unsafe sex."[163] She relies on sensationalism, reductive medical information, carefully selected and scripted ethnographic subjects, sentimental narrative techniques, and powerful social punishments to deliver her thesis about the HIV/AIDS epidemic and gay men's sexual culture.

In the end, *The Gift* is neither a sustained examination of a subculture nor an "ethical exploration of self-other relations."[164] Instead, it is a gift for those who would like to see the always-threatening HIV-positive body derogated, desexualized, and disempowered; for those who would like to glorify the HIV-negative body and praise the heterosexual community's prevention efforts; and for those who would like to see the gay male community and their efforts dismissed and blamed for continuing the epidemic. *The Gift* does offer education, but the lesson is an old one. Instead of viewers adopting "benign sexual variation" to learn about the ethics and pleasures of a sexual subculture, they expose themselves to Hogarth's reductive thesis—one that blames gay men for the AIDS crisis and works to ensure a derogated HIV-positive existence.

We can find a response to Hogarth's narrative in Cooper's *The Sluts*. Cooper provides a platform from which the bug chaser, gift giver, and barebacker can speak back and communally negotiate how dignity can flourish alongside queer excess. Interestingly, it is through the poz subject (pre-TasP or -PrEP) that Cooper gives voice to alternatives: because these individuals remain ineligible for reintegration within dignity's limits, they can provide possibilities unstained by dignity's rhetoric and allure. While the novel does not engage deliberate HIV infection exclusively, Cooper's handling of the erotic practice offers divergent possibilities and problematizes Hogarth's rendering of HIV/AIDS and the erotic practice of intentional transmission, as well as of the murky relationship among sexuality, language, representation, and death.[165]

Influenced by his own participation in sexual subcultures and his general anarchist disposition, Cooper depicts the erotic practice by featuring its central values and pleasures. Praising Cooper's uncompromising rawness and honesty, Robert Gluck posits, "The authenticity of [Cooper's] work is related to how far [he] will go, how much [he] will say."[166] If a sexual subculture saturated with imperatives of silence can be represented ethically at all, Cooper perhaps gets us as close as possible. Anticipating Dean, Cooper displays his proximity to the subculture and fluency with its ethics, meanings, and pleasures. Cooper suggests something similar when asked about his aesthetic choices: "My aesthetics developed the way they have because I conducted so many different mental and physical experiments on such a specific area of interest, I guess. I mean in my fantasy life, in my life itself, and on the page."[167] The result is that sexual variance in all its complications, messiness, and exhilarations ooze from the novel.

As a studied participant who recognizes the impossibility (and undesirability) of harnessing the erotic charge of sexual subcultures through language, Cooper is equipped to represent the misunderstood or inaccessible practice of deliberate HIV infection without resorting to curative discourses. Resisting the invasive impulse that saturates Hogarth's film, Cooper highlights the subculture's egalitarian ethos, foregrounds the disparity between virtual self-identification and behavior to probe an engagement with fantasy, and centralizes ideas about kinship and consent to display the subculture's ethics and possibilities. Consequently, the text has the potential to undercut Hogarth's promise of truth and to question her reductive—yet seemingly transparent—"findings." Cooper refuses to moralize and deploy the bug chaser as a rhetorical instrument to consolidate ideas about normative sexual expression, which costs him readers. He notes, "People develop expectations of my work because of their own preconceptions about sex and violence, and they don't like what I've determined in the name of progress."[168] Perhaps for the same reasons, he has a faithful following—one that craves an alternative representation that resembles the practices they value. He provides such a counternarrative to resist the restraints of normative dignity touted by more popular representation.[169]

Attempting to examine the subculture respectfully and to represent it complexly, Cooper lets it speak on its own terms. He does not unearth his characters from their communities—refusing to isolate them. Instead, he sets his novel in the digital spaces in which this subculture often flourishes. The characters in *The Sluts* interact with their communities through sex ads, message boards, voice chats, emails, and faxes. Moreover, Cooper does not translate subcultural argot for his readers, most of whom recognize the "signaling (revealing . . . to initiates who know the code)."[170] While Hogarth can only gain entrance to these website's homepages and while a particular interviewee might narrate for her in hindsight, Cooper traffics in these spaces and represents them in an unadulterated manner—showcasing his fluency with the communities about which he writes. Without the formula of admission and subsequent moralism, he allows his characters to reside and play in their spaces of contact. They are decidedly not alienated or lonely. By utilizing a variety of voices, he foregrounds the egalitarian ethos of the bug-chasing/gift-giving underworld. Since the only requirement to join is the willingness to embrace risk as a way of connecting, many markers of discrimination (race, masculinity, age, beauty imperatives, or HIV status) do not carry nearly as much currency in a community with a radical openness to alterity. While Hogarth's ethnographic subjects remain removed from their communities and reflect alone, Cooper's characters remain in their erotically charged, subcultural space and engage one another without considering the needs of an "outsider."

Additionally, Cooper does not distance his readers from the subcultural activity in which his characters participate. His characters are *actively* engaging in the practice—not in "recovery" and not reflecting on their behaviors with guilt-laden hindsight bias for an "outside" interviewer to educate mainstream audiences as in Hogarth's work. Furthermore, Cooper avoids Hogarth's normative gaze that frames, invades, and moralizes. Instead, the lights are turned down low in their "playrooms," and the subcultural activity is vibrant. When Hogarth "documents" the subculture, the lights are on, the playrooms are empty, and the action is over (or dormant). Cooper's text, by contrast, is populated with bodies—with orifices being filled up and desires being filled in. As a result, readers have little of the "safe" distance that animates Hogarth's film.

Cooper refuses to have his characters confess with a hint of apology; they do not repent to receive reintegration into mainstream society or to provide education. HIV is treated as an erotic component of one's life and not a rhetorical device used to launch conservative rhetoric. Cooper does not frame his narrative through the model of confession that offers a possibility of cleansing; instead, his characters unapologetically express their pleasures in the most candid of fashions: "Gorgeous poz top seeks cute, slender, 18–20 year old neg bottoms for breeding. I'll pound your throat and ass raw with my fat 11″ cock and then shoot huge loads of poz cum in your ravaged holes. Sero-conversion guaranteed. Also seek serious relationship with a cute, 18–20 year old poz bottom into pneumonia scenes, death dances, lesion wearing, and grave chase."[171] Rather than crying and admitting their mistakes to beg for reentrance into the normative social order, Cooper's characters unabashedly share their erotic imaginations and behaviors: "My thing was and is bareback sex—breeding, bug chasing, and so on. Yeah, I like the 'I might be sentencing someone to death when I cum inside him' thing a lot. . . . I love how gay guys can be like straight guys who wonder how many illegitimate kids there could be out there with their DNA. I love imagining my ex-fucks out there in the world infecting others."[172] Because of his unwavering commitment to sexual variance—finding meaning in the body's perilous contours—Cooper embraces an unadulterated excess without apology or stigma.

In surveying the body's possibilities, Cooper centralizes major tenets of the erotic practice of deliberate HIV transmission: creative self-(re)making and kinship building through consensual acts of exchange. Dean explains a similar practice of transformation when he describes the work done on self *and* others. He argues that these subcultural participants showcase queer creativity when they transform an agent of infection into something life-giving—something communal—something to connect rather than to separate them. Why was this queer creativity needed in the first place? As we traced in chapter 1, the violence committed by the state, which allowed the virus to flourish, created a situation in which a community was ravaged; those within it turned on each other, and their sexuality became plagued by fear and death.

Thinking about *how to do things with a virus*, these bug chasers and gift givers reimagine their ability to form kinship and connection, to reproduce by sharing copies of the virus. Cooper's characters exhibit how gay men who seek to share HIV with one another reconceptualize models of kinship with their infected DNA. More than that, they embrace the painful pleasures of thinking about their ex-lovers out in the world spreading the microbe (that is a part of their own genetic material). Although this practice might resemble and even invoke the vocabulary of heteronormative reproduction, the important difference lies in establishing kinship with people one has never even met or never could meet because those people might already be dead. Not only does this contact transgress racial and class boundaries, but it also crosses temporal constraints, producing a dynamic notion of togetherness. As such, cumming together in real time and space mends the wounds of the past and overcomes missed opportunities due to the toll of death and loss wrought by the early years of the HIV/AIDS crisis.

In a similar vein, discussing viral sharing in tandem with heterosexual reproduction, Lev suggests, "The Poz practices, rituals, and fetishes are darker, but no more fetishistic, than those that surround the breeding, signification, and signifying of children, which are perpetually disseminated, apotheosized, and naturalized within heteropatriarchal culture."[173] As Cooper's characters and their fantasies demonstrate, these notions of kinship are also linked to an openness to radical alterity. Part of the thrill might come from creating one's own narrative about the paternity of one's viral strain and contemplating the various bodies through which the virus has passed and from which it has mutated in its own unique ways—for better or worse.

Committed to the dynamics of the sexual subculture, Cooper also foregrounds the issue of consent/mutual pleasure, which is paramount in the subcultural circles as a governing principle. Whereas *The Gift* presents the gift giver as seductive, manipulative, and bitter/angry about his HIV status, Cooper emphasizes consent. As *The Sluts* reveals, when a member in this subculture neglects his responsibility to get consent, other members check his participation. More importantly, these community members educate others about such a shortsightedness so that everyone can make sounder decisions. This kind of ethos of care—what we can center as an ethical approach to Delany's contact—is not a part of Hogarth's sensationalism. Her omission is telling, for such an inclusion would undercut her reductive condemnation of the erotic practice.

Even as Cooper displays fluency with the subculture's complexities and even as he offers a valuable perspective, we must also account for the fact that he is writing fiction. We must at least ask if Cooper could offer his subcultural knowledge and his dangerously transgressive viewpoints if he were engaging with human subjects in the documentary film genre. Since the ethos of the erotic activity revolves around a valuation of silence and because it is so heavily stigmatized (and even criminalized in certain locales), we wonder if Cooper could produce the same results if he were to venture into a genre with real bodies and different expectations. That Cooper writes fiction perhaps illustrates how the work attempts to imagine a world that could or might exist, that aspires to a transgressive value system, and that makes it readable to a broader public. In this way, Cooper gestures toward a possible future. Hogarth operates in a genre that capitalizes on notions of truth, yet her truth is always already infected by particular ideological motivations and lessons that reify normative power. Hogarth values that which existed before AIDS, and she locks us into a conservative logic of limits and recovery.

It would be a danger to argue that Hogarth's depiction is *wrong* and that Cooper's portrayal is *right*. We are more interested in thinking about the audiences for these representations and the messages the representations send; in pondering each creator's proximity to a transgressive sexual practice or each creator's fluency with the subcultural values, ethics, and meanings; and in contemplating the various investments, desires, and ideological agendas that suffuse each text. Without question, *The Gift* and *The Sluts* ignite powerful debates on all sides, but while the former reinforces conventional deployments of dignity that remain fundamentally exclusionary, the latter challenges them, exposes their limits, and gestures toward alternatives unstained by dignity. Since "the bug-chasing phenomenon is likely to continue to exist outside the doors of clinics, hospitals, and doctors' offices," we need texts like *The Sluts* to provide a divergent narrative that resists medicalizing discourses, curative impulses, and sensationalist (mis)representations, which all deny dignity.[174] As we ponder whether or not "it is anyone's place to police others' personal choices, however extreme or [supposedly] self-destructive," we should examine the ideological undercurrents of our assertions and the fears motivating our attempt to govern others, particularly when participants prioritize consent.[175]

Conclusion

In this chapter, we considered how deployments of dignity by governing authorities and how internalization of these notions within LGBTQ+ communities influence contemporary efforts to establish queer kinship. In an era when HIV has been transformed into a chronic and manageable illness, the range of acceptable sexual practices may have broadened, and public health messaging has become more nuanced. Nevertheless, these broadened practices and more nuanced messages are still mediated through the concept of restraint, which remains coded as dignified. For example, insofar as many contemporary bathhouses or apps promote such restraint by encouraging a sociality of networking—in their visual presentations of space and financial parameters of access—they may bolster the normativity that neuters the transgressive potential for which Delany and Dean hope. While some of the independent bathhouses or less common apps do nod to the connections afforded by contact and illustrate an ongoing tension between normative power and capacities for resistance, that they remain at the margins indicates the broad force of normative dignity. Indeed, by maintaining certain boundaries, the most corporatized bathhouses and the most popular apps encourage a networking culture. The design and structures of corporatized bathhouses and the most popular apps establish expectations and promote behaviors that conform to the parameters of dignity by reducing opportunity to encounter difference, strangeness, and risk.

Public health messaging around PrEP and TasP is equally important to address. While these medical innovations could alter the normative logics of dignity and facilitate queer kinship bonds, which HIV/AIDS eclipsed, dominant public health narratives reveal how much these two preventative approaches have been incorporated into the state's definition of dignified behavior. The dominant narrative has become that responsible LGBTQ+ persons take PrEP or maintain an undetectable status. And because existing inequities in healthcare persist along class, gender, and race lines, access to dignity does as well. Black and Brown bodies, in particular, continue to fall beyond dignity's limits; the state's deployment of dignity reinforces structural inequalities and white supremacy.

Consequently, the medical surveillance required for PrEP and TasP access, the market-based parameters of pharmaceutical research that enabled the discovery and disbursement of PrEP, and the exclusionary access that follows from health insurance coverage in the United States call into question whether PrEP or TasP can help queer men reconnect to liberating conceptions of queer excess. By contrast, an older and ongoing subcultural practice of intentional transmission, because it challenges what the state defines as dignified behavior and asserts agency over what can be done with our bodies, reclaims queer logics of the past that move beyond the limits of dignity as it has been deployed by governing authorities. Perhaps the underground subculture that eroticizes intentional transmission, because it is deliberate, grounded in choice, and beyond the state's watchful eye, creates alternatives not mediated through the limits imposed by dignity.

Ultimately, contemporary attempts that might, at first glance, appear to recapture the transgressive potential of the past are often saddled by the state's deployment of dignity. This potential—which may be most robustly performed by subcultures of intentional transmission—may be foreclosed by how LGBTQ+ institutions such as bathhouses and apps have been inflected by dignity's generative work. Put differently, what looks initially like a resuscitation of seemingly lost queer alternatives often proves difficult to realize because those alternatives are mediated by authorities invested in maintaining systems of power inequity. While this influence is pervasive, Robert Reid-Pharr reminds us of the value of consistently reaching for queer alternatives: "What often passes as the LGBTQ community has been largely networked. . . . The good news . . . is that the . . . desire still remains untamed. . . . And when it arrives, reeking of promise and invention, it whispers the same naughty word to those with enough temerity—and hope—to hear: contact!"[176] The questions that remain are how we can inspire and nurture such temerity and how we can compel governing authorities and LGBTQ+ communities to rethink contact as a guiding principle to shape public health policy, cultural production, and law.

PART II

Promoting Sameness or Embracing Difference

Distinct Visions of Dignity in Popular Culture

3

Isn't Straight Still the Default?

The Politics of Restraint in Love, Simon

After a pivotal bullying scene in Greg Berlanti's 2018 pop culture sensation *Love, Simon*, the vice principal of Simon Spier's high school, Mr. Worth, verbalizes both a key tenet of contemporary efforts to represent LGBTQ+ lives in media and a guiding principle of the film.[1] As he ostensibly lacerates the protagonist's homophobic peers and seemingly supports two of the film's LGBTQ+ characters, Mr. Worth engages in a clearly rehearsed Q&A about the school's values. Prompting the bullies, he asks, "At Creekwood High, what do we believe in?" The bullies reply "Tolerance" in disinterested unison. Although the scene is meant to champion diversity and inclusion—albeit in a clunky way—Mr. Worth's explanation of the school's values reveals an obdurate cultural logic that often animates how media authorities render LGBTQ+ persons legible and acceptable: these persons are *tolerated* only if they tame or restrain themselves in line with the normative strictures of dignity as defined by the demands of the majority.[2]

Shortly after *Love, Simon*'s 2018 release, viewers, critics, and marketing blurbs touted the film's progressive message about difference in ways that echoed Mr. Worth's message.[3] One of the film's key phrases went viral: "Why Is Straight the Default?" The social media moment became a mantra of sorts—replete with hashtags, media campaigns, and merchandise.[4] But Mr. Worth's bullying intervention and the subsequent questioning of heterosexuality's ubiquity exemplify how the film promotes a particular brand of market-based respectability politics that comports with the work performed in and through the contemporary deployment of dignity. *Love, Simon* reflects and reproduces a hegemonic conception of neoliberal dignity that understands dignified behavior as restrained behavior.

For readers less familiar, *Love, Simon* is a feature film that follows the romantic and sexual growth of its title character and his impact on family, friends, and the larger community.[5] As Simon navigates his senior year of high school as a closeted teen, he stumbles on an anonymous blog post from a classmate who admits to being gay. Curious and longing for romantic connection, Simon creates a pseudonym and responds to him, and they build a connection over email. While their relationship grows online, Simon searches for the real identity of his budding love interest as he also tries to keep his sexuality a secret from those closest to him. His journey takes a turn, however, when another classmate finds the emails and uses them as blackmail. As Simon faces the threat of exposure, he begins lying, manipulating, and damaging his relationships with his family and friends. Finally, when the blackmailer outs him publicly, Simon has to face his fears, learn how to embrace himself, and mend his fractured relationships. By the end, Simon finds love, rejoins his family and friends as an improved version of himself, and becomes a model for members of his community who are battling their own secrets.

Certainly, with box office totals that have surpassed other recent films that bring attention to sexual exploration and adolescence (such as *Call Me by Your Name*, *Moonlight*, and *Carol*), a fairly large international wide release, and with GLAAD Media Awards, MTV Movie + TV Awards, and Teen Choice Awards to its name, the film showcases moments of potential.[6] Indeed, the dialogue it provokes is cause for marking progress toward LGBTQ+ acceptance. As Matthew Tinkcom contends, "Film has historically been widely accessible and therefore has been a medium in which many queer people have gained the first inklings of the possibilities that new kinds of sexuality and gender might become a reality within their lives."[7] In the same breath, he also warns against uncritical celebration: "However, we should not assume that a film—any film—is transparent in its operations and in the ways it seeks to represent the world to its audiences. . . . Such an assumption is dangerous because film, like any other cultural medium, contains within it ideas and techniques that demand our critical and analytical attention."[8] A critical look at the political work done by *Love, Simon* reveals how it operates under the guise of progress while demanding sameness and negating the transformative potential of difference.

Ultimately, Simon's narrative is one of caution—the pathway to powerful social rewards comes at a grave cost and at the expense of intra-communal bodies and worldviews that remain ineligible for declarations of dignity. To expose this trade-off, we make two moves in this chapter. First, we contrast the film with the original source material on which it is based, the young adult novel *Simon vs. the Homo Sapiens Agenda* by Becky Albertalli.[9] In this comparison, we ask questions about what *Love, Simon* includes, what it amplifies, what it dilutes, and what it erases relative to Albertalli's novel.[10] We examine who gets narrative focus and voice in each, who earns powerful social rewards, and why. Relatedly, we reflect on what happens to characters who do not assuage audiences' anxieties about difference. We explore what happens to difference in the process—how particularity and transgression can be absorbed and drained of their subversive potential. Finally, we investigate the differences between the novel's and the film's treatment of queer iconography and allusions to queer culture, and we critique moments in which Simon is introduced to queer culture. Perhaps more importantly, we amplify the film's silences and elisions, reading as much for what the film circumscribes as for what it centralizes, especially concerning queer culture and queer community-building.

Second, we turn the film critically slantwise to read through a peripheral LGBTQ+ character: Ethan, the African American student who is both gender non-conforming and gay. In so doing, we reveal how the film's celebration of Simon is contingent on his adoption of a non-threatening sameness and a disavowal of difference that is firmly related to race and power. A comparative reading of Simon's and Ethan's characters (and of racial politics more broadly) reveals that the film's entire message of inclusion and Simon's attendant protection by authority figures—his teachers, principal, parents—depend on his unequivocal rejection of Ethan's Black queer excess. As Treva Ellison reminds us, "Blackness functions as both central to and in excess of what is legible."[11] Reading through Ethan's character involves reckoning with how whiteness is shaped by overdetermined narratives of Blackness in general but, more specifically, also grappling with how single-issue queer politics (i.e., sexuality as just about sexual object choice) in contemporary representation vacates serious conversations about structural violence along racial lines in favor of a color-blind community. To be sure, the film's posturing needs Ethan's Black queer excess desperately, but at the same time, the film refuses to have the conversations necessary to discuss how that excess shapes the world in particular ways for Ethan. Ethan's excess consolidates Simon's normative power, but it remains "too much" for the film to explore how Ethan's Blackness and queerness intersect to produce specific lived realities for him. Doing so would rupture any neat alignment of him with Simon under the umbrella of sexual orientation and would expose how Ethan's experience is far from the universalizing one that the film requires to foster relatability with mainstream audiences.

Simon's story arc from a single closeted teen to an out gay teen with a boyfriend keeps him ensconced in the trappings, expectations, and requirements of heteronormativity. After the disruption of his outing, Simon is welcomed back into a world whose dynamics of racism, gender conformity, and class privilege remain fundamentally undisturbed by Simon's personal development. Simon adopts the uncritical stance of homonormativity.[12] As Roderick Ferguson argues, "The formation of homonormative subjectivities and social relations name homosexuality's entrance into white supremacy."[13] If Simon conforms to the gender and sexual norms of the majority by practicing a single-issue sexuality animated by queer restraint, he can wash the one stain off of his whiteness and his cisnormativity that marks him for exclusion. He can regain access to the privileges that he feared losing in the first place should he "come out."

Ferguson highlights who pays the cost of the white homonormative subject's reentry into white supremacy: "As homonormative formations achieve cultural normativity by appealing to liberal capital's regimes of visibility, the immigrant, the poor, and the person of color suffer under the state's apparatuses—apparatuses that render them the cultural antithesis of a stable and healthy social order."[14] In the arena of representation—one characterized as the "cultural marketplace of sameness" by Kaila Adia Story—*Love, Simon* illustrates Ferguson's contentions through Simon's development and concomitant acceptance.[15] The film also shows how the consequences for this growth are paid by the more marginal Black queer body—namely, Ethan's.

Our reading can be difficult for the audience to see because of how the film embraces representational diversity; the cast is multiracial, but the narrative is saturated in whiteness. In this way, Black embodiment is hypervisible and invisible at once. To be sure, *Love, Simon* engages in the trend of multicultural casting, as Simon has two friends who are read as Black or Brown. He also has a love interest who identifies as Black (which he announces to Simon during a climactic scene, but Simon seemingly ignores his claim to Blackness). At the level of visibility, a viewer of *Love, Simon* could think that they are witnessing a moment of progressive politics on screen. But as Alison Reed warns, we must be wary of any visibility trap that confuses race for racism: "The popular conflation of race and racism produces what I call a 'spectacular absence,' which locates an eerie evacuation of discussions of systemic racism in the everywhere-there-ness of race."[16] Within the context of critiquing white queer theory, Reed offers a salient point: "Race as a theoretical fetish satisfies an institutional need for multicultural representation and theoretical diversity, while perpetuating colorblind logics that foreclose possibilities of justice by denying the existence of white supremacy."[17] Because *Love, Simon* is rich in Black and Brown bodies but devoid of sustained analyses of institutional racism and its links to queerness within the narrative, the film can be a particularly dangerous iteration of contemporary queer politics. It appears far more progressive and transformative than it is.[18]

Without doubt, *Love, Simon* qualifies as a mainstream visibility project—one met with loads of cultural approbation as a testament to how progressive the current moment has become—precisely because it conforms to and bolsters a narrative of progress. But when read slantwise through the lens of Ethan (or, in Reed's terms, through "spectacular racialized embodiment" and its attendant absences), audiences can discern how the film neuters progressive politics, becoming instead a story that demands neoliberal depoliticization.[19] Since the film requires an understanding of queer politics as single-issue oriented, it renders clear what Ferguson theorizes as a "one-dimensional queer." As Ferguson notes, "Multidimensional gay politics transitioned to a single-issue and one-dimensional platform" and "divorc[ed] queer liberation from political struggles around race, poverty, capitalism, and colonization. . . . Put simply, by mainstreaming queerness—making it conform to civic ideals of respectability, national-belonging, and support for the free market—gay rights and gay capital helped to renew racial, ethnic, class, gender, and sexual exclusions."[20] Ferguson importantly distinguishes between depoliticization and being apolitical: "This depoliticization did not represent the absence of politics so much as the regulation of politics."[21] Depoliticization "work[s] to confine the political to those standpoints approved by established systems. Part of depoliticization's maneuvers was to neutralize thinking and actions that tried to transcend the status quo."[22]

The single-issue orientation that Ferguson laments and critiques because of its violence against queer and trans people of color is at the heart of *Love, Simon*, for as Simon announces in the film's opening sequence, "I am just like you" except for *one* "huge-ass secret."[23] That orientation becomes all the more complicated when it is swathed with appeals to generative (and seductive) concepts like diversity and dignity. The single-issue-oriented white gay male—one who qualifies for homonormativity under the dictations of heteronormativity—is eligible for dignity. He is complicit in the structural violence enacted by the neocolonial, white supremacist, capitalist (hetero)patriarchy.[24] Simon is that person. His story is presented as universal and serves a universalizing function; he is presented as the model. He is a character who prevails through emotional trials, but his experience is particular to his whiteness, cisnormativity, and class position.[25] His perceived universality "promote[s] forms of racial, gender, and class exclusions that le[ave] people of color, the poor, and queers of color to be victims of those exclusions."[26] By situating the white cisgender gay man as the model of dignity worthy of acceptance at the expense of a queer Black body, the film's creative team showcases the exclusionary force of dignity, for it privileges certain raced, classed, and gendered ways of living.

In short, *Love, Simon* features a turn toward homogeneity that permits only a slight divergence. Simon can rejoin the mainstream as a gay teen worthy of happiness and safety so long as he contorts himself into an already-existing model of normativity with a slight twist: he can change only the pronoun of his partner without threatening *to change or transform* heteronormative logics or worldmaking practices. To earn the (literal) applause of heteronormative characters and, by extension, of mainstream audiences at the film's end, Simon cannot be *too much—too different*. He cannot threaten how the world works. He can appeal for entry into the world as is and can have his one "huge-ass secret" accommodated, but alternatives that could disrupt, destabilize, or reformulate existing power structures must be denied.

By reading the film in these two ways—through comparison with its original source material and through the eyes of its characters marginalized by race and gender—we reveal the inextricable connections between racism and heteronormativity in mainstream LGBTQ+ representation. We draw attention to these connections by examining four aspects of the film: (1) its structural circularity that promotes character stasis rather than transformation, (2) its choices concerning narrative time and focus, (3) its universalization of Simon's experience of coming out as a relatable practice for all, and (4) its deletion, alteration, and erasure of certain characters that satisfy diverse casting aspirations but refuse to promote content that politicizes the narrative. All of these features advance a narrative that severs Simon from opportunities to learn about and engage multidimensional queer community and history, an isolation that exists in stark contrast with the character's development in the novel on which the film is based.[27] Indeed, the film's references to that community and its artifacts are either left on the cutting-room floor or played for laughs. This severing from history, context, and particularity permits Simon to be easily reincorporated into normative familial and social dynamics after his coming out disrupted them. Furthermore, it permits hierarchies and dynamics of power to remain unquestioned and to go unchallenged. Finally, it forecloses the coalition building across difference that could fortify multidimensional queer communities to resist a culture of normativity more powerfully and to fight for a more equitable future.

Incorporation without Disruption: Reading *Love, Simon*'s Circular Structure

Even as *Love, Simon* concludes by blaring a pivotal line from the song "Wild Heart" by Bleachers—"Well, everything has changed"—a careful viewer might realize that very little has changed.[28] The film's circular structure positions Simon in a similar place to where he began. In fact, the opening and closing sequences of the film operate as mirrors of each other; the only difference worthy of note is that Simon has a boyfriend by the end. This structure works in tandem with the film's opening lines (which market the film in taglines and trailers) to present a decontextu-alized, dehistoricized view of identity—namely, that LGBTQ+ folks are just like everyone else except they have, as Simon tells us, "one huge-ass secret" that needs to be revealed and accommodated (or domesticated) so that normal life can continue. This pervasive idea not only comforts mainstream audiences, but it also operates as a sound bite that reduces the complexity of LGBTQ+ identities and elides how sexual orientation has a far-reaching impact in the making of the self and queer commu-nities; it starkly characterizes the one-dimensional queer and renders conflicts around sexuality as private and personal matters rather than public and political ones. It anesthetizes any potential for queer resis-tance and liberation.

When the movie begins, before viewers even meet Simon in the nar-rative present, we hear his voice-over deliver the film's first lines: "I'm just like you. For the most part, my life is totally normal."[29] Additionally, as family movie footage of Simon getting his first car unfolds, he nar-rates his normativity for viewers: "My dad was the annoyingly hand-some quarterback who married the hot valedictorian. . . . I have a sister I actually like. . . . And then there's my friends. Two of them I've known since pretty much the beginning of time, or at least kindergarten. One of them I just met a few months ago, but it feels like I've known her forever. We do everything friends do. . . . So, like I said, I'm just like you."[30] Each of these opening details—along with the visual image of him putting his pants on (literally) one leg at a time—characterizes him as a readable normative subject with whom audiences are famil-iar and with whom they can more easily empathize. Without doubt, Simon emerges as the attractive, lovable, jock-adjacent white male high schooler. And despite the fact that the book on which the movie is based begins with the blackmail story line that serves as a catalyst for Simon's coming-out experience, the film begins instead by situating him firmly within the framework of the nuclear family structure and within larger heteronormative kinship bonds with his friends. The difference speaks to what is the ideological center of each text—the heteronorma-tive family of the film and the queer teenagers and their relationship in the novel.

When Simon repeats the same lines delivered only moments ago, but this time to his email correspondent and eventual love interest, Blue/Bram, he offers an additional detail: "So, like I said, I'm just like you. I have a totally perfectly normal life. Except I have one huge-ass secret."[31] From this space of being normal with a secret, Simon begins his daily routine: entering the family kitchen to grab a bite on the go from his little sister, heading out the door to pick up his friends Nick and Leah, stopping for four iced coffees, picking up Abby, and driving all of them to school. In this beginning shot, Nick muses about a dream he had the night before, and Abby provides a reading of the dream that suggests Nick is missing something that is right in front of his eyes. Experiencing wild discomfort with Abby's reading, Simon cranks up the music to end the conversation before anyone can possibly inch any closer to his "huge-ass secret."

To complete its circular logic, the film's ending returns to this daily routine. Move by move, the sequence of the scene is nearly identical. This time, however, Simon picks up *five* iced coffees instead of the usual four and makes a new last stop to complete the carpool: he picks up his boyfriend, Bram. At least three details are worthy of note in this final scene and its relationship to the film's opening: most obviously, Simon has added a passenger. Moreover, his secretive and tense characteristics so visible in the opening have subsided. Finally, his destination is not school; rather, Simon tells his friends that he has an adventure planned, and based on the closing shot of the city of Atlanta, viewers can assume that Simon and company are leaving the so-called safe, mundane day-to-day happenings of their suburban senior year for a wild exploration within the playground of the major urban center of the Southeast.[32]

The film's circularity highlights the underlying logic of the film: Simon's owning the truth of his sexual orientation is merely a matter of adding a variable to a ready-made formula and is decidedly a personal matter. Consequently, Simon remains rooted deeply in his nuclear family and nestled within all heteronormative kinship configurations of his past. While this might initially read as a moment to celebrate, we question whether the hard work of inclusion involves only adding a new variable to patterns of normativity, and we spotlight how this narrow notion of inclusion stands on the necks of other further marginalized queer folks. Furthermore, we see the dangers of considering sexual orientation only through the prism of privatization, for such an approach promises a kind of depoliticization that animates the film. By presenting Simon's story as only a personal one rather than a political one, *Love, Simon* falls victim to the kind of depoliticization that Ferguson sees as central to the constitution and deployment of the one-dimensional queer: "As such, depoliticization denoted the attempt to sever the links between the public and the private as well as between one type of struggle and other sets of struggles. Thus, depoliticization denotes the process by which social grievances become private and discrete matters."[33] In Simon's case, the grievances are solved in his personal life.

Fundamentally, though, Simon never transforms in substantial and disruptive ways, and he never demands that the ordering of the world transform either. More specifically, he never threatens the order of the status quo; the systems, institutions, and logics that uphold power and that continue to delineate which bodies and lives matter and which don't are never called into question. Importantly, he also neglects to account for any queer experience that differs from his own, particularly one in which access to power differs. The film's completed circular structure facilitates incorporation without disruption because *Love, Simon* merely asks that Simon's difference in sexual object choice be acknowledged and (to invoke Mr. Worth) be tolerated.

Perhaps even more importantly, that tolerance is marketed as an institutional value—as a winning value system—that will diversify Simon's educational institution. In reality, though, it will do little to make life more equitable (and livable) for queer people. As Sara Ahmed notes in her work on institutional diversity initiatives, the lip service and, indeed, labor that institutions perform around diversity and inclusion often uphold institutional power / the status quo (racism in her study) rather than dismantle power: "Feminists of color have explored the relationship between diversity and power by showing how diversity is incorporated by institutions: 'diversity management' becomes a way of managing or containing conflict or dissent."[34] Instead of undoing and redoing institutions alongside the "diversification" of them, institutions demand that diverse "others" contort themselves into an existing order—just adding a little color or "flavor" to the institution as it is. And while these institutions might begin looking different (though not much different) and while their leaders might claim to be laboring for a more just place/space, these marginalized bodies actually become marketing projects—branding posters, if you will—while the values, needs, power structures, and majority bodies remain firmly intact.

Whose Story Is This? Narrative Time and Focus in Novel and Film

By perpetuating the tendency to drain the transformative power of queerness in favor of adopting a non-threatening sameness, Berlanti and his creative team render clear the dangers of incorporation without disruption. *Love, Simon* puts on full display the seductive quality, potential dangers, and consequences of a feigned inclusion project, especially one that masquerades as a progressive representation of LGBTQ+ life. This draining of the subcultural potential of queerness becomes evident when viewers compare what occupies narrative time in the film versus what topics pace Albertalli's novel. Indeed, this comparative approach illustrates how *Love, Simon* demands neoliberal restraint instead of welcoming any kind of queer excess to establish its narrative focus and thus communicate its value system and priorities. Instead of celebrating difference in all its disruptive fervor through a detailed depiction of the queer romance, the film centers the heteronormative family and broader heteronormative peer groups.

In Albertalli's novel, the narrative focus is split between the email exchange and the subsequent relationship building between Simon and Blue/Bram and the rest of Simon's life. Roughly 45 percent of the novel's chapters (before the characters meet in person) are devoted to their email exchanges. By contrast, about 10 percent of the film—roughly eleven minutes of narrative time—details their email exchanges. Readers of Albertalli's novel follow two teens as they build community with and love for each other. Their exchange is protracted and expansive; it is full of possibility. In the film, the emails are chopped up and remixed, and they are blended with other scenes in Simon's life, which fractures the already-reduced narrative focus on their budding romance. Viewers of *Love, Simon* might have more difficulty understanding how the two teenagers form such a powerful bond. In short, their exchange and relationship are deprioritized in favor of the heteronormative family.

Just as important as the quantity of their exchanges is the *content*. In Albertalli's rendering of this budding teenage romance, Simon and Blue/Bram openly discuss queerness—specifically queer history and queer critiques of power. As they embrace their emerging sexualities, they converse about queer history and important figures in queer subculture. For instance, they discuss Oscar Wilde and consider Casanova's alleged bisexuality: "So, you know how you hear stories about people coming out to their parents, and the parents say they already knew somehow? Yeah, my dad isn't going to say that. I'm officially certain that he has no idea I'm gay, because you will not believe what book he picked out to give me. *History of My Life* by Casanova. . . . Maybe I should have asked him to exchange it for Oscar Wilde."[35] Decidedly, the queer content discussed is not necessarily rooted in respectability; Wilde is one of our earliest decadent figures and represents an infamous case of criminalization. Later in the novel, after the two have met in person, they share an intimate moment alone in the school's empty theater, and Bram returns to the subject of their earlier email discussion to talk to Simon about what else he learned about queer history: "Oh, and guess who was apparently bisexual? . . . Casanova."[36] Even though this moment is fleeting, it showcases an ongoing conversation between two queer young people as they grapple to quilt together a history that is not regularly offered to them in everyday conversation, school curricula, or mainstream cultural representation. And similar to the example of Wilde, mentioning Casanova is particularly interesting because our extant cultural narratives regularly obscure or erase Casanova's bisexual leanings to present him as a premier ladies' man. Although these characters are not necessarily engaging with queer elders and learning about their histories in protracted ways, they do discuss them casually among the many quotidian details of their lives as they share space together.

Relatedly, Albertalli's narrative insists on providing space for queer sexuality to flourish unapologetically, mainly through Simon and Blue's horny innuendos. While the two teenagers exhibit the awkwardness of a growing awareness of their bodies and desires, they do *openly engage in sexual dialogue*. They have a noteworthy exchange that is ostensibly about typos and autocorrect. Simon begins this conversation by responding to Blue's inquiries about his Halloween costume: "A ninja? *Suck* a good guess, but no dice."[37] He immediately attempts to correct the error, but he makes another fumble: "Aaah—autocorrect fail. *DICK* a good guess."[38] Finally, he concludes with one more correction: "SUCH a good guess. SUCH. Jesus Christ. This is why I never write you from my phone."[39] Of course, readers could reason this away as a typo, but Blue's response solidifies its sexually charged function: "Are you doing anything interesting this weekend? We're supposed to have *suck* nice weather. Excuse me, *dick* nice weather."[40] While this is only the beginning of their open display of sexuality, the queer teens amplify their sexual attraction to each other as the novel progresses. More specifically, they bounce back and forth with their direct references and sexual wordplay. For instance, as Blue/Bram probes Simon to guess what he is eating (part of their bonding over Oreos), Simon does not take the bait. Instead, Simon responds, "You have me curious. A banana? Hot dog? Cucumber?"[41] To make the point clearer, Blue/Bram responds with more phallic wordplay: "More like a giant baguette."[42] Then Simon makes his most pointed reference to take the conversation to its fullest logic: "I love your giant baguette."[43] References to hard cocks abound, and these characters express sexual desire for each other openly and without apology, even as they display trepidation.

The email exchanges eventually move beyond the realm of metaphor. Simon and Blue/Bram start sharing that they like to think about each other in a sexual context. Simon makes a purposeful shift when he pivots from food talk to sex explicitly: "Isn't it funny the way you fantasize about junk food when you're a kid? It's really all-consuming. I guess you have to obsess about something before you know about sex."[44] Blue/Bram then ups the ante: "I have to admit I like to imagine you as a kid fantasizing about junk food. I also like to imagine you now fantasizing about sex. I can't believe I just wrote that. I can't believe I'm hitting send."[45] Spoiler alert—he does hit send and, as a result, intensifies their open embrace of queer sexuality.

Albertalli does not actualize a sex scene between the two characters, which could be a limitation of the young adult genre itself or could be explained by the characters' own lack of familiarity with queer sex, especially in a world without models. Nevertheless, Albertalli does pen a scene narrated by Simon that could convincingly be read as a masturbation experience. On the heels of the email exchange in which Blue/Bram reveals that he likes to imagine Simon fantasizing about sex,

Simon shares a private moment in his room: "HE LIKES TO IMAG-
INE ME fantasizing about sex. That's something I probably shouldn't
have read right before bed. I lie here in the pitch-darkness, reading that
particular line on my phone again and again. I'm jittery and completely
in knots. . . . And I'm hard."[46] Just a few lines later, Simon continues by
wondering about what it would be like with Blue in person:

> I picture it. He kisses me, and it's nothing like Rachel or Anna or
> Carys. . . . His tongue is in my mouth. His hands slide up under my shirt,
> and he trails his fingers across my chest. I'm so close. It's almost unbear-
> able. *God.* Blue.
>   My whole body turns to jelly.[47]

Albertalli's language—particularly within the context of their intensifying sexual conversations and their budding sexuality—is clear: not only
is Simon masturbating while thinking about a sexual encounter with
Blue/Bram, but he also cums, which paves the way for the erotically
charged energy between the two of them when they meet in person.
We must foreground here, though, that Albertalli's rendering of Simon
and Blue's relationship is not *only about sex*; rather, she characterizes
their relationship as multidimensional, involving intellectual, emotional,
and physical desire. Because two common sound bites often characterize queer relationships in our social, cultural, and political spheres—one
of the hypersexual, insatiable queer character and one of the domesticated and desexualized queer character as a sidekick—Albertalli's
characterization of queer desire strikes a balance. She is neither afraid of
sexualizing Simon and Blue, nor is she limited to thinking about their
connection *only* in sexual terms. While connections focused on sex
alone or asexual connections have validity, Albertalli's narrative suggests
an awareness of a crisis of representation that locks queer relationality
into an either/or binary, especially for young queer people. She provides
a dynamic, young queer couple: two people who make each other laugh,
make each other swoon, and make each other hard.

By sharp contrast, the sexual components of their budding romance
are almost omitted altogether from the film—save a kiss or two in a
fantasy or on a Ferris Wheel at the film's climax in front of applauding
peers. In fact, readers of Albertalli's novel who watch *Love, Simon* may

find themselves looking in vain for many of the scenes that form such integral parts of Simon's relationship with Blue. In Berlanti's version, viewers will find no innuendos to hard dicks—no bananas, hot dogs, cucumbers, or (giant) baguettes—and no explicit mentions of imagining each other fantasizing about sex. Furthermore, viewers of the film will not find any mention of each other's bodies, save for one brief reference to kissing from Blue to Simon and a brief retelling of their first celebrity crushes (in quite demure terms). Conversation about sex is not only nearly absent between the two characters, but the movie is also devoid of scenes in which they experience sexuality together. Unlike in the novel, the two do not sneak into empty theaters at school, and they are not left home alone to explore their bodies together. Rather than centering on their sexual desire for each other or any type of autoeroticism with the other in mind, Berlanti focuses most of their interaction around the pinnacle "coming out" scene on the Ferris Wheel.

Interestingly, instead of Simon and Blue's sexual interaction or their relationship more broadly being the focal point of Berlanti's narrative, mending the nuclear family is the priority of *Love, Simon*. From its opening shots, Berlanti's film situates Simon firmly within the context of the heteronormative family. The narrative tracks the fractures suffered by the family as a result of Simon's "huge-ass secret." The family is initially together but not perfect, then fractures, and then repairs to emerge better than before. When we look through the lens of genre conventions, Berlanti neatly follows the script of a comedy-romance in the sense that everything is peaceably resolved by the end and the family has healed. Importantly, though, for the nuclear family to heal, Simon has to follow a strict set of prescribed behaviors to render his difference acceptable and not disruptive. To do so requires decentering the queer relationship. While Albertalli's novel foregrounds the young queer characters and their community-building, *Love, Simon* focuses much more on centering Simon's role as son, brother, and even friend.

The relationship between Simon and Blue/Bram does not even constitute the secondary narrative in the film. In addition to the mending-the-family narrative that emerges as the primary focus, the secondary narrative is Simon's relationship with the heterosexual characters, such as his friend group and Creekwood High School more broadly. Just like his relational trajectory with his family, Simon is also part of an establishing scene showing him and his peers as being together but with minor tensions, then experiencing moments of fracture, and then repairing their relationship to emerge better than before. While audiences might celebrate a queer young person being reintegrated into a supportive family unit and peer group, several elements of these narrative trajectories remain troubling: First, what must Simon deprioritize, what must he change, what must he adopt, and what must he perpetuate? Second, for Simon to remain legible as an eligible candidate for reintegration, who must be left behind? Third, what logics and histories must be elided, erased, or even firmly disavowed? Fourth, whose values, logics, histories, and institutions must be centered?

Coming Out Is *Not* a Trend: Resisting the Universalizing Work of *Love, Simon*

Continuing to compare Albertalli's novel to *Love, Simon* further reveals which narratives are eligible for mainstream success and endorsement. When readers of both texts examine the filling of narrative time and what that communicates about narrative focus and narrative priorities, what quickly comes into view are salient differences about what qualifies as content worth exploring and representing. To be sure, these decisions are often determined by whose logics and needs are privileged and by whose gaze is most prominent. Even though Berlanti's foregrounding of the heteronormative family and peer group is clear in the use of narrative time, the primacy of heteronormative audiences and their needs is perhaps made most obvious in how Simon experiences coming out and how he finally meets his love interest outside of their email exchanges. In both the film and the novel, Simon is blackmailed by a classmate named Martin, even though the characterization of Martin varies in each text. Importantly, Simon's response to his forced outing and how he proposes and experiences his first in-person meeting with Blue differ intensely from book to film, and these differences matter.

In Albertalli's narrative, Simon's journey does not end with his meeting of Blue and their finale kiss to applause from heterosexual onlookers. In fact, instead of their coming together serving as public entertainment for their heterosexual peers in which all are included, Simon actually contacts Blue/Bram privately—true to their private email communications throughout much of the novel—and, importantly, also meets Blue privately at the carnival:

> I'm not going to pretend I know how this ends, and I don't have a freaking clue if it's possible to fall in love over email. But I would really like to meet you, Blue. I want to try this. And I can't imagine a scenario where I won't want to kiss your face off as soon as I see you. . . . So, what I'm trying to say is that there's an extremely badass carnival in the parking lot of Perimeter Mall today, and it's apparently open until nine. For what it's worth, I'll be there at six thirty. And I hope I see you.[48]

In the novel, rather than meeting on a Ferris Wheel, Blue reveals himself in the flesh by joining Simon on a Tilt-A-Whirl with just the two of them. Unlike the meeting scene that constitutes the film's apex, the couple's first in-person meeting and their first acts of intimacy in the novel are not broad public knowledge via a "Creek's Secrets" blog post and certainly are not showcased at the top of a Ferris Wheel in front of everyone to the sounds of their hoots and hollers of approbation.

This comparison and the film's crucial edits/additions to the original source material deserve critical attention for a number of reasons: (1) in Albertalli's novel, Simon's "coming-out" scene and first acts of intimacy are not moments of spectacle for heterosexual audiences to be included in, to applaud, to learn from, or to appropriate; (2) the coming-out moment does not serve as the pinnacle of Simon's narrative in the novel, as the novel continues for several chapters with important moments for the couple; and (3) their first intimate exchange in the novel is not animated by the logic of the fairy-tale script with a changed variable of sexual object choice.

In Berlanti's rendering of Simon's journey, a significant part of the climax is Simon's open display of affection for Blue on the very same digital platform that Martin used to force his outing in the first place. Because Simon endured a painful coming-out experience on the "Creek's Secrets" blog and because Blue has deleted the email account he used during their exchanges, Simon takes to the blog himself to write back and detail his digital love affair with Blue. Furthermore, he orchestrates their dramatic in-person meeting on this public platform and thereby becomes a source of inspiration for his peers. (Notably, the same peers who congratulate him are the ones who sit by mostly silently when he experiences bullying after Martin initially spills Simon's Tea). Crucially, however, although the blog post facilitates Simon's meeting with Blue, Simon does not address the post to Blue directly. Actually, Simon addresses the post to *everyone in the community*—to the "Students of Creekwood High."[49] From the blog post scene to the Ferris Wheel scene, Simon's heterosexual peers remain involved and stay informed each step of the way. They even help with high fives and words of encouragement.

Furthermore, in an odd moment of guilt/salvation, Simon's heterosexual blackmailer provides the last ride tickets to keep Simon on the Ferris Wheel so that he can have his romantic moment with Blue. Due to narrative pacing, Martin offers the money for Simon's last ride tickets—with his last dollars, to be sure—right before Blue arrives. According to the logic of the film, Martin ironically provides the gay couple with the resources to share their public moment.

After the gay couple earns the applause of their heterosexual peers, Simon's coming-out experience becomes more significant public property in Berlanti's closing sequence of *Love, Simon*. As Simon starts his daily routine, he receives a phone call from his best friend, Leah, in which she shares the news that he has gone viral again. This time, however, Simon is neither forcibly outed nor publicly detailing his love affair for a heterosexual audience to read. Rather, Leah explains that Simon's coming out has become a source of inspiration for his peers to also, as it were, "come out." Archiving their truths with the hashtag "#thxsimon," his peers offer their own signed "confessions" for their "huge-ass secret[s]."[50] Furthermore, they thank him for his bravery and share their own hard truths. They offer testimonies about going to rehab, having an eating disorder, or having dreams that depart from familial expectations. Even though Leah hints at six signed confessions, the dialogue centers one confession from Taylor, Simon's co-star in the school production of *Cabaret*: "My parents didn't come see me in *Cabaret*. They hate that I want to be an actor. I don't know if they'll ever be proud of me. #thxsimon."[51] From Leah's narration, we learn about Taylor's confession, but we also learn that Simon's coming out has been translated and appropriated by others and their specific experiences. Indeed, to a smiling Simon, Leah proclaims, "You're a trendsetter now, Spier."[52]

Through this specific repurposing of Simon's coming-out experience from novel to film, the particularity of queer folks and their experiences navigating expectation versus desire are erased in favor of a *universal* message. Everyone "comes out" about something. Relatedly, in his open letter on the "Creek's Secrets" blog, Simon actually writes the following: "At first, I thought it was just a gay thing, but then I realized that no matter what, announcing who you are to the whole world is pretty terrifying."[53] In Berlanti's fictive world, Simon's journey is not rooted in the particularity of queer experience, nor does it foreground the budding queer community and romance between Simon and Blue/Bram. Departing significantly from the novel, Simon's coming out is unquestionably public but, imperatively, not in a way that broadly criticizes heteronormative logics or the systems and institutions that uphold them.

The universal messaging of *Love, Simon* is inextricable from the construction of Simon as a universal (white, cisnormative, middle-class) subject, especially since "the universality of the citizen exists in opposition to the intersecting particularities that account for material existence, particularities of race, gender, class, and sexuality."[54] We could argue that everyone dilutes undesirable parts of themselves to achieve particular personal and political goals—one thinks of Kenji Yoshino's theories of "covering"—but similar to Yoshino's conceptualizations, *Love, Simon* does not interrogate various dimensions of intersecting identities and embodiments and, more importantly, how those inflect material existence in structured social, political, and economic worlds.[55] This is a dangerous move, but one at the heart of our contemporary politics of visibility and representation. As Kaila Adia Story warns, "The quick move to have a 'kumbaya' moment across racial difference that disavows difference altogether, coupled with a move toward racial normativity, has created a culture in which taglines such as 'Gay is the New Black' or 'Gay Civil Rights' flourish."[56] In Story's formulations, difference is collapsed across racial lines to ignore historical context and particular dynamics of power in the quest for a false togetherness around a politics of injury.

Story's warnings bear a haunting resemblance to *Love, Simon*'s universalizing narrative around "coming out," for such a conflation of experience relies on decontextualizing and dehistoricizing to produce a kind of false consciousness about our material worlds. Furthermore, this approach functions in a way that is antithetical to altering these realities so that marginalized folks can live in a more just and equitable world. Even as the impulse to share experience and to build collectives is tempting, this cannot happen without engaging with difference on more ethical terms, which necessitates grappling with particularity and power—even within already marginalized communities. Cathy Cohen explains as much when she details the complexities of forming resistance movements across difference: "Thus, identities and communities, while important to this strategy, must be complicated and destabilized through a recognition of the multiple social positions and relations to dominant power found within any one category or identity."[57] For *Love, Simon*, that recognition would reveal how Simon's experience differs both from his heterosexual classmate who wants to be in *Cabaret* and from multiply marginalized folks like Ethan, whose queer experience is complicated by his gender expression and race.

Critique of power is not the goal in Berlanti's film, though, regardless of the film's marketing and social media campaigns, which might lead viewers to believe so. Unfortunately, the goal is to domesticate the coming-out experience—to neutralize it as a threat to power—by translating the act of coming out into an experience for *everyone*. Everyone has to do it in some way, so really, we are all the same. Berlanti's film aims to ensure that heterosexual audiences are not left out of a narrative that, in material reality, they *do not* actually experience because specific logics, systems, and institutions punctuate coming out for queer folks in particular (and often violent) ways. As a result of Berlanti's rendering, Simon is severed from the specific experience of difference and a celebration of said difference in favor of translating the experience into a universal one of which everyone can be a part.

In the novel, Simon and Blue/Bram's first meeting is not fairy-tale-like, and it is also messy and awkward yet full of beauty, intimacy, and communal care. Instead of the public and sweet meeting on a Ferris Wheel that ends in a public kiss, Bram makes himself physically ill from the incessant spinning of the Tilt-A-Whirl ride and almost vomits afterward. As Simon narrates this scene, he highlights these details: "We step off the ride and make it to the curb, and he leans all the way forward, tucking his head between his knees. I settle in beside him, feeling awkward and jittery, and almost drunk."[58] In Albertalli's narrative, the couple does come together and does share intimate moments in person, but these moments are not romanticized. Once Bram's nausea settles and Simon has ensured his well-being, their moment becomes more intimate: "I scoot closer to Bram, until our arms are almost touching, and I can feel him twitch just slightly. Our pinky fingers are maybe an inch apart, and it's as if an invisible current runs between them."[59] While their coming together is heartwarming in its own quirky way, Albertalli does not write a scene that abides by the dictates of the heteronormative romantic comedy—a scene to be shared in front of a live, mostly heterosexual audience—as *Love, Simon* does. Even though proponents of the film might champion the publicness of Simon and Blue's love affair on account of breaking silence, let us be clear: Albertalli neither shies away from the awkwardness of their initial encounter nor forces them into a kind of closeted love affair. Her novel lets them reveal themselves to each other on their own terms and on their own time—for their own benefit.

After they meet each other in person within the context of their budding romance, in the novel, they openly share space in their classes and other public places as a couple well beyond the initial reveal. Nevertheless, they do not immediately render themselves readable to broader heterosexual publics. In Berlanti's film, queer desire conforms to a particular brand of permissible visibility—a hypervisibility, one might argue. Berlanti's creative vision involves translating queer desire and domesticating that desire for acceptable consumption by heteronormative publics. He prioritizes the majority culture's needs and politics. By contrast, in the novel, Simon's friends and family thirst for the details of his queer romance, and importantly, he does not satiate their curiosity or prioritize their needs over his relationship with Bram.

Simon's decisions are clear when he reflects on his friend Abby's insistence that he tell her about his love life: "I text her and tell her I'll talk to her tomorrow. I think I want to keep the details to myself tonight. Instead, I call Bram."[60] Albertalli's novel extends this conversation by featuring a scene at the school the following day: "'All right,' Abby accosts me at my locker. 'I'm about to lose it. What the heck is going on with you and Bram?'"[61] Through these scenes and several others like it with family and friends, Simon chooses to keep details to himself, but he does not choose to do so out of shame; rather, he consistently refuses a heteronormative gaze and privileges his own queer relationship. And, yes, Simon's friends (and family) do revel in the couple's growing love affair, but Simon and Bram build their relationship on their *own* terms, regularly steal time for *themselves*, and assert their *own* needs as a new couple irrespective of others' comfort levels and curiosity. Unlike *Love, Simon* and its Ferris Wheel scene, their first meeting in-person and the early stages of their in-person relationship do not function to inspire heterosexual characters in Albertalli's novel. In her rendering, their coming together is for them in a world otherwise dominated by the needs, desires, and demands of heterosexual folks.

As the novel progresses, Bram is integrated more firmly into Simon's life, including meeting his two sisters and his parents. Instead of concluding with the gay teen kiss, *Simon vs. the Homo Sapiens Agenda* explores their relationship in greater depth. Following their initial "reveal" meeting at the carnival, they build their relationship further—replete with moments of flirting in English class, a trip outside of the school for a special lunch together alone, private phone chats, and even an impromptu make-out session in the empty theater at their school. In fact, it is in that impromptu make-out session that Albertalli breathes life into the newest stage of their relationship. As Simon experiences the intensely sexual moment, he communicates it to the reader: "His hands fall to my waist, and he pulls me in closer. He's only a few inches taller than me, and he smells like Dove soap, and for someone whose kissing career began yesterday, he has seriously magical lips. Soft and sweet and lingering."[62] Albertalli then layers the scene: "And then we pull out chairs, and I twist mine around sideways so I can rest my legs across his lap. And he drums his hands across my shins, and we talk about everything. Little fetus [Bram's soon-to-be half-sibling] being the size of a sweet potato. Frank Ocean being gay."[63] In a space that they steal for themselves within the confines of a traditional institution, Simon and Bram combine the digital community that they formed throughout the novel with their newfound in-person interaction. In so doing, Albertalli refuses to reduce their relationship to a public kiss in front of others, and consistent with their coming-together moment on the Tilt-A-Whirl, she refuses to separate their sexual attraction from their community-building with each other.

By contrast, the early stages of Simon's relationship with Blue in the film undergo moments of diluting. For example, in the novel, Simon's oldest sister, Alice, actually arranges a secret plan to keep his parents away from the family home so that Simon and Bram can go spend two hours of unsupervised time together at home. Informing Simon of the plan, Alice's new boyfriend explains everything: "So, Alice is in the lobby, but she sent me in with a message for you and, uh, Bram. . . . She wanted me to tell you that your parents are about to invite you to some place called The Varsity, and you're supposed to say you can't go. . . . She's giving you two hours at home unsupervised."[64] Instead of working neatly within harmonious relationships with family and respectability, Alice and Simon actually conspire to work *around* that authority to make space for queer desire to flourish, even in the teenage years. Admittedly, Albertalli does not write a sex scene per se, but she mentions passionate make-out sessions, freely roaming hands and body contact, and hard dicks—all outside of the gaze of heteronormative authority and/or surveillance. In fact, the site in which the nuclear family consolidates its power—the family home—becomes a space in which queer sexual contact can happen and, notably, can happen by way of the sibling who contests heterosexist systems and institutions pointedly throughout the novel. Even though the novel ends with the suggestion that Simon's parents will begin to set boundaries in his newfound relationship, Albertalli ends her narrative with the couple expressing queer sexuality in the home outside of the view of others. Berlanti's kiss on a Ferris Wheel to a round of applause is not enough for Albertalli. While one might cite differences in medium and limitations of condensed narrative time, the edits that Berlanti makes are telling, particularly when one thinks through market-based respectability politics and the imperatives of dignity.

Who Stays and Who Goes: Exploring Character Additions, Alterations, and Erasures

Love, Simon introduces characters who do not exist in Albertalli's novel and eliminates others who are pivotal to the novel's political message. Both decisions communicate important information about how the film operates in our current moment and about how Simon becomes a character behind whom audiences can rally—ultimately demonstrating the imperatives of dignity for queer folks and dignity's potential limits as a strategy to advance queer worth. Out of all the changes to the character list from novel to film, the two most striking decisions are the changes related to Simon's siblings and the creation of the character of Ethan in the film.

In Albertalli's novel, Simon is the middle child; more specifically, he is the brother of an older sister named Alice and a slightly younger sister named Nora. As readers of *Simon vs. the Homo Sapiens Agenda* learn details about Simon's life, we realize the centrality of family, but in a slightly different way than the film suggests. When we meet Alice and Nora in the novel, they are both quite involved in Simon's life as almost peers, and they do much to guide him in life. Most notably, his older sister, Alice, is a student at Wesleyan University and is characterized as an outspoken, politically active woman who speaks truth to power, including Simon's misguided parents. Indeed, some of the sharpest critiques of systems and institutions that disempower women, queer folks, and people of color come from Alice and her studied approach to living an inclusive feminist life. For example, when Simon's father makes insensitive and inappropriate comments about Simon's sexual orientation, Alice critiques him by immediately intervening to stop the behavior and explain her objections: "Dad, stop it. . . . That's so offensive."[65] While Simon's father tries to refuse responsibility on account of humor, Alice does not waver in her resistance: "Your heterosexist comments aren't lightening the mood."[66] As "Alice is getting political," she invokes the vernacular of social justice projects; she identifies their father's commentary as heterosexist and demands better for her brother, her family, and society.[67]

Albertalli makes it clear that this commitment to speaking truth to power is not limited to questions of Simon and sexuality. Alice's resistance is her foundational trait within the novel. When Simon reflects on his own use of problematic language regarding women, he thinks of Alice's influence: "I know perfectly well that if Alice heard me using that word [bitch], she would call me out, too. Alice is pretty hardcore about when it's appropriate to use the word 'bitch.'"[68] Simon's description of Alice being "hardcore" about power imbalances and about holding people accountable continues to animate his reflections about her and her relationship with their well-meaning but problematic father. In another context, Simon wonders, "I never know if my dad says that kind of stuff because he means it, or if he's just trying to push Alice's buttons."[69] Regardless of intent, Alice never sways in her critical posture. Because of Alice's studies, the intellectual and political community she has formed at school, and her own penchant for using her voice for change, she names and contests the power that seeks to oppress folks— regardless of intent or intensity—and refuses to retreat into silence to keep familial peace.

Alice and her activist role as ally are written out of the film entirely. Moreover, the character of Nora is transformed into a much younger sibling who adores Simon and wants nothing more than to be a successful chef and feed her family her culinary creations. She also cares for Simon and tries to comfort him during emotionally intense moments, but when things get tense, she mostly cries or expresses her discomfort in less political terms (even if flavored with frustration). Finally, and importantly, she just wants everyone to get along and for peace to be restored in their family. By removing the sharpest critique of logics, systems, and institutions that allow heterosexism to flourish through erasing Alice's character and by recharacterizing Nora as a non-threatening younger child, Berlanti ensures that audiences will drown in the pathos-inducing figure of the child, desperately want the family to mend, and never be offended by pointed political critique of heterosexism. In short, Berlanti's changes fundamentally depoliticize Albertalli's novel, which has lasting implications for how we read and understand Simon's character and his experiences.

In addition to the depoliticizing work done by Berlanti's film with the erasure of Alice and recharacterization of Nora, the casting edits also add to the film's insistence that Simon's journey as a queer person is an individualized one. Crucially, this individualization is countered a bit in the novel. In Albertalli's narrative, even when Simon tries to retreat into his bedroom alone after an awkward family exchange, Alice insists on sharing space with him. When Simon initially holds tightly to his emotions, Alice says, "I'm your big sister and you need me."[70] A few minutes later, she encourages him to engage in dialogue with her: "Talk to me, bub!"[71] Unlike the novel's focus on community between Alice (the activist) and Simon, the film transforms this sequence into a quick scene in which Nora comes into Simon's room, he treats her insensitively, and she runs out crying. In this representation, the focus shifts from Simon's experience with coming out and navigating heterosexist power to foregrounding how his actions distress his innocent young sister, whom he makes cry, again reinforcing for him how his coming out is affecting the family (rather than how it is affecting him or other queer people).

When this scene is coupled with Berlanti's decision to follow it with Blue's deletion of his email account and his attendant abandonment of Simon, a vital narrative thrust from the film becomes clear: Simon's "huge-ass secret" is tearing his family apart and isolating him. And if the nuclear family is to mend, Simon must go on an individualized journey to learn how to make his sexuality less problematic for majority culture—to reduce his difference. Only then can Simon be reunited with a (healed) family and be eligible for romantic love. Contrary to the novel's focus on community-building between Simon and Alice and on a collective journey against heterosexist power, *Love, Simon* tells a different story: it is the heteronormative nuclear family that is impacted by Simon's secret and needs to heal. If Simon can adjust alone, then his sister can stop crying, he can earn his friends back, and he—finally—can have his boyfriend. In short, Simon must learn to behave or suffer disruptive and unwelcome consequences.

Not only does Berlanti's film eliminate and recharacterize pivotal characters from *Simon vs. the Homo Sapiens Agenda*, but it also creates characters who do not exist in Albertalli's fictive world. The addition of the character Ethan to *Love, Simon* provides a pathway through which Berlanti's invocation of dignity and its limits become clearest. Although Ethan appears nowhere in Simon's life in the novel, his character does crucial work for Berlanti's film as another gay teenager in Simon's high school. Within the first ten minutes of the film and during its opening, viewers meet Ethan outside of the school building. This introduction performs generative work as an establishing sequence. As Simon and his friends are pulling into the parking lot, Ethan appears in a confrontation with two cisgender heterosexual students who toss shade at him—which he returns with a devastating read—and then they call him a "fag."[72] Even though Simon witnesses the scene, he does not intervene or express empathy or cross identification; rather, he remarks, "I wish Ethan wouldn't make it so easy for them."[73] This scene begins a side-by-side comparison of Simon and Ethan, one that renders Simon legible as a dignified gay teen worthy of safety, happiness, and inclusion on the back of Ethan's othering.

Because Ethan is characterized as African American and more gender non-conforming than Simon, he acts as a foil to Simon—someone from whom Simon distances himself. To be sure, Ethan neither plays a significant role within the context of the plot nor delivers key moments of dialogue. Rather, he operates on the periphery of the film as a figure of queer excess—a haunting for Simon and his life goals and a fundamental "too much" that the film must contain or reject. This very negation of Ethan's queer excess serves to characterize Simon in acceptable ways that will render him, by way of contrast, a successful candidate for inclusion in mainstream culture and reentry into white supremacy. If audiences read the film from the perspective of Ethan's character and thus from the queerer margins, then what dignity requires and what exclusionary byproducts it creates in queer communities become quite evident.

While one might suggest that Simon's initial response to Ethan has everything to with where he is in his own coming into consciousness, and while one might also argue that Simon moves beyond this mental space once he "grows" into his own public gay identity, those readings do not hold. As the film progresses, Ethan continues to experience violence from peers who harass him as well as from peers who inflict damage by remaining silent. Not only does Simon initially blame Ethan for his own oppression, but Simon also characterizes Ethan as a person for whom everything is so easy. Ethan is simultaneously at fault for the violence inflicted upon him for being "too gay" and subjected to the pervasive controlling image of being superhuman, an image that often refuses to engage with the pain and, more expansively, the humanity of Black folks. In either case, Ethan's realities remain unchanged.

This violence becomes clear when viewers see Simon discussing Ethan in one of his emails to Blue: "I mean, Creekwood's resident gay kid seems to be doing just fine. When Ethan came out, no one even cared."[74] The careful movie viewer needs to cross-reference this assessment with the bullying scene that Simon witnesses in the film's opening, where Ethan was clearly called a "fag" and Simon's cisgender and white privilege enables him to reason the violence away by blaming Ethan for making it too easy for his attackers. Furthermore, and more importantly, Ethan's pain is never addressed with deliberation, and a reckoning never occurs that is specific to him and his intersectional queer experiences.

Simon's misreading or inability to see Ethan beyond the purview of his own whiteness is indicative of what Black philosopher Charles Mills describes in the racial contract, the unwritten contract that ensures white supremacy will be the unnamed structuring principle of the modern world. As Mills argues, "*Thus, in effect, on matters related to race, the Racial Contract prescribes for its signatories an inverted epistemology, an epistemology of ignorance, a particular pattern of localized and global cognitive dysfunctions (which are psychologically and socially functional), producing the ironic outcome that whites will in general be unable to understand the world they themselves have made.*"[75] This acculturation in and through whiteness applies to Simon, too, even though he is gay. Mills goes on further to explain how and why Simon's understanding of self relies on his inability (or refusal) to see and reckon with Ethan's lived experience (and his pain): "As a general rule . . . *white misunderstanding, misrepresentation, evasion, and self-deception* . . . are among the most pervasive mental phenomena of the past few hundred years, a cognitive and moral economy psychically required for conquest, colonization, and enslavement."[76] Indeed, while Simon might not be preparing to colonize Ethan per se, his thoughts, comments, and behaviors certainly represent the neocolonial byproducts of a sustained racial contract.

Read through the arguments by Mills, the narrative trajectory of *Love, Simon* showcases how overdetermined fantasies of Blackness are needed both to constitute whiteness and to render its supposed superiority legible by way of comparison. Simon cannot understand himself outside of the lens of Ethan, and his power is impossible without Ethan's subjugation. As such, the film ignores Ethan's pain in the service of Simon's journey of white gay injury. Not until Simon is outed and becomes the target of bullying do school authorities intervene to stop the homophobic attacks. While Ethan is also a part of the climactic bullying scene with Simon, Simon's body and experiences are centered and are the impetus behind the protection from school authorities.

Even though the bullies say "Hey, Ethan" as they stage their nonsense, they focus on Simon, and importantly, the scene is situated in the part of the film in which Simon's "normal" life is broken because his "huge-ass secret" is out and he has not yet earned reentry into the world of norma-tivity in which he resided previously.[77] If readers consider the logic of the narrative and the focal point of the bullying—along with the subsequent (and sustained) intervention from the drama teacher—they might think that it is only Simon who deserves protection from homophobic vio-lence. Because of Ethan's outsider status as a queerer and dark-skinned Black body, he does not qualify for the kind of safety, access, and voice that Simon enjoys. When compared to Ethan, Simon is "not that gay." As such, bullying endured by Simon can be read as more excessive or, perversely, as somehow less justifiable. Put differently, because Simon does not contest normative worldmaking by way of his very being or by any queer behaviors, he enjoys powerful social rewards that accom-pany normativity. Whereas Ethan revels in queer excess—contesting normative gendered scripts and unapologetically speaking truth back to heterosexist power while refusing to conform—Simon practices queer restraint.

Though the film had immense potential to provide a bullying inter-vention scene that centers progressive politics for queer students, Ber-lanti and his creative team again miss the mark during the scene in Vice Principal Worth's office. But it is not just the sloppy apology encounter and the awkward embrace of the rhetoric of tolerance that frustrate view-ers searching for more progressive politics in *Love, Simon*. The exchange between Simon and Ethan outside of Mr. Worth's office exists as the one time that the two gay characters share space in conversation, and it holds within itself endless possibilities for consciousness raising, community building, and an accounting of the violence endured by Ethan during the narrative. Yet none of this takes place. In the short scene, Simon feels inconvenienced by having to encounter his bullies, which he demon-strates when he exclaims, "Can't we just let this shit go?"[78] His frustra-tion softens when he turns to address Ethan. Although Simon begins with what seems like an apology that addresses Ethan's experience and maybe even accounts for his own complicity, he instead centers himself again: "I'm sorry, Ethan; none of this ever happened when just you were out."[79] And instead of Ethan defending himself and speaking back to Simon to remind him of the endless violence he has endured for years, the writers shockingly give Ethan a response that forces him to swallow his own blood to reflect Simon's experience back to him: "One gay is a snooze; two are a hilarious hate crime."[80] Even though viewers just witnessed moments in the film in which Ethan is bullied, called a "fag," and kept on the outside of the narrative focus, he and Simon both ignore the violence that Ethan endures before Simon's coming out. The core difference that neither addresses, in fact, is that someone actually intervenes only when Simon is involved.

To be generous to the film, Simon does finally admit his jealousy of Ethan, but he explains his jealousy by noting that Ethan's life as openly queer always seemed so "easy." This admission reflects Simon's earlier assessment of Ethan's life as "just fine" in an email to Blue. If we replace Simon's characterization of easy with a recognition of Ethan's ability to deflect, endure, and choose a different value system to affirm himself, then Simon's admission might make sense. This, however, is not the reality of the scene. While Ethan admits a piece of his struggles with his mother, what never happens in the film is an apology for Simon's complicity, an account of Simon's privileges, a moment of recognition or transformation on Simon's part, or any attempt at queer community building that pays attention to the particularities of Ethan's specific experience of being gender non-conforming, queer, Black, and young in the South.

Instead of a coming-into-consciousness moment for Simon in light of his interaction with Ethan, what transpires is an awkward apology from the bullies, a firm embrace of milquetoast tolerance in the school's (and the film's) approach to engaging difference, and a firm refusal of Ethan and Simon as a couple. After a disavowal of any romance between Ethan and Simon, the characters never share close space in a scene again. Aside from being one of the many to read Simon's "Creek's Secrets" blog post and to cheer for him at the carnival, Ethan is never considered again in any sustained way. Reading with a careful eye on Ethan's character and his centrality to Simon's legibility as a life worth fighting for, we ask a number of questions—with implied answers—that reveal the imperative of restraint in the face of undignified queer excess: Why can't Ethan and Simon become friends? Out of all the minor subplots throughout *Love, Simon*, why isn't Ethan's life worth exploring in detail, especially since he's specifically added to the film's cast of characters? Why doesn't Ethan find romance or happiness—or experience sexuality at all? How is Simon's eventual love interest, Blue/Bram, similar to or different from Ethan's queerness? Why doesn't Simon account for his privilege or apologize for his complicity? Ultimately, can we imagine a world in which Ethan does not serve as a foil for a cisgender, jock-adjacent white gay teen? Can we fathom a narrative in which the violence he endures is accounted for, privilege is addressed, and someone else's power isn't consolidated on his back? Can we conceive of a narrative that centers his experience, gives him voice, and features him as a character eligible for safety, resources, sexuality, and community?

Why Multicultural Casting Is Never Enough: Reading at the Intersections

Furthering its overall reduction of difference in the service of a more universalized, dehistoricized, and decontextualized project that elides the violence of normative logics and institutions, *Love, Simon* also omits—or at least substantially softens—Albertalli's handling of racial politics in the novel. While Albertalli's text nods to a more intersectional understanding of identity, one that amplifies how race both impacts the life of cisgender heterosexual Black young women and cisgender queer Black young men, Berlanti's film casts more Black and Brown bodies in front of the camera without attending to the particularity of their experiences. But as Alison Reed warns us, "The structural problem of turning toward race while evacuating conversations about racism encourages risky readings."[81] Just as *Love, Simon* avoids blatant critiques of heterosexism—with the elimination of the character of Alice from the novel—the film also ignores how its Black and Brown characters move through the world in specific ways because of how race has been made to mean, particularly in the film's setting of Georgia. As a result, Berlanti's film presents itself as "diverse" through casting, but it also substantially de-races its characters through its content by removing specific racial commentary from Albertalli's novel and adding Black characters of its own while never attending to how race shapes their lives.

Such a move demonstrates how "colorblindness operates . . . through a dangerous swapping of terms, namely a substitution of sustained conversations about systemic racism with race as such, particularly spectacular racialized embodiment."[82] And if Berlanti avoids a careful exploration of race as a category of difference in isolation, he certainly never takes a more nuanced approach that reveals how race intersects with the characters' other registers of experience as queer people or women. Thus, at the level of the visual, "this fetishization of blackness produces its own logics of disavowal, reinforcing hegemonic understandings of race by articulating embodiment in post-racial terms. Whiteness, then, goes unacknowledged and unexamined, while uncritically reproducing multiculturalist logics that mainstream visibility politics can smooth over ongoing injustices, precisely by exploiting the hypervisibility of black bodies for a white queer politics of injury."[83] In this way, a Black queer/quare reading of *Love, Simon* reveals the limits and even dangers of mainstream visibility politics and "diversity" aspirations in casting, particularly when they buttress the values of the neoliberal state.[84]

Berlanti most notably removes the specificity of race from Albertalli's novel through the character of Abby, a friend of Simon's. In the novel, as a young Black woman, Abby experiences the setting differently than the majority of white, middle-class characters; Albertalli explicitly explores her particularity, and some of the novel's sharpest critiques of power emerge in Simon's commentary about how race impacts her life. For example, early in the novel, Albertalli employs Simon's narration about Abby's life to discuss the geography of Georgia and explain how space is racialized: "Rehearsal ends, but Abby and I dangle our feet off the edge of one of the platforms. . . . The south county late bus doesn't leave for another fifteen minutes, and then it's another hour until Abby gets home. She and most of the other Black kids spend more time commuting to school each day than I do in a week."[85] Albertalli takes the racial critique further by extending Simon's reflections: "Atlanta is so weirdly segregated, and no one ever talks about it."[86] Importantly, Simon's narration about Abby and about how racialized space impacts her life does not end with one passing reference early in the text. In fact, Albertalli threads this critique throughout the novel as Simon and Abby share their quotidian experiences as young teenagers. For instance, when they get closer to the opening of their school's theater production, Abby has to navigate concerns that other students never think about: "Abby doesn't have a car tonight, so she comes home with me after school on Friday and brings her overnight bag. I know it must suck for Abby living so far away."[87] Finally, when Simon's bullies unexpectedly truncate play rehearsal due to their violent nonsense, Simon shares how this uncontrollable circumstance will disproportionally impact Abby's life: "So, Abby's stuck at school until the late bus leaves, and I feel really terrible about that."[88] By repeatedly mentioning details about Abby's life—amid many other details about her character and experiences—Albertalli highlights how contemporary racial politics and the deep history of race in Georgia dictate geography, housing, and access to resources like education for one of her characters. Said differently, Albertalli refuses to characterize one of her novel's key players along racial lines without thinking through (at least a little) how that specific register of difference might influence her daily life.

In addition to pointing to Abby's difficult commute to school, Albertalli directly positions her in a particular geographical locale. Instead of remaining ambiguous about where Abby lives or falling into the trap of referencing a kind of non-descript "ghetto," Albertalli gives Abby the dialogue to talk about her home space. When she and Nick take Simon into the city to introduce him to queer space and community, Abby discusses taking a drunk Simon back to her house; when her passengers inquire about the direction in which she is driving, she says without hesitation that she is driving "to my house . . . College Park."[89] For those familiar with the segregated geography of Georgia, this is identifiably Black space. For those who are not familiar, College Park is a culturally rich and economically complex locale near the Atlanta airport. According to the Decennial Census of Population and Housing of 2010 (by decade), College Park has a demographic makeup of over 80 percent African Americans.[90] Not only is College Park dominated by African American citizens, but it also plays a unique role in the development of Black cultural expression, particularly in the development of hip-hop in the South with the SWATS (Southwest Atlanta, too strong).[91] At its most expansive, the term *SWATS* refers to the population, geography, and cultural traditions of College Park and East Point.[92] Drawing on her own knowledge as a Georgia resident, Albertalli contextualizes Abby's life in a racially inequitable world and is explicit about how race complicates her life, especially in comparison to the more privileged cisgender, upper-middle-class white characters.

In sharp and revealing contrast, Berlanti's film presents Abby's character as somewhat de-raced, and her difference is firmly reduced. Even though her character is played by a biracial actress (Alexandra Shipp) and despite her character making a passing comment about her old school and a knife fight, the film removes Albertalli's critique of racialized geography in Georgia. Instead of mentioning Abby's long commute to school or College Park and its racial past and present, Berlanti depicts Abby as living close to Simon, Leah, and Nick.[93] Though she does not live in their neighborhood, Simon picks her up easily on their way to school. Not only does Berlanti refuse to situate her in an identifiably Black locale like College Park, but he also removes direct references to how race impacts her life. She never comments on her Blackness, and when she discusses her past or family, she does so in "color-blind" ways: for instance, she talks about a father who cannot remain faithful and how difficult it is for her to trust and fall in love. Abby's personal disclosures could easily come from any other character's mouth without substantial changes. By comparing the translation of Abby's character from novel to film, we suggest that this is yet another instance in which Berlanti's film insists on a universalized messaging strategy that robs characters of their history and particularity. Because *Love, Simon* aims to reach the hearts and minds of the masses, the film demands a firm reduction of difference that refuses to engage racist systems and institutions and how they affect certain characters differently than others. As a result, Abby and other Black characters in the film serve as embodied instances of diversity that nod to a progressive visibility politics without doing the work of confronting power to push for a more equitable future, especially for the most marginalized.

Simon and Blue/Bram also discuss matters of race in Albertalli's novel in ways that are removed from—or at least fundamentally altered—in *Love, Simon*. In Albertalli's work, Simon and Blue discuss race openly, and crucially, they mention how access to power is divided along racial lines. Even though they do not describe themselves in racial terms during their digital love affair, they do discuss identity in explicit ways: most noteworthy is how they begin to discuss the intersection of race and sexuality. When Simon begins his now-viral questioning about why straight is the default, Blue responds to include attention to racial difference: "It is definitely annoying that straight (and white, for that matter) is the default, and that the only people who have to think about their identity are the ones who don't fit that mold."[94] Albertalli extends this conversation when she gives Simon the opportunity to reflect on race and its impact on desire. After the two characters meet in person and Simon realizes that Blue is actually Bram—an African American guy in his larger peer group—they discuss how they did or did not guess the other's identity in real life. When Simon reflects on why he did not guess that Blue was Bram, he shares the following through narration: "I'm an idiot. I was looking for him to be Cal [a white jock in the group]. And I guess I assumed that Blue would be white. Which kind of makes me want to smack myself. White shouldn't be the default any more than straight should be the default. There shouldn't even be a default."[95] In harkening back to Blue's earlier edit to Simon's original focus on just sexuality ("Why is straight the default?"), Simon demonstrates a consciousness-raising moment. In fact, he learns from his interaction with Blue/Bram that race matters. Even though he is seemingly "woke" with regard to Abby's life, he recognizes how he himself coded desire in racist terms. In so doing, Simon demonstrates how embodying one register of difference (non-normative sexuality) does not preclude folks from ignoring or even disempowering others, particularly those with intersectional experiences. Through Bram, Albertalli continues her focus on how difference is made to mean and how her characters' specific identities dictate the value placed on their bodies and what their bodies can and cannot do. Through her young queer couple, she educates her readership on identity and power.

The discussions about race between Simon and Blue are largely missing from the film. Blue/Bram's character is played by a biracial actor (Keiynan Lonsdale), but his character's experiences do not attend to how race impacts his life, especially as a queer person of color. While Albertalli gives Blue/Bram narrative space to discuss how race intersects with sexuality, Berlanti's film only centers sexuality through the character of Simon and his pivotal question: "Why is straight the default?" In the film, Blue/Bram does not add to Simon's critique of heteronormativity by adding a focus on white supremacy. Additionally, during the film's pivotal scene in which the two young men meet in person, Simon does not reflect on how his desire might be racialized. He does not even address Blue/Bram's Blackness.

While Simon does not seem to recognize race as a category of difference, Bram's character does briefly mention his Blackness in the film. During the Ferris Wheel scene, Simon mentions, "And you're Jewish, which is cool," and then Bram replies, "And I'm Black, too. And gay. It's kinda crazy, huh?"[96] A moment or so later, Bram asks Simon if he's disappointed that he is Blue, and Simon sweetly answers that he is not disappointed. On the surface, the inclusion of this brief exchange, coupled with the casting choices for these characters, might look like progressive messaging—a kind of "love is love" platform.[97] But what remains telling about the scene (and the film) is that Simon does not engage with Bram's assertion of his multiple identities at all. When Bram mentions his Blackness, Simon replies by shifting the conversation entirely: "I didn't think you would come."[98] To be sure, Simon cannot even imagine reckoning with his own whiteness, his investment in white supremacy, or how his own understanding of self relies on overdetermined fantasies of Blackness, for as Reed suggests, "since whiteness defines itself by contrast, white Americans actively disinvesting in white supremacy would equal nothing short of reenvisioning their basis for identity."[99] Importantly, Bram's assertion of his own Blackness and queerness is also devoid of a reckoning with power—of conversation about "default" identities and invisible power. For Berlanti, it seems to be enough that he has cast a biracial character and that the character announces his multiple identities and finds love with someone white (who does not seem to even consider his race when choosing to love him back).

Ultimately, when considering Albertalli's specific critique of racial politics and of how race informs desire, and when coupling this elision of race with the de-racing of the character of Abby, Berlanti's film falls victim to a kind of color-blind, universalized narrative of love. And it does so at the level of the individual to somehow suggest a newfound multicultural harmony at the societal level. To do so showcases "the struggle to recognize institutional racism . . . as part of a wider struggle to recognize that all forms of power, inequality, and domination are systemic rather than individual."[100] By giving Simon a biracial love interest and de-racing him, Berlanti's film presents a risky reading of our contemporary landscape. Such a narrative elides how race, gender, and sexuality are intertwined with power and how they are firmly rooted in systems and institutions that control how folks think, what bodies can do, and who is valued.

Instead, *Love, Simon* proffers a "we're all human" position that demands sameness instead of celebrating difference on its own terms and reckoning with how difference has been made to mean. Such an obfuscation of difference (particularly racialized, gendered, and classed differences) in the service of a universal figure like Simon centers the white cisgender male (even if gay) as the stand-in for that which is universal. If we follow Ahmed's lead and look critically at "what diversity does by focusing on what diversity obscures," then we learn a crucial lesson about universalizing narratives as well as institutions that claim to value diversity: "How they circulate matter is a reflection of what matters."[101] In this way, then, we see how Ahmed's arguments about institutional diversity efforts being an instrument of consolidating white supremacist power under the guise of "inclusion" have a direct relationship to representation in our current neoliberal moment. As Ahmed explains clearly, "Diversity becomes about *changing perceptions of whiteness rather than changing the whiteness of organizations.* Changing perceptions of whiteness can be how an institution can reproduce whiteness, as that which exists but is no longer perceived."[102] If we apply Ahmed's insight by changing "organizations" to "narratives" or think about how narratives work in the service of organizations, we can see how Ahmed's lamentations about institutional diversity work pay dividends for analyzing contemporary representations of LGBTQ+ life, like *Love, Simon.* The film attempts to change perceptions of discriminatory logics and inequalities but does not wrestle with power to do the very kind of destabilizing work required of such goals.

Not only does Berlanti's film de-race the Black characters in Albertalli's novel and elide their intersectional experiences shaped by power, but his film also adds its own Black characters and never attends to how race specifically impacts their lives. Most notably, Ethan, whom we discussed above, is added. As a character who is Black, gender non-conforming, queer, and young in the Deep South, Ethan resides firmly at the intersections of racism, cisnormativity, and homophobia. While Berlanti could have utilized Ethan's character to provide a rich avenue through which the film could discuss the particularity of queer folks of color, he uses his character provide the marketable value of queer subcultural practices—like sharp reads / throwing shade at the bullies—instead. Most importantly, Berlanti misses key opportunities to discuss explicitly how being raced in a white supremacist America complicates Ethan's life.[103] Of course, this elision becomes more frustrating when viewers recognize how the film profits from subcultural practices as "extra flavor" while it "undermine[s] some of the strategies that people of color had developed to speak to the materiality of their condition," which furthers the dehistoricizing, decontextualizing, and depoliticizing thrusts that shape the film's worldview.[104]

Furthermore, through the combination of casting and narrative form/content, Berlanti and his creative team seem to fall into the traps of a colorist value system—assigning value to Black and Brown bodies based on their proximity to a white supremacist ideal. To be sure, Ethan's character—whom we have already described as depicting a kind of undesirable queer excess—is the person with the darkest skin, which directly contrasts with the main characters of color, who are biracial and operate quite differently in the value system created by Berlanti's fictive world. By casting Ethan as the character with the darkest skin and constructing him as a character who serves merely as a narrative foil through which to consolidate Simon's status as the right kind of (restrained) queer, Berlanti and his film firmly embrace the logic of colorism. While some of the biracial characters find love by the end of the film, Ethan does not. Indeed, it is not only Ethan's gender presentation or his sexuality that render him excessive; his Blackness, especially his darker skin, is always already codified as excessive in an America that stratifies based on one's proximity to a Eurocentric ideal.[105]

Just as the film removes Albertalli's inclusion of Simon reflecting on how race shaped his thoughts about desire, Berlanti remains silent about desire's place in Ethan's life. The only moment in which Ethan is sexualized at all is in the bullying scene. His "likeness" appears in the bullies' role-play scene as a sexual partner penetrating a fictive Simon from behind. Thus the only time Ethan's character is sexualized at all, the scene is saturated with violence—one in which he is defiling Simon's white manhood by being played as the hypersexual Black buck—the big Black dick.[106] Even this sexualized representation happens outside of his own body, as his identity is puppeteered by a bully. In this moment, Ethan has no autonomy over his own body and narrative, especially as the scene is centered on Simon's reaction to the bullying and not Ethan's. Even as the film does permit Ethan briefly to discuss his home life and the fact that his mother lies to his grandparents about all the girls he is dating, he never mentions how race and a broader Black sexual politics inform this dilemma. Instead, Ethan frames it briefly as a kind of "My mom isn't proud of me" moment, which is a fundamentally universalizing move. If the film were to consider how Ethan's hypervisible Blackness inflects his life, audiences could think through how colonial/imperialist imposition on Black sexuality has specific consequences for Black queer folks and their battle against a respectability politics that is inseparable from white supremacy.[107]

For a progressive politics to emerge, it is not enough merely to cast a Black body, specifically a darker-skinned actor. It is irresponsible to pimp the value of Black queer subcultural practices (like reading/shading) for the film's humor and to capitalize on controlling images that haunt Black sexuality (like the buck) to amplify the emasculation of the white protagonist.[108] If *Love, Simon* aims to educate and open hearts and minds, then a clear confrontation with how power shapes the daily life and possibilities for Ethan is crucial. To be frank, the stakes are high for Black queer bodies, and silence (or glaring omissions) is not an option. As E. Patrick Johnson urges, we need a "theory in the flesh" to supplement the discourse around identity as socially constructed: "Identity, although highly contested, manifests itself in the flesh and, therefore, has social and political consequences for those who live in that flesh."[109] But because this kind of attention to difference and power would necessitate that Berlanti historicize and contextualize non-normative characters, he avoids the question altogether.

Just as a broader national politics—as well as a mainstream gay and lesbian politics—regularly ignores the particularity of race, Berlanti demands that his character stay silent about how race specifically impacts his life. At the same time, though, Ethan's presence operates as the figure of haunting excess that helps render the film's cisgender white gay protagonist as legible, dignified, and valued—a value that is most clearly displayed when Simon's mom tells him, "You deserve everything you want."[110] Ethan has no visible reckoning with his parents or his peer group, and viewers find no indication that he finds widespread acceptance. Doing so would require *Love, Simon* to tend to difference and power in ways that could alienate or offend a mainstream viewership that still, by and large, fails to account for the value of Black queer lives.

Severed from Community and History: Why Simon Doesn't Know the Lyrics

If reading through the lens of Ethan's character does not render the generative work of dignity and its exclusions clear, viewers might consider the broader depictions of queer community, space, and care in the film. The film's engagement with these themes is brief, played for laughs, and abandoned or rendered unnecessary. Tellingly, the film presents queer identity as a matter of individual experience and choice. It is not, as Albertalli presents it, something that has a rich history, can be a deeply communal experience, and is replete with an ethics of care.

This difference becomes clear during the fantasy scene in which Simon imagines a sort of "It Gets Better" moment.[111] As Simon writes an email to Blue about why he has not come out yet, he makes a promise to no one in particular: "When I go to college in Los Angeles, I'll be gay and proud. I promise."[112] Indeed, tucked away in the safer space of the imagination and situated in the geographical distance of California, Simon contemplates his "gay and proud" life in college. The fantasy sequence—played to the soundtrack of Whitney Houston's queer anthem "I Wanna Dance with Somebody (Who Loves Me)"—showcases what Simon thinks "being gay" looks like: posters of so-called hot guys, a nod to Judy Garland, and Whitney Houston in the middle of the montage.[113] While we absolutely live for a solid Whitney bop from the late 1980s, a number of details in this scene captivate our critical attention. First, Simon's only understanding of queer culture is deeply rooted in symbols from the commercialization of gay identity post-Stonewall, for his room and the surrounding areas in which he travels in the scene are drowning in the rainbow paraphernalia common to Pride parades that have overwhelmingly fallen victim to corporatization. Second, in Simon's "out and proud" imagery, viewers will find very little historical consciousness or politicization that is not rooted in a kind of rainbow capitalism.[114] For example, viewers will not find a nod to ACT UP in Simon's version of "being gay."[115]

This fantasy scene continues to pay dividends for a critical reading of *Love, Simon* when viewers attend to Simon's wardrobe, his body's choreography, and his firm disavowal of queer excess—the very kind Ethan embraces and showcases. Simon dresses in a muted neutral palette, while the folks that join him as soon as he exits his dorm room drench themselves in bold, bright (one might even say "loud") colors. Even though Simon is fantasizing about a more liberated and open future, the creative team continues to situate him in neutral, ill-fitting clothes, and he remains set apart from the other unapologetically queer folks. Simon does not read as comfortable with his own body. Rather than imagining a scene in which Simon embraces Whitney's energy, Berlanti continues to situate Simon in a position animated by restraint. The dance sequence, in which Simon barely participates, is "too gay." Even though he is blocked in the center of the choreography, which is a spot usually reserved for the strongest dancer or captain, he achieves no harmony with the group—in step or emotion.

When Simon's invocation of imagery, wardrobe choices, and awkward choreography are all read alongside the use of narrative time and Simon's dialogue, a deliberate posturing emerges. As the imaginary scene begins, viewers hear the opening riffs that anyone "in the life" recognizes immediately as Mama Whitney, but as the scene speeds forward, Berlanti edits the song to include only the chorus and a brief snippet of the outro.[116] Just as Berlanti edits and abbreviates the anthem, Simon's embrace of unapologetic queerness is halfheartedly performed in the scene and firmly rejected by the scene's end—characterized as "too much." Simon's dialogue breaks through the music to punctuate the end of the fantasy: he stops dancing, looks directly at the camera, and issues one of the most revealing lines of the film: "Yeah, maybe not *that gay*."[117]

Similar to the decision to cut Whitney off—reducing her queer anthem to an abbreviated sound bite to which most viewers can sing along—the film's logic also restrains Simon's knowledge and embrace of queer knowing and living. Simon does not know—and does not seem to want to know—the verses of the song; by extension, he is not interested in queerness beyond sexual object choice or fashion advice. Furthermore, his restraint is expressly compared to the queer excess that surrounds him—in his fantasy sequence by way of the backup dancers and in the narrative present by way of Ethan's unapologetic queerness. In both instances, Simon turns in another direction. Simon's restraint is rewarded by power, and that which he denies is derogated both in the plot and in Berlanti's crafting of narrative time and space. Because he denies queer excess, Simon can consolidate his power as the "right" kind of different.

In addition to Simon's failure to form queer community with Ethan and his inability to keep in step with the presumably queer folks in his fantasy dance scene, Simon remains severed from queer consciousness and queer community in *Love, Simon*. However, this is not the case in Albertalli's novel. In that rendering, Simon experiences important moments of queer community outside of his relationship with Blue at least twice. First, when Simon is navigating the limitations of others after he is outed by Martin, he is exposed to the care and solidarity often found in queer cultures, regardless of who knows whom. Simon reflects on this unexpected support by sharing, "These two lesbian girls I don't even know come up to me at my locker and hug me and give me their phone numbers."[118] Even though these girls are not part of his life, they express solidarity with him against the violence of heterosexism and offer their support.

Additionally, in the novel, Simon, Abby, and Nick venture into the city so that Simon's two friends can introduce him to vital queer locales to nurture his coming into consciousness. First, they take him to a queer bookstore to help him get resources and provide him with a sampling of the vastness of queer identity. As he comments on their trip, he notes, "Abby and Nick want to take me to this feminist bookstore that evidently has a lot of gay stuff."[119] In such a place, replete with cultural materials and like-minded folks, Simon could learn about the queer past, engage with a queer present, and ruminate about a queer future. In addition to visiting what is presumably the real-life Charis Books—an Atlanta staple for queer and feminist knowledge and community—they also take Simon to a restaurant/bar, which is presumably either Joe's on Juniper or Einstein's—both steps from Atlanta's queer intersection of Tenth and Piedmont.

During this restaurant scene, Albertalli depicts the value of queer community and queer joy most clearly. Moments after arriving, Simon meets a college-aged gay guy named Peter and is folded into his queer friend group. Simon is trying to pass for a college student and attempting to join a specific queer bar culture before he is legally able to drink, and Peter and his friends welcome Simon until they realize he is a high school student. Before they realize Simon's age, he enjoys their interaction and experiences the joy of gathering in queer space: "Peter's friends are loud and funny, and I laugh so hard I'm hiccupping. . . . It's this strange other universe. . . . And it feels amazing."[120] While in their company, Simon is firmly situated in queer space, and he flourishes there. Indeed, readers of Albertalli's novel could easily make the case that Simon's introduction to queer space provides some of the most intense joy he experiences in the narrative. And Simon would likely agree with such an assessment himself. As he relishes in the night's experiences, he shares, "I love it here. . . . It's a perfect night. Everything is perfect. It's not even cold out anymore. It's a Friday night, and we're not at Waffle House, and we're not playing *Assassin's Creed* in Nick's basement. . . . We are out and we are alive."[121] In Simon's reflections on the night, he both expresses queer joy and points to a more dynamic definition of queerness that is not limited to sexual object choice. Vitally, he explicitly compares the joy experienced in distinctly queer space with the presumably worn happenings in largely heterosexual-dominated spaces in his hometown—like Waffle House and his friend's basement.

In addition to showcasing queer joy in purposeful queer space, Albertalli also illustrates the communal care Simon experiences in these unfamiliar places. Not only does Simon enjoy his time with Peter and his friends, but they also care for him, especially in a vulnerable moment. As soon as Peter learns that Simon is a bit too young and has had a bit too much to drink, he does not shame or embarrass him. As Simon narrates the night, he drunkenly explains, "He helps me up and holds my hand, and the room keeps lurching, but I end up in a chair somehow. Next to Abby and across from Nick, in front of an untouched cheeseburger. . . . 'Goodbye, cute Simon,' says Peter, hugging me, and then kissing me on the forehead. 'Go be seventeen.'"[122] Even though Simon cannot remain in their company, Peter does not leave him without support. He identifies Simon's friends in the corner of the establishment, gently returns Simon to their care, and makes sure that Simon is safe. This is another instance of queer community and care rooted in particularity.[123]

Unfortunately, these elements of queer community-building are entirely absent from *Love, Simon*. Although Berlanti and his team recorded a scene in which Simon is placed in queer space—namely, a queer bar—the scene was cut from the film's final edit because, according to Berlanti, it fit neither the narrative trajectory for the film nor Simon's character development.[124] Berlanti's assessment is indicative, for contextualizing Simon in queer history and in queer ways of knowing/being is not a priority for the film.[125] Characterizing Simon in and through particularity and giving him the opportunity to embrace queer community are antithetical to the film's normative thrusts.

Compounding this glaring absence of queer community, some of the novel's key character moments—especially as they relate to understanding the value of particular spaces—are rewritten to center heteronormative audiences. For example, Simon is not placed in a "party scene" or a "drunk scene" in queer space in the film as he is in Albertalli's novel, but he does experience a scene filled with partying and underage drinking. This scene, though, is at a house party at which he celebrates Halloween with his mostly heterosexual peers. While a scene like this does appear in the novel, it is not prioritized in the same way, nor does it function similarly in terms of character development. In the film, Simon is cared for by his childhood best friend, Leah, and brought back into his (heteronormative) home and put to sleep. Furthermore, the heterosexually dominated spaces that Simon devalues in comparison to queer space in the novel become central locales for Simon in the film. Indeed, they are even referenced in the opening to establish Simon's normativity. The elimination of queer space from Simon's life and the additional edit of placing him at a house party full of underage teenagers do generative work for the film's thematics and its neglect of political questions.

To be sure, for Simon to win the "hearts and minds" of majority audiences and their politics, he needs to be decontextualized and his experiences universalized.[126] Heterosexual peers and locales need to be prioritized in his life. While audiences of *Love, Simon* could be alienated by or disinterested in the value of queer space and queer community and care, they can easily identify with a house party full of heterosexual teen debauchery. Regardless of whether we consider Albertalli's rendering of queer space *or* Berlanti's filming of—and cutting of—a scene at a queer bar, an explicit focus on queerness cannot find a home within *Love, Simon*. Crucially, the only engagement with queer identity must be in the service of finding a boyfriend.

Additionally, the absence of distinct queer space and queer community and care in *Love, Simon* is reinforced by the rhetoric of two of the primary adult figures in Simon's life: Mr. Worth and Simon's mother, Emily, who is played by Jennifer Garner. Through these important authority figures in *Love, Simon*—the mouthpieces from the two major institutions of the home and the school—the film elides or erases the value of collective queer history, space, and care in favor of representing sexuality as a matter of private experience.

The character of Mr. Worth, particularly his relationship with Simon, provides us with yet another angle from which to explain how the film remains saddled by a troubling tension: on the one hand, the film gestures in seemingly progressive ways, but on the other hand, the film consistently falls short of centering progressive politics. From some of the earliest scenes in the film, Mr. Worth is characterized as an awkward, slightly intrusive, but mostly caring school administrator. Additionally, he is depicted as an adult who is having trouble with aging, particularly as a single, cisgender man in an increasingly digital age. Because of his aging crisis and because of Simon's clear social currency as the attractive, young white guy in the school (before being outed as gay), Mr. Worth pays extra careful attention to Simon.

This relationship extends beyond being understandable for any protagonist with the school as a major setting. Mr. Worth consistently pops up in Simon's life to police his cell phone usage, which furthers the plot of Simon's digital queer romance. But Berlanti and his creative team characterize Mr. Worth as almost admiring Simon or as wanting to return to a previous version of his younger self through his interaction with Simon. During their scenes together, Mr. Worth talks about his personal life far too often, including his dating life and details about his home life. Indeed, Mr. Worth informs Simon that they have a lot in common: "I know I am hard on you, but it's only because I really see myself in you."[127] When Simon expresses his doubts about their similarities, Mr. Worth hammers home his comparison: "No, I see it: it's obvious, it's obvious."[128] As a primary authority figure in Simon's life, Mr. Worth continues to pay close attention to Simon, and the film continues to place the administrator and Simon in close proximity.

In addition to the scene in which Mr. Worth "disciplines" the bullies and acts as an "ally" by promoting "tolerance," another scene that precedes the bullying reveals some of the film's political shortcomings. Mr. Worth's relationship with Simon fractures in important ways after

Simon is outed during their Christmas break. Once they all return to school after Simon's social currency is at its lowest, Mr. Worth wears a rainbow pin affixed to his suit jacket to signal his ally-ship (the first time this detail has appeared on his wardrobe or anyone else's, for that matter). He delivers some telling lines to Simon during a crucial point in the film. After briefly asking Simon if he is OK, he spends the rest of their interaction by harkening back to earlier moments in which he had compared the two of them: "Um, for the uh, for the record, when I was saying that we have a lot in common, you know, I wasn't, really, that's not what I was talking about. But yeah, just, ugh, just FYI, just for the record."[129] As soon as Simon is dethroned as the jock-adjacent teenager who is presumably heterosexual and cisgender, Mr. Worth no longer wants to align himself with Simon. Instead, he distances himself from Simon.

Even as Mr. Worth boasts of his ally status with his rainbow pin, he disavows Simon's status as "other." Importantly, though, Mr. Worth does not separate himself from Simon in order to acknowledge his own privilege in a heteronormative institution and world. Moreover, if we keep in mind the film's structural details, this scene is the first interaction back at school that contains dialogue, and the dialogue is quite abbreviated. Out of everything that Mr. Worth could have said to Simon, he chose to negate queerness and reconsolidate his own heteronormative power. In other words, a supporting character—one who represents institutional authority—feigns inclusion while also slipping into regressive, oppressive tendencies. Mr. Worth's insistent disavowal of queerness to solidify his own compulsory heterosexuality demonstrates the clear limits of tolerance—and the limits of dignity as well.[130]

In another realm of authority—the home and family—Simon's mother, Emily, reveals how normative notions of what constitutes dignity prioritize individualism over community. With an emotional speech during a turning point in the film, she tries to get Simon back on track, as it were. This restorative scene comes after Simon has been outed, is facing bullying at school, has lost his friend group, has been abandoned by Blue/Bram, and—perhaps most importantly to the film—has disrupted the harmony of the nuclear family with his "huge-ass secret." As the paramount moment of mending, Simon's mother delivers a monologue to the teary-eyed teenager: "As soon as you came out, you said,

'Mom, I'm still me.' I need you to hear this. You are still you, Simon. You are still the same son who I love to tease and who your father depends on for just about everything. And you're the same brother who always compliments his sister on her food, even when it sucks."[131] Then she delivers one of the most revealing lines in the film: "Being gay is your thing. . . . There are parts of it you have to go through *alone*. I hate that."[132] While this scene invokes an emotional response and while Garner's star power adds to the gravity of this moment, the monologue uncovers what is chiefly problematic about *Love, Simon*'s representation of queerness. In fact, the monologue makes clear the film's politics; when his mother speaks to him, she exercises the kind of neoliberal restraint that animates the film at the level of the individual character (Simon) but also at the level of the communal (a larger queer community). As Emily reflects Simon's identity back to him, she situates him in the logic of the nuclear family: to her, Simon is first and foremost a son (to his mother and to his father) and a brother (to a cute little sister). His mother's characterization of him focuses on stasis rather than transformation; in her view, Simon is still the *same*, and the family is still the *same*, which ameliorates Simon's earlier fears about change should he come out. Through Emily's speech—something that looks like progress—she reinforces sameness and consolidates the power of the family as it is.

Perhaps more important than Emily's mantra of sameness is her observation that Simon must go through parts of his "huge-ass secret" alone. On the heels of resituating him within the logic of the nuclear family and the home space, she suggests that there are versions of Simon's identity with which she (and the family) cannot help. Due to the limitations of her own consciousness about a rich queer history and dynamic queer communities, she cannot imagine any other option for Simon than his being alone. This is, in part, because the family would fail him here—because she would fail him here. Since her experience is constricted by the boundaries of normative kinship and belonging, in her understanding, Simon must have to navigate his queerness alone. His mother's views become all the more perplexing (or at least discouraging and frustrating) when audiences consider her broader characterization from the film's beginnings: not only is she a mental health professional, but she is also depicted as a politically conscious one, readying herself to march against the patriarchy and fight for justice. But just as she misspells the word "patriarchy" on one of her posters for an unscreened march, she also has glaring gaps in understanding about queer histories and collectives—much less about building coalitions across various movements and marginalized communities. Although she is in a profession that could lead Simon toward a consciousness-raising moment in which he learns about his queer history and could introduce Simon to a like-minded community, she delivers a message that isolates Simon or at least estranges him from queer particularity. By both resituating him firmly within the logic of the family and by denying him the value of a queer community, his mother's monologue—as affectively charged as it is—furthers the dangerous work of *Love, Simon*. Unfortunately, she teaches Simon (and other queer young people or confused parents) how to reduce his difference and reintegrate himself back into systems and institutions that can only incorporate his difference without disruption or transformation.

Emily's speech joins a sequence in which Simon quests to learn how to deal with his difference, which is rendered most clearly for viewers through his solitary trip to the coffee shop to get only one iced coffee and through his trip to look at the carnival alone from the outside. Indeed, the goal of this sequence is for Simon to learn how to be absorbed back into heteronormative structures and institutions—the family, the school, and his mostly straight peer group—without being excessively different, without being *too queer* or *too much*. His goal is to demonstrate sameness with a slight variation. Put differently, the film accommodates the *only thing* that keeps him from continuing to enjoy his life of normativity. If Simon can figure out how to accommodate his "huge-ass secret," his world can return to normal.

While we, too, tear up and nod in agreement when Emily tells her son, "You finally get to exhale, Simon," we worry about the broader ideas presented by the mother's monologue, particularly when it functions as an ostensibly progressive moment in the film's supposed focus on inclusion.[133] We hesitate when we see how the valorization of the individual continues to shape the film's choices in form and content. The uneasiness we experience when watching this monologue is compounded by Berlanti's decision to erase iterations of queer community, omit engagements with queer space, and elide references to queer history—all of which are central components of Albertalli's novel.

Indeed, the absence of queer particularity and a strong focus on the valorization of the individual struggle highlight some of the central pathologies of our current neoliberal moment and its relationship to queer representation. As Marian Meyers posits, "It is the mainstream media . . . that has been the most effective in selling an agenda and ideology that supplants as societal goals the notions of 'democracy,' 'equality,' 'the common good,' and 'community' with neoliberal ideas of 'freedom,' 'individualism,' and 'choice.'"[134] Emily's speech cements the narratives of personal responsibility, self-regulation, self-empowerment, self-improvement, and self-invention that saturate Simon's journey.[135] This decontextualization of Simon's queerness in favor of his individual journey primes him for the universalizing thrust that constructs him as a dignified gay who can be reintegrated back into normative power structures. Under the auspices of progress and inclusion, Simon emerges as a dehistoricized, decontextualized character whose journey to find himself can become universally applicable to broader audiences. As a result, his difference—his particularity—is reduced, and structural change never happens.

Conclusion: Page Not Found; or, Looking for Road Maps and Finding None

As we argued in the previous section, Berlanti's Simon has no road maps and no historical understanding of queerness. His only options during his pivotal moments of becoming are Google searches as his guides. Once he decides to be "gay and proud" outside of the confines of his imagination and not in the *elsewhere-ness* of California, he Googles "How to dress like a gay guy" and is presented with images of Anderson Cooper and Andy Cohen and a series of tight T-shirts with minor variances in each of their styling details.[136] Of course, having visible queer celebrities can serve a noteworthy function, but the only part of queer identity that concerns Simon or the film is how to dress. Instead of searching online for instances of queer history to learn or using the democratic potential of the networked age to establish queer community beyond the confines of geographical boundaries, age limitations, or even material safety concerns, Simon looks *only* for fashion advice. If we were to take this scene to its fullest logic, we might realize the devastating irony of *Love, Simon* and its contribution to visibility politics: at the same time that we are watching a touted representation of contemporary LGBTQ+ teen life and witnessing a young queer searching—literally—for guidance, that representation itself is limited to exhausting and exhausted stereotypes. Representations of gay men as concerned with only fashion and aesthetics have saturated shows like *Will and Grace* and have limited depictions of queer life to images that comfort and amuse the majority; perpetuate reductive, flawed understandings of our lives and experiences; and anesthetize the otherwise radical potential of queer critique so that normative dynamics remain undisturbed.[137]

Perhaps the most violent consequence of the film's reimagining of Simon's story is that it severs Simon—especially in this formative stage in his coming into consciousness about his sexuality—from queer history and specific queer community. Doing so accomplishes ideological work: it tells audiences that queer identity need not disrupt heteronormative values, priorities, and institutions. By reading the box-office hit film *Love, Simon* in comparison to *Simon vs. the Homo Sapiens Agenda*, this political work becomes apparent. Berlanti's production reflects and constitutes normative notions of neoliberal dignity as restraint and individualism. It ignores queer values, communities, and histories. It positions certain iterations of queerness as excessive, and the film reduces difference in favor of sustaining sameness.

Ultimately, the circularity of Simon's narrative captures this deployment of dignity; his gay identity is incorporated so long as it does not challenge normative notions of coupling, romance, and sexual restraint. Because the concept of dignity (and its generative work) resides at the level of the individual and aspires to be a universalistic good, it severs the individual from historical, communal, and cultural contexts that offer meaning and value. As a result, queer communities, distinct histories, and unique epistemologies are refused and often fall out of view, thereby orchestrating a purposeful generational fracture that leaves young queer folks without context, road maps, and elders. The film makes this concept of dignity quite manifest.

While the film appears at one level to be a progressive comment on contemporary teen life—because it has a multicultural cast that includes numerous Brown and Black actors, because it is the first mass-marketed film centered on a gay teenager, and because it can be read as a primer for how straight parents and friends might respond to and continue to love queer young people—our reading reveals that this progressivism elides how marginalized groups navigate power. Rather than centering the ostensible focus of a budding queer romance, the film privileges a heteronormative gaze: its logics, institutions, and experiences constitute the film's narrative focus. Furthermore, the film reduces its young gay protagonist to maintaining and mending the heteronormative family, and as such, he must work in service to that ideal rather than counter it with any substantive voicing of queer alternatives. Instead, the film reaches for a message legible to the widest audience. Consequently, *Love, Simon* flattens the particularity of a queer coming-out narrative to a universal "just like you" claim that works to decontextualize, dehistoricize, and erase the spaces and narratives that constitute the queer self and communities.

We acknowledge that *Love, Simon* has the potential to start conversations about the experiences of young queer people. It offers the possibility to reflect on dating across racial lines. It could even ignite a conversation about the devastating effects of bullying. But many of these opportunities already followed from the groundbreaking inclusion of a central gay character in the series *Dawson's Creek* in 1999, for which Berlanti was a show runner.[138] From our contemporary vantage point twenty years later, this aspiration seems limited. Berlanti's *Love, Simon* is a byproduct of our contemporary pivot toward and internalization of dignity as respectability. To be deemed worthy of dignity is so seductive that it hinders us from thinking beyond its limits and recognizing what we sacrifice for it.

Our aim in this chapter is to reveal those sacrifices and open up the possibility of imagining alternatives in the popular culture landscape. As Cathy Cohen argues, "Many of us continue to search for a new political direction and agenda, one that does not focus on integration into dominant structures but instead seeks to transform the basic fabric and hierarchies that allow systems of oppression to persist and operate efficiently."[139] Such radical new directions—particularly with mainstream representation of LGBTQ+ lives—will necessarily involve a shift in content creation, an opening up of who enters into the writing room, who directs productions, and who sits at the table of production meetings. Despite its popularity, unfortunately, Berlanti's film does not gesture toward such radical new directions. Instead, *Love, Simon* offers only a coming-of-age narrative about a gay teen that does little to critique the lonely, unfamiliar, and isolated position in which Simon finds himself. Rather, it reinforces this lonely, unfamiliar position and even, at times, uses it for comedic effect. Not only does *Love, Simon* neglect to unpack Simon's predicament of navigating the world as a queer person without knowledge of queer history or community, but it also furthers the universalizing logics and the valorization of the individual. If *Love, Simon* discussed the importance of queer history and community and contested individualist values, the film could better explain Simon's isolation and offer him pathways toward a more dynamic future rooted in queerness.

4

Doing the Most

Pose *and the Value of Queer Excess*

Within the first two minutes of the pilot of FX's *Pose* (created by Ryan Murphy, Brad Falchuk, and Steven Canals), Elektra Abundance—one of the show's protagonists—passionately announces, "It's time we remind the world who we are."[1] Though her comment has specific relevance for the plot, her insistence moves beyond the narrative time of the 1980s. Indeed, her pronouncement reverberates into contemporary discussions about queer representation in popular culture and serves as a foundational mantra that motivates this chapter. Countering the politics of respectability centered in *Love, Simon*, which we discussed in the previous chapter, FX's *Pose* marks a turning point in mainstream representation of queer lives. Instead of endorsing and perpetuating a pathway to neoliberal dignity that prioritizes individualism, dehistoricizes and decontextualizes queer folks, and severs community ties that might offer queer alternatives, *Pose* bolsters a value system of its own. The show articulates an oppositional posture that furthers our exploration of dignity and its relation to contemporary LGBTQ+ life.

Set in New York City in the late 1980s, the drama explores the underground ball scene that gained increased attention in the early 1990s by way of Jennie Livingston's documentary *Paris Is Burning* and Madonna's hit song "Vogue." Focusing primarily on the lives of Black and Brown queer and trans people, *Pose* showcases the details of "house" culture and foregrounds the action of the balls that proliferated beyond the purview of queer life in the Village. Featuring two central "house mothers" (Blanca Evangelista and Elektra Abundance), the master of ceremonies and Black queer elder (Pray Tell), and "house children" (like Damon and Angel Evangelista), the show depicts their particular challenges and joys during this turbulent era of queer life in one of its largest epicenters. In so doing, *Pose* also juxtaposes two distinct worlds developing along similar timelines. By comparing the impact of the HIV/AIDS crisis and its ravaging of queer communities to the increasing corporatization of New York City, the drama foregrounds a disparity between lack and luxury and issues arguments about whose bodies matter and why. Furthermore, by engaging the ballroom's focus on "realness" alongside characters who exist outside of the balls, *Pose* asks hard questions about which world's inhabitants live more authentically and why.

Taking cues from Elektra's statement that opens the pilot, we argue that *Pose* emerges as an excavation of a denigrated queer past and as a building block for a fierce queer future. As Roderick Ferguson asserts, to forge pathways toward a more liberated future, we must center "the aliveness of historical alternatives, the need for queer politics to identify and activate those alternatives, the role of queer history as grist for the mill of political theorizing, and the confluence of social struggles as part of the observations of a multidimensional queer politics."[2] By surveying the show's construction, its thematics, and its relationship to mainstream representational histories of queer lives, we contend that *Pose* not only abandons dignity as it is currently defined—as a singular quality that compels a universal sameness—but also directly critiques this notion of dignity precisely because the concept demands an unquestioned adoption of heteronormative logics. To be sure, the show does not create a world in which dignity's seduction is absent. Nevertheless, through form and content—namely, by way of characterization—*Pose* highlights either dignity's inapplicability to queer bodies and worldmaking practices or, at very best, its fragility as a foundation for building self and communal worth and for protecting queer folks economically, politically, or socially. Whereas *Love, Simon* adopts a contemporary neoliberal notion of dignity as integral and inherent to the self, as "universal," and as independent of history, *Pose* redefines dignity as earned and sustained through ethical communal praxis.

Without a doubt, the series slays because it does not center a token representative "other" crafted to assuage normative anxieties about difference. It refuses to fuel imaginary progress narratives about a universal togetherness and to deploy the queer subject as an instrument of the state. As Reina Gossett, Eric A. Stanley, and Johanna Burton remind us, "Aesthetics and image matter deeply and can exist against the current instrumentalization of trans visibility as an advertisement for the state,"[3] especially as we practice navigating, examining, and "resisting increasingly complex modes of incorporation and repression."[4] Similarly, Ferguson has noted that "it has historically been women of color, queer of color, and trans movements and actors that have illustrated the violence that underpins those narratives of progress."[5] Because the show resists a domestication of difference that rarely alters the material conditions of marginalized queer and trans folks—particularly of color—*Pose* stands in sharp contrast to *Love, Simon*. Simon's acceptance relies on his conforming to white supremacist heteronormative logics that demand sameness, exemplifying how a calculated restraint of queerness excludes too many ways of being and perpetuates the myth of whiteness as universal. *Pose* chooses to revel in queer particularity and excess that make life more livable even as they foreclose access to neoliberal dignity. Indeed, *Pose* exposes dignity's limits, particularly for Black and Brown queer and trans people.

Through the show's embrace of queer excess, its amplification of queer history, its resistance to institutional authority, and its adoption of alternative notions of kinship and belonging, *Pose* articulates and advocates for a divergent pathway to dignity. Whereas neoliberal deployments of dignity promote restraint, *Pose* showcases the value of excess. Whereas neoliberal deployments of dignity favor a dehistoricized, decontextualized, and universal subject, *Pose* insists on the importance of learning and connecting to a queer past. Whereas neoliberal deployments of dignity demand compliance to institutional authorities, *Pose* defies the dictations of traditional sources of power. And whereas neoliberal deployments of dignity valorize individual and private success, *Pose* models alternative kinship and community praxis. Taken together, these contrasting value systems reveal *Pose*'s distinct vision of dignity as negotiated and earned through ethical engagement with and accountability to others.

Pose's defiant vision is made possible (at least in part) because the writing room and production sets are saturated with artists and activists who often do not exist in close proximity to normativity and who, perhaps, have always been deemed unfit for dignity. With these content creation choices, the show avoids many of the representational shortcomings of contemporary approaches to "diversity and inclusion" in media—namely, what Gossett, Stanley, and Burton call the "trap door" of representation,[6] what Juliana Huxtable refers to as the "consumption of marginality"[7] or what Che Gossett describes as a "scattering of people [in front of the camera] without any redistribution of power."[8] As trans activist CeCe McDonald notes in a conversation with LGBTQ+ legend Miss Major Griffin-Gracy, "The stereotypical narrative and the rhetoric that plays out with it soothes society, which then acts out in ways that can be even more violent, or transphobic, or homophobic, or queer-phobic toward our communities."[9] Because "visibility is being used to sabotage actual engagement with real questions of structural negligence and discrimination and violence,"[10] *Pose* offers a "queer politic based on analyses of power."[11] By centering the voices and perspectives of folks who live at the intersections of race, class, gender, sexuality, and ability, *Pose* offers frank (and gritty) conversations about what it means to live on the fringes of the American body politic. The show's creative process structurally alters whose narratives, voices, and bodies matter and exemplifies McDonald's assessment: "If there were more trans, queer, and GNC [gender non-conforming] people of color having agency in mainstream spaces, then our narrative definitely could change."[12] Key to this change is how *Pose* embraces difference without compromise and places value on surviving and thriving in collectivity and particularity. In this way, the show emerges as a counter-representation of the dominant discourse of sameness offered in the chase for dignity in market-ready representations of queer lives. *Pose* remains firm in its refusal to drain the transformational potential of difference as it explores "theoretical and historical trajectories that further imaginative capacities to construct more livable Black and trans worlds."[13]

The Category Is . . . Showing All the Way Up

In the opening ten minutes of *Pose*'s debut episode, viewers can find many of the features that will animate the show's first two seasons at the level of form and content. The first image that we see is a close-up shot of a giant disco ball that is not in the middle of a party or a club but resides in the middle of an apartment. As the camera zooms out and surveys the room, what comes into view are the controlled, structured, and practiced dance moves of voguing—a community-specific dance practice and communication style—being rehearsed in community by

Cubby and Lemar (two minor characters in the ballroom world). This disco ball provides an entryway into reading the relationship between form and content and becomes a structuring principle through which components of the opening episode tell its viewers what matters. Not only is the disco ball—all bright and shiny—a figure of excess, but it also becomes the centerpiece of the ballroom to create a link among ballroom, family, community, and alternative versions of "home."

As the show moves to its opening credits, audiences hear the clacking of heels and the voice-over of Pray Tell. Invoking the linguistic rhythms and vocabulary of the community, he performs the show's tagline: "The Category Is . . . Live . . . Werk . . . Pose."[14] As he speaks, a nondescript room fills the screen, and a huge sign spelling "Pose" in capital letters with bright-pink neon lights appears. As he gets closer to the dramatic finale of the tagline, the word gets brighter and more focused, and the room brightens with pink lights until the whole sign explodes—flooding the screen with glitter. As glitter flies through the air, the music starts and credits roll.

Drenched in the excess of pink neon lights and a glitter storm, the show's opening would shine and sparkle on its own, but a careful reader will observe that excess is not being used gratuitously. Rather, the pink neon lights that spell the word "Pose" and the additional pink lights on the periphery of the screen that encircle the show's name are the very same lights that appear in the pivotal ballroom, which anchors the show's narrative, foregrounds its specific queer history, and houses much of the community-specific education offered to viewers. Furthermore, the non-descript room with the wooden floor is the empty ballroom space itself. And finally, the same disco ball that focuses the opening shot in the House of Abundance and adorns the middle of the ballroom floor is the one that reflects the lights and glitter in the explosive opening.

Taken together, the neon pink lights, glitter shower, massive disco ball, and all the cadences and extravagant visuals of the ball scene constitute the show's first representation of itself. And its core identity is one shaped by a commitment to queer excess. Through aesthetics and content, the world of *Pose* will take most viewers where they have never been before. In so doing, it will not limit its characters, plot, or audiences by tempering queerness. Instead, the show emerges as a representational corrective and healing balm for communities that face demands to tone it down, straighten up, or make themselves smaller in a world not built for them.

In this way, it is no surprise that Janet Mock, one of the show's executive producers, writers, and directors (and the first openly trans woman of color in the writing room and director's chair in Hollywood), arrived at the 2019 Met Gala in a disco-ball gown with a coordinating shiny clutch that read "The Most." Sharing details about her look on social media, Mock informed her Instagram followers that Alberta Ferretti's designer gown was made from four hundred multisized sequins and over one thousand hand-dyed feathers. True to form, Mock also explained why her fashion choice matters: "I wanted to pay homage to the iconic Josephine Baker while showcasing voluminous texture that allows us to take up more space in a world looking to shrink us . . . [and] bring in my own disco ball mirroring the ones in ballroom that radiate our collective brilliance—with the intent to show *all the way up by doing the most*. #metgala."[15] Pointing specifically to excess, Mock comments thoughtfully in dress and words on what it means to live an unrestrained life and on how important it is to demand space in a world that brands Black people and/or queer people as "too much." By glamorizing excess and tying it to Black and queer histories of resistance, Mock urges her followers to reconceptualize "doing the most" as valuable and as a movement toward fuller liberation.[16] She models how to resist and how to make it fashion.[17]

Even though Mock makes a compelling case for an unadulterated centering of excess, original show creator Steven Canals often articulates how a rhetoric of excess almost kept the show in the womb. While the early versions of his script for the pilot episode of *Pose* won him recognition in college, industry executives would not greenlight the project because it was "too niche": "The meetings were varying degrees of 'We love the characters and we love the world, but what else do you have?' to 'You're never going to get this made because it's a period piece and too Black and too brown and too queer and too trans.' It was just too much."[18] Before Ryan Murphy saw the script, Canals had shopped it to over 150 executives, and the industry was clear: stories about Black and Brown queer and trans folks that centered the value of *showing all the way up by doing the most* were not welcomed or understood as profitable. Luckily, Canals knew the value and remained unequivocal in his decision to represent LGBTQ+ folks in unrestrained and communally specific ways. Indeed, Canals and Mock agree that *Pose* provides a moment—maybe the *only* moment for the foreseeable future—for queer and trans folks of color to see themselves in an uncompromising representation that does not translate them for mainstream acceptance. From the writers' room and director's chair to the actors' spotlight, the *Pose* team foregrounds excess at the level of narrative time and focus, costuming and dialogue, and music.

This embrace of excess realized in narrative time and music is perhaps most obvious in Damon's dance audition scene in the pilot episode. In a scene that could be read alongside the fantasy dance sequence from *Love, Simon*, *Pose* offers its own take on the same classic queer anthem "I Wanna Dance with Somebody (Who Loves Me)" by Whitney Houston.[19] Unlike the dance number in Greg Berlanti's film that features an out-of-step Simon, an abbreviated version of the song, a disregard for the song's importance to queer history and community, and a firm disavowal of queerness—Simon explicitly rejects the fantasy as too gay—*Pose*'s dance sequence offers a profound counternarrative. Within the context of an audition to access an impressive dance school, Damon dances to the Whitney bop and gets his entire life. By proxy, the audience gets life as we witness him welcoming all that has rendered him supposedly sinful, wayward, and beyond the purview of a family's love—beyond the parameters of a life worth living, of dignity.

Pose dedicates almost its last ten minutes of narrative time in the pilot to this audition and over four minutes to the song itself and Damon's performance. At the level of structure, the show's creative team renders its focus clearly: queer excess is valued and is a gift. As Treva Ellison argues, folks can find "potential and creativity in being surplus . . . or reworking and repurposing the signs, symbols, and accoutrements of Western modernity."[20] Though Damon initially shows signs of hesitation and worries that he is not good enough, house mother Blanca informs him that "we don't have the luxury of shame," and she encourages him to "take" his moment.[21] Instead of thinking through an inclusion strategy that promotes incorporation without disruption, *Pose* argues that entry into these spaces requires that those institutions transform based on the particularity of queer bodies and logics. *Pose* makes space for queer people to bring this particularity, know their worth, and insist that exclusive institutions rethink themselves. To be sure, Damon goes into one of the most stressful moments of his life and succeeds *as a result of—not in spite of—his queerness*. His queerness is not characterized as something to abandon or even restrain for the comfort of others, especially those in power. In *Pose*, his unabashedly queer movements and queer experiences (the fierceness and pain) are what make him valuable.

Exhibiting the show's embrace of excess, the audition scene features Damon dancing to almost the entirety of Whitney's five-minute dance track and, in so doing, embracing all of his Black queer fierceness in front of an audience of powerful figures. Instead of reducing the scene to a few key clips of his audition or to a sound bite of the song that mainstream audiences could sing along to, the narrative stays with Damon through the song's intro, first verse, pre-chorus, chorus (multiple times), bridge, and—most importantly—even the extended outro. During Damon's routine, all of Whitney's signature riffs and the song's key transitions are on full display, as are his abilities and queer ways of expressing himself. Even Whitney's beloved movement from the pre-chorus to the powerhouse chorus happens not once in the scene but twice—concluding both the first verse and the song's bridge. While this may seem like an insignificant move, it pays critical dividends when viewers pay attention to Damon's growth alongside the song. As Whitney builds in intensity, lets herself go to the beat, and starts living her best life, so does Damon. The transformation is clear: at the beginning, Damon is unsure and hesitant, but as the song progresses, so does his willingness to thrive—to feel his oats. Through Damon, we see that "maintaining the capacity for joy is critical to the struggle for justice."[22]

At the beginning of the dance, the dean of dance reminds Damon to smile for the judges—to abide by expectations and conventions common to auditions. He tries for a moment, but his movements are riddled with a lack of authenticity, and this moment smacks of a performance of respectability. Damon cannot keep this up and succeed. He walks away from his audience, turns his back, and fortifies himself to do it his way. As Whitney begins her first verse, he spins around with an attitude, a renewed conviction to defy expectations. Afterward, he spends the rest of the routine liberating himself to dance in a way that makes sense to him. He embraces his so-called feminine movements, he flirts with the white (presumably cisgender man) teacher when the song's lyrics call for it, and he even booty bumps the white (presumably cisgender woman) teacher. The tables that are supposed to separate him and establish the judges' authority become props—part of his dance floor. With his defiant choices, Damon embodies what Kaila Adia Story refers to as a "politics of deviance": "a more radical form of political struggle in which we do not 'subscribe to a predatory/institutionalized heterosexuality' and where we dance in the delight of difference . . . throw[ing] shade on normativity, sashay[ing] away from a politics of respectability."[23] By playing with them to the beat and lyrics, Damon displays non-normative desire, toys with gender expectations, and stresses power dynamics.

If viewers pay careful attention to the spatial dimensions of the scene, particularly the camera movements, we can make better sense of how Damon occupies physical space and what that might mean for the narrative. When the scene begins, the camera's focus is much wider, and Damon's body is seemingly swallowed by the space. Without a doubt, he has not learned how to occupy the room yet—how to take up the space that he deserves. As the scene develops, the camera's focus tightens, and Damon commands the room. In so doing, he releases that which the world has demanded he restrain, and he flourishes as a result. He learns to claim space.

In addition to Damon's body in space, the structural specifics offer more insight when we consider the symbolism of the cassette tape that reads "Whitney! <3."[24] Importantly, Damon gets his audition music from Blanca, who is his newly minted "house mother" and the conduit through which he learns about queer community and history. She passes the cassette down to Damon to help him, which also sets into motion the intergenerational relationship that will guide him. Living through the music, Damon receives some of the earliest glimpses of the value of his femme energy, sass, and slender physique. What his birth father demonizes about him earlier in the episode—he's too soft, too dainty, too sissy, too artistic—is precisely what flourishes. The fundamental *too much* or *too different* that disgusts his father and causes his parents to disown and evict him from their home is what sets him apart in the audition. By releasing the restraint demanded by his father and by embracing what Blanca begins to teach him, he shows the dean of dance his spirit and talent. After his performance, she sees his future as someone who can alter the trajectory of the field by infusing a presence heretofore denied.

Pose does not limit moments of queer excess to individual story lines or character arcs. Several of the most convincing and indicative embraces of excess occur at the level of the community. While audiences could turn to a number of instances of excess embraced in groups, a key scene from "Mother of the Year" emerges as telling.[25] In this episode, nearly thirty minutes of the action—roughly half of the entire episode—features the "Princess Ball." Even though the narrative arc of the show continues, most of the narrative action happens on the ballroom floor, and dialogue does not necessarily reign supreme; rather, serving face, giving the children flawless looks, and slaying dance are all key components. Indeed, this thirty-minute segment is replete with a powerful "house versus house battle," an intense "femme queen vogue" dance-off, and an emotional "Mother of the Year" crowning.

With this episode, queer excess is on full display, and it is a group affair. The clearest example of this is perhaps the epic battle between the House of Evangelista and the House of Ferocity. The action is protracted, filled with multiple categories in which smaller numbers of each family face off in different challenges to emerge as the most sickening group. Importantly, *Pose* devotes almost five full minutes of narrative time to this competition because the details matter: it is in the details that a house sets itself apart. During battle, dialogue among characters does not necessarily happen verbally. The ballroom floor and its happenings *constitute the narrative.* As the end nears, Pray Tell initiates a chant in which everyone repeats "pose" and, in so doing, serves a pose. This happens about twenty times and includes an intensification in the final lap—"pose double time"—in which the chant gets faster and the invitation to pose speeds up. The self-reflective chant takes the embrace of excess to its fullest logic: *Pose* devotes over thirty seconds of narrative time to the same word being repeated over and over while the battle contestants strike poses that showcase their beauty, power, and artistry.

Importantly, this posing extravaganza moment is not limited to the contestants in the "house versus house battle." Just like the broader ballroom community members insert themselves into the action of categories by snapping in affirmation, shouting endorsements, and per-forming their own numbers on the sidelines, they also find their way into the "pose" chant. As the chant builds in intensity, the camera moves from tighter shots that feature the main cast members battling to shots that spotlight the wider ballroom world. By the end, the community is posing together and doing the absolute "most" in unison (while main-taining uniqueness). *Pose* allows this moment of togetherness to take up its due time and space. Furthermore, the embrace of excess brings the community together, especially after a divisive house battle.

What is most telling about this scene is Pray Tell's punctuation of its end. In all of his own excess—in volume, extended enunciation, and high drama—he concludes the battle and subsequent "pose" moment with the ultimate endorsement: he shouts out to the energetic crowd, "Ovahness personified!"[26] While "ova" or "ovah" can have many differ-ent iterations, at its core, it is a statement of affirmation that recognizes someone is deep in their truth and has reached a pinnacle of living that is absolutely right. Additionally, it can be used to snap for someone who has flawlessly executed a performance or served a sickening look, but even then, the celebration has a layer of praise that signals elevated truth. To tell someone that they are "ova" or "ovah" is a high form of intracommunal praise, and it is deep praise. "Ova" or "ovah" goes well beyond a more casual "werq" or "yaasss" to note that someone is doing the damn thing—that is, they are ascending to their highest truths and living as a model for others. When Pray Tell provides the capstone moment of queer excess on full display, he tells the group that they have become a living embodiment of "ovah."[27] By conferring this upon them, he encourages them to applaud one another for reaching the highest level of self and communal actualization.[28]

Before the action of the Princess Ball, Pray Tell primes the scene for an unadulterated celebration of queer excess—one that runs counter to the state's demand for queer restraint during the height of the HIV/AIDS crisis. As Pray Tell greets the crowd and starts to energize them for a night of celebration, sickening looks, and fierce competition, he deliv-ers a key revaluation of excess: "Now, listen, somebody had told me that the Department of Health had closed down the bathhouses, but from where I'm standing, it looks like they just dumped you bitches right on out here in front of me."[29] For the purposes of our conversation about dignity's boundary-making potential, Pray Tell's specific reference to the Department of Health and his mentioning of the state-directed closure of queer community space serve vital functions for understanding *Pose*'s interventions. As we detailed the history of bathhouse closures in chapter 1—amplifying the state's motivations and surveying the consequences for queer communities—we argued that these dynamic and life-giving communal spaces were often characterized by those outside of them as immoral, dirty, diseased, and excessive. A fundamental *too much* informed the critique of these spaces and led to the shuttering of them. In fact, an argument about devalued excess led the state (and other queers) to blame gay men for the crisis.

Pray Tell responds unequivocally to this rhetoric by calling direct attention to the state's violent action and by revaluing so-called excessive behavior. While the state (and the broader mainstream society) has branded his community as excessive and denigrated them as a result, Pray Tell offers the ballroom as a harbor, one in which they do not have to restrain themselves to find belonging and safety. Importantly, his response to the state comes from the microphone on the ballroom floor—literally amplifying the message—and it also opens the Princess Ball. By way of form and content, *Pose* refutes the state's actions, issues its counternarrative about excess, and centers a celebration of excessive behavior in community at the balls. Because this is a distinctly communal space in which folks find belonging, value, and affirmation, *Pose* provides the ballroom floor as another spatial possibility for folks mourning the loss of the dynamic space of the bathhouses. When the state wreaks havoc on already-vulnerable queer spaces, *Pose* says to bring all of that denigrated "too much" into this space and snatch trophies for it.

"Know Your History, Children": *Pose* as Historical Primer

From Elektra's opening lines of the pilot, *Pose* begins its meticulous and loving rendering of a collective queer past, especially for Black and Brown queer and trans folks. Her proclamation "It is time we remind the world who we are!"[30] joins Pray Tell's consistent refrain: "Know your history, children."[31] In addition to exhibiting characteristics common to period pieces, *Pose* takes deliberate steps within and beyond the narrative to spotlight the value of learning or being reminded of lessons from a distinctly queer past. While our current neoliberal moment and many representations of contemporary LGBTQ+ life rendered through its lens argue for a dehistoricized, decontextualized queer subject that propagates a simultaneously universal and individualized message, *Pose* saturates its show in queer particularity. The need to remember joins *Pose*'s embrace of excess to nuance the show's oppositional approach.

As L. H. Stallings notes, "If transgender and transsexual history and culture depend upon what has been published, visible, legible, and authorized enough to be archived, then we might query what has been omitted as a result of the conditions of illiteracy, criminalization, or poverty."[32] C. Riley Snorton joins Stallings in thinking through the challenges of trans (and queer) history building, especially for Black and Brown folks, noting that "the circumstances of omission that Stallings identifies are . . . conditions of possibility."[33] Through its unrelenting focus on history, *Pose* excavates a rich past—one that is fractured and from which we have been severed, like Stallings argues—to remind us of where we have been and to show us where we could go next, like Snorton suggests. Specifically, through its history-building, the show has the potential to ignite individual and collective consciousness, heal, and politicize.

From the pilot of season 1 to the "In My Heels"[34] finale of season 2, *Pose* operates as a primer for audiences to learn about queer history—narratives that are usually elided, abandoned, erased, or revised to support white supremacist renderings of progress. Teaching the children how to read, this primer offers key lessons about central issues, debates, icons, cultural contributions, communal values, and distinct vocabulary. The show distributes these lessons to audiences through a variety of techniques: (1) episodes that focus on dramatizing specific historical events, (2) episodes that feature moments of history-building that are not immediately tied to the plot, (3) more protracted narrative arcs that reveal historical events and introduce community concepts and values, and (4) extratextual discourse on social media that continues the lessons—sparking further reading and dialogue among the show, audience, and real-life historical figures. By examining examples of each, we demonstrate how *Pose* becomes a vehicle to remember the past and contextualize community. As such, the show resists the universalizing narratives of dignity that often demand that we forget or never learn about our queer past.

Specific Historical Events Retold by Pose

The first major category of history-building showcases how particular episodes focus on specific historical events from our collective queer past. Episodes like "Acting Up" and "Butterfly/Cocoon"[35] perform this archival work,[36] even though some of the historical references are more apparent than others. From the opening in "Acting Up," *Pose* articulates one of its key foci for the show's second season. Pray Tell and Blanca travel to Hart Island to reveal an often-untold story of HIV/AIDS history: mass and unmarked burials. Traveling by ferry, they reach "the most remote part of New York," according to Pray Tell.[37] He is referring to an island in the northeast Bronx that is about a mile long and occupies space at the western part of Long Island Sound.[38] Throughout history, the remote space has served many functions—from a Civil War prison camp to a psychiatric ward and from a tuberculosis sanatorium to a rehabilitation center, but by the mid-1980s, the area served as a spot to bury folks who died from HIV/AIDS complications. While the area initially acted as a quarantine spot for HIV/AIDS deaths, once the science of transmission became clearer and the epidemic reached new heights, Hart Island became more of a mass burial site. Indeed, historians know that the number of bodies is well into the thousands, but the exact number is not clear. In fact, Hart Island may be the largest mass burial ground of people lost to HIV/AIDS. Acting as a potter's field, the ground holds the remains of those lost to the virus who died in poverty or who went unclaimed by their shamed families. Many of them are marked only by a number and sometimes by their assigned sex at birth.[39]

In an act of excavation, *Pose* sends its main characters to the island to tell the buried history of their communities and to pay their respects to the many untold stories and lives not given the honor that they deserved. As they travel, they confront visuals of cheap pine boxes that are spray-painted with numbers and piled on top of one another by men in HazMat suits—both showcasing the mass death visually and displaying the lack of value bestowed on these lives lost. The visual images join dialogue with a state bureaucrat to demonstrate the state's position. This unnamed worker tells a tough truth to Blanca and Pray Tell: "Here's the thing—names don't matter here. Just a bunch of pine boxes in a ditch."[40] She continues, "Welcome to Hart Island: just a mass grave for people whose families couldn't afford a burial or unclaimed bodies from the morgue. Infants are out back in Potter's Field. We've quarantined the ones who died of AIDS—don't want them infecting anyone else, you know."[41] After interacting with this dismissive state authority, Pray Tell and Blanca depart on a mission to pay their respects to their friend.

As they search for their friend, they take the audience on the journey with them—surveying the landscape and displaying the emotions that a lonely mass graveyard produces. While the show is unequivocal in its condemnation of this blatant disregard for life, *Pose* does not end this act of remembering the queer past on a somber note of victimhood. Rather, the sequence dares to remember and mourn but then centers resilience and survival by way of communal care and action. Before Pray Tell and Blanca leave the island, they find a space of possibility—a cross made of decorated rocks that sits on a tiny hill. Each of the rocks, brought by a loved one, commemorates someone lost and buried on the island. Though the rocks tell individual stories of love and loss, they collectively form a symbol of faith. Importantly, as Pray Tell and Blanca leave a rock in their friend Keenan's memory, they fortify themselves and each other for the survival work ahead of them in the episode. This work includes Pray Tell's politicization through ACT UP (AIDS Coalition to Unleash Power) and the group's participation in the reimagined Stop the Church demonstration—direct action that critiqued the Catholic church's interference in the HIV/AIDS crisis, which we will detail later in this chapter.[42]

From the trip to Hart Island and the ACT UP meeting to the restaging of Stop the Church and the "Silence = Death" slogan that functions as an epigraph for the episode, *Pose* devotes the majority of its season 2 premiere to remembering a queer past that is shaped by pain, anger, resilience, and communal organizing.[43] By delving deep into history often sidelined, maligned, or erased, *Pose* provides audiences with a history that is desperately needed even as they are entertained. Finally, and importantly, the show also makes small interventions into the representations that do exist of this early AIDS activism by displaying Black and Brown queer and trans participation—a presence often elided even in those queer histories that do circulate.[44]

If "Acting Up" is loud and deliberate in its sharing of HIV/AIDS history, the episode titled "Butterfly/Cocoon" might be the quietest episode of the series that centers findings from the queer archives. In this episode, Elektra gets herself into trouble when one of her sex-work clients dies on her watch. Because the world reads him as a heterosexual white man with money, Elektra and her friends know that she cannot go to the police, regardless of her innocence.[45] Rather than appealing to the police, Elektra and Candy go to Ms. Orlando, a woman in their community who handles difficult situations. As Elektra and Candy wait for guidance, Ms. Orlando goes to the store for supplies, comes back to the girls, and shares the plan: "I got some goodies to play with. . . . The lye: it's for the smell; the pleather: it's easy to work with, and, most importantly, it doesn't leak. . . . We're gonna wrap him up, we're gonna sew him in, and we're gonna put him in that closet with some boxes over. And I promise you . . . no one will ever know. A beautiful little cocoon."[46] Then the episode continues to provide the step-by-step process of cocooning the dead body and hiding him in Elektra's new luxurious closet to escape being blamed for his death and to avoid imprisonment on Rikers Island. Even though the episode appears to center a heartless act, *Pose* is careful to contextualize this decision by highlighting important dimensions of power.

The plot of "Butterfly/Cocoon" takes on an added layer of significance when viewers learn that the inspiration comes from the real-life story of Dorian Corey (one of the most memorable faces and voices of *Paris Is Burning*) and the mummified body found in a trunk of hers after her own death.[47] The details of the Corey affair are fairly unresolved, but historical records show that Corey's friends found a dead body with a gunshot wound to the head mummified in the back of her closet. Additionally, records also indicate that the body was that of her ex-lover Robert Worley. Beyond the details of the location of the body, who found it, and who he was, the "endorsed" facts begin to blend with conflicting community renderings of events. What we can be sure of is that Corey used her skills as a fashion designer and as a woman trying to survive to hide the evidence of a crime that she may have committed.[48] And

Pose leaves clues that could guide curious viewers to the archives for this real-life unsolved mystery—one that is perhaps most noteworthy for its lesson in creativity, talent, and resilience.

Calling back to the trunk in the back of Corey's real-life closet, Elektra describes her hiding place for Paul: "We put him in an old trunk. I moved boxes around to try to hide him. I worry that the others can smell him. . . . He's mine now. He will be with me for the rest of my life."[49] Similar to Corey, who kept Worley's corpse for some fifteen years until he was discovered after her own death from AIDS-related complications, Elektra plans to keep a cocooned Paul so that she stays out of state authority's unfair and unjust reach. In addition to narrative parallels, *Pose* ends this episode with a direct reference to Corey in an epigraph. Not only does this episode nod specifically to the famous queen, but it also links Elektra to Corey to contextualize their plights and to demonstrate how they both prioritize sisterhood to survive. In this way, the episode deepens its lessons by acknowledging power disparities and displaying communal love. Refusing to decontextualize Elektra, *Pose* protests routine criminalization of trans and queer folks of color and—arguably—situates them as morally superior.[50]

Brief and Subtle Historical References in Pose

The second major category of *Pose*'s take on queer history features brief moments in an episode that invoke specific historical references or that teach mini-lessons about a queer past—even if they are not immediately relevant to the story lines of that episode. Sometimes, the references are subtle (quiet nods to the ballroom past), and other times, the references are more direct (louder offerings from the queer archives). Both types work together with the show's other iterations of history-building to demonstrate how deliberate *Pose* is in explaining what has value and why. Many of these historical references, specifically when they involve ballroom culture's history, are largely possible because of the purposeful consulting relationships that Murphy, Canals, and others create behind the scenes. Under the guidance of folks like the late Hector Xtravaganza, Jose Xtravaganza, Jack Mizrahi, and even Jennie Livingston, the show's architects steep themselves in the deep history that the show centers and pull experiences from the past to make multiple episodes a lesson in learning.[51] For example, in the first two episodes of season 2, we see both direct and indirect moments of history-building beyond the episode's historical conversation of ACT UP's fight against AIDS and Madonna's interest in the balls.

In "Acting Up," Pray Tell features a more direct pedagogical moment that punctuates the end of a deeply historical episode. As chief elder and master of ceremonies, he clears the floor and centers an important moment from the queer archives with additional commentary: "So, listen, I just want to take a moment to acknowledge one of the pioneers of the ballroom. In 1970, *pop, spin, dip* was introduced right here on the ballroom floor. Now, as legend would have it, Paris Dupree was flipping through a *Vogue* magazine and saw the poses that the models were doing. She brought it right back here to the ballroom floor—imitating the models to the beat. This is the category as we know it today. Know your history, children. Now . . . let's voggggueee like Paris."[52] Importantly, as Pray Tell provides this history lesson, Lemar—one of the show's most historically fluent dancers—physically enacts the communally specific vocabulary from the lesson. As he mentions "pop, spin, and dip," Lemar embodies the movements, which allows Pray Tell to provide both visual and auditory experiences for the eager learner. As the act of deliberate remembering proceeds, other characters join Lemar in the center of the ballroom floor to execute a precise, accurate, artful, and choreographed display for the children at the ball and those watching on their screens. All of this, of course, happens to the soundtrack of Madonna's hit song both to keep in time with the plot's treatment of her current ascendancy and to make clear the discrepancy between her mainstream fad and the deep subcultural history on which it depends. To place even greater focus on this moment, *Pose*'s creators give the final moments of the premiere over to this history and—crucially—let it take up significant narrative time.

The season's next episode, "Worth It," features a more indirect, nonverbal example of teaching from the ballroom archives.[53] In this particular iteration of the past, *Pose*'s creative team makes queer history *fashion*. As part of the show's love letter to Hector Xtravaganza, who died between seasons 1 and 2, "Worth It" features an iconic sartorial moment of his.[54] During the opening scene, Pray Tell announces the category:

Fashionable Femme Queens. From the start, he centers the relationship among fashion, creativity, and self-worth. When Lulu Ferocity hits the floor, Pray Tell builds anticipation and prepares the audience for an important reveal, instructing, "Pay attention."[55] Narrating the moment, he takes the children through Lulu's walk: "Aww, come on, Miss Lulu Ferocity. What'chu got yo'self cookin' up on tonight? I can tell something going on. Oh, she said, 'Hold on a minute. I got a thing to do.' Whatta you doin'? What are you serving us?"[56] When Lulu moves to the back of the floor, she takes off her tulle skirt to reveal her shiny, form-fitting pants underneath. The gag of the century is this: the skirt that she removes stands up on its own—opened up—as a stage prop. She stands beside it to serve body, face, and fashion to the beat, leaving everyone gagged by her innovation, creativity, and execution. Lulu's standing skirt is inspired by Xtravaganza's real-life tulle skirt ballroom gag.[57]

Though the show never points to this history explicitly, viewers fluent in the ballroom world might recognize the reference. To provide guidance, especially for some of the quieter historical references, *Pose* offers another clue by way of the epigraph that closes each episode of season 2. Bringing Xtravaganza directly to the fore for audiences, the creators use his words to form the epigraph that ends "Worth It": "Blood does not family make. Those are relatives. Family are those with whom you share your good, bad, and ugly, and still love one another in the end. Those are the ones you select. —Hector Xtravaganza, 1965–2018."[58] As Grace Dunham laments, "With so many trans [and queer] people disappeared and forgotten, few remained alive long enough to carry accounts of resistance into canonical histories."[59] Knowing this intimately, the show celebrates our known elders and reaches for those about whom we know little. Centering Xtravaganza's words, *Pose* draws a heart around its loving tribute to a grandfather of ballroom who left an indelible trace on the show's aesthetics, politics, and communal ethos.

Pose's Narrative Arcs Tell Our Queer Past

The third major category that organizes *Pose*'s contribution to remembering a collective queer past happens in protracted story lines that develop across episodes. Story lines that track Pray Tell and Blanca's experience with HIV/AIDS, the rise of Madonna's "Vogue"[60] and its impact, and Angel's modeling career all serve as chief examples. While the first and second categories focus on an isolated historical event (such as ACT UP's Stop the Church) or a moment in time (such as Xtravaganza's "standing skirt" stunt), this third category explores extended histories that often contain many developments and nuances across time and space. To be sure, such extended treatments of history raise fundamental questions about why the *Pose* creative team wants to return to these specific histories at this particular moment.

Pose starts its series in 1987 in the midst of the HIV/AIDS crisis—mainly through the lens of its two main characters, Pray Tell and Blanca. Though Pray Tell does not receive his HIV diagnosis until episode 4, "The Fever," he is the main conduit through which viewers engage this history.[61] Before his diagnosis, he communicates information through his dating life and shares his reflections through his friends' experiences with the virus. His character takes viewers into the halls of St. Vincent's Hospital, which served as an epicenter for the epidemic in New York City.[62] From his eyes and through his conversations with medical staff, we learn about the underfunded facility and the overworked medical providers. Additionally, we see images of patients neglected—some even dying in the hallways. From Pray Tell's meditations, *Pose* issues its strongest critique of governmental neglect and the politicized healthcare system. In so doing, Pray Tell offers unrelenting examinations of how race, gender, sexuality, and class inform Black and Brown queer and trans experiences with HIV/AIDS in America.

Furthermore, with scenes that detail specifics about access to medication in "Acting Up," *Pose* does not homogenize all queer people and their experiences with HIV/AIDS. By showing that access to the antiviral drug AZT for many Black and Brown queer and trans bodies relies on the generosity and deaths of upper-class white queer folks with HIV/AIDS—that remaining medicine was taken from those who passed and redistributed to those who could not afford access—the show demonstrates how economically stratified the epidemic has always been and what the valuation of life looks like, even *within* the queer HIV-positive community. Indeed, this dimension of the crisis is underrepresented, even though Black and Brown trans and queer communities were hit the hardest (and still are the most impacted and under-resourced).[63]

Through Pray Tell and Blanca, we also learn about how marginalized communities made a way out of no way. From Pray Tell and Blanca's friendship and their elder status as survivors, viewers do not receive only a bleak picture of dehumanization and victimization.[64] Pray Tell and Blanca speak out against systemic violence specific to the crisis, and they organize at the community level to make life more livable. In episodes like "Love Is the Message" and "Love's in Need of Love Today," they form partnerships to provide music, community, and fundraising to help those suffering most from the ravages of the disease.[65] Importantly, too, they help each other navigate their own experiences with the disease: they motivate each other to date and claim sexuality, and they offer accountability and inspiration when the world sees them as disposable.

Pose juxtaposes this protracted history of the epidemic for Black and Brown queer and trans folks in the late 1980s with the increasing gentrification and corporatization of New York City.[66] As audiences move from scenes of lack to scenes of excess, we are challenged to compare and contrast these two simultaneously developing worlds and to ask hard questions about what is present and absent in each. Certainly, *Pose* challenges viewers to identify which world is *real* and which world is *well*. Yes, HIV/AIDS is decimating Black and Brown queer and trans communities, but as *Pose* places two worlds side by side, viewers get the message that the communities suffering the most from disease (and the communities most often characterized as diseased) are far healthier communities in that they value love, collective survival, and living life openly and honestly, regardless of consequences. In contrast, characters in the world of access, power, and material wealth spend their time lying, manipulating, spending trivially, drowning in toxic masculinity, and prioritizing the plight of the individual above all else. Interestingly, these characters consistently find themselves attracted to the authenticity of folks in the ballroom world, but they cannot admit this openly and risk losing their power by embracing their desires.[67] By situating the drama in this queer history and by juxtaposing it with a corporatized New York City, *Pose* makes firm statements about power, access, equity, and authenticity.

As *Pose* continues its focus on extended history, the creators depict a quest for mainstream visibility and assess its limitations for those "represented." More specifically, season 2 tracks Madonna's ascendency and her interest in the ballroom world through her hit song "Vogue" in the early 1990s. With "Vogue," *Pose* introduces the possibility of mainstream visibility and maps crucial intracommunal debates about the value of mainstream acceptance. While Blanca, Angel, and Damon commit to capitalizing on this visibility, Pray Tell and Candy insist that Madonna is the latest example of appropriation without structural change.[68] As the season develops, viewers experience both the rise and fall of Madonna's "Vogue." The dance craze ends almost as quickly as it begins: opportunities fade, and the pang of being dropped plagues many characters. Afterward, the ballroom community must reestablish its own values, reinvigorate its own community, and reclaim its own power and worth.

By developing this history across a season, *Pose* accomplishes vital representation work. First, the show tells the fraught history of Madonna and her unethical appropriation of subcultural material and unfair use of marginalized bodies. Second, the show places this critique within a broader history of mainstream appropriation of subcultural innovation for a quick thrill and for the insidious production of profits for the people who need them the least. *Pose* uses Madonna's behavior to exemplify a history of abusing marginalized communities and exploiting their bold experimentation and innovation. The show thereby amplifies a rarely told history and shares a genealogy of influence that places credit where it belongs. *Pose*'s rendering of events exposes how queer histories of Madonna's icon status often sideline the contributions of queer and trans people of color and remain silent about their pain—what Snorton calls "erasure from historical memory to 'hegemonic whiteness.'"[69] Because "a narrative, formally and as a vehicle of ideology, accrues its meaning by constructing other forms of knowledge as unthought," the narratives we tell about our histories matter.[70] What *Pose* makes clear is that, again, available histories of queer culture further the same kind of white supremacist work that Madonna showcased when she told the world to "strike a pose."[71] And this story line chips away at those histories to offer a counternarrative that recovers artistic and political cultures sidelined.

The show furthers its exploration of visibility—its seduction and traps—through the character of Angel and her desire to be a model without getting clocked. From the season 2 premiere to the finale, the show features Angel's quest to become a beauty seen by the world. What starts as a "Fresh Face" campaign contest ends in a disappointing fall from grace as Angel is "outed" for being trans during a photoshoot and then blacklisted. As the show explores this arc, which is influenced by the real-life trans beauty pioneer Tracey Africa Norman, viewers see another instance in which Black and Brown trans and queer folks fight for visibility and dare to dream in a world not ready for them.[72] Through Angel's journey, *Pose* displays the darker sides of the world of glitz and glamour. She begs for a chance, appeals to white women's curious fascination with "voguing," and endures the sexual trespasses of unethical photographers who fetishize and extort trans bodies. Even as Angel experiences moments of success, she must live stealth—in constant fear of being exposed—and she must fight against the seduction of expensive drugs that saturate the modeling world. By the end of the arc, someone has taken control of her narrative, aired her "Tea," and ensured that work will be scarce in the United States. Nevertheless, true to form, *Pose* does not punctuate Angel's story with only loss and hopelessness. With Lil Papi and Ms. Ford lending helping hands, Angel ends her season 2 narrative by booking modeling work overseas. Importantly, this new work in the modeling field does not demand the silencing of her trans identity; rather, her identity is a gift.

Though she is never named explicitly, Norman serves as a historical influence for Angel's story line as she was the first major Black trans face on marketing for beauty products. In the 1970s, Norman appeared as a face for Clairol hair products and booked a major contract with Avon.[73] Similar to Angel, she was outed during a photoshoot, and her career took a tremendous hit, at least initially. Like Angel, she found success internationally (in Paris and Milan) and redefined her career. Most crucially, she also has found the most success after sharing her truth with the world, and like Angel, she found vital life-giving support from the ballroom community. Angel's story line spotlights Norman's pioneering bravery and her decision to endure heartbreak in and through community.[74] Like the Madonna story line, *Pose*'s depiction of Norman's history does much historical reparative work, particularly in a culture that reasons through trans identity from an ahistorical lens or that characterizes trans folks as a recent phenomenon. As Morgan

Page argues, "The media that make us visible simultaneously obscure our presence in history by continually framing trans people as new, as a modern, medicalized phenomenon only now coming to light in the topsy-turvy post–gay marriage world."[75] This is especially true for Black trans and queer folks, for as Snorton reminds us, "within New World grammars, blackness was defined as always out of time, out of place, wrong anyplace and anytime."[76] Refusing this ahistorical tendency, *Pose* nuances Angel's narrative and offers trans pioneers like Norman their rightful place as vital predecessors and boundary-breakers within their proper context.[77]

Pose *Gets "Social" and Connects with Queer Media to Retell Our History*

The fourth major category of remembering comes from extratextual sources—namely, the show's social media accounts and queer media's coverage of aired episodes. While the in-text citations, if you will, do much to expand the historical consciousness of its characters and viewers, *Pose* expands its centering of queer history by continuing the lessons beyond the immediate narrative of the show. In thinking through the potential and pitfalls of visibility and history, Huxtable discusses the value of technology: "I think social media is expanding the possibilities for both archiving the present and finding ways of revisiting and reading the past."[78] Through social media projects like #PoseFxFact and the "On This Day" feature, *Pose* uses its social media platforms on Facebook, Twitter, Instagram, and more to further historical references in the show and to extend the knowledge base of its audiences.[79]

At times, #PoseFxFact shares behind-the-scenes details, but often, the show will inform audiences more about a quieter nod to the past in the show. The posts might link to specific folks from history or to people who currently work in the community or might center a community organization, past or present. "On This Day" also spotlights facts from queer history.[80] These facts, as the name suggests, will match the date of the initial post and (oftentimes) be at least indirectly connected to the plot.[81] With these tools, the creative team keeps audiences engaged in between shows and ignites interest in what is to come, but these tools also serve important pedagogical functions to help audiences understand the historical content of the show.[82]

Pose's social media platforms also use animations blended with text to provide audiences with more visual explorations of ballroom knowledge. In particular, terms mentioned by Pray Tell (like *dip*, *pop*, and *spin*) get individual treatment on social media so that audiences can revel in the specifics and learn and practice some moves themselves. For example, one such post features the term *pyramid* and instructs followers carefully: "a triangle or pyramid-shaped formation, with two or more members of a house, executing arms and poses to the beat of the music."[83] As followers read the instructions, they can watch animations of the movement. Finally, the text of the social media post itself often encourages *Pose* lovers to get their own lives alongside these animations—to join the community with their own movements. Mel Chen notes a similar function of a networked world: "The internet allows . . . [trans folks] to make their archives usable, not as moribund repositories, but as generative resources for identity."[84] Using social media expansively, *Pose* makes learning the past a distinctly communal affair.[85]

Additionally, queer media works with *Pose* to ignite further dialogue about queer history. Outlets like Logo's *NewNowNext* or *Out* will regularly follow up an episode of *Pose* with more contextual details about a plotline or a historical reference in the show.[86] For example, when *Pose* aired "Butterfly/Cocoon," queer media continued the conversation by contextualizing the narrative with a story about Dorian Corey to take audiences further into the queer archives.[87] When the show tackles historical experiences from queer icons who are still with us, queer media outlets will link together the show's historical material with interviews and Q&As with those folks today. In the case of Angel's story line and its relationship to the real-life experience of Tracey Africa Norman, the show's social media and larger queer media outlets worked together both to nuance the plot of the show and to elevate the historical experiences and contemporary work of Norman.[88] And without a doubt, by providing all of this extratextual material, *Pose* continues to educate audiences well beyond the confines of the narrative and has the potential to raise the consciousness of other queer readers who may or may not be watching the show.

Throughout each of these major categories, *Pose* makes its goals clear: history matters, and the past is ever-present. As the show develops, the creative team becomes more deliberate in its efforts to recover an often-elided or incomplete queer past, particularly for Black and Brown queer and trans communities. Miss Major spotlights the drastic need for this when she says, "We have a history of trans people that didn't just start with me, or with Laverne Cox being on the cover of *Time*; it started *years* ago."[89] While representations of contemporary LGBTQ+ life like *Love, Simon* present queerness as ahistorical and only a matter of divergent sexual object choice, *Pose* insists on a more dynamic view of queerness that is steeped in history and context and that reckons with power. *Love, Simon*'s title character sees little value in a collective past—except for Googling fashion tips—and grows into his sexuality without historical consciousness or elders.[90] And without any reckoning of power, he never accounts for his privilege and furthers the work of white supremacy. Simon successfully enters into the mainstream mostly because he rejects the need for queer particularity and assumes an ahistorical and non-threatening posture.

Contrastingly, the characters in *Pose*'s re-created world need the lessons of the past to move through an inequitable present and build an equitable future. To be sure, one could cite varied uses of narrative time to reason away these differences between *Love, Simon* and *Pose*, but *Pose*'s return to the past is not about nostalgia. Rather, *Pose* offers guidance for the present through its recovery of a denigrated queer past.[91] As Page argues, "Yet, despite all this visibility, trans people remain largely historically isolated, adrift on the sea of history, with little access to knowledge of where we came from and who got us there."[92] Through its dynamic representation of queer history, the show attempts to fill this gap and encourages audiences to ask questions about whose perspectives and narrative priorities influence content creation and shape consciousness. Furthermore, *Pose* motivates questions about how furthering white supremacy relies on boasting certain perspectives and sidelining others, especially when offering incomplete progress narratives.[93] Page's discussion of building trans history highlights the importance of race: "Racist transphobic harassment in the archive adds another layer of inaccessibility to trans history."[94] For the characters in *Pose*, intersectionality matters, and progress narratives remain questionable at best: health disparities in HIV/AIDS care persist, institutional violence continues to impact them disproportionately, and their histories remain sidelined for white-washed narratives of the past.[95] A *Love, Simon* approach just won't do.

"The System Is Never on Our Side": *Pose*'s Critique of Institutional Authority

In addition to embracing excess and foregrounding queer history, *Pose* establishes an oppositional position toward state power and broader institutions that symbolize and/or perpetuate inequities for Black and Brown queer and trans communities. As Dunham argues, "Trans political life was not born out of institutions; it rubbed up against and resisted them."[96] Beginning with the pilot, Canals, Murphy, and Falchuk prepare audiences for that resistance and for what to expect from the show by penning a scene of disruption. In the opening sequence, the House of Abundance breaks into a New York City museum to steal its art exhibition—one that features costumes of royal powers—so that they can walk in a ball category called "Royalty."

For our conversation, several components of this scene emerge as crucial. First, during its introduction to the world, *Pose* features key characters acting as figures of disruption. Refusing to abide by normative time, they enter into the museum right before closing time, hide in the building, and then emerge to do their generative work when the lights go down. Second, the ball category and museum exhibition bring power and the unequal distribution of wealth into explicit focus. Third, the strategy that the House of Abundance adopts is not one of asking or begging; instead, they take. When Lulu asks Elektra what they should take from the museum, she answers, "Everything."[97] Fourth, as they attempt to leave the darkened museum, they find themselves trapped inside. To get out, they literally have to bust through the glass. From their entrance to their exit, the characters disrupt and exercise force to get what they need.

In addition to depicting how the House of Abundance demands access and occupies space—where low-income trans and queer folks of color are not welcomed—*Pose* also demonstrates a transferal of power from the confines of a Midtown museum to the balls uptown.[98] The characters do not just remove the royal costumes from the highly sur-veilled museum; they also transfer and repurpose them—and all the power that they historically represent—to an epicenter of queer power. Indeed, Elektra and her children don the mopped finery to break necks at the ball and slay the judges—earning tens across the board. They take these prized possessions where they are not supposed to and assign alternative value to them.

Even when the cops finally bust into the ball to arrest the members of the House of Abundance, the writers pace the narrative to ensure that the House of Abundance receives communal adulation before facing state authority. Moreover, the cops do not stop the party as much as they punctuate the ending of a fierce ballroom showing. While the writers could have easily written a scene in which the cops raid the room, snatch wigs (in the undesirable way), confiscate the booty, and violently apprehend the "criminals," instead they construct a scene in which Elektra incorporates the police into her stunning performance of royalty. Pray Tell participates in Elektra's use of police presence by intensifying the moment through narrating Elektra's use of state authority as props. He solidifies this when he notes "and that's how you do a ball" as the House of Abundance files out in handcuffs.[99] His concluding remark, which precedes the first explosive opening credits, reveals a deep truth about *Pose*: while the community will have its own standards, rules, and priorities that will be managed accordingly, resistance to state authority and institutional powers will be centered and celebrated.

Pose's oppositional position should not be viewed as advocating anarchy. The characters' encounters with institutional authorities do not promote an inability to follow rules, act orderly, or behave respectfully. Because *Pose* emphasizes equity and justice, engagements with author-ity are contextualized and developed to showcase the injustices of sys-tems and structures.[100] Each one highlights systemic disparities fueled by combinations of various *isms* that disempower the show's queer and trans world. While examples are plentiful, an indictment of the criminal justice system in "Butterfly/Cocoon" and "Never Knew Love like This Before"[101] and a disruption of violent religious doctrine in "Acting Up" serve as illustrative.[102] Since these characters live at the intersections of marginalized identities, racism, sexism, homophobia, transphobia, ableism, and classism shape their lives, and the show addresses and critiques these.

Perhaps the clearest example of *Pose*'s anti-state position occurs in its condemnation of the justice system in "Butterfly/Cocoon" and "Never Knew Love like This Before." In the former, Elektra has a sex-work client die in her workplace, so she goes immediately to Blanca and Candy for advice.[103] In "Butterfly/Cocoon," the show presents a narrative arc that centers Black trans women having an explicit conversation about their unique place in the system. While Blanca urges Elektra to call the cops, Candy provides an alternative narrative about the justice system: "Call the po-po's, and ya definitely going to jail. . . . Ain't no way that your broke ass is beating the best lawyers that white money can buy."[104] When Blanca stresses that Elektra is innocent and the police will protect her, Candy continues, "They not gonna believe a bunch of transsexuals, girl."[105] Candy insists that Elektra ask girls before turning herself in to the police.

Echoing Candy's lack of faith is Euphoria. Euphoria, as someone who has navigated the criminal justice system as a Black trans sex worker, shares a hard truth: "Miss Elektra crossed the one line that our kind ain't allowed to ever cross. We're the ones supposed to get beat up and die, not them. . . . And I don't care if they got the guy dying on video. You gonna take the fall. For girls like us, the system is never on our side."[106] To solidify her assessments, which she ultimately characterizes as a prison industrial complex, she tells a story about her encounter with an older white John and law enforcement. In her narrative, the man attacked her first, and she fought back. And even though the cops witnessed him beating her, she took the fall. Because the cops were systemically primed to see her as a criminal and as an object of deceit—disposable or at least not worthy of protection—the John drove away, and she was sent to jail.

The episode's indictment of state power continues as Euphoria gives a testimony of her time in jail: "On my first day in Rikers, I got beat up. On my second day, a guard tells me he could keep me safe—even sneak in some cosmetics . . . maybe even a good wig. But it wasn't kindness: he was just makin' me pretty so he could pimp me out."[107] With Euphoria, *Pose* reveals the criminalization of trans sex workers and amplifies the violence they face once incarcerated. Ultimately, *Pose* also spotlights how authorities partake in their own hypocritical version of the sex trade.[108] Indeed, one's race, gender, sexuality, or class status can lead them into vulnerable underground economies and position them in a dangerous relationship to a state power that, in Euphoria's words, already wants to "rough [them] up a little."[109]

Pose further explores the fundamental devaluation of Black and Brown trans and queer lives by institutional authority in "Never Knew Love like This Before." In this heart-wrenching episode, the rambunctious but communally minded Candy Ferocity is murdered by one of her Johns and left dead in an abandoned hotel room.[110] Resisting a trauma-porn approach, the majority of the episode focuses on the value of Candy's life, the community's response to loss, and its resilience rather than on the murder per se.[111] However, the episode does amplify the main tenets of the #BlackTransLivesMatter movement—one that centers disproportionate violence faced by Black trans women, which is often ignored or mischaracterized by state power and elided in conversations about institutional violence against cisgender Black lives.[112]

Depicting this specific epidemic of violence, the episode centers indictments of several interrelated systems and institutions that contribute to the unabated murders. First, Elektra's commentary exposes the lack of care from state power for these murders. Specifically, Elektra notes, "The NYPD doesn't care about a murdered transsexual. We've never been treated with respect or dignity. Candy's death isn't any different."[113] Second, "Never Knew Love like This Before" showcases how the institutional violence does not stop with a lack of protection of trans lives or justice for their deaths. After her death, Candy's communally defined family structure cannot even gain access to her body to give her a proper burial. Indeed, the episode is careful to show how the law does not extend rights to alternative configurations of family in a time of loss. When Nurse Judy, Elektra, and Blanca appeal to the state for access to Candy's body, the state employee responds, "I'm sorry for your loss, but you're asking me to break the law."[114] By appealing to the employee's own queerness, Judy convinces him to break the law, but *Pose* shows that this is further injustice and causes more emotional labor during a painful time. Third, Candy's death raises the issue of dead-naming or misgendering trans or gender non-conforming people as a final act of systemic violence.[115] During the ceremony, the community emphasizes

Candy's self-identity without question—no matter who tries to identify her otherwise.

Not only does the episode unequivocally denounce the inequities created and maintained by state authority, but it also demonstrates how cultural logics and state (in)action mutually inform each other. Before the communal healing work begins, Pray Tell offers an opening speech to the mourners that demonstrates an uncomfortable truth: because these marginalized communities cannot appeal to the state for safety and protection, they must assume the responsibility themselves. As Pray Tell's notes, "We are charged to continue on living through this tragedy so that *we can fight our hardest to protect our sisters* from the hands of men who are weak—who are afraid to deal with their desires."[116] With his speech, he empowers the community to protect themselves, indirectly critiquing the state's refusal to serve.

Furthermore, he dispels an often-touted defense used by those who do harm to trans and gender non-conforming folks. Rather than entertaining a narrative of justification that paints trans women as objects of deception that induce "trans or gay panic" on the part of unsuspecting cisgender heterosexual men, *Pose* critiques these men for their inability to confront their non-normative desires.[117] Taking Miss Major's logic seriously—"society's got to be accountable for building this type of fear"—the show indirectly indicts a culture that treats trans women as disposable objects and refuses to make affirmative space for trans-loving folks.[118] All the while, the episode explains who pays the price for these structural problems, especially in the closing uncredited epigraph that provides staggering statistics and concludes the somber but therapeutic episode.[119] Depicting what Snorton calls "an alchemy of black criminalization, violence, disappearance, and death," *Pose* refuses to "mask the links between criminalization, carcerality, and death that produce blackness and transness as objects of necropolitical valuation."[120] To be sure, in "Butterfly/Cocoon" and "Never Knew Love like This Before," *Pose* continues its antithetical position toward institutional power and rejects a narrative of respectability that translates Black and Brown trans and queer folks into agents of the state.

Not only does *Pose* indict the criminal justice system, but the show also articulates its oppositional relationship to other iterations of institutional violence by featuring a disruption of violent religious doctrine in "Acting Up."[121] While the episode illustrates broader governmental neglect and the political value of ACT UP's fight against HIV/AIDS, the narrative centers a rendering of ACT UP's Stop the Church demonstration, which occurred on December 12, 1989.[122] Though the chronology is altered, *Pose*'s decision to foreground queer opposition to religious institutions is noteworthy in its efforts to foreground power. "Acting Up" situates Pray Tell in an ACT UP meeting in which the organization plans the Stop the Church protest.[123]

Articulating the community's concerns with the church, the character of Syd notes the following: "The Catholic church has spent millions of dollars putting the false message into the world that condoms don't work and that abstinence is the only way to fight HIV. That is a lie, and that is morally wrong. So, we're staging a die-in in the middle of that congregation as a peaceful protest against the annihilation of our community."[124] Syd spotlights the church's power and its harmful rhetoric that links public health to religious views of morality. As Syd ignites Pray Tell's consciousness, they offer the following closing observation: "We will not allow . . . racist, sexist, homophobic ideologies to affect the health of every single person on this planet."[125] Now politicized, Pray Tell takes the information back uptown, and he and Blanca recruit for the protest. With Syd's commentary and Pray Tell and Blanca's recruiting, "Acting Up" does crucial work. The episode suggests a disruption of business as normal to show that the church's beliefs, actions, and power pose a direct threat to Black and Brown trans and queer folks.

The episode hammers home an oppositional relationship to religious violence by reimagining the protest and inserting its lead characters in St. Patrick's Cathedral. From the protestors' entry into the church, the writers expose the church's financial power. When Lil Papi marvels, "This look like a lot of money," Angel responds, "Mmhmm, and you know they ain't payin' taxes on any of this shit."[126] From the outset, viewers juxtapose the Evangelistas' fundamental lack of resources with the immense wealth and political power of the church.

After bringing this structural critique to the fore, "Acting Up" dramatizes moments from the actual demonstration in which protesters made mock programs like those common at a religious service. Instead of featuring conventional details like scriptures, schedules, or lyrics to a religious song, the program details ACT UP's critique of the church in enumerated fashion. Foregrounding details of institutional violence, the camera zooms in to reveal the text in the program. In the largest font at the top, we see the following headline: "END CHURCH INTER-FERENCE IN OUR LIVES."[127] Then the brochure provides a subtitle and a list detailing how the church uses its power to damage the lives and futures of queers. As the mock program details "THE SINS OF THE CARDINAL AND CHURCH POLITICIANS," it lists affronts ranging from blaming queer people for AIDS to discouraging condom use and needle exchange programs.[128] The critique intensifies as Angel argues, "Abstinence is not a human solution," and as Pray Tell shouts, "Arrest the cardinal; he's the criminal."[129] Modeling "Silence = Death," *Pose* indicts religious leaders and reverses narratives about moral health and criminality.[130]

Examining the justice system and the church, *Pose* demonstrates how institutions not only regularly fail to support Black and Brown queer and trans communities but also consistently victimize them.[131] In *Pose*'s rendering, institutional authority does not protect and serve and does not sanctify or provide salvation. For these characters, institutions fail and must be exposed and critiqued. Furthermore, since "institutional thinking replicates hierarchy and puts power in the hands of the state in ways that problematically devalue community and place-based power," alternatives must be developed intracommunally.[132] In short, characters must succeed *in spite of institutions rather than because of them*.

While one might suggest that *Pose*'s institutional critique is limited to the historical era that it depicts, placing the show against *Love, Simon* pays critical dividends once more. As we argued in chapter 3, Simon's cisgender white body qualifies for institutional protection, even though the gender non-conforming Black character, Ethan, remains unprotected. When Ethan is bullied, institutional authority never intervenes, and violence is not acknowledged. Simon even blames Ethan's "excess" for the bullying. When Simon's body becomes the target, institutional powers respond immediately, and the film centers a lesson about bullying and gives it narrative prominence.

Even though *Love, Simon* never fully realizes and responds to Ethan's pain, careful viewers can discern which bodies matter and which do not for institutional authority. Perhaps the harshest irony is that a Black woman teacher acts as a figure of authority to rescue Simon. While the film touts a progressive message of inclusion, it actually reinscribes the long-standing mammy trope and showcases how institutions neglect to protect queer and trans folks equally across racial lines.[133] The Black queer body in *Love, Simon* is also failed by institutions, but the film's anti-disruptive posture snuffs this critique in favor of a progressive narrative about inclusion. But Micha Cárdenas makes a convincing case for when visibility is problematic and when it is effective: "An abolitionist trans politics requires that visibility for trans [and queer] people of color not be promoted in the absence of anti-prison, antipolice, and anticolonial critiques, because it is precisely this absence which allows neoliberalism to manage the determination of which trans people are acceptable . . . and which trans people are disposable."[134] If we combine *Pose*'s anti-institutional critique and *Love, Simon*'s elision of power, we see that what looks like progress can be deceptive. Perhaps *Pose* supplies lessons in defiance and also provides alternative ways to reread other texts celebrated as progressive.[135]

"Houses Are Homes": Belonging beyond the Nuclear Family

In addition to *Pose*'s strong anti-institutional stance toward the criminal justice system and the church, the show also assesses the narratives of the nuclear family and features a series-long exploration of what it means to establish alternatives for kinship and belonging. Throughout both seasons, *Pose* foregrounds extended conversations about what constitutes community-building to spotlight what facilitates it, what impedes it, and what forecloses it. Furthermore, the show regularly performs comparative work to expose the limits of the nuclear family, especially its failure to attend to the specific needs of Black and Brown queer and trans people.[136] As Brittney Cooper suggests, "Queer Black folks have survived precisely because they have refused to let traditional ideas about what love and relationships look like dictate what is possible."[137]

Whether viewers look at Damon's abandonment by his birth family, Angel's birth father's physical and mental abuse, or Blanca's birth brother and sister's emotional and physical abuse during their birth mother's death, *Pose* demonstrates the harm of the nuclear family.[138] In many of the critiques, though, the focus is structural; *Pose* does not demonize individuals in nuclear families as much as it resists the rigid narratives that structure the family—ones that render queer folks as excessive.[139] With instances like Blanca's birth mother and Candy's birth parents struggling to love their children across difference, viewers realize how these rigid narratives limit everyone—even those who fit within its parameters.[140] What becomes clear is that these culturally endorsed scripts are harmful to all. Rather than presenting the nuclear family as an institution that queer folks should reincorporate themselves back into, *Pose* shows the cost of that approach. Because reincorporation delimits queer folks and demands that they contort themselves into existing frameworks that do not serve them, *Pose* argues for "coming together in ways that don't replicate the state's moral imperatives" and fighting against contingent tolerance.[141]

Not only does *Pose* expose the limiting narratives that inform the nuclear family, but the show also builds other possibilities that sustain and nurture queer folks as they are or want to be. More specifically, *Pose* offers queer alternatives as a healing balm and as a model for a more liberatory future. With its reparative work, *Pose* centers alternative models of kinship, explores the impact of queer elders, prioritizes the well-being of the communal, and promotes a politics of accountability to the group. While broader cultural discourse denigrates, diseases, or disregards queer configurations of kinship and community as inauthentic or as less than, the show amplifies the unique structure, logics, and ethics of care that saturate them.[142]

Continuing its educational work, *Pose* provides divergent paths to community by introducing the deliberate development of houses as alternatives to the nuclear family. Mainly through Blanca's construction of the House of Evangelista, audiences learn about the specifics of ballroom—from its family structure to its vocabulary and from its responsibilities to its conflicts.[143] From the pilot episode forward, Blanca (as house mother) offers the most careful and endorsed model of what ballroom culture means and why it is so important. With her relationship with her house children, Blanca teaches audiences how Black and Brown queer and trans folks face intersectional obstacles that require attention and support.[144] She "emphasize[s] the critical need to care for other trans [queer] people in rich and variant ways."[145] She provides shelter, culturally competent resources, and inspiration, but she also requires accountability.

In the House of Evangelista, the members bind together to cultivate physical as well as emotional well-being. They share resources, divide roles and responsibilities, problem-solve together, navigate trauma collectively, and listen and hold one another closely. For instance, when Damon's birth family renders him homeless, Blanca provides him with shelter. When Angel feels the unrelenting pain of childhood trauma, Blanca intervenes to help her re-remember. When Elektra finds herself abandoned by her "daddy," Blanca functions as a refuge.[146] In example after example, *Pose* makes clear how house families operate as a corrective in a world that seeks to crush Black and Brown queer and trans folks or to hold them accountable to heteronormative standards that do not apply. As the exemplar of house culture, Blanca's home alleviates homelessness, prevents starvation, curbs addiction, and helps build dreams for queer people on their own terms. Finally, the show uses her character and house more broadly to evaluate the values of other houses and to critique those that have embraced neoliberal values that harm—rather than support—communities already under siege.

Extending its reimagining of family, *Pose* focuses on the presence of elders to rethink who takes responsibility for future generations. Rather than young people receiving guidance from their birth parents, church leaders, or teachers, house mothers and fathers join other manifestations of queer elders to lead the community. Furthermore, when particular communities cannot rely on the government and other institutions for their education and protection, elder presence takes on more significance. In communities that suffer from racism, sexism, transphobia, homophobia, poverty, and the AIDS crisis, the term *elder* undergoes further redefinition. These elders come from unconventional places, and their profiles differ. Blanca is not even in her late thirties, yet she is an elder figure due to increasing death tolls and reduced life expectancies.[147] In this way, *Pose* rethinks who is responsible for whom and redefines elders for an endangered community.

From the pilot to the finale of season 2, *Pose* illustrates how important elders are to a vulnerable younger generation. While the lessons concerning elder presence persist, episodes like "Blow" offer pointed depictions of how elders anticipate needs, respond to verbal and non-verbal signs of crisis, and challenge young people to grow.[148] These elders must learn how to love and how to prepare young queer folks for a world that does not love them back. In this episode, Madonna's "Vogue" promise has faded, and Damon, Ricky, and Lulu have lost their purpose and confidence. Seeing this, Blanca and Pray Tell gather them, give loving critique, and provide a pathway for rediscovering themselves.[149] The plan that the elders initiate—which encourages the younger generation to design a political protest, one that reimagines the actual ACT UP protest of covering Senator Jesse Helms's home with a giant condom—serves multiple objectives: the young folks rediscover their purpose, collaborate with the community for resources, and resist an external world full of logics that rob them of life. Instead of being rescued by an outsider, queer folks save themselves—guided by their elders—and take ownership for leading an uncertain future.

Additionally, the show also demonstrates how queer elders can find their own purpose and value in their leadership role. In the case of Blanca and Pray Tell, this is a distinct purpose that gives them a will to live. Because both principal elders are HIV-infected, *Pose* nods to how they can find peace by making imprints on the future generation with their time remaining. This is clearest in the season 2 "In My Heels" finale when Blanca fights a health crisis with an uncertain future.[150] Since her house children have all found their paths, Blanca finds herself in an empty House of Evangelista and ready to surrender to the virus. But by the end of the episode, she discovers renewed purpose in two new young characters who need the benefits of a loving house family. Similar to how she finds and nurtures a discarded and endangered Damon in season 1, Blanca introduces herself to the new potential children and perks up as she realizes she is needed again. Gesturing toward the pilot in which Blanca processes her HIV diagnosis and finds purpose by starting her house, "In My Heels" reminds Blanca of why she must fight for life and of how queer and trans young people are abandoned and need elders.[151]

It is no accident that Blanca joins Pray Tell to care for the new young characters, for it is Pray Tell who initially tells Blanca during the pilot episode how and why house families will always be needed in queer spaces. In a full-circle moment, "In My Heels" ends with that very message from Pray Tell in 1987 by way of an epigraph. The self-referential moment for the show demonstrates to audiences how consistently *Pose* centers the role of queer elders and why: the elder role amplified in *Pose* is queer and provides queer and trans young people with the specific guidance they need to navigate the world in the bodies and identities they inhabit.[152] The elders do not demand queer restraint and do not leave the young folks to navigate their differences solo.

A common refrain from *Pose*'s alternative models of kinship and belonging is that folks must prioritize the communal over the individual. Taking a stance against the valorization of the individual and the rhetoric of capitalism that lobbies for solo success regardless of who must be sacrificed, *Pose* argues that communal well-being takes precedent.[153] Whether it is a question of money, other material resources, duties and responsibilities, professional accomplishments, or physical and emotional health, the show remains steadfast in its insistence on "we" language. To belong to the House of Evangelista, individuals must agree to contribute to the fabric of the collective; relatedly, individuals cannot selfishly choose to partake in any activities that could harm the whole group (i.e., lying, stealing, or doing drugs). Viewers should not mistake this ethos for respectability, though. For example, sex work is not judged, but doing/selling drugs is because it could infect the house with police presence or violence or addiction.

In the House of Evangelista, everyone contributes based on their skills and opportunities. For example, when Angel makes money from the piers or modeling, she provides financially. When Elektra joins the house and has a stable income, she helps pay the rent. Similarly, when characters lack capital, they must provide otherwise. For instance, when Lil Papi does not have money, he provides discounted or free food from his job at a bodega. When characters can provide neither money nor food, they contribute by cleaning, cooking, shopping, and doing errands to prepare for a ball. This group mentality becomes obvious in the smallest of activities, like preparing meals. As a structuring principle, *Pose* uses these meal times and the symbolism of dinner tables to handle communal business, often at the beginning or end of an episode.[154] In these moments, they divide labor and problem-solve collectively, regardless of the issue at hand.

Pose's focus on a communal ethos/praxis extends beyond material survival. When characters strive for professional success or artistic accolades, they strive to achieve communal benefits. And if a particular character errs on the side of individualism, a character like Blanca or Pray Tell will often reframe the quest for success in light of what it could bring to the group. For example, when Damon finds success as a dancer, the expectation is that his win is a communal win. The group will help him get there, but he will also bring those skills to the balls. Furthermore, he will build a House of Evangelista overseas once his dance career takes him beyond the United States.[155] In the same vein, Angel becomes a "fresh face" model, but she will bring that experience back to the balls, and she will help inspire careers like that displayed by Lil Papi and the formation of his talent management company.[156] More often than not, the Evangelistas articulate *Pose*'s commitment to necessary and fulfilling communal victories. Even when an individual snatches a trophy at the balls, they are doing it for the house rather than for themselves.

Although the House of Evangelista serves as a model example of belonging, *Pose* does not necessarily romanticize its articulation of community. Instead, the show deliberately depicts the labor of building these types of spaces. Inasmuch as Blanca's house provides a model, her house conflicts also remind viewers of how important it is to promote a politics of accountability. Certain characters are held accountable by other members of the community, especially when a character falls victim to chasing individual success. Additionally, all characters are held accountable by the narrative arc, as *Pose* makes the values of the show clear to audiences.

While examples of communal accountability abound, two narrative threads that promote accountability address drug use and sexual health. In the first, characters battle the presence of drugs in their community. Even though Blanca demands a drug-free house and children, things do not always go according to plan. When Blanca evicts Lil Papi in "Pink Slip" because he lies and sells drugs, she makes it clear that his behavior puts everyone at risk; then the events in the show make it clear to him that his chosen path is a dead end and far riskier than Blanca's survival strategies (like sex work).[157] Likewise, when Damon tries to guide Angel toward sobriety in "Blow" and "Revelations," he privately warns her of the dangers to her and the house, but when that does not work, he publicly confronts her because the well-being of the house is more important than his private loyalty to her. In the same arc, Blanca reasons away the accusations against Angel, but Angel accepts the accountability Damon demands; then, in turn, she holds her house mother accountable for favoritism. The stakes are high for Angel, but she takes responsibility for her drug use and challenges Blanca to hold all Evangelistas to the same standards.[158]

While drug use anchors several accountability arcs, sexual health and the HIV/AIDS crisis form another important narrative thread that emphasizes responsibility. From the earliest episodes, *Pose* makes it clear that community members need to take care of themselves and protect one another, especially because institutions will continue to fail. Characters like Pray Tell or Blanca hold other characters accountable for being tested, practicing sex in ways that reduce risk, and seeking medical care. Since no character is immune to accountability, Blanca and Pray Tell even hold each other accountable for managing their HIV infections.

Beyond these refrains about sexual health, the show addresses the HIV/AIDS crisis and accountability in a few pointed ways. For example, when Ricky tells Pray Tell that he's had unsafe sex with another partner behind Damon's back, Pray Tell holds Ricky accountable for being tested and communicating openly with Damon. This is not just a moralizing moment for Pray Tell; he goes the extra mile to take Ricky to get tested. When the result is positive, he again reminds Ricky of how vital it is to inform Damon.[159] Importantly, though, *Pose* does not provide a directive as much as it advises that one must disclose when and how one feels safest but never put another community member at risk and rob them of the ability to make informed choices.

"Acting Up" features the loudest accountability lesson when Pray Tell confronts Elektra for abandoning her community during a health crisis. Directly and intensely, Pray Tell unequivocally rejects Elektra's valorization of the individual and her misguided priorities in the French Revolution–themed ball scene.[160] Through a public exchange, Pray Tell uses the ballroom floor and his position as MC to shame Elektra, bolster a communal value system, and condemn a toxic approach. While Pray Tell quietly holds Ricky accountable, he publicly snatches Elektra's wig to demand better. This is due to the generational differences between Ricky and Elektra; however, Pray Tell's louder approach also makes sense as a response to Elektra because characters regularly hold her accountable for being communal, even though she mostly fails to remain in step. Loud or quiet, *Pose* insists that a sound community only sustains itself if everyone is invested and embraces accountability. But because *Pose* depicts the messier sides of community-building, it provides a dynamic view of the labor required to unlearn and relearn what it means to live without centering the self.

Pose challenges its characters to rethink their values and question a solo victory, particularly when it requires sacrificing any component of the community, and the show also urges a rethinking of the progress narratives that animate current queer politics. It asks viewers to consider who *exactly* is progressing.[161] Relatedly, with its unwavering philosophy of what constitutes success, progress, and liberation, *Pose* asks us to reconsider how we celebrate cultural representation and how we might uncritically conflate visibility with advancement. Equipped with the lessons offered by *Pose*, we can reread supposedly progressive narratives—like *Love, Simon*—that saturate our current representational landscape, especially through the lens of community. *Pose* insists on a communal ethos and creates space for alternative configurations of kinship and belonging, but *Love, Simon* remains firm in its commitment to the nuclear family and the valorization of the individual. In Berlanti's film, Simon's secret fractures the nuclear family, and he must repair it—namely, by learning how to reintegrate into an existing structure without disrupting it too much.[162] That is his primary work in the film. And even though Albertalli's novel (the film's source) places Simon in queer space and centers queer community, the film minimizes his difference and promotes sameness.[163]

Furthermore, as we discussed in chapter 3, Simon's mother's emotional monologue continues to inform our ongoing critical discussion, particularly as it relates to community. When his mother tells him that being gay is "his thing" and that he must go through parts of it "alone," she presents his queerness as something that necessarily isolates him. What she or the film cannot imagine for him—namely, a community that might support him—is exactly what *Pose* offers its characters as the primary resource for their survival and success. Indeed, for the folks in *Pose*, the power of joy comes in and through belonging to a queer kinship network. Since *Pose* is not interested in the nuclear family that fractures because of a queer child, the show can focus firmly on the queer subject and their needs.

"You Maintained Your Dignity": *Pose* Redefines Dignity through Community

While the alternative kinship structures in *Pose* provide the characters with material resources, physical safety, and emotional comfort, they also provide a distinct framework through which to rethink dignity. And the show's alternative conceptualization of dignity stands in stark contrast to the dominant neoliberal deployment of dignity that valorizes individualism, private success, and heteronormative family and monogamy.[164] Even though these tendencies are applauded in narratives like *Love, Simon*, *Pose* lobbies for another path. Indeed, *Pose*'s oppositional understanding of dignity is clear: striving for a version of dignity that relies on abandoning communal praxis does not lead to collective liberation and demands sacrifices too great to make.

While *Pose*'s alternative value system is clear, not every character thinks or acts in opposition to the normative thrusts of neoliberalism. Mapping the character development of its central Black trans women—Blanca, Angel, and Elektra—brings to light *Pose*'s critique of dignity. Whereas Blanca articulates her inability to "pass" and how that impacts her life, Angel and Elektra are both characterized as women in close proximity to a cisgender norm and who are closest to the possibilities of neoliberal dignity. By triangulating among the three, we argue that *Pose* demonstrates how seductive conventional narratives of dignity can be and showcases that alternatives emerge from folks who do not qualify under current prescriptions.[165]

As the show's moral center, Blanca champions a community-first approach, perhaps because she exists most beyond the limits of neoliberal dignity. From the opening scenes, she sets her eyes on building a house, but she is not doing so only to snatch trophies or bolster her ego. Unlike the Elektra-led House of Abundance, Blanca's House of Evangelista has one primary objective: creating a space full of resources, safety, guidance, accountability, and belonging. Because Blanca was orphaned after sharing her trans identity, she knows intimately the dangers of homelessness, joblessness, and starvation. Beyond those immediate needs, she recognizes how harmful it can be to move through the world without a sense of worth, purpose, and belonging. The culture she builds and models for others is animated by those values. When characters need to learn hard lessons about what to prioritize and value, Blanca is never far from the conversation. Whether she is protecting the integrity of community in her own home or in the broader world, she emerges as a mirror of the show's philosophies and politics and as a role model for others. Blanca joins Pray Tell as one of *Pose*'s teachers who stresses alternative conceptions of dignity.

Perhaps Blanca's relationship to dignity is most evident when she attends the funeral of her birth mother in "Mother's Day."[166] Even though Blanca's birth siblings attempt to bar her from mourning because they perceive her presence as disruptive, she demands space and reclaims her right to grieve in community with the House of Evangelista. She goes to the funeral and does not attempt to "butch it up" to satisfy the expectations of her birth family. Throughout the experience, she is misgendered, characterized as a threat, and physically harmed, but she insists on her right to mourn and occupy space fully.[167] After the ceremony, Damon directly invokes the language of dignity to support Blanca: "I couldn't have done it. I would have been too scared. You maintained your dignity, and I'm proud of you."[168] Through his assessment, Damon gestures toward how Blanca's dignity is not contingent on the nuclear family's approval of her. Instead of attending the funeral in ways that satisfy the expectations of her assigned sex at birth—or not attending altogether—Blanca maintains her dignity through the assertion of her trans identity and the support of her chosen family. Through this reference to dignity, *Pose* suggests that dignity does not derive from conformity to respectability; instead, the show argues that Blanca maintains dignity precisely because she *refuses* to conform.[169] Finally, her negotiation of dignity happens firmly in and through the members of her chosen family.

While Blanca occupies an almost-unwavering communal position, other characters struggle with where to assign value. As *Pose* tracks their journeys into consciousness, it continues to reiterate an alternative understanding of dignity. Angel serves as an interesting example in character development. Even though she initially does not follow Blanca to the House of Evangelista, by the end of the pilot, Angel moves toward Blanca's version of motherhood and community. But Angel's transition to Evangelista does not signal her adoption of Blanca's ideas around community and belonging and their relationship to dignity.

As season 1 progresses, Angel finds herself entangled with Stan, an upwardly mobile finance professional who is cisgender, straight, married, and white. He is trans-attracted and does not know how to process his desires. Initially, Angel looks to him for financial safety, but they start to build a romance that is turbulent, passionate, and revealing. As their relationship intensifies, Stan offers Angel the status of a kept woman.[170] Angel responds, "I should refuse you, right? Demand commitment? But I've also learned how to keep my dignity, even when I'm kneeling down for scraps—under the table."[171] In this provocative conversation, she toys with the idea of demanding something akin to the heterosexual norm of romance precisely because of her ability to pass and integrate into normativity. Unlike Blanca, Angel can imagine herself as occupying a space in the normative family structure. But unlike Elektra, she is not entirely convinced that her womanhood will go uncontested. Consequently, Angel does not demand that Stan change. She conforms to his demands rather than demanding that he value her. In other words, she, too, invokes the specific language of dignity to recognize how that world should change and to articulate what Black and Brown trans women deserve. But instead of demanding change as Blanca does in "Mother's Day," Angel conforms to dignity's limits to access Stan's world.

In the early stages of their relationship, Angel communicates how seductive it can be to chase individual success, secure what you need, and then shut yourself off from the world. In fact, Angel initially vocalizes to Stan that she wants a nice place to lay her head, money to live comfortably, and a man to make her feel desired. In this way, Angel articulates a deep yearning for validation and belonging according to scriptures of normativity. As their relationship develops, Angel moves from seeking only safety to indulging in the potential for a luxurious life. When her success with Stan is at its height, *Pose*'s architects actually move Angel from the physical space of her community in the House of Evangelista to her own apartment with all the trappings of 1980s luxury.[172] Though Angel originally celebrates the apartment, she quickly realizes that what looks like progress—what looks like safety and validation and even dignity—is not what it seems. In the episode "Giving and Receiving," *Pose* situates Angel in her fancy new apartment alone, lonely, and waiting for Stan, which operates in direct contrast to the plentiful community at the House of Evangelista. Once she leaves the space characterized by individualism, she finds joy, love, and healing at Blanca's. While this incident alone is not enough to shift her values, "Giving and Receiving" provides key moments of transition.[173]

As their arc continues, Angel tries to share her communally shaped world with Stan by taking him to the balls. However, he wants to move her away from that life because it does not speak to his worldview.[174] He wants to move her to the suburbs, bring children into their lives, and protect and provide for her according to narratives of the nuclear family and masculinity.[175] While Angel is tempted, *Pose* insists on placing her in situations in which she must compare and contrast living individually with plentiful material access and living communally with enough to sustain herself and others. By way of constant comparison and contrast, Angel makes a pivotal decision: at the end of season 1, outside of the balls, Angel rejects Stan's offer to live a normatively dignified life as a suburban housewife.[176] While she could have justifiably rejected him due to abandonment, she goes further and tells Stan that she already has a family—already has purpose, safety, and belonging. Angel transforms by rejecting individual success, which is seductive but empty (and fragile), and by embracing Blanca's route.[177]

As a final point on *Pose*'s characterization triangle, Elektra occupies a third position distinct from Blanca and Angel. With the greatest ability to "pass" as cisgender and enjoy the luxury of New York City life through financial support provided by her "daddy," Elektra feels the least amount of responsibility to contribute to her community. Additionally, Elektra is the oldest of the three trans women and has experienced a life informed by a different historical context and different goals. For Elektra, success means moving through the world unclocked, having material luxury, and living safely.[178] In short, she aims to move through the world according to normative notions of what it means to be dignified. Furthermore, she feels the need to define herself against other trans women, especially those who cannot pass and who threaten her carefully sought dignified status.[179] As Elektra develops, viewers see her battle to transform. She experiences an ebb-and-flow consciousness journey that moves between moments of brief transformation and then regression as she tries to unlearn and relearn what constitutes success.

In a few major moments of conflict, Elektra realizes the fragility of her privilege and learns hard lessons about why queer community is important. At the beginning of season 1, we see Elektra's life of luxury and learn that her financier, Dick, provides for her. But as Elektra contemplates having gender affirmation procedures, she learns how contingent Dick's "love" is. When she decides to have bottom surgery to reconcile her gender identity and her body—a decision that gives her a deep sense of happiness and self-actualization—Dick drops her like "a Hefty bag filled with last night's takeout containers."[180] Because his desire and his "care" rely on his being in control and objectifying her difference, he is no longer interested once she loses that "little something extra."[181] Searching for a similar arrangement, she experiences the rejection of powerful men because she no longer conforms to their fetishes: she is no longer the hot "chick with a dick" that saturates the porn industry. When Elektra loses everything, Blanca rescues her by practicing communal ethics. With this narrative, *Pose* critiques Elektra's individualistic values, showcases the limits of such a value system, and even illustrates how she does violence to other trans women in pursuit of individualism.

Even though the end of season 1 finds Elektra turning a corner—and starting to think a little more communally—she does not maintain this approach for long. When she finds a new lucrative job, she gets a steady cash flow, rediscovers her finery, and again is lured into a life of individual success.[182] Importantly, *Pose*'s creative team does not let her remain there for long. By "Butterfly/ Cocoon," Elektra once again realizes that her valorization of the individual will never sustain her, especially when she needs help dealing with a dead body to avoid being unfairly criminalized.[183] Elektra relearns that the world will remind her that she is Black and trans no matter how much she approximates cisnormative standards of beauty and class.

Quite purposefully, *Pose* employs Elektra's character to show that no matter how well she dresses, how pretty she is, how sophisticated she acts, or how elevated her speech is, the world still hates her and wants to erase her. Indeed, when her embrace of neoliberal notions of dignity fail her, Blanca and Candy and other trans women of color repeatedly mobilize to help her, illustrating *Pose*'s message of dignity through community. In yet another moment of conflict and despair—very much connected to her quest for individual success—community saves her and shows her the value of another way of establishing worth and purpose.[184] Currently, Elektra is still growing, but she has moved closer to Blanca and Angel's position, as illustrated by her mothering in "Life's a Beach" and her sisterhood solidarity during the "In My Heels" finale.[185]

By triangulating Blanca, Angel, and Elektra, *Pose* demonstrates how seductive neoliberal discourses of dignity are and how difficult they are to resist. Furthermore, the show also illustrates how adopting a communal ethos can shape a distinct rethinking of dignity. Importantly, the drama highlights how characters' proximity to normativity influences their ability to resist, see, and lobby for alternative value systems. Because Elektra has the unquestioned ability to pass and is most deeply steeped in dignity's rhetoric due to her generational status, she has the strongest allegiance to neoliberal understandings of dignity. And she has the most to learn. Similarly, Angel approximates normativity, and her womanhood goes mostly uncontested, but she does not have the same confidence or generational situatedness as Elektra. As a result, she is tempted to live according to neoliberal dignity, but she learns faster than Elektra about its limits and turns to community for dignity.

Contrastingly, Blanca consistently articulates her inability to pass and her ineligibility for normative dignity. Thus she rarely entertains dignity's work; rather, she serves as the point of contrast for the other women to see the errors of neoliberal thinking and being. As Sara Ahmed argues, "We learn about worlds when they do not accommodate us. Not being accommodated can be a pedagogy. We generate ideas through the struggles we have to be in the world; we come to question worlds when we are in question."[186] Due to her situatedness, Blanca emerges as the teacher who articulates *Pose*'s oppositional understanding of dignity. By building the House of Evangelista, Blanca provides a framework that stands in contrast to discourses that demand that dignified lives be restrained, ahistorical, compliant with institutional power, private, and individualistic.[187] When this triangulation and its relationship to alternatives is taken to its fullest logic, *Pose*'s alternative ways of seeing can be inextricably related to the folks in the writing room and how they— due to distance from normativity and neoliberal notions of dignity—can see differently, place value elsewhere, and offer oppositional representations of LGBTQ+ life.[188]

Pose's unique definition of dignity seems to reside between neoliberal notions of dignity as respectability (which suggest that dignity is conferred by the state) and more pre-political understandings (which insist that dignity is innate, inherent, and irrevocable). For *Pose*, a violent state apparatus cannot confer dignity, especially onto hypercriminalized communities. Similarly, dignity is not a natural or God-given quality that one cannot lose. *Pose*'s references to dignity suggest that it is earned, negotiated, and assessed through communal praxis. Finally, one's ability to remain dignified requires unlearning the lessons of the state and relearning care for others.

Conclusion: "Welcome to Our World"

Because *Pose*'s architects understand that "representations do not simply re-present an already existing reality but are also doors into making new futures possible," viewers will find an embrace of queer excess, a centering of queer history, a critique of institutional power, and a rethinking of kinship that all contribute to redefining dignity through communal ethos and praxis.[189] In particular, this alternative definition recognizes the importance of community members speaking for themselves and through their own vernacular. Indeed, what *Pose* accomplishes has been much needed and long sought. Rooted in a carefully researched and executed particularity, the show serves the children a depiction of queer life that refuses to apologize for itself or to translate itself for heteronormative audiences and their needs. As Mock asserts, "There's no over-explaining of our experiences. . . . It's just: 'Welcome to our world.'"[190] With this welcome, *Pose* celebrates our collective past and offers a primer for an alternative future of representation that features queerness on its own terms and that refuses to perpetuate white supremacy. Indeed, the show addresses trans activist CeCe McDonald's concern about audience expectations and how they shape mainstream representation of LGBTQ+ life. As she asserts, "Our narratives aren't really for those people. . . . They're not for them to consume in such a way that makes them feel better about themselves. Our narratives should make them get their shit together."[191] In contrast to *Love, Simon*, which makes heteronormative audiences comfortable and centers their concerns, *Pose* decenters this audience. Additionally, *Pose* demands that its audiences critique the institutions and values that are deemed "universal" but that bolster whiteness. As Che Gossett highlights, "Visibility politics, or the kind of queer and trans politics we might call neoliberal, cannot account for ways that blackness ghosts and haunts the normative."[192] Instead of aspiring toward integration without disruption or chasing understandings of dignity that mandate erasure of particularity, *Pose* demands structural change that addresses inequities intersectionally.

Pose emerges now and looks back—so purposefully and meticulously—to this turbulent era of queer life to do reparative work at this critical juncture. At a moment in which trans lives are still explicitly devalued—even during a representational "tipping point"—the show intervenes to remind queer folks of where we have been, who we are, and where we might go next.[193] In its first two seasons, *Pose* unquestionably reveals how the queer penchant for difference persists even at a cultural moment that celebrates films like *Love, Simon* with its particular valorization of sameness as a marker of progress. *Pose* reclaims the historical potential of transgression to instruct queer communities on a dynamic, firmly contextual, and diverse polyvocal path forward.[194] As far as we can tell, audiences are here for it.[195]

PART III

Respect versus Respectability

The Court's Definitions of Dignity

5

Liberal Rulings for Conservative Ends

Manipulating Dignity from Decriminalization to
Marriage Equality

Shortly after his election in 2016, Donald Trump sought to reassure LGBTQ+ Americans by stating that he was "fine" with same-sex marriage. In an interview on *60 Minutes*, the then president-elect said his personal opinions were "irrelevant" and the question of marriage equality was "done." He continued, "These cases have gone to the Supreme Court. They've been settled. And I'm—I'm fine with that."[1] This position contradicted the Republican Party's 2016 platform, which called for overturning two Supreme Court decisions that recognized same-sex marriage: *United States v. Windsor* (2013), which ruled that the federal government must recognize marriages where they were already recognized by state governments, and *Obergefell v. Hodges* (2015), which required recognition of same-sex marriage throughout the United States.[2] In particular, the platform disparaged *Obergefell*, noting how "in the words of the late Justice Antonin Scalia, [it] was a 'judicial Putsch'—full of 'silly extravagances'—that reduced 'the disciplined legal reasoning of John Marshall and Joseph Storey to the mystical aphorisms of a fortune cookie.'" According to the Republican Party, in *Obergefell*, five unelected lawyers robbed 320 million Americans of their legitimate constitutional authority to define marriage as the union of one man and one woman.[3]

In this context, the position taken by Trump's first Supreme Court nominee, Neil Gorsuch, was all the more surprising. In hearings before the Senate Judiciary Committee, Gorsuch sided with Trump and against the national platform. His position also contradicted the justices who dissented in *Windsor* and *Obergefell*—namely, Scalia, John Roberts, Samuel Alito, and Clarence Thomas. Gorsuch called same-sex marriage "absolutely settled law."[4]

Why would a Republican president and his Supreme Court nominee to the seat once held by the anchor of contemporary conservative jurisprudence, Scalia—who was a vociferous dissenter in decisions such as *Romer v. Evans* (1996), which struck down state limits on anti-discrimination protections for lesbians, gays, and bisexuals, and *Lawrence v. Texas* (2003), which ruled criminalization of consensual adult same-sex intimacy unconstitutional, as well as the marriage equality rulings—take positions at odds with Republican orthodoxy?[5] Alignment with public opinion is one possibility. Public acceptance of same-sex marriage has skyrocketed in recent years.[6] Perhaps Gorsuch did not want to appear out of the mainstream, a criticism that Senator Chuck Schumer (D-NY) used to justify filibustering the confirmation vote.[7] But Gorsuch and Trump maintained Republican opposition to abortion access even as nearly 80 percent of the public supported legal abortion access under some or all circumstances.[8] Consequently, their distinct stance on marriage equality indicates that strategic alignment with public opinion is a less compelling explanation.

An alternative answer may lie in the jurisprudential tradition that *Obergefell* draws upon and the conservative ends to which it could be put. *Obergefell* speaks to petitioners' claim to dignity and represents a judicial deployment of dignity. The petitioners rested their demand on previous rulings that invoked dignity.[9] Many of these precedents were crafted by Justice Anthony Kennedy, who spoke for the majority in *Obergefell* and built a gay and lesbian rights jurisprudence over two decades that rests on dignity as a constitutional value.[10] However, we contend that dignity, at least as defined and deployed by Kennedy, proves a problematic foundation for LGBTQ+ equality.[11]

Our skepticism about Kennedy's notion of dignity rests on four claims. First, these rulings refuse to engage with queer values. Insofar as these decisions have defined dignity within heteronormative and neoliberal values that promote privacy, romance, and coupled monogamy, dignity functions as a constraining force that inhibits a robust conception of sexual justice. It limits the scope of what behaviors and identities can be recognized as deserving respect. In other words, dignity denies the history and value of queer social practices.

Second, the justification for equal treatment for gays and lesbians and for a fundamental right to marry a same-sex partner does not follow the pathways of equal protection jurisprudence that were cut for race or sex equality since the mid-twentieth century. What constitutional law scholars refer to as the doctrines of tiered scrutiny and suspect class or suspect classification, which are central to race equality jurisprudence as well as sex and gender equality jurisprudence, are not followed in the Supreme Court's rulings on gay rights and marriage recognition. We contend that this divergence does important work to promote a neo-liberal conception of equal rights, or what we see as a vision of limited government action to sustain formal equality rather than a more robust notion of government responsibility to promote equity and counter long histories of structural inequality.

Third, dignity—with no clear grounding in constitutional text or even an agreed-upon definition—is malleable and has been used to support outcomes that challenge progressive values and that potentially undermine equal rights for LGBTQ+ people.[12] Legal analyst Jeffrey Rosen noted this possibility even before the Court ruled in *Obergefell*. Writing after oral argument in that case, Rosen offered a cautionary assessment: "There is no doubt that Justice Kennedy accurately and movingly describes the indignity and stigma that bans on same sex marriage impose on the right of LGBT citizens to define their own identities and to claim the benefits of equal citizenship. But constitutionalizing that injury with broad abstractions like dignity may lead to results in the future that liberals come to regret. . . . The right to dignity—now celebrated by liberals for what it means to gay rights—could ultimately produce other decisions in unrelated cases that they would not be so quick to celebrate."[13] Indeed, the Court has invoked dignity to limit abortion access and curb policies that would racially integrate public schools. As such, dignity bolsters the objectives of the conservative legal movement. Unsurprisingly, as one scholar has found, dignity has been invoked with greater frequency by justices on the conservative Roberts Supreme Court than those in earlier Courts, and liberal jurists use the term as much as conservative ones, even with substantial disagreements over what the term connotes.[14] Furthermore, actors in the executive branch have utilized the malleability of dignity to promote political aims to curb equal treatment for LGBTQ+ individuals.

Fourth, even as the Supreme Court has deployed dignity as the foundation for gay and lesbian rights, the term has proven unable to resolve some contemporary questions for LGBTQ+ communities. This failure is illustrated by the Court's 2018 ruling in *Masterpiece Cakeshop v. Colorado Civil Rights Commission*.[15] In that case, recourse to dignity did not provide a means to balance the rights of the same-sex couple seeking equal treatment in commerce against First Amendment speech or religious expression rights. The more recent victory for gay, lesbian, bisexual, and transgender persons in *Bostock v. Clayton County, Georgia*, which ruled that the 1964 Civil Rights Act Title VII ban on sex discrimination in employment protects against discrimination based on sexual orientation and gender identity, further supports our critique. Not only did *Bostock* avoid the word *dignity* entirely, but also Justice Gorsuch, writing for the majority, mapped how future decisions could curb the ruling's potential.[16] In other words, *Masterpiece* failed to answer the substantive question, How should the dignity of the LGBTQ+ person be balanced against the dignity of the religious believer? *Bostock* similarly leaves that question for another day, yet it mentions how the dignity of religious believers might be elevated.

In this chapter, we trace the jurisprudential development of a dignity doctrine from *Romer* to *Obergefell*, and we illustrate how dignity could ironically prove useless, if not dangerous, to LGBTQ+ equality claims. Through textual analysis of these decisions, we show (1) how the gay rights rulings diverge from standard Fourteenth Amendment equal protection and due process analysis, (2) why this divergence enables the gay rights rulings to support conservative legal aims rather than to bolster progressive objectives—women's rights, abortion access, affirmative action—which are often understood as politically linked with LGBTQ+ rights aims, and (3) how these rulings ultimately reveal the limits of dignity.

How the Court Denies Queer Kinship

The Supreme Court's invocation and deployment of dignity create boundaries of respectability that exclude queer intimacy and practice. Legal scholar Yuvraj Joshi refers to this as "respectable queerness," or the circumstance where "the newfound public recognition of gay people and relationships is contingent upon their acquiring a respectable social identity that is actually constituted by public performances of respectability and by private queer practices."[17] This idea has its roots in legal theorist Carl Stychin's notion of the "good gay," which he developed in the 1990s to denote strategies by which outsiders seek inclusion within the imagined community of a nation on the very basis of their exclusion.[18] Consequently, the demand that queers be "respectable" or "good" to be recognized by the Court or other public and private authorities as deserving of rights is not new.[19] The notion that marriage requires a domestication of queer practice that might impede any aspiration to queer liberation is also not new.[20] Indeed, much of the movement for LGBTQ+ equality has been premised on the claim that inclusion within marriage might inhibit the expansive potential of gay and queer liberation.[21] Either such inclusion might render invisible all the familial forms that queers create and value outside of traditional marriage or it might stigmatize those queers who do not conform to normative notions of romantic love and monogamy.[22] And queer critique of litigation strategies involved in *Lawrence, Windsor,* and *Obergefell* and the subsequent rulings is not new.[23] Nevertheless, the Court's decision to tether dignity to marriage and to conceptualize dignity as constituted in recognition by others is important. As Joshi states, "Never before, however, has respectability been more salient in queer politics than at this moment of recognition."[24]

Dignity—as Justice Kennedy invoked it in the Court's marriage equality jurisprudence—follows from recognition by others. First, it does not inhere in the individual per se; instead, it is constituted in a relationship—particularly, in a relationship between two individuals that is sanctified through marriage. Second, marriage recognition is granted to gays and lesbians in the context of that sexual minority's relationship to the majority; public opinion demonstrates that the majority has increasingly accepted gays and lesbians over time. Third, dignity is granted by the state. In Kennedy's formulation, dignity depends on state recognition and thereby signifies the status of the relationship between the state and the LGBTQ+ community.

As scholars have argued, state power is deployed through marriage, and insofar as dignity inheres in marriage, state power determines the boundaries of dignity.[25] Put differently, dignity is conferred by the state through its willingness to recognize, sanction, and promote relationships characterized by their adherence to heteronormative notions of romance, intimacy, coupling, and privacy. Consequently, the power to anoint with dignity is grounded in the potential to mark as unequal particular ways of living, which exposes dignity's exclusionary limits.

On June 26, 2015, speaking for the Court majority, Justice Kennedy ruled in *Obergefell* that petitioners "were ask[ing] for equal dignity in the eyes of the law. The Constitution grants them that right."[26] As we recognize the achievement that marriage represents as a legal and cultural matter—that it extends to gay and lesbian couples a range of economic benefits, privileges, and responsibilities previously denied to them and that it confers a sense of cultural legitimacy to their relationships that could serve as the foundation for other recognitions of familial equality such as parenting rights—we must acknowledge that such recognition reinforces neoliberal political aims. As Yasmin Nair contends, "Gay marriage is seen as the core of a new kind of privatized and personal endeavor—the rights of LGBT individuals to enter into a private contract. This ignores the fact that the U.S. is the only major industrialized nation to tie so many basic benefits like health care to marriage."[27] Marriage deepens neoliberalism's privileging of self-reliance and the state's limited scope of responsibility to its citizens.[28] By suggesting that dignity inheres in marriage, dignity supports neoliberal values of individualism and limited governance, which also, as Matthew Hindman contends, "draws problematic boundaries around the proper limits of citizenship."[29]

Furthermore, the marriage equality decisions refuse to recognize queer notions of intimacy. To transgress the private, coupled, and romantic relationship that is the normative foundation for marriage and family is to be dismissed as childish, irresponsible, and undignified. By including gays and lesbians within the privatized heteronormative construct of marriage, the Court transforms a particular kind of same-sex intimacy—which falls within the same parameters of the extant cross-sex marriage institution—into something capable of being dignified. Same-sex intimacy must correspond to values of romance and monogamy in order to be seen as respectable and dignified.[30] All other forms of intimacy are left unacknowledged and unvalued, and the potential for a substantive critique of marriage as an institution is jettisoned in the name of inclusion.[31] Furthermore, as Elizabeth Baia argues, "defining LGBTQ rights as including these values, or requiring them to be present to extend protection, has the effect of eroding the potential for future rights claims."[32] Falling outside of these values weakens litigants' abilities to make cognizable arguments about their own equality.

Writing prior to *Obergefell*, Noa Ben-Asher contends that *Windsor* "completed a three-decade transformation of the legal homosexual from an individual whose sexual conduct the state could punish as morally blameworthy, to a couple whose marriage the State can find 'worthy of dignity.'"[33] Here the first sense of dignity as relational, as constituted within an intimate and romantic relationship, is exposed. The same-sex relationship is like the cross-sex relationship, and insofar as similarity can be established, the worthiness of the same-sex couple follows. As Mary Bonauto and Douglas Hallward-Driemeier, the *Obergefell* plaintiffs' co-counsel, contended during oral argument before the Supreme Court, "The intimate and committed relationships of same-sex couples, just like those of heterosexual couples, provide mutual support and are the foundation of family life in our society."[34] Justice Kennedy rearticulated this claim: "The nature of marriage is that, through its enduring bond, two persons together can find other freedoms, such as expression, intimacy, and spirituality. *This is true for all persons, whatever their sexual orientation.* There is dignity in the bond between two men or two women who seek to marry and in their autonomy to make such profound choices."[35]

That this intimacy could be transformed from criminal to dignified, from so-called disgusting to publicly valued, in such a short time is remarkable. It is a credit to advocates within the LGBTQ+ community and to its allies who sought inclusion within marriage as their goal.[36] Nevertheless, Ben-Asher criticizes "dignity" as articulated in *Windsor*—and restated in *Obergefell*—as weak because the Court does not conceptualize dignity as inherent in the individual.[37] According to Ben-Asher, to suggest that dignity is conferred by the state through marriage recognition implies that those who are unmarried are somehow not fully dignified or, alternatively, that certain relationships must be privileged above others. For Kennedy, since marriage "always has promised nobility and dignity to all persons," the state's refusal to grant them access to marriage leaves gays and lesbians "condemned to live in loneliness, excluded from one of civilization's oldest institutions."[38] For Kennedy, to marry becomes the most valued form of a relationship. As Joshi argues, "it is only *this* choice to marry—not *any* choice about marriage, including the choice *not* to marry—that is dignified."[39]

Consequently, certain forms of connection and kinship are unrecognized, if not debased, by the public and governing authorities. Here Kennedy's second notion of dignity as relational is exposed. Dignity depends on the public recognizing that gays and lesbians should have access to marriage. Access depends on the majority determining that a certain kind of gay and lesbian intimacy is socially acceptable. In *Obergefell*, Kennedy traces a "shift in public attitudes toward greater tolerance" of gays and lesbians, and in light of these changes, as he recounts in *Windsor*, certain states decided to grant legal recognition of same-sex couples, which constituted "a dignity and status of immense import."[40] But resting dignity upon social acceptance is dangerous: "The absence of social approval becomes an excuse for disregarding dignitary injuries."[41] Of course, the whole notion of governing authorities engaging in dignity-taking would suggest that Kennedy's conception, however troubling, is empirically accurate.[42]

Finally, insofar as the connections at the heart of a queer ethic of public sex—anonymous, present, and momentary—embrace a sense of time and space antithetical to the supposed commitment inherent in marriage, the reification of traditional marriage within LGBTQ+ communities may undermine and counter queer logics. Marriage recognition becomes the legal pathway by which the heteronormative can absorb the transgressive potential of queer politics and transform it into a narrow notion of homonormativity.[43] Privileging marriage only perpetuates the indignity of refusing to recognize queer logics of contact and intimacy.

Thus the third notion of dignity as relational is exposed. When it is tethered to marriage, dignity would seem to be conferred, bestowed, and controlled by the state, permitting the state to shape the boundaries of acceptable gay and lesbian identities.[44] Without such recognition, the state commits an indignity. For Kennedy, the state humiliates gays and lesbians: "Excluding same-sex couples from marriage thus conflicts with a central premise of the right to marry. Without the recognition, stability, and predictability marriage offers, their children suffer the stigma of knowing their families are somehow lesser. They also suffer the significant material costs of being raised by unmarried parents, relegated through no fault of their own to a more difficult and uncertain family life. The marriage laws at issue here thus harm and humiliate the children of same-sex couples."[45] Justice Thomas lambasts this conception of dignity as conferred by the state in dissent. In chapter 6, we explore his notion of dignity as inherent in the individual and thereby untouchable by the state or other authorities.

Gay Rights Rulings Abandon the Usual Framework

When Chief Justice John Roberts dissented in *Obergefell*, he contended that the majority strayed from accepted interpretations of the Fourteenth Amendment's equal protection and due process clauses: "Petitioners contend that the Equal Protection Clause requires their States to license and recognize same-sex marriages. The majority does not seriously engage with this claim. Its discussion is, quite frankly, difficult to follow. The central point seems to be that there is a 'synergy between' the Equal Protection Clause and the Due Process Clause, and that some precedents relying on one Clause have also relied on the other. Absent from this portion of the opinion, however, is anything resembling our usual framework for deciding equal protection cases."[46] What Roberts calls the "usual framework" refers to a doctrine of suspect class or classification and the resulting judicial review of tiered scrutiny.

Whether one views the offense in question as affecting a suspect class or a suspect classification is important because the phrases—often conflated—mean different things and carry distinct implications. The doctrine of suspect class holds that should a law affect a class of persons that either or in combination (1) has suffered a history of discrimination, (2) has a distinguishable or immutable characteristic irrelevant to the objective but on which the discrimination is based, and (3) has been rendered politically powerless, then laws affecting this class must be evaluated by the Court with heightened scrutiny.[47] Suspect classes have included African Americans, and the Court has considered women to form a quasi-suspect class. For a law that affects these classes to be constitutional, it must be narrowly tailored to achieve a compelling government interest (strict scrutiny, which traditionally applied to laws affecting African Americans) or be substantially related to the achievement of an important government interest (intermediate scrutiny, which traditionally applied to laws affecting women).[48]

As we detail later in this chapter, by the late 1980s, the Court began to shift this doctrine of suspect *class* toward suspect *classification*. Suspect classification is less concerned with whether the law is affecting a particular group and whether that group can be recognized as suffering histories of discrimination and political powerlessness. It is more concerned with whether the law makes a classification on the basis of either race or sex as categories. In other words, a racial classification in the law is automatically subject to strict scrutiny regardless of whether that classification is seeking to remedy histories of subordination and unequal treatment or whether that classification aims to perpetuate such unequal treatment. Suspect classification moves the Court from considering histories of inequality to promoting an abstract universalized principle that holds any classification to be constitutionally suspicious. In other words, suspect classification privileges a colorblind understanding of the constitution and its guarantees, which promotes what we see as a problematically abstract universalism.[49] A colorblind approach to the constitution is notable for "its refusal to engage history"; the assertion of colorblindness "actively erases the significance of history, because it claims that past institutional and cultural discrimination must not direct our attempts to remedy their current manifestation."[50]

Obergefell goes beyond advocating an anti-classification approach; it avoids both suspect class and classification altogether. Indeed, the Court never asks if gays, lesbians, or bisexuals are a suspect class or if a law that classifies by sexual orientation, such as a marriage statute that only permits cross-sex marriage, is suspect. Instead, the Court grounded the *Obergefell* decision in a vague—if uplifting—concept of dignity.[51] In so doing, it further develops dignity as a guiding jurisprudential principle that had already been anchored in rulings in *Lawrence* and *Windsor*.

In his criticism of the majority in *Obergefell*, Roberts echoed Scalia's dissent in *Windsor* issued two years earlier:

> If this is meant to be an equal-protection opinion, it is a confusing one. The opinion does not resolve and indeed does not even mention what had been the central question in this litigation: whether, under the Equal Protection Clause, laws restricting marriage to a man and a woman are reviewed for more than mere rationality. In accord with my previously expressed skepticism about the Court's "tiers of scrutiny" approach, I

would review this classification only for its rationality. As nearly as I can tell, the Court agrees with that. . . . The sum of all the Court's nonspecific hand-waving is that this law is invalid (maybe on equal-protection grounds, maybe on substantive-due process grounds, and perhaps with some amorphous federalism component playing a role) because it is motivated by a "'bare . . . desire to harm' couples in same-sex marriages."[52]

The confusion was captured by Judge Christopher Piazza of Arkansas when he struck down a state ban on marriage: "Attempting to find a legal label for what transpired in *Windsor* is difficult."[53] The legal label is difficult to identify inasmuch as it does not comport with the traditional tiered-scrutiny approach. Nevertheless, *Lawrence*, *Windsor*, and *Obergefell* contain an internal logic: a reliance on some conception of dignity. Taken together, these cases create what might be called a contemporary "dignity doctrine."

This dignity doctrine marks a shift in equal protection and due process jurisprudence. Legal scholars have explained that gay rights rulings since *Romer* illustrate how the Court views anti-gay discrimination as grounded in an unconstitutional animus.[54] The Court has held laws targeting gays and lesbians for unequal treatment to the lowest level of judicial review—rational basis, whereby a law must be rationally related to a legitimate government purpose. Consequently, gays, lesbians, and bisexuals, as a class of people who have suffered a history of discrimination and/or political powerlessness grounded in an immutable trait—as scrutiny doctrine demands—have not been so identified by the Supreme Court.[55]

Some scholars have contended that *Romer*, *Lawrence*, *Windsor*, and *Obergefell*, taken together, announce an anti-harm or anti-humiliation principle as the foundation for rational basis review.[56] They suggest that equal protection jurisprudence is intact but also hold that these rulings may be more elegant than traditional suspect class analysis because the dignity/anti-harm/anti-animus principle does not require the designation of suspect class status, which can prove exclusionary. As Kimberlé Crenshaw critiques, "The paradigm of sex discrimination tends to be based on the experiences of white women; the model of race discrimination tends to be based on the experiences of the most privileged Blacks."[57] Scrutiny doctrine does not recognize the intersectional nature of identity; discrimination is understood as experienced either as a woman or as an African American, but experiences of a Black woman resist legibility because a discrimination claim may elide the singularity of race or sex.

Since the gay rights rulings do not invoke an identity group as the operative concept but instead suggest that an individual's dignity is denied, the underlying logic is often lauded. By focusing on the individual's identity and proclaiming a universal, inviolable quality of dignity, the difficulties of wrestling with intersecting group identities are altogether avoided, and a seemingly progressive promotion of equal rights is achieved.[58] Laurence Tribe's assessment of *Obergefell* is illustrative: "Justice Kennedy's decision represents the culmination of a decades-long project that has revolutionized the Court's fundamental rights jurisprudence. . . . *Obergefell* has definitively replaced . . . [the] wooden three-prong test focused on tradition, specificity, and negativity with the more holistic inquiry."[59] Indeed, this approach, which abandons any need to consider histories of discrimination or tiers of scrutiny, was applauded by legal journalists in the weeks prior to the *Obergefell* decision. For example, Emily Bazelon has found the scrutiny tiers to be a cumbersome architecture to evaluate discrimination:

> I'll refrain from droning on about the higher levels of scrutiny the court accords to laws that appear to discriminate on the basis of race, ethnicity, religion or sex—but not, thus far, sexual orientation. I'm with Justice Scalia: "Strict scrutiny, intermediate scrutiny, blah blah blah blah." The government should have a pretty decent reason for passing a law. Singling out one group based on a fundamental and unchangeable aspect of its identity is usually not a decent reason. I think Justice Kennedy gets this. His opinions striking down laws that discriminate on the basis of sexual orientation, going back to 1996, basically say that you can't kick people to the curb, under the law, because you don't like them for a reason that's beyond their control or none of your business. Good enough for me! And good enough for generally protecting gay people from discrimination, I think.[60]

Similarly, legal journalist Adam Liptak referred to scrutiny doctrine as a "legal fog machine" and contended, "Justice Kennedy has proved perfectly capable of striking down laws that discriminate against gay people without specifying whether his scrutiny was rational, heightened, strict or some combo sandwich built of animus-detection and dignity-protection." He nevertheless acknowledges, "There would be a symbolic value to placing gay people on the other side of a legal line meant to protect groups that have suffered grave discrimination at the hands of the government."[61]

We argue that this acknowledgment is more than symbolically important. We contend that the lack of this acknowledgment is problematic, as it leaves individuals exposed to ongoing discrimination. Perhaps most importantly, we posit that Kennedy's route to strike down discrimination against gays, lesbian, and bisexuals without invoking tiered scrutiny and instead offering a dignity principle does more than allegedly improve our ability to counter discrimination as Bazelon and others suggest. *Lawrence*, *Windsor*, and *Obergefell*'s dignity principle is individualized and universalized such that grappling with the context and structure of inequality is rendered unnecessary. Put differently, dignity becomes a neoliberal response to the enduring liberal commitment to tiered scrutiny and suspect class analysis. Consequently, dignity can function as a jurisprudential principle that can serve conservative legal aims.

When Kennedy states in *Lawrence* that criminalization of same-sex sexual relations is unconstitutional, he does not suggest that the long history of discrimination against gays and lesbians, which he nevertheless traces, merits that the Court must be more skeptical of the statute than it would otherwise be. Rather, he states a universal principle—namely, that "adults may choose to enter upon this relationship in the confines of their own homes and their private lives and still retain their dignity as free persons."[62] The ruling does not apply to gays or lesbians as gays or lesbians but broadens to apply more generally such that the historical context of discrimination proves unnecessary to the articulation of a universal principle. Similarly, in *Windsor*, Kennedy writes that the Court strikes down the Defense of Marriage Act (DOMA) because through it the federal government seeks only to "disparage and to injure those whom the State, by its marriage laws, sought to protect in personhood and dignity."[63] Dignity is again invoked as a universal good, one that follows from personhood itself, and as such, no complicated rubric of tiered scrutiny that requires attention to historical, political, or cultural context needs to be applied.

This *ideational* turn gestures toward an *institutional* development regarding the role of the Court in a democracy and the neoliberal turn to limited governance since at least the 1980s.[64] The gay rights rulings illustrate that to identify inequality, the Court no longer needs to examine the factors that underlie scrutiny doctrine—namely, histories of discrimination and powerlessness. This move repositions the Court's role in US democracy as it has developed over the twentieth century. The fourth footnote of *United States v. Carolene Products* (1938) captures this role.[65]

Recognizing that laws flowed from a flawed system, the Court indicated in the fourth footnote that it would be more skeptical of laws that appeared to have a disproportionate impact on particular groups, especially groups who could demonstrate that their voice was not duly heard when the law was crafted.[66] That role, and its corresponding doctrine of targeted skepticism, was institutionalized as the tiered-scrutiny doctrine, which operated as the framework for the interpretation of mid- and late twentieth-century Fourteenth Amendment equal protection.

The gay rights rulings, because they do not utilize the context-specific identification of suspect class designation or higher scrutiny and instead articulate a universal claim to dignity, follow a discernably distinct logic, and they provide a distinct basis for the unelected Court's institutional standing in a democracy. The twentieth-century interventionist frame grounded in the assessment of process and structure, which underlaid so much of the race and sex equality litigation, now competes with a newer invocation of universalism that is purposively abstract and grounds gay and lesbian rights litigation. By advancing individual dignity as a principle animating the Fourteenth Amendment, the gay and lesbian rights and marriage equality decisions articulate a privatized, individualized, and abstractly universal notion of dignity that potentially curbs the Court's ability to recognize, regulate, and limit subordination.

Without the scrutiny doctrine properly applied, gays and lesbians continue to be unrecognized as a suspect class, and their rights remain vulnerable to both state infringement as well as citizen-to-citizen bias. By refusing to apply the doctrine, the Court also deepens its commitment to a conceptualization of rights rhetorically grounded in neoliberal logics of individual autonomy and self-reliance rather than equal protection. Dignity—given its philosophical and moral foundation in the individual and its appeal as a universal principle—fits with the neoliberal logics embraced by an increasingly conservative Court. These logics are at odds with the more proactive government-based actions that flowed from the mid-twentieth-century judicial liberalism of which suspect class analysis is emblematic.

In short, dignity may appear as a universalistic good—the self-evident foundation of equal treatment and due process. Because it appears timeless, it can stand as a seemingly neutral concept. Therefore, it may help reorient the legitimate role of the judge in a democracy, which, at least rhetorically, has been one objective of the conservative legal movement.[67] It did provide a way for Justice Kennedy to achieve his desired result in gay rights rulings without employing the cumbersome and critiqued scrutiny doctrine. And it gained traction when scrutiny doctrine was being creatively reworked to achieve ends seemingly antithetical to its purpose.

Manipulating Ideas for Antithetical Ends: The Conservative Reimaging of Scrutiny Doctrine

Building on political scientist Rogers Smith's conception of US political culture as comprising multiple traditions—liberal, republican, and a set of ascriptive prejudices—Stephen Skowronek has argued that entrepreneurial actors create "cultural composites, ideas characterized by the interpenetration of these antithetical ends," and thereby foster a new developmental trajectory; these new formulations are "constitutive of action along lines all their own."[68] In other words, Skowronek shows how formerly racist ideas can be transformed in new contexts and put to liberal ends.[69] This "audacity to be found in the play of ideas over time" is illustrated in how certain conservative justices redefined scrutiny doctrine from an effort to remediate discrimination against particular suspect classes to an effort to call any classification constitutionally suspect, thereby undermining attempts to advance targeted remedial policies.[70] Indeed, between 1990 and 2003, 73 percent of race-conscious statutes were struck down through the use of strict scrutiny, and "almost every single law that was struck down in that period was one that sought to ameliorate the status of racial minorities, such as affirmative action."[71] In short, the idea of suspect class as developed in scrutiny doctrine has been put to antithetical effect. And that shift can be traced in the deliberate moves of particular justices.

We uncover this process to demonstrate how justices can transform received understandings of constitutional commitments, here the meaning of the Fourteenth Amendment's equal protection. The deliberate movement made from suspect class to suspect classification reveals a conservative aversion to identity group designation (which requires attention to process, structure, and history) and privileges the abstract individual (which requires no such attention). Such privileging provides an opportunity to develop a dignity doctrine.

How justices have relied on *Loving v. Virginia*, the case striking down bans on interracial marriage, illustrates how rulings can be reimagined to serve particular ideological aims. Liberals cheered *Loving*, but the decision provided a foundation for later moves that overturned policies meant to counter racial subordination. Historian Peggy Pascoe notes that while Chief Justice Earl Warren was careful in his ruling for the unanimous Court to stipulate that Virginia's miscegenation law was an invidious discrimination on its face and that overruling the law constituted an anti-subordination act, she also reveals "a tendency to regard the *Loving* decision as proof positive to Justice John Marshall Harlan's famous 1896 assertion that 'our constitution is colorblind.'"[72]

Liberals had long touted colorblindness and sought to overturn miscegenation law as it was racially classified to subordinate. Classifications in the law, which enabled this subordination, were at odds with the Constitution's guarantee of equal protection. But conservative jurists could utilize the anti-classificatory language of *Loving* to read the equal protection guarantee as a broad principle against any classification, regardless of its purpose (something Kennedy would come to do). Insofar as the remedy in *Loving* required that states could no longer classify by race, conservatives on the Court could use *Loving* to challenge affirmative action and busing cases that relied on classification to achieve ends that countered discriminatory subordination and unequal treatment. As Pascoe writes, "In several highly controversial cases on these issues, references to *Loving* lined both sides of a deep judicial divide. In affirmative action cases, liberal justices returned to the position Earl Warren had originally taken in *Loving*, and began to insist that when it came to race classifications, purpose really did matter. . . . Conservative justices, however, insisted on treating the race classifications in affirmative action programs as if they were exact parallels to the race classifications in segregation law."[73] This anti-classificatory reading of *Loving* confuses suspect class with suspect classification. Nuanced attention to histories of racism is replaced with the simpler concern of whether a law classifies by race. Conservatives have argued that any classification is illegitimate, whereas liberals have tried and failed to hold to the idea that a classification that responds to and attempts to remedy a history of discrimination could be constitutionally permissible. The ironic result has been that a scrutiny standard developed to monitor the context in which law was crafted so that subordination may be detected and countered has been transformed into a decontextualized doctrine of abstract principle to guard against any classification that indicated difference.[74]

The conflation of class with classification is exemplified by the ruling in *City of Richmond v. J.A. Croson Company*.[75] The Court struck down Richmond's Minority Business Utilization Plan, which required the city to hire a percentage of minority business enterprises. Justice Sandra Day O'Connor, with separate concurrences from Scalia and Kennedy, read the Fourteenth Amendment's equality commitment not as a remedial responsibility but as requiring race neutrality or colorblindness. According to O'Connor, "The standard of review under the Equal Protection Clause is not dependent on the race of those burdened or benefited by a particular classification."[76] By focusing on classification (race) rather than the class to be protected from subordination (African Americans), Kennedy and Scalia concur with O'Connor. For Kennedy, "the moral imperative of racial neutrality is the driving force of the Equal Protection Clause."[77] For Scalia, "strict scrutiny must be applied to all governmental classification by race, whether or not its asserted purpose is 'remedial' or 'benign.'"[78]

Justice Thurgood Marshall saw this shift from class to classification as a significant misdirection: "Today, for the first time, a majority of this Court has adopted strict scrutiny as its standard of Equal Protection Clause review of race-conscious remedial measures. This is an unwelcome development."[79] According to Marshall, "A profound difference separates government actions that themselves are racist, and governmental actions that seek to remedy the effects of prior racism or to prevent neutral governmental activity from perpetuating the effects of such racism."[80] The majority's claim that African Americans were not a minority for purposes of remedial policy was ahistorical and out of line with doctrine: "We have identified *other* 'traditional indicia of suspectness': whether a group has been 'saddled with such disabilities, or subjected to a history of purposeful unequal treatment, or relegated to such a position of political powerlessness as to command extraordinary protection of the majoritarian political process.'"[81] Marshall clings to the established understanding of scrutiny as grounded in context, as committed to recognizing histories of discrimination and powerlessness. The majority, by contrast, creates a universal principle that any classification is hostile to equal treatment.

Ultimately, Marshall contends that O'Connor's move to classification and away from class reorients the Fourteenth Amendment, as well as the Thirteenth and Fifteenth Amendments, toward an end antithetical to its original purpose: "To interpret any aspect of these Amendments as proscribing state remedial responses to these very problems turns the Amendments on their heads."[82] To read these amendments as requiring a blanket ban on classification in the law undermines the remedial aims sought by their framers. Marshall characterized *Croson* as "a full-scale retreat from the Court's longstanding solicitude to race-conscious remedial efforts."[83] This retreat continued with *Adarand Constructors v. Peña* (1995).[84] Asserting that *Croson* established the principle that any racial preference must be reviewed with consistent skepticism, O'Connor cemented the suspect classification rendering of the Fourteenth Amendment's command. Importantly, she grounded her principle of skepticism in the claim that "the Fifth and Fourteenth Amendments to the Constitution protect persons, not groups."[85] That statement rejects the notion that the Court would engage in more searching scrutiny when the law affects insular and discrete or suspect classes.[86]

If O'Connor is the entrepreneurial jurist who reconfigures the aims of the Fourteenth Amendment from an engagement with the context and history of discrimination to the application of an abstract principle against any kind of classification, then Kennedy is the innovator who grasps a new concept—dignity—to push O'Connor's move further.[87] O'Connor shifts from class to classification, and Kennedy does not even seek to classify. Nowhere is this universal aspiration to an individualized notion of equal personhood more evident than in Kennedy's reliance on dignity in the gay rights rulings.

The Dignity Alternative: The Distinct Pathway of Gay Rights Jurisprudence

Dignity as a textual constitutional value, or "a social value that has been expressed—explicitly or implicitly—in the constitution of the state," gained popularity in the wake of World War II.[88] Post-war constitutions and treaties are replete with references to dignity as the foundation for rights. However, dignity is not explicitly part of the US constitutional text, even as it has been mentioned periodically in US constitutional decision-making. The Supreme Court has invoked the concept of dignity, perhaps more in dissents than majority rulings, since the 1940s. The earliest uses, however, hardly amounted to a consistent doctrine or definition; scholars have called the use of dignity "episodic and underdeveloped," "tentative," and "fragmented."[89] Aharon Barak summarizes the trend of the Court: "The Justices point out that their decisions are an attempt to realize human dignity, but they do not explain what human dignity is, what it covers, and what are the elements that comprise it."[90] Barak points out that at least three Supreme Court justices are crucial to the articulation of dignity as a constitutional value: William (Frank) Murphy, William Brennan, and Anthony Kennedy. Indeed, Kennedy has turned dignity into the rhetorical cornerstone of contemporary gay rights discourse in *Romer, Lawrence, Windsor,* and *Obergefell.*

The *New York Times'* banner headline on June 27, 2015, of "Equal Dignity" was taken from Kennedy's ruling in *Obergefell.*[91] Kennedy characterized the plaintiff's desire for marriage as asking for "equal dignity in the eyes of the law. The Constitution grants them that right."[92] In *Obergefell,* the majority decision invoked the phrase "equal dignity" twice, and that phrase marked how distinct *Obergefell* and other gay rights rulings seemed to be. For example, *Loving v. Virginia,* the decision that forty-eight years earlier had struck down state bans on interracial marriage, never used the word *dignity.* The phrase "equal dignity" was utilized once in *Windsor* when the majority declared that "the history of DOMA's enactment and its own text demonstrate that interference with the equal dignity of same-sex marriages, a dignity conferred by the States in the exercise of their sovereign power, was more than an incidental effect of the federal statute. It was its essence."[93] The phrase was not used at all in *Lawrence*. Nevertheless, *Lawrence* did mention *dignity* twice, *Windsor* nine times, and *Obergefell* nine times. While all of these discussed the fundamental dignity of gays and lesbians to love whom they choose, none identified gays and lesbians as a suspect class or sexual orientation to be a suspect classification.

The first refusal to identify gays and lesbians as a suspect class came in 1996, when the Supreme Court struck down an amendment to the Colorado constitution that prohibited adoption or enforcement of any statute "whereby homosexual, lesbian or bisexual orientation, conduct, practices or relationships shall constitute or otherwise be the basis of or entitle any persons or class of persons to have or claim any minority status, quota, preferences, protected status or claim of discrimination."[94] Kennedy argued for the majority in *Romer* that the state constitutional amendment under review unconstitutionally "named [a] class, a class we shall refer to as homosexual persons or gays and lesbians," and restricted the rights of these persons and no other.[95] The amendment unjustly imposed a "broad and undifferentiated disability on a single named group," cutting that group out of the democratic process.[96] The imposition was so broad that it could not be explained by any other motive than "animus toward the class it affects."[97] While the Court appears to be beginning to characterize gays, lesbians, and bisexuals as a suspect class by identifying them as a discriminated class, Kennedy holds that the class status is created by the state of Colorado for unconstitutional, purposeful discrimination; the state created a class in order to discriminate against it. The Court, it would seem, has no intention of compounding this action by utilizing traditional suspect class analysis. Instead, it states that Colorado cannot put forward a legitimate interest to justify its constitutional amendment. The Court declared the amendment a "status-based enactment divorced from any factual context from which we could discern a relationship to legitimate state interests; it is a classification of persons undertaken for its own sake, something the Equal Protection Clause does not permit."[98]

Kennedy's refusal to employ the established principles of traditional suspect class/classification doctrine carried forward into *Lawrence*, *Windsor*, and *Obergefell*. *Lawrence* has been called the *Brown v. Board of Education* and the *Loving v. Virginia* moment of the gay, lesbian, and bisexual rights movement.[99] Unlike *Brown* and *Loving*, though, Kennedy explicitly ruled that *Lawrence* was not decided primarily as a matter of equal protection.[100] Rather, he subsumed an equal protection claim under a construction of fundamental rights as protected by due process: "As an alternative argument in this case, counsel for the petitioners and some amici contend that *Romer* provides the basis for declaring the Texas statute invalid under the Equal Protection Clause. That is a tenable argument, but we conclude the instant case requires us to address whether *Bowers* itself has continuing validity."[101] Kennedy sought to reverse *Bowers v. Hardwick*, and to do so, he had to engage *Bowers* on its own assumptions.[102] By subsuming equality under due process liberty, *Lawrence* stands primarily as a ruling about *individual* freedom, autonomy, and ultimately what the Court called dignity rather than a ruling about equality or about recognizing histories of discrimination and mistreatment of a particular class.

This distinction is heightened by *Lawrence*'s failure to determine whether gays and lesbians constituted a suspect class such that any equal protection claim made would be reviewed under a higher scrutiny threshold. Kennedy's ruling makes no mention of scrutiny levels. By avoiding an equal protection argument, the Court sidestepped addressing if sexuality was a suspect classification, if gays, lesbians, or bisexuals constituted a suspect class, or if scrutiny needed to be applied. This evasion did not go unnoticed. As Scalia pointed out in dissent,

> Though there is discussion of "fundamental proposition[s]," . . . and "fundamental decisions" . . . nowhere does the Court's opinion declare that homosexual sodomy is a "fundamental right" under the Due Process Clause; nor does it subject the Texas law to the standard of review that would be appropriate (strict scrutiny) if homosexual sodomy *were* a "fundamental right." Thus, while overruling the *outcome* of *Bowers*, the Court leaves strangely untouched its central legal conclusion: "[R]espondents would have us announce . . . a fundamental right to engage in homosexual

sodomy. This we are quite unwilling to do." Instead the Court simply describes petitioners' conduct as "an exercise of their liberty"—which it undoubtedly is—and proceeds to apply an unheard-of form of rational-basis review that will have far reaching implications beyond this case.[103]

Rather than adhering to tiered scrutiny, Kennedy spoke to how criminalization statutes denied gays and lesbians their dignity: "Adults may choose to enter upon this relationship in the confines of their homes and their own private lives and still retain their dignity as free persons."[104] The Court relied on dignity as an operative concept: laws that violate dignity are grounded in no other motivation than animus and thus are unconstitutional.

Kennedy's reliance on dignity surfaced again in *Windsor*. When ruling that the federal government must recognize same-sex marriages already recognized by state governments, Kennedy indicated this requirement was necessitated by dignity. He began by noting, "It seems fair to conclude that, until recent years, many citizens had not even considered the possibility that two persons of the same sex might aspire to occupy the same status and dignity as that of a man and woman in lawful marriage."[105] He stipulated that when a state recognizes marriage, it "confer[s] upon them a dignity and status of immense import."[106] The state enhances the "recognition, dignity, and protection of the class in their own community."[107] He characterized DOMA as creating an "injury and indignity" that "is a deprivation of an essential part of liberty protected by the Fifth Amendment."[108] He considered New York's decision to recognize same-sex marriage as constituting "further protection and dignity to that bond" and as representing a determination by the state that same-sex couples were "worthy of dignity in the community equal with all other marriages."[109] He contended, "The history of DOMA's enactment and its own text demonstrate that interference with the equal dignity of same-sex marriages, a dignity conferred by the States in the exercise of their sovereign power, was more than an incidental effect of the federal statute."[110] Furthermore, he argued that marriage creates responsibilities and rights, which "enhance the dignity and integrity of the person," that DOMA denies.[111] Finally, he declared the statute invalid because "no legitimate purpose overcomes the purpose and effect to disparage and to injure those whom the State, by its marriage laws, sought to protect in personhood and dignity."[112] While Kennedy utilized the phrase "legitimate purpose," his reliance on dignity elides the formal structure of scrutiny tiers. He did not articulate the level of scrutiny applied. Given his discussion of animus, dignity, and legitimate purpose, the ruling suggests that there is no *rational basis* for the federal government to deny recognition to same-sex marriage.

On June 26, 2015, the second anniversary of *Windsor* and the twelfth anniversary of *Lawrence*, Kennedy issued another ruling that would endear him to gay and lesbian rights activists. Kennedy delivered the ruling for the five-justice majority in *Obergefell*, which held "that same-sex couples may exercise the fundamental right to marry. No longer may this liberty be denied to them."[113] As in *Lawrence* and *Windsor*, in *Obergefell* Kennedy premised the decision on dignity; he defined marriage as a union that "always has promised nobility and dignity to all persons, without regard to their station in life."[114] He discussed how marriage has transformed to recognize the "equal dignity" of women in cross-sex marriages. He suggested, reiterating *Lawrence*, that personal intimate choice was a marker of that dignity. He referred to marriage as a status where "there is dignity in the bond between two men or two women who seek to marry and in their autonomy to make such profound choices"; he called state recognition of marriage a "basic dignity." He then defined the action sought by petitioners: "They ask for equal dignity in the eyes of the law. The Constitution grants them that right."[115] The word *scrutiny* appeared once in the majority decision, and only in a description of the Hawaii ruling granting marriage recognition in 1993. The phrases "suspect class" or "protected class" did not appear.

Lest Kennedy's turn to dignity and abandonment of tiered scrutiny be considered the musings of one individual, it is important to note that these ideas have traveled to the executive branch. The Department of Justice during the Obama administration tellingly abandoned the multiple contextual considerations employed by scrutiny doctrine for a general dignity claim.

For example, in 2011, before *Windsor* and *Obergefell*, Attorney General Eric Holder announced that the administration would not defend DOMA in federal court. President Obama concluded that section 3 of the law, which defined marriage as a union between one man and one woman, was unconstitutional. According to Holder, President Obama determined that gays and lesbians constituted a suspect class, that laws affecting that class should be held to heightened judicial scrutiny, and that DOMA would not survive that level of scrutiny: "Given a number of factors, including a documented history of discrimination, classifications based on sexual orientation should be subject to a more heightened standard of scrutiny."[116] Holder's statement is significant because of how closely it held to the traditional equal protection analysis; it recognized gays and lesbians as a suspect class even as it acknowledged that the Supreme Court has not.

When Attorney General Loretta Lynch commented in 2016—after *Windsor* and *Obergefell*—on whether and how a North Carolina law, the Public Facilities Privacy and Security Act, or HB2, violated existing federal civil rights statutes or the Fourteenth Amendment's guarantee of equal protection, she did not employ scrutiny doctrine. Instead, she invoked dignity. The law, which prevented municipalities from passing anti-discrimination ordinances that would include sexual orientation and gender identity and specifically banned transgender individuals from public restrooms that correspond to their gender identity, was deemed "in direct opposition to federal laws prohibiting discrimination on the basis of sex and gender identity." Because North Carolina responded by suing the federal government, the Department of Justice brought a countersuit. Explaining part of the rationale for that suit, Lynch stated the following: "This action is about a great deal more than just bathrooms. This is about the dignity and respect we accord our fellow citizens and the laws that we, as a people and as a country, have enacted to protect them—indeed, to protect all of us. And it's about the founding ideals that have led this country—haltingly but inexorably—in the direction of fairness, inclusion and equality for all Americans."[117] She went on to invoke a long history of discrimination that the Court has invalidated, ranging from Jim Crow laws to bans on same-sex marriage.

By framing HB2 as a legislative backlash against LGBT rights recognition, Lynch channeled Kennedy. She characterized the law as "inflict[ing] further indignity on a population that has already suffered far more than its fair share. This law provides no benefit to society—all it does is harm innocent Americans."[118] First, Lynch's rhetorical invocation of dignity and how she defined dignity parallels *Obergefell*—namely, without reference to suspect class status or political powerlessness, which indicates that Kennedy's ideas traveled to another branch. Second, like Kennedy, Lynch indicated that LGBTQ+ persons have suffered a history of discrimination, but she did not translate that recognition into a claim of suspect class or higher scrutiny. That move is in stark contrast to Holder's statement from 2011. Third, Lynch referenced how an appeal to dignity was inherently not class specific; instead, the Department of Justice's actions were meant to "protect all of us." In short, the invocation of dignity refuses to consider discrimination historically and contextually as suspect class doctrine requires.

Our argument does not speak only to how Kennedy has innovated equal protection jurisprudence by abandoning a contextual remedial approach and replacing it with an abstract universalism of dignity that can more easily keep status quo biases and discrimination in place. We further suggest that dignity can be turned to antithetical ends. Even as it has been developed and asserted in the context of Supreme Court gay rights jurisprudence, the Court can and has invoked it to support readings of law that could curb LGBTQ+ claims and progressive aspirations toward racial justice and gender equality. While that idea is developed in the next section, it is important to note that the Trump administration invoked dignity to this end. On June 12, 2020, the Department of Health and Human Services (HHS) finalized a rule that overturned an Obama-era directive that had, through the Affordable Care Act, guaranteed equal access to healthcare regardless of sexual orientation and gender identity.[119] Explaining this change, which endangers the health of anyone who identifies as LGBTQ+, Roger Severino, director of the Office of Civil Rights within HHS, defended the move: "HHS respects the dignity of every human being, and as we have shown in our response to the [COVID-19] pandemic, we vigorously protect and enforce the civil rights of all to the fullest extent permitted by our laws as passed by Congress."[120] The statement posits that since sexual orientation and gender identity are not named categories in federal civil rights law, HHS cannot guarantee individuals with those identities equal treatment. The potential impact is that the federal government cannot compel treatment providers to care for these individuals if such treatment violates the caregiver's beliefs. Doing so may violate that believer's dignity. In other words, dignity—which has most fully grounded gay and lesbian rights—can be invoked and manipulated to serve ends that harm gay, lesbian, bisexual, transgender, and queer people.

Dignity: Its Value to Politically Conservative Aims

Conservative thinkers, lawyers, and political actors may come to accept *Obergefell* and the broader gay and lesbian-rights jurisprudence because of how its underlying rationale, which places dignity at the center of equal protection, can serve the ends of the conservative legal movement. This movement refers to interests that coalesced since the 1970s to challenge New Deal and civil rights–era liberalism. These include corporate interests seeking to limit federal regulatory authority of the economy,[121] conservative interests opposed to remedial policies aimed at promoting racial equity,[122] and religious interests enraged by the Supreme Court's sanctioning of contraception and abortion, decriminalization of homosexuality, and recognition of same-sex marriage, as well as its curbing of public prayer.[123] While dignity in US constitutional jurisprudence has been primarily developed by Kennedy in recent gay rights rulings, the ill-defined and perhaps inchoate notion of dignity is malleable and has been utilized by Kennedy to strike against affirmative action and abortion access, positions lauded by political conservatives. In other words, dignity, the cornerstone of progressive rulings on gay rights, can ironically become the foundation of an equal protection jurisprudence that undermines other progressive objectives.

Gorsuch hinted at how conservatives might utilize *Obergefell* when he stated, during his confirmation hearings, that he was not inclined to consider persons as fitting into a particular class. Gorsuch's position fits the Court's conservative rereading of the Fourteenth Amendment since at least the *Adarand* ruling. When Senator Dick Durbin (D-IL) asked whether Gorsuch had any record of "standing up for those minorities [he] believe[s] are not being treated fairly" and whether the judge could "point to statements or cases [he had] ruled on relative to that class," Gorsuch rejected the notion of class or group identity entirely: "Senator, I've tried to treat each case and each person as a person—not a 'this kind of person,' not a 'that kind of person'—a person. Equal justice under the law. It is a radical promise in the history of mankind."[124]

With this statement, Gorsuch challenged one of the defining frameworks of equal protection jurisprudence—namely, suspect class and scrutiny doctrine. He also signaled his alignment with a conservative legal movement that has, since the late 1980s, reshaped this doctrine away from class and toward classification. In so doing, conservative jurists have shifted it from its original purpose of striking against subordination of discrete classes to a doctrine that is skeptical of any identity-based *group* classification of *individuals*. In other words, suspect *class* has been replaced gradually with suspect *classification*; whereas the former might consider laws that harm African Americans constitutionally illegitimate, the latter considers any law that classifies by race to be illegitimate.[125] Whereas the former notion would compel striking against oppression of groups of people who have faced historic and ongoing discrimination, the latter would treat attempts to remedy that discrimination with identity-based policies—for example, bussing for school integration—as constitutionally suspect.

The Supreme Court's gay rights rulings since *Romer* have achieved equal rights recognition without relying on scrutiny doctrine, and as such, they may lay the foundation for a conservative alternative to suspect class/classification doctrine. These decisions have discussed how government regulations, such as criminalization statutes or marriage bans, harm the *dignity* of the gay or lesbian *individual* rather than consider gays or lesbians a suspect class deserving of constitutional protections. Already, the Court has deployed dignity to challenge an evaluation of discrimination that would pay close attention to histories of discrimination and powerlessness and invoke a universalized and individualized notion of liberty that is hardly attentive to context. Ironically, dignity can become the foundation of a legal tradition that undermines strides toward other progressive objectives. Kennedy has invoked dignity as a basis to strike *against* racial equality and abortion access, positions lauded by political conservatives.

Consider Kennedy's invocation of dignity in his dissent in *Stenberg v. Carhart* (2000).[126] The Court struck down a Nebraska prohibition on late-term abortions. Kennedy considered the ban constitutional in part because he claimed the abortion procedures bore a striking relation to infanticide and undermined the dignity of the physician performing the procedure and the dignity of the fetus: "A State may take measures to ensure the medical profession and its members are viewed as healers sustained by a compassionate and rigorous ethic and cognizant of the dignity and value of human life, even life which cannot survive without the assistance of others."[127]

Kennedy revived this argument seven years later in *Gonzales v. Carhart* (2007), which upheld the Federal Partial-Birth Abortion Ban Act of 2003. That statute banned a particular late-term abortion procedure known as dilation and evacuation.[128] While abortion access had been, to this point, litigated under the fundamental right of privacy and thus laws affecting it held to heightened scrutiny, Kennedy reviewed this federal statute under the lowest threshold of rational basis review. He contended that a right to abortion access was not at stake; rather, the state's right to ban a medical procedure was. Such a ban fell within the domain of government's power to regulate so long as the regulation had a rational relationship to a legitimate purpose. Kennedy spoke to the need to maintain human dignity as this legitimate purpose. He characterized the federal statute as "express[ing] respect for the dignity of human life" and stated, "No one would dispute that, for many, D&E is a procedure itself laden with the power to devalue human life."[129] His dignity concern was limited in scope and application. According to one legal scholar, "The dignity interests of women confronted with an unwanted pregnancy went largely unacknowledged."[130] Kennedy was concerned with the dignity of the physician and of fetal life; he considered the dignity of the woman only insofar as she should be saved from the emotional trauma of choosing the procedure: "It seems unexceptionable to conclude some women come to regret their choice to abort the infant life they once created and sustained."[131] Other legal scholars called the ruling "remarkable" for "its almost complete indifference toward the holders of those rights: women" and argued that "abortions seem only, in the eyes of the Supreme Court to involve the 'abortion doctor,' 'the fetus,' and 'the cervix.'"[132]

Also consider how Kennedy has claimed that classification of any kind undermines dignity. In *J.E.B. v Alabama*, which struck down a state law that limited women's ability to serve on a jury, Kennedy wrote that the discrimination violated women's dignity.[133] When evaluating whether an individual suffered race-based discrimination in exercising the right to vote in *Rice v. Cayetano*, Kennedy contended that racial classifications violated dignity: "One of the principle reasons race is treated as a forbidden classification is that it demeans the dignity and worth of a person to be judged by ancestry instead of by his or her own merit and essential qualities."[134]

Treating any and all racial classification as constitutionally suspect is no more evident than in Kennedy's concurrence in *Parents Involved in Community Schools v. Seattle School District No. 1 et al.*: "To be forced to live under a state-mandated racial label is inconsistent with the dignity of individuals in society."[135] Kennedy's aversion to classification suggests that it can be treated with skepticism and that the Court can avoid reinforcing it through its rendering of the Fourteenth Amendment's equal protection guarantee as a group-based right, with groups defined either as classes or by classifications.

Instead, Kennedy sounds the conservative chord of equality at the level of individuals—that all individuals should be treated the same before the law. Dignity, as expressed in the gay rights decisions, offers that potential. Unsurprisingly, it also undergirds conservative aims to challenge abortion access and eliminate affirmative action. Even though political progressives might applaud Kennedy's dignity doctrine in gay rights decisions, one must understand that it has also grounded conservative rulings.

Whose Dignity Matters More? Conflicting Rights Claims

Since Kennedy crafted *Romer*, *Lawrence*, *Windsor*, and *Obergefell*, his repeated invocation of dignity may be mere personal proclivity, an attempt to fit gay, lesbian, and bisexual equality within a set of personal values that do not correspond to the identity group politics on which scrutiny doctrine rests.[136] Indeed, much has been made of Kennedy's use of dignity in gay rights, abortion, and death penalty jurisprudence and of how dignity occupies a position within Kennedy's Catholicism.[137] It is also possible—though more investigation of Kennedy's papers would be needed—that his reliance on dignity purposively recalls the position of another Republican-appointed judge increasingly out of step with the ideological trajectory of the conservative movement: John Paul Stevens.[138] Stevens dissented the following in *Bowers*:

These cases do not deal with the individual's interest in protection from unwarranted public attention, comment, or exploitation. They deal, rather, with the individual's right to make certain unusually important decisions that will affect his own, or his family's, destiny. The Court has referred to such decisions as implicating "basic values," as being "fundamental," and as being dignified by history and tradition. The character of the Court's language in these cases brings to mind the origins of the American heritage of freedom—the abiding interest in individual liberty that makes certain state intrusions on the citizen's right to decide how he will live his own life intolerable. Guided by history, our tradition of respect for the dignity of individual choice in matters of conscience and the restraints implicit in the federal system, federal judges have accepted the responsibility for recognition and protection of these rights in appropriate cases.[139]

His conceptualization of sexuality was distinct from that of the other justices, who understood homosexuality only as a sexual act either entitled or not to occur in the private home. For Stevens, privacy could not capture the stakes of the criminal sanctioning of intimacy. Instead, he suggested that sexual intimacy is an expression of dignity. By replacing privacy with dignity, Stevens, if only for himself and Justices Brennan and Marshall, who joined his dissent, embraced a richer conception of how sexuality defines selfhood across private and public spheres.

But does the recognition of gays and lesbians' dignity validate rights claims beyond the bedroom or the confines of their relationships? The Trump administration's rule that limits access to healthcare for LGBTQ+ individuals indicates that the answer is no.[140] The Supreme Court decided otherwise. On June 15, 2020, in *Bostock v. Clayton County, Georgia*, a six-justice majority ruled that federal law prohibited discrimination in employment based on sexual orientation and gender identity; the existing ban on sex discrimination in Title VII of the 1964 Civil Rights Act protects a gay, lesbian, bisexual, or transgender person from employment discrimination. As Justice Gorsuch made clear, "An employer who fires an individual for being homosexual or transgender fires that person for traits or actions it would not have questioned in members of a different sex. Sex plays a necessary and undisguisable role in the decision, exactly what Title VII forbids."[141] Tellingly, Gorsuch never uttered the word *dignity*.

Perhaps Gorsuch avoided dignity because whatever dignity doctrine Kennedy developed fails to provide a clear answer to this recent front in gay and lesbian rights. This front takes rights claims fully into the public sphere: equal treatment in employment, housing, and public accommodations. Kennedy's doctrine pits one conception of dignity (that of the religious believer or the speech expresser) against another (that of the individual seeking to live free from discrimination). Historically, when the Court has construed gay rights claims to conflict with First Amendment claims to freedom of expression, the latter have won.[142] Furthermore, Kennedy's reliance on dignity could be used to curb rights claims—particularly those that take expression of sexual identity beyond the heteronormative bounds of the private romantic bedroom, household, and family—precisely because the term can be so easily manipulated.

Masterpiece Cakeshop v. Colorado Civil Rights Commission provided an opportunity to grapple with this problem and to provide a direction to where a dignity doctrine might lead.[143] Unfortunately, as Kennedy deployed dignity in *Masterpiece*, the concept seemed to lead nowhere, which is to say it was not (and could not?) be used to resolve the dispute. The case involved a same-sex couple, Charlie Craig and David Mullins, who sought the services of Jack Phillips, owner of Masterpiece Cakeshop, to design a wedding cake. This occurred in 2012, when same-sex marriage was not yet recognized in Colorado (before *Obergefell* recognized same-sex marriages throughout the nation). The couple sought to wed in Massachusetts, where marriages were recognized, and then to hold a reception for family and friends at home in Colorado. Phillips indicated that he would sell them other baked goods, but he could not bake them a custom wedding cake because same-sex marriage violated his beliefs.

Craig and Mullins filed a claim under the Colorado Anti-Discrimination Act (CADA), which prevents discrimination in public accommodations, defined as any "place of business engaged in any sales to the public," based on a set of protected characteristics, including sexual orientation. The Colorado Civil Rights Commission (CCRC) investigated and found probable cause for discrimination. The alleged violation of CADA was referred to the Office of Administrative Courts. An administrative law judge found for Craig and Mullins. Phillips appealed to the CCRC, but the CCRC affirmed the administrative law judge's ruling. Phillips appealed to the Colorado Court of Appeals in 2015, but this court also found for Craig and Mullins. The Colorado Supreme Court denied Phillips's request for review, so Phillips appealed to the US Supreme Court.

In their written brief to the Supreme Court, lawyers for Phillips argued that CADA interfered with Phillips's free religious expression and that any statute that conflicted with this First Amendment right would have to survive strict scrutiny (the state can only restrict his right to religious exercise if there is a compelling government interest, and they can only do so through the least restrictive means available). They maintained that the CCRC's objectives to prevent discrimination, to enable equal access to public accommodations, and to maintain the same-sex couple's dignity did not meet the strict scrutiny threshold. They argued that baking a custom cake constituted a form of free speech and/or expressive conduct.

The CCRC countered that CADA would survive strict scrutiny but that it need not be applied, as the law at issue affected *commercial conduct* and not speech. Phillips violated the law not because he held certain beliefs but because he refused to serve an entire class of persons who were a protected class as defined by CADA. Significantly, *both sides claimed dignitary harm*; Phillips claimed that CADA harmed the dignity of religious believers, and Craig and Mullins argued that the denial of services undermined the dignity afforded to gays and lesbians by law.

Kennedy's decision for the majority of seven justices neither engaged the level of scrutiny applied nor ruled on whether CADA violated First Amendment rights. Kennedy did recognize the tension in the competing claims to rights in his summary of the question at hand: "The case presents difficult questions as to the proper reconciliation of at least two principles. The first is the authority of a State and its governmental entities to protect the rights and dignity of gay persons who are, or wish to be, married but who face discrimination when they seek goods or services. The second is the right of all persons to exercise fundamental freedoms under the First Amendment, as applied to the States through the Fourteenth Amendment."[144] At issue for Kennedy was how to balance the Constitution's requirement of equal treatment against the Constitution's requirement of free religious exercise and free expression. Rather than answer this question, Kennedy restated the quandary throughout his ruling. He reaffirmed the dignity of gays and lesbians: "Our society has come to the recognition that gay persons and gay couples cannot be treated as social outcasts or as inferior in dignity and worth."[145] This imperative must recognize, as he wrote in *Obergefell*, that "those who adhere to religious doctrines, may continue to advocate with utmost, sincere conviction that, by divine precepts, same-sex marriage should not be condoned. The First Amendment ensures that religious organizations and persons are given proper protection as they seek to teach the principles that are so fulfilling and so central to their lives and faiths, and to their own deep aspirations to continue the family structure they have long revered."[146] Consequently, Kennedy continued in *Masterpiece* with the following: "At the same time, the religious and philosophical objections to gay marriage are protected views and in some instances protected forms of expression."[147] Nevertheless, Kennedy contended that these religious objections cannot extend to rights in commerce: "It is a general rule that such objections do not allow business owners and other actors in the economy and in society to deny protected persons equal access to goods and services under a neutral and generally applicable public accommodations law."[148] Back and forth, Kennedy articulated the two positions that seemed locked in unresolvable tension.

As Kennedy worked through the issue at stake, the balance of the two principles seemed to tip in favor of the same-sex couple. A blanket exemption to equal treatment on the basis of free exercise of religion goes too far: "If that exception were not confined, then a long list of persons who provide goods and services for marriages and weddings might refuse to do so for gay persons, thus resulting in a community-wide stigma inconsistent with the history and dynamics of civil rights laws that ensure equal access to goods, services, and public accommodations."[149] He imagined reasonable limits on public accommodations to be possible: "Any decision in favor of the baker would have to be sufficiently constrained, lest all purveyors of goods and services who object to gay marriages for moral and religious reasons in effect be allowed to put up signs saying 'no goods or services will be sold if they will be used for gay marriages,' something that would impose a serious stigma on gay persons."[150] Indeed, Kennedy articulates a distinction on which to act. Legal journalist Emily Bazelon has also specified this principle. When responding to the idea that churches might be compelled to officiate same-sex marriages, Bazelon dismissed it: "I think there's an easy reason that the answer is no: There's a clear legal line between a for-profit business and a nonprofit organization."[151] Kennedy did not pursue this distinction even as he acknowledged its logic. He resorted to philosophical considerations of pluralism, noting how each side has articulated reasonable positions to be gauged.[152]

Instead of resolving the conflict, Kennedy's ruling for the majority in *Masterpiece* called attention to a process failure that avoided the substantive matter. He claimed that the CCRC failed to provide due respect to and neutral consideration of Phillips's objections to same-sex marriage. Hostility was allegedly evident in the statement from a CCRC member: "If a businessman wants to do business in the state and he's got an issue with the—the law's impacting his personal belief system, he needs to look at being able to compromise."[153] That statement could be positing that the businessman engages in the balancing that Kennedy suggests the Court must perform, but Kennedy read it as hostile because of a subsequent statement made by a CCRC member: "I would also like to reiterate what we said in the hearing or the last meeting. Freedom of religion and religion has been used to justify all kinds of discrimination throughout history, whether it be slavery, whether it be the holocaust, whether it be—I mean, we—we can list hundreds of situations where freedom of religion has been used to justify discrimination. And to me it is one of the most despicable pieces of rhetoric that people can use to—to use their religion to hurt others."[154] This declaration is said to have revealed bias because it called faith "despicable" and implied that belief was insincere. But does the statement suggest that reading? The commissioner was drawing attention to how religious beliefs have been used to justify a broad range of policies—from slavery to bans on interracial sex and marriage to bans on same-sex intimacy—that would now be understood as grounded in animus.[155] Can the observation of a well-evidenced historical pattern be an indication of undue prejudice against a religious believer?

By focusing on the alleged procedural breakdown at the CCRC review, Kennedy avoided the substantive issue. He did not (and perhaps could not) offer the balancing for which he called. Maybe this is because dignity does not admit of a metric that can provide such balancing. If everyone holds or is entitled to be recognized as having dignity, then no one's dignity can be said to be more valued without denying a principle of equality.[156] Kennedy reached for a process critique perhaps because his dignity jurisprudence had hit a substantive dead end. Thus he ended the decision where he began, by noting that the Court will have to balance the issues to which Kennedy proved unwilling or unable: "The outcome of cases like this in other circumstances must await further elaboration in the courts, all in the context of recognizing that these disputes must be resolved with tolerance, without undue disrespect to sincere religious beliefs, and without subjecting gay persons to indignities when they seek goods and services in an open market."[157] Put differently, everyone has or is entitled to being recognized as having dignity, so the case could not be resolved by resorting to the idea of equal dignity. In this sense, *Masterpiece* reveals the dead end of dignity when applied to rights in commerce.

The *Bostock* ruling tees up a future case that could compel a resolution to this quandary. That decision was a significant victory for the LGBTQ+ community: until this ruling, it was legal to fire someone for their sexual orientation and/or gender identity in about half of the US states.[158] Nevertheless, Gorsuch placed caveats on his ruling for the majority by ruminating on circumstances not presented in *Bostock* or its companion cases.[159] He opined that should such cases come before the Court, the limits of *Bostock* could be elucidated:

We are also deeply concerned with preserving the promise of the free exercise of religion enshrined in our Constitution; that guarantee lies at the heart of our pluralistic society. . . . As a result of its deliberations in adopting the law [the Civil Rights Act of 1964], Congress included an express statutory exception for religious organizations. This Court has also recognized that the First Amendment can bar the application of employment discrimination laws "to claims concerning the employment relationship between a religious institution and its ministers." And Congress has gone a step further yet in the Religious Freedom Restoration

Act of 1993 (RFRA). That statute prohibits the federal government from substantially burdening a person's exercise of religion unless it demonstrates that doing so both furthers a compelling governmental interest and represents the least restrictive means of furthering that interest. Because RFRA operates as a kind of super statute, displacing the normal operation of other federal laws, it might supersede Title VII's commands in appropriate cases.[160]

The case before the Court did not require resolving a conflict between an LGBTQ+ claim to equality and the right of a religious believer to hire, fire, promote, or demote whom they choose because of religious belief. It did not present a balancing of dignity claims. While Kennedy avoided such balancing in *Masterpiece* by recourse to a procedural critique, Gorsuch avoided it because the question was not present. Nevertheless, Gorsuch voiced ideas he foreshadowed in his *Masterpiece* concurrence. The First Amendment and the Religious Freedom Restoration Act could supersede Title VII, thereby suggesting that the dignity of religious expression may be more valued than the dignity guaranteed to gays and lesbians in *Obergefell* and reiterated in *Masterpiece*. Gorsuch mapped the road for the conservative legal movement to take. While the decision is a victory for LGBTQ+ rights, it nevertheless contains valuable ideas for conservatives on how to curb its potential.[161] Our point is not to resolve the conflict or critique the resolution at which he hints. Rather, we argue that the recourse to dignity fails to offer a resolution.

Conclusion

Kennedy's oeuvre of gay rights rulings—*Romer, Lawrence, Windsor*, and *Obergefell*—does critical work to supplant the tiered scrutiny doctrine with a paradigm grounded in dignity. When we consider how Kennedy has deployed the term in other arenas of liberty, it becomes clear how conservative justices can adopt dignity to curb the aspirations of the political left, which has been at the forefront of LGBTQ+ rights advocacy. Dignity has already been used to support outcomes that challenge progressive values and bolster substantive legal and political objectives associated with the conservative legal movement in the United

States. Consequently, we are skeptical of dignity as a useful principle in US constitutional decision-making.

That skepticism rests on three additional claims. First, dignity as formulated in Kennedy's marriage equality rulings creates boundaries and constraints that rely on neoliberal respectability and refuse queer sociality. As queer theorist Tim Dean, summarizing Michael Warner's arguments, reminds us, "The campaign for same-sex marriage . . . confer[s] on erotic relations a measure of respectability by privatizing intimacy. Queers confront a kind of Faustian bargain, whereby we tacitly agree to renounce public sex—or to sell downriver those who find value in it—in return for the legitimacy afforded by the right to marry."[162]

Second, because gay and lesbian rights jurisprudence is grounded in dignity rather than the suspect class/classification and tiered scrutiny doctrines that ground race and sex equality, it can be conceptualized as part of a longer trajectory pursued by conservative jurists to abandon any further elaboration of those doctrines. But more than that, it also builds the foundation for an alternative approach that embraces the individualistic as well as community-negating and context-ignoring pathologies of our neoliberal moment. The Court's turn away from suspect class and toward suspect classification, which began in the late 1980s, is a crucial step in a broader neoliberal aspiration to valorize individual rights and abstract universalism while discarding the needed attention to context and history that might compel government action to promote equity. Chief Justice Roberts's consideration of bussing in *Parents Involved* is emblematic.[163] His aphoristic notion that the way to stop discriminating on race is simply to stop doing so reduces racism to "an individual phenomenon that need only be confined to the private realm to render it constitutionally irrelevant."[164] Conceptualizing discrimination this way absolves the justices of any need to consider how racism or sexism or anti-gay or anti-transgender bias may be structurally reproduced in policies or law. Any attention to "the institutional, cultural, and economic embedding of racial discrimination and its production of intractable patterns of hierarchy [and] exclusion" is tossed aside.[165] Kennedy's embrace of dignity as an abstract and universal right—in his concurrence in *Parents Involved* and in the gay rights and marriage equality rulings for which he is the primary author—takes the move from class to classification one step further. It avoids any reckoning with histories of structural inequity by promoting a universal principle—dignity—that already favors a particular way of being in the world but also appears as both aspirational and deceptively neutral.

Third, dignity—at least in Kennedy's body of decisions—does not resolve critical disputes, particularly with regard to equal treatment in commerce, housing, and public accommodations for LGBTQ+ individuals.[166] The *Masterpiece* ruling is illustrative. The decision reveals the limits of the dignity jurisprudence, or at least Kennedy's unwillingness to resolve the implications of the doctrinal tradition for which he seems singularly responsible. While he stipulates that gays and lesbians cannot be denied their dignity and that denial of services grounded in their sexual orientation would constitute an indignity, he nevertheless avoids this conclusion by taking refuge in a contestable diagnosis of a process failure.

Perhaps Kennedy's unwillingness to follow his own ideas to their logical conclusion is unsurprising, since he repeatedly refused to do so in his gay rights decisions. From *Romer* through *Obergefell*, Kennedy declined to designate gays and lesbians as a suspect class and to subject laws that discriminate against them to higher scrutiny even as he argued that they meet the criteria: they suffered a long history of discrimination (*Romer*, *Lawrence*, *Windsor*, and *Obergefell*), the discrimination has often rendered them politically powerless (*Romer*), the discrimination is grounded in an immutable trait (*Obergefell*), and the trait was irrelevant to government aims (*Lawrence* and *Obergefell*). Instead, Kennedy turned to dignity, a move that many legal scholars applauded in the immediate wake of *Obergefell* as an improvement on the tiered-scrutiny doctrine that defined race- and sex-based equality jurisprudence. *Masterpiece* reveals that perhaps this praise was immature, though. At most, *Masterpiece* shows that the Court is unsure about in which direction a dignity doctrine might lead, and the omission of dignity in the *Bostock* ruling suggests that perhaps the inchoate doctrine leads nowhere.

The conservative logic of the liberal victory of same-sex marriage—grounded in a dignity status to which gay and lesbian individuals can aspire—embraces a neoliberal notion of self and universality that decontextualizes the individual and strips the individual from historical and structural contexts. Ironically, that logic may restrict the recognition and exercise of the marriage right itself. Consequently, we must consider whether dignity is a dead end, especially as a foundation for LGBTQ+ equal treatment.

6

Is Dignity a Dead End?

Alternative Notions of Dignity and the Promise of
Our Anti-racist Constitution

Dignity has become a dominant lens through which LGBTQ+ rights have been viewed in the United States. Nevertheless, in light of the critiques raised in chapter 5, we must consider whether dignity is a dead end as a constitutionally useful concept. Is it too slippery a term that can be turned against the aspirations of LGBTQ+ communities and their allies? Can dignity provide a strong foundation for LGBTQ+ equal treatment?

To answer these questions, we begin by returning to the jurisprudential line of *Lawrence v. Texas, United States v. Windsor, Obergefell v. Hodges*, and *Masterpiece Cakeshop v. Colorado Civil Rights Commission*, which all speak of gay, lesbian, and bisexual rights as grounded in some form of a dignity claim.[1] Importantly, dignity does not even maintain a consistent meaning in this line. In *Lawrence*, the term suggests that certain identities or actions must be respected regardless of whether others approve, which links dignity to autonomy and individual choice. In *Windsor* and *Obergefell*, the term seems to reference the notion that certain identities or actions are respectable or considered worthy and approved of by others.[2] The dignity doctrine that emerges from these Supreme Court cases conflates these two distinct and, indeed, oppositional meanings, leaving dignity a muddled concept.

To wade through the confusion, we make three moves. First, we consider Justice Clarence Thomas's alternative construction of dignity, which he provides in dissent in *Obergefell*. We turn to Thomas's dissent because his is the only one that specifically explores the meaning of dignity and directly rebuts the majority's conception of the term; other dissenters do not address dignity to any substantial degree. According to Thomas, "human dignity is innate," and he rejects Kennedy's characterization of the term, claiming that it problematically positions dignity as "com[ing] from the Government."[3] For Thomas, dignity is unaffected by the actions of others and certainly unaffected by state action. We contend that Thomas's conception of dignity as pre-political and intrinsic to the individual only reifies the concept's exclusionary potential. It ignores how dignity can be harmed by state action, and it serves a conservative political objective of limiting government's responsibility and accountability to its citizens.

Since we reject Thomas's understanding, we explore legal and popular responses to dignity that would build or extend the meaning of the term as Kennedy deployed it in *Windsor* and *Obergefell*. In particular, we examine how advocates of consensual non-monogamy (CNM) and plural marriage build on these rulings to expand dignity's potential.[4] Importantly, CNM and plural marriage should be distinguished. CNM advocates do not necessarily advocate for plural marriage, instead often adopting more feminist and queer critiques of the institution's limits and inequities. We focus on plural marriage advocacy, since marriage currently requires recognition by the state. Plural marriage is illegal in the United States, but it has garnered sustained exploration in legal and political theory as well as increasing visibility in popular culture.[5] Extant research has revealed how both legal strategies and more popular-level advocacy for plural marriage have invoked tropes of dignity previously utilized in the political mobilization and litigation strategies for same-sex marriage. In other words, dignity's seduction of equality through sameness, or the access it provides to respectability, often overtakes or inflects attempts to construct alternatives that challenge coupled hetero- and homonormativity.

Finally, as we ask if dignity can be salvaged as a useful constitutional principle, we conclude by considering whether and how dignity could ground equality without the limits imposed by respectability. Our inquiry leads us to an exploration of the Constitution's Thirteenth Amendment rather than the more traditional foundation for equal protection—namely, the Fourteenth Amendment. We read the Thirteenth Amendment as an anti-stigma provision, which is a rendering supported by original and more modern understandings at the popular, legislative, and judicial levels. If it is so understood, this amendment may prove a useful foundation for a dignity claim. Nevertheless, even as we survey this possibility, we are skeptical of its potential. Our reading requires a set of reorientations toward racial justice that the contemporary Court seems unlikely to make. In total, this chapter examines three alternative notions of dignity: the pre-political conception offered by Justice Clarence Thomas, the seemingly transgressive possibilities of plural marriage advocates, and our own exploration of and advocacy for an expansive anti-racist reading of the Thirteenth Amendment. In so doing, we assess whether dignity is a dead end as a viable constitutional principle that can serve progressive aims.

From Where Does Dignity Come? Evaluating the Thomas Dissent in *Obergefell*

In both *Windsor* and *Obergefell*, Justice Anthony Kennedy, writing for the majority, discusses the recognition sought by same-sex couples as explicitly linked to dignity. While Kennedy deploys dignity as the cornerstone of *Lawrence*, *Windsor*, and *Obergefell*, the term carries a different meaning in *Lawrence* than it does in the marriage cases. In *Lawrence*, some scholars suggest that dignity is a synonym for respect of individual choice.[6] Kennedy writes, when declaring unconstitutional any criminalization of consensual same-sex intimacy between adults, that "the petitioners are entitled to respect for their private lives." This respect is linked to dignity: "It suffices for us to acknowledge that adults may choose to enter upon this relationship in the confines of their homes and their own private lives and still retain their dignity as free persons."[7]

Dignity serves different ends in the marriage rulings. In these decisions, dignity does not imply respect for personal choices; rather, it implies respectability via verisimilitude to heteronormative romance and marriage. As legal scholar Yuvraj Joshi notes, whereas "respect connotes acceptance of difference," respectability, by contrast, "connotes acceptance of the norm" or "follow[s] a normative standard of behavior in public, while being mindful of continual evaluations against that standard."[8] Consequently, *Windsor* and *Obergefell* stand for the proposition that dignity is conferred upon same-sex relationships by others ("continual evaluations") so long as they resemble those that the state already recognizes and privileges.

Political scientist and legal scholar Connor Ewing takes this distinction further by focusing on how and by whom dignity is conferred in *Windsor* versus how and by whom it is bestowed in *Obergefell*.[9] In *Windsor*, Kennedy describes how, in recognizing the marriages of same-sex couples, the state of New York "conferred upon them a dignity and status of immense import."[10] Elsewhere in the ruling, the justice held that marriage, because of the responsibilities and rights this status provides, "enhance[s]" the dignity of those who enter into it.[11] In *Windsor*, marriage bestows—or at least enhances—dignity, but so, too, does the state through its power to recognize marriage. Indeed, Kennedy notes that when the federal government denies marriage recognition where the state has already granted it, such refusal "demeans the couple . . . whose relationship the State has sought to dignify."[12] Thus in *Windsor*, Kennedy imagines state actors as taking purposeful action either to bestow dignity upon its citizens by publicly recognizing their marriage or to deny that dignity by refusing such recognition. Even Chief Justice John Roberts, in his dissent in *Windsor*, conceded the state government's authority to confer dignity by recognizing marriage: "No one questions the power of the States to define marriage (with the concomitant conferral of dignity and status)."[13] As Ewing argues, the decision "stresses the positive role of the state in augmenting the dignity of their citizens through the regulation of rights and responsibilities attending marriage."[14]

Ewing contends that the *Obergefell* ruling offers a different idea about how and by what authority dignity is bestowed. For Ewing, in *Obergefell*, Kennedy retreats from his earlier characterization of the state's awesome power to confer dignity upon same-sex couples. Instead, Ewing reads Kennedy's statement—"The lifelong union of a man and woman always has promised nobility and dignity to all persons, without regard to their station in life"—as contending that marriage itself dignifies the bonds of a couple.[15] Marriage, not the state, does the dignity-granting work. Another passage from Kennedy proves illustrative:

> From their beginning to their most recent page, the annals of history reveal the transcendent importance of marriage. The lifelong union of a man and a woman always has promised nobility and dignity to all persons, without regard to their station in life. Marriage is sacred to those

who live by their religions and offers unique fulfillment to those who find meaning in the secular realm. Its dynamic allows two people to find a life that could not be found alone, for a marriage becomes greater than just the two persons. Rising from the most basic human needs, marriage is essential to our most profound hopes and aspirations.[16]

Kennedy characterizes petitioners as understanding and committing to "the enduring importance of marriage."[17] He argues that same-sex couples do not seek to transform marriage; instead, they want to be brought within and included in its embrace: "It would misunderstand these men and women to say they disrespect the idea of marriage. Their plea is that they do respect it, respect it so deeply that they seek to find its fulfillment for themselves."[18] Through marriage, same-sex couples can find a dignity to which they would otherwise have no access: "There is dignity in the bond between two men or two women who seek to marry."[19] By reading marriage as the dignity-conferring institution, the final lines of *Obergefell*—"They ask for equal dignity in the eyes of the law. The Constitution grants them that right"—stands not for a claim of awesome state power but instead for the proposition that marriage is a dignity-granting institution to which there is no rational reason to deny same-sex couples.[20]

In *Obergefell*, Kennedy conceptualizes marriage as having so much capacity to bestow dignity upon those who enter it that those who find themselves, for whatever reason, unmarried should be pitied. He describes individuals who are unable to marry as "condemned to live in loneliness."[21] He suggests, rather forlornly, that they may despairingly "call out only to find no one there."[22] The statement creates a hierarchy of valued status: to be married is to be more complete. The content and tone of these statements are reminiscent of how New York City mayor Ed Koch disparaged gay men who sought kinship in the bathhouses: "It must be horrific, horrendous in its actuality to witness."[23] The statement betrays an inability to conceptualize fulfilling kinship structures and practices beyond romantic marriage. To be unmarried is rendered horrifying; it is to reside only in the darkness, alone and without emotional support or community. Both Kennedy and Koch seem either unable or unwilling to imagine forms of kinship, family, or connection that may be as, or even more, emotionally satisfying than state-sanctioned marriage and that may not be romantic, coupled, or even sexual.[24]

The distinction that Ewing draws between the state's authority to confer or enhance dignity (which he contends follows from *Windsor*) and marriage's independent capacity to have this effect (which he suggests is the implication of *Obergefell*) perhaps assuages fears of an overly powerful state.[25] The difference might also be explained as an artifact of the distinct facts that motivate the two cases. In *Windsor*, New York recognized the same-sex marriage of the petitioner, but in *Obergefell*, Ohio did not.[26] In *Obergefell*, the state was not trying to confer dignity, whereas in *Windsor*, the state was. Ohio was degrading the citizen and denying their dignity through its refusal to permit access to marriage.[27] This difference in the state action under review may have compelled Kennedy to offer an alternative conceptualization of dignity.

If Kennedy is trying to retreat from the implications of *Windsor* by narrowing the source of dignity in *Obergefell*, then this effort is lost on the dissenting justices. Evaluating these dissents is important insofar as chapter 5 has already highlighted a set of problems with Kennedy's conception of dignity. Do the dissents offer an alternative that prevents manipulating dignity for the conservative and even anti-LGBTQ+ political ends described in the previous chapter?[28] In *Obergefell*, the four dissenting justices pen their own dissents even as they join those of their brethren, yet only Roberts and Thomas discuss dignity explicitly.

Roberts's acknowledgment of dignity is curt, and he dismisses the term as irrelevant. After noting that there is no "'Nobility and Dignity' Clause in the Constitution," he focuses most of his dissent on critiquing the majority for removing the question at stake from democratic deliberation.[29] He sees the *Obergefell* majority as another instance of problematic decision-making that exemplifies judicial overreach.[30] By contrast, Thomas advances a substantive claim about the meaning of dignity. His notion of dignity denies any government authority or capacity to grant, take, or otherwise alter an individual's dignity. Dignity is pre-political and innate.

Thomas's dissent addresses four concerns. First, he argues that any claim of a right to marriage that includes same-sex couples misinterprets the Constitution's meaning of liberty. Second, he argues that this misinterpretation illustrates the dominant theme of Roberts' dissent: the majority is imposing its own political values. Third, he distinguishes same-sex marriage regulations from other marriage cases, especially *Loving v. Virginia*, which ruled that bans on interracial marriage were unconstitutional by terms of due process liberty and equal protection in the Fourteenth Amendment.[31] Fourth, he condemns the majority's conception of dignity. All arguments speak to an aspiration of the conservative movement to limit federal governing responsibility.[32]

Thomas begins his dissent by summarizing what Roberts discussed extensively—namely, that by "treating the Due Process Clause as a font of substantive rights," judges can "roa[m] at large in the constitutional field guided only by their personal views as to the fundamental rights protected by that document."[33] The *Obergefell* decision is thereby cast as supplanting a democratic process to determine something on which the dissenters contend that the Constitution is silent. This is a perennial criticism of judicial decision-making, particularly when the Court decides the extent of a fundamental right.[34] Judicial authority to declare the meaning and content of a fundamental right has been understood to follow from the due process liberty clauses found in the Constitution's Fifth and Fourteenth Amendments. That authority, known as the doctrine of substantive due process, is controversial, in part, because it seemingly permits a judge to impose personal values. For Thomas in this instance, it also promotes a misreading of liberty.[35] Thomas defines liberty in its negative sense only, as freedom from government action.[36] For him, the liberty spoken of in these amendments has been "almost uniformly construed . . . to refer only to freedom from physical restraint."[37] For advocates of marriage recognition to claim that they have a right under due process liberty to their marriage is to expand grossly the scope of this term.

Thomas's position is unconvincing. Even if we grant Thomas's cramped understanding of freedom as negative and as limited only to freedom from *physical* restraint, which he contends is the most appropriate reading of the term, the denial of marriage recognition creates the precise physical restraint against which persons should be guarded.[38] Refusal to allow marriage impedes physical movement and limits freedom even in Thomas's narrow sense. By his terms, denying marriage recognition is to deny liberty—even when liberty is unnecessarily narrowly construed.

In the pre-*Obergefell* marriage regime, same-sex couples married in, for example, New York could not move to a state where their union was not recognized without jeopardizing the state and federal rights and responsibilities of their marriage.[39] Such a move would have consequences for their financial well-being and might jeopardize the integrity of their family unit; parental custody rights as well as spousal rights, such as the ability to make health-related decisions, could be destabilized if not ceded altogether by moving from a marriage-recognition state to a non-recognition state.[40] In short, the legal presumptions that flow from marriage evaporate when a same-sex couple moves, and that consequence limits freedom of movement.

Thomas simply ignores this situation in his dissent. By contrast, he contends that the state in no way restrains gays and lesbians from living as they choose: "They have been able to cohabitate and raise their children in peace. They have been able to hold civil marriage ceremonies in States that recognize same-sex marriages and private religious ceremonies in all States. They have been able to travel freely around the country, making their homes where they please. Far from being incarcerated or physically restrained, petitioners have been left alone to order their lives as they see fit."[41] Thomas's characterization of LGBTQ+ life is wildly and, indeed, offensively inaccurate.[42] As legal scholar Christopher Leslie has documented, "The *Obergefell* dissenters presented an overly optimistic portrait of the lives of same-sex couples who cannot legally marry."[43] Thomas's claims that same-sex couples can equally codify their relationships in a public ceremony, equally raise children, "hold themselves out as married," and access legal documents that ensure the rights of marriage without any official state sanctioning of marriage are all wrong.[44] We might ask, What does "hold themselves out as married" even mean? That gays and lesbians can pretend to be married for the benefit of friends and families while being held apart and denied the rights and responsibilities to community that marriage brings hardly counts as equality.

Furthermore, Thomas's emphasis on negative liberty serves a broader political commitment to limiting government authority. His response to and rejection of the majority's notion of dignity make this goal manifest. For Thomas, if dignity is conferred by the state through marriage recognition, then any realization of dignity depends on state action, which means dignity can be granted by the state as much as it can be taken away by the state. But for Thomas, the Constitution captures a "vision of mankind in which all humans are created in the image of God and therefore of inherent worth."[45] Consequently, dignity exists irrespective of whether and how others recognize an individual: "Human dignity has long been understood in this country to be innate."[46] It follows from the Declaration of Independence's assertion that people are "endowed by their Creator with certain unalienable Rights" and that these rights exist irrespective of government. Dignity, for Thomas, is the shorthand denotation of this unalienable quality. If it comes from nature or the creator prior to the existence of any state, then the state cannot in any way deny, damage, or destroy it. As Thomas writes, "Human dignity cannot be taken away by the government. Slaves did not lose their dignity (any more than they lost their humanity) because the government allowed them to be enslaved. Those held in internment camps did not lose their dignity because the government confined them. And those denied government benefits certainly do not lose their dignity because the government denies them those benefits. The government cannot bestow dignity, and it cannot take it away."[47] Even as this notion may be alluring as an assertion of independence and personal autonomy—a kind of constitutional version of how "sticks and stones may break my bones, but names (or what we may think of as assaults or disparaging of dignity) will never hurt me"—Thomas troublingly ignores the sentence in the Declaration that follows the one he quotes. The document does stipulate self-evident truths, such as "all men are created equal, that they are endowed by their Creator with certain unalienable Rights, that among these are Life, Liberty and the pursuit of Happiness." But it then immediately declares that "to secure these rights, Governments are instituted among Men, deriving their just powers from the consent of the governed." If we follow Thomas's claim that inalienable rights include dignity, then the purpose of government is to secure and protect dignity. We might then ask the following: If government can have no effect on dignity, as Thomas maintains, then how could it possibly protect and secure it? By extension, if government can and should protect dignity, surely the need for protection suggests that some actors, even the state itself, can harm, take, or deny dignity.

To argue that government action has no effect on dignity is preposterous from an empirical standpoint. Even if we were to concede that dignity cannot be bestowed by the state, to suggest that it cannot be taken or damaged by state action would seem more of a normative aspiration than reality. When a government takes, for example, property, it does not necessarily harm the individual who owned the property, particularly if some just compensation is offered. But as Bernadette Atuahene has extensively argued and documented, when such a material taking is premised on marking the owners or occupiers as "sub persons," then dignity is damaged and/or denied through the material taking.[48] In fact, public criticism of Thomas's dissent often focused on his refusal to acknowledge this very point.[49]

Importantly, the assertion that dignity is so innate to an individual's identity as to be untouchable by governing authorities does critical political work to limit the powers and responsibilities of the state. This idea not only curbs the state's authority—it has no capacity to harm individual dignity—but also absolves the state of accountability for any harmful actions it may take. To the extent that state action may result in harm against a person or particular community, the injury is minimized by the supposition that it did not and could not affect one's dignity because, by definition, doing so is impossible. The cut can never be very deep. As for reparative action, Thomas's notion of dignity would seem to restrict, if not negate, its need. No dignitary harm was produced by state action, for it could not be; therefore, no dignity-restorative measures need be undertaken. And inasmuch as reparation is "time-consuming, complicated, and expensive," the denial of dignitary harm proves efficient and economical.[50] The conservative impulse to inhibit the capacity and motivation for robust state action is maintained.

In summary, Thomas's conception of dignity proves no less problematic—and potentially more so—than Kennedy's in *Obergefell* and *Windsor*, although for different reasons. Whereas Kennedy's notion is nebulous enough to serve antithetical ends—used to undermine LGBTQ+ equality even as it is developed to recognize that equality— Thomas's alternative falls short because it denies the empirical reality of extensive state-sponsored discrimination and violence, and it denies responsibility and capacity to respond to those dignitary harms.

The overarching ambition of Thomas's dissent is to limit the capacity and responsibility of state actors. Its cramped understanding of liberty ignores the long record of limits and restraints upon same-sex couples; as one legal scholar has pointed out, the dissent "is not an accurate chronicle of history but . . . a cautionary tale of how the desire to discriminate can be so powerful as to blind people to historical truths."[51] Thomas's definition of dignity absolves the state of accountability for the harm and violence that it has committed against individuals and groups deemed unworthy. It rejects the possibility of reparation not as pragmatically unworkable but as principally unnecessary. The limits that follow perpetuate the capacity for dignitary harm precisely because it ignores the possibility of dignitary harm. To that end, Thomas's ideas prove useless at best and dangerous at worst; they speak more to politically conservative ambition to curb state power, responsibility, and accountability than to the need to describe and assess the realities of inequality and inequity.

The Specter of Polyamory: Dignity as Respect or Respectability

The other *Obergefell* dissenters did not engage the majority's discussion of dignity. Rather, they focused on the alleged implications of the majority's position or its slippery slope, which is a rhetorical device in the dissents in *Lawrence* and *Windsor* as well. All, to varying degrees, contended that the rulings accelerate moral decay. In *Lawrence*, Justice Antonin Scalia feared the loss of any principle by which to identify appropriate or valued behavior: "State laws against bigamy, same-sex marriage, adult incest, prostitution, masturbation, adultery, fornication, bestiality, and obscenity . . . [are] called into question by today's decision; the Court makes no effort to cabin the scope of its decision to exclude them from its holding."[52] For Scalia, decriminalization of consensual adult same-sex sexual intimacy would lead to recognition of same-sex marriage even as Kennedy placed limits on *Lawrence*'s holding.[53] Scalia's dissent was prescient, for we can now see that Kennedy's later rulings in *Windsor* and *Obergefell* rely on the dignitary framework laid out in *Lawrence*.

The later recognition of same-sex marriage by certain states shifted the dangerous specter at the end of the slippery slope. In his dissent in *Oberge-fell*, Roberts raised plural marriage as the new horror that would follow:

> It is striking how much of the majority's reasoning would apply with equal force to the claim of a fundamental right to plural marriage. If "[t]here is dignity in the bond between two men or two women who seek to marry and in their autonomy to make such profound choices," why would there be any less dignity in the bond between three people who, in exercising their autonomy, seek to make the profound choice to marry? . . . If not having the opportunity to marry "serves to disrespect and subordinate" gay and lesbian couples, why wouldn't the same "imposition of this disability," serve to disrespect and subordinate people who find fulfillment in polyamorous relationships?[54]

Thus in their respective dissents, Scalia and Roberts rely on the idea that the behavior—the outcome toward which a ruling would seem inevitably to lead—is irresponsible, dangerous, unrestrained, and to be avoided.

The majority who ruled in favor of same-sex marriage recognition would seem to agree with the dissent's supposition. Indeed, Kennedy limits the implications of his rulings for the majority. For example, he ends the *Lawrence* ruling by stipulating that the case does not involve matters such as same-sex marriage. As if to prevent any implication that recognizing same-sex marriage would lead to recognizing plural marriage, Kennedy maintains couplehood and cisgender normativity as crucial characteristics of what the state is being asked to recognize in *Windsor* and *Obergefell*. In *Windsor*, he says the word *couple* thirty-one times. Using a similar tactic of factual distinction as he did in *Lawrence*, Kennedy placed boundaries on the ruling in *Obergefell*: "Indeed, with respect to this asserted basis for excluding same-sex couples from the right to marry, it is appropriate to observe these cases involve only the rights of *two* consenting adults whose marriages would pose no risk of harm to themselves or third parties."[55] The matter before the Court did not involve third parties as may present in plural marriages.

While the majority sought to distance its ruling from plural marriage because such consensual non-monogamy is freighted with allegedly undignified notions of excess, the dissenters wanted to keep it within sight for the same reason. Indeed, legal scholars have explored how these rulings could lead to legal recognition of plural marriage.[56] Some suggested a constitutional right for plural marriage before *Windsor* or *Obergefell*.[57] While some theorists attend to supposed inequalities and inequities that may emerge in plural marriage, they also explore how to mitigate this potential.[58] For example, recognizing plural marriages affords the state the authority to regulate them and provides an opportunity to counter domestic abuse.[59]

However, to contend that the same-sex intimacy decriminalization and marriage equality rulings—deploying dignity—lay a path for recognition of plural marriage is to read those rulings as offering a consistent and coherent conception of dignity, and they do not. Again, dignity is a powerful rhetorical device that can be deployed to indicate what actions and identities should be respected and what practices and identities should be viewed as respectable. Whereas the former use of dignity places the onus for action on others to avoid obstructing individual choice, the latter puts the onus for action on the individual to conform to notions of worth determined by others who occupy positions of power. These two distinct meanings appear to go unnoticed, or unremarked upon, in the majority holdings in *Lawrence*, *Windsor*, and *Obergefell*. Instead, the dignity doctrine that emerges conflates these meanings, especially as the decisions on marriage equality, which seem to define dignity as respectability, cite as precedent earlier rulings that define dignity as requiring respect for individual choice.

The legal scholarship that advocates for plural marriage reads the dignity doctrine primarily, if not solely, as a doctrine of respect for individual choice. For example, political theorist and legal scholar Ronald C. Den Otter has noted that the dignity sought and granted in *Windsor* need not be restricted by number: "What too many liberals fail to see is that the compelling reasons that support same-sex marriage, such as the value of *personal choice* in selecting a marital partner and the importance of equal treatment, also support a right to plural marriage. The slope from same-sex to plural marriage may be slipperier than many liberals notice or are willing to admit."[60] Legal scholar Mark Goldfeder agrees: "The real beauty of *Windsor* though is that it not only opened the door for polygamy, but it also established a desperately needed framework for how to deal with it."[61] If, as Goldfeder contends, *Windsor's* outcome is predicated on the idea that the state cannot criminalize same-sex intimacy, nor can it offer a rational reason for banning same-sex couples to marry, then a similar path can be followed for poly relationships: first, decriminalization, and second, marriage recognition.[62]

If bans on plural marriage are only predicated on moral opprobrium, *Lawrence* would seem to undermine the logic of any such ban. We then come to policy concerns for restricting marriage. As Den Otter points out, these concerns range from the supposed inequality that could take place within a plural marriage (inequalities may abound within a married couple) to protection of children (evidence does not suggest that plural marriage would harm children; it may support a healthy upbringing, and even if it did cause harm, the state could regulate against child abuse in a plural marriage as it does in a two-person marriage).[63] If the state restriction on plural marriage follows only from a bare desire to harm the socially or politically unpopular, then it serves no legitimate interest and violates either or both the due process clause and the equal protection clause of the Fourteenth Amendment. Pointedly, political theorist Sonu Bedi has argued that bans on plural marriage "must be about the intrinsic moral superiority of two-person couplings over couplings of three or more. This is what underlies extant prohibitions on plural marriage."[64]

What if dignity does not mean respect for individual choices? Again, the dignity in *Lawrence* is quite distinguishable from the dignity in *Windsor* and *Obergefell*. If dignity connotes respectability, then *Windsor* and *Obergefell* do not necessarily lead to plural marriage, because those rulings in no way challenge the heteronormative and coupled requirements of state-sanctioned marriage. Instead, those rulings indicate that same-sex couples who adhere to these requirements—coupled, private, outwardly romantic, and monogamous—are entitled to civil marriage. In other words, legal advocates of plural marriage rely on *Lawrence's* dignity but not necessarily on *Windsor's* and *Obergefell's* dignity. Den Otter makes this reliance clear: "Constitutionally, the issue ought to be whether competent adults should be free to choose such a marital relationship and not whether it would be wise for most people to do so, whether the legal recognition of different types of plural marriages would irreparably damage the traditional institution of marriage, or whether the licensing of only two-person marriages would produce better overall consequences. Constitutionally, their personal reasons are their own and should be presumed valid."[65] But the Supreme Court's conception of the right to marriage is not grounded only in a right to choose. Civil marriage is not merely an instrument to access public rights, benefits, and responsibilities. It is a conferral of a recognized status. In his critique of *Goodridge v. Public Health*, the Massachusetts Supreme Court ruling that compelled recognition of same-sex marriage in that state, political philosopher Michael Sandel highlights the fallacy of understanding marriage solely as a freedom to love whom one chooses: "Autonomy and freedom of choice are insufficient to justify a right to same-sex marriage. If government were truly neutral on the moral worth of all voluntary intimate relationships, then the state would have no grounds for limiting marriage to two persons; consensual polygamous partnerships would apply."[66] Marriage is a determination of what the state values. Tethering marriage to dignity positions certain actions and behaviors as dignified or respectable and positions others as not.

In her exploration of civil marriage, Tamara Metz concedes that marriage "functions as a special symbolic resource that individuals can use to say something about who they are to themselves, their partners, and their communities."[67] Indeed, the Supreme Court famously stipulated as much when it ruled in 1888 that civil marriage was "more than a contract." Instead, it is understood as a status whose value reaches beyond the individuals who enter into it, and "it partakes more of the character of an institution regulated and controlled by public authority, upon principles of public policy, *for the benefit of the community*."[68] But it is for these reasons that civil marriage recognition can carry with it a demand for respectability; civil marriage, because it has meaning beyond the persons who enter into a particular marriage contract, can be loaded with expectations of certain behavior. The state, through its capacity to sanction marriage, becomes involved in creating and affirming a moral hierarchy among its citizens.

Same-sex couples can be recognized as married for the reason that Kennedy highlighted in *Obergefell*: they do not seek to disrupt its normative requirements. Indeed, he states numerous times that same-sex couples seek access to the institution to respect and maintain it. This makes our point that dignity, as used in the marriage cases, is premised upon the heteronormative exclusion of consensual non-monogamous relationships. Those limits help explain why the strategies and tactics of advocates for plural marriage recognition have often mimicked those efforts of the successful movement for same-sex marriage recognition, which minimized difference, emphasized love, and sought inclusion within—not a redefinition of—marriage.

The Limits of Transgression within Neoliberal Dignity

We began our study with a discussion of how bathhouses functioned as a counterpublic in which gay and queer men might explore relational forms and kinship structures that transgress heteronormative practices and assumptions, which cement compulsory heterosexuality and privilege monogamy, couplehood, romance, marriage, and privacy in sex.[69] Insofar as dignity is conceptually linked to this heteronormativity, poly or CNM relationships, given their refusal of monogamy, may resist heteronormativity and the limits of dignity as respectability.[70] Indeed, we note that the potential for transgression among advocates of poly or CNM relations is perhaps greater than those who advocate for plural marriage because the latter requires the sanctioning and imprimatur of the state. Seeking formal recognition fosters conformity to the norm. Put differently, within the range of poly relations, CNM relations that do not aspire to marriage potentially embrace a more queer critique of normative expectation than does plural marriage.

Nevertheless, if the specter of poly relations or plural marriage frightens some Supreme Court justices, nothing implicit to plural marriage necessarily resists reproducing aspects of heteronormativity. Recent scholarship on consensual non-monogamy highlights how people in these relationships often aspire to the dignitary conferral achieved by the same-sex marriage movement and attempt to define their relationships within the boundaries promoted in *Windsor* and *Obergefell*. They do not embrace a politics of transgression.[71] In other words, advocates for plural marriage have worked to render their identities and relationships legible as normative.

CNM relationships—whether their participants aspire to marriage recognition or not—are hardly as culturally taboo as Supreme Court justices have contended. Their cultural visibility has proliferated in recent years. As Nathan Rambukkana notes, "The tricky thing about non-monogamy is that as soon as you start looking for it, you see it everywhere."[72] Both CNM relationships and plural marriage have been depicted on television. HBO's *Big Love* follows a polygamous family within the Fundamentalist Church of Jesus Christ of Latter-Day Saints living in Utah, and TLC's *Sister Wives*, Showtime's *Polyamory: Married and Dating*, and Netflix's *Sense8* all explore these relationships, showing their active role in the pop culture imaginary.[73] These CNMs are also discussed in anthropological, sociological, and legal research, which has focused on non-monogamy as a subculture and sociopolitical movement that maintains norms, ethics, shared meanings, and a rights-based agenda.[74] Revealing a normalizing tendency, options for relationship status on LGBTQ+ oriented social media apps have multiplied to include open and poly relationships.[75] Opportunities to build subcultural institutions have proliferated.[76]

Nevertheless, CNMs carry all sorts of negative connotations in the public imagination, which is why the Supreme Court justices' invocation of the slippery slope seems to resonate. As Mimi Schippers notes, "To the extent that the monogamous couple is held up as the ideal and only viable relationships structure for emotional and sexually intimate relationships, those who violate the norm of monogamy are often constructed as immoral or inferior."[77] Consequently, much of the media representation depicts how CNM defies normative expectations of excess, harm, or irresponsibility. In short, the visibility aims to showcase responsibility. For example, when describing the show *You Me Her*, produced by Netflix, one cultural critic writes, "Any representation is great, and the show tackled the issue with responsibility, showing that a poly relationship takes as much time and effort as any relationship."[78] The representation is considered valuable because it conforms to what social norms define as dignified; it highlights that those within CNM relationships face similar struggles as those in other relationship types. The "just like you" framing, which also undergirds representations like *Love, Simon*, does important work.[79]

Such framing would seem a strategic reaction to what Lital Pascar and others have found—namely, that many popular depictions of CNM relationships center tropes of cheating, thereby promoting conceptual linkages between these relationships and promiscuity, dishonesty, or greed.[80] In an innovative study of public attitudes about CNMs, Lea Seguin found that respondents often considered them to be unsustainable, perverse, amoral, or deficient even as some noted they were acceptable or valid and beneficial. After they were exposed to literature that dispelled common misunderstandings about these relationships, respondents continued to associate them with negative qualities.[81] Furthermore, Pascar shows how these negative depictions correlate with already disparaged identities associated with race and class.[82]

Given these common depictions and assumptions, advocates for plural marriage are often compelled to adopt a publicity strategy that emphasizes how these relationships align with normative conceptions of dignity. The cultural assumptions that plague CNM—made manifest in the *Obergefell* dissents' invocation of slippery slopes—explain why plural marriage advocacy specifically, and consensual non-monogamy more broadly, was considered, by some, to be a liability to the same-sex marriage movement.[83] That this movement would separate itself from potentially more inclusive transgressive values reveals that the movement was bounded by dignity's limits, which remain raced, classed, and gendered. Kaila Adia Story makes this critique: "The activist and intellectual pursuit of legalized marriage and respectability by the marriage equality movement is nothing but a racialized ruse for class ascension linked to racist heteronormative notions of citizenry. . . . The marriage equality movement excludes more than it includes. Namely, it privileges marriage over desire, gay and lesbian identity over bisexual and transgender identity, and white queer middle-class men over poor and working-class queer people of color."[84] Rather than confront and challenge these limits, some plural marriage advocates have adopted strategies and tactics that parallel the normalization efforts of the same-sex marriage movement. They have sought inclusion within dignity's limits instead of exposing and resisting them.

Pascar points to rhetorical parallels between CNM relationships and LGBTQ+ identities made manifest in the rhetoric of compelled closeting: "The narrative of the CNM closet, similar to that of the LGBT closet, suggests that social misconceptions and prejudice lead some CNM people to hide their CNM practices, which they often see as their 'true self.'"[85] Pascar also notes how some within the CNM community adopt a "born this way" narrative to suggest that being CNM is natural or inherent.[86] Another strategy of the plural marriage movement that parallels the normalization strategy of the same-sex marriage movement is the reliance on those who are "able-bodied, heteronormative (feminine-presenting women and masculine-presenting men), cisgender (in contrast to trans or genderqueer people) and somewhat conventionally attractive."[87] And this tactic is paralleled in the poly community when they challenge any expectation that they necessarily transgress norms of sexual restraint. Olivia Goldhill notes this performance of conventionality when reporting on Tableaux, a social event that caters to this community:

> Throughout the 1960s and 1970s, Americans who rejected monogamy typically did so in an effort to throw off mainstream, normative culture and politics. But the attendees of Tableaux fit in with the rest of privileged, gentrified Brooklyn: They match the dark, tattered-glamor aesthetic of the room; wear dark-grey clothes and plenty of eyeliner; and are overwhelmingly white. . . . Most there present as cis; most queer women as femme. Sex is no more prominent here than at any other party in middle-class Brooklyn. We discuss vegan burgers and holiday destinations. Gin and tonics appear and disappear rapidly, and the abundance of iPhones and fast fashion suggests polyamorists have no problem with consumerism.[88]

Research on CNM parallels this assessment of homogeneity, particularly along racial, class, and cisgender lines.[89] Research also suggests that this may be a political strategy of normalization.

The plural marriage movement—not to be conflated with CNM, as it is seeking explicit recognition and sanction from the state and may be less inclined to transgress and more inclined to seek inclusion without disruption—has adopted a "love is love" message to counter the same worries of promiscuity and lack of social restraint that plagued the same-sex marriage movement. Importantly, sociologist Myrl Beam has revealed how the political strategy to achieve marriage equality by relying on "a story that would validate and re-affirm the moral rightness of straight people's own identities and life choices" and thereby empha-sizing "love, freedom, responsibility, and *sameness*" to straight values diminished positive affirmation of queer difference, alienated, and excluded.[90] According to Beam, "Many queer people active in the cam-paign did *not* feel compelled or included in this vision of the good life the campaign sought to mobilize."[91] To achieve a goal on the majority's terms, queer identities were narratively abandoned. For Pascar, plural marriage advocates often execute the same strategy.[92]

In his research on the movement, Christian Klesse reveals how CNM advocates increasingly adopt a definition of "responsible non-monogamy" to distance themselves from those queer values of contact and promiscuity, which dominant norms code as irresponsible, danger-ous, and undignified. Klesse notes how the emergent poly emphasis on "love" and "intimacy" as defining and dignified traits of poly relation-ships inhibits "a truly pluralistic sexual ethics that may embrace the diversity of non-monogamous sexual and intimate practices."[93]

The parallel strategies, tactics, and messages of the same-sex marriage and CNM normalization efforts illustrate how each works to remain included in the boundaries of dignity's limits. The common reliance on "love" as an animating feature is particularly revealing. As Klesse notes, "The current celebration of love and intimacy usually bolsters the hege-monic ideal of the monogamous long-term couple."[94] Insofar as CNM relationships endorse kinship forms that rely not on romantic love but on other kinds of connection, they could transgress and expose the lim-its of dignity.[95] However, Klesse's scholarship on the CNM subcultures and the politico-legal movements for normalization and plural marriage reveals a "central role of love and intimacy in polyamory discourses," which seems to embrace the logics of heteronormativity and dignity as respectability rather than resist or challenge them. Klesse contends that this "renders them vulnerable to being appropriated by normative and assimilationist ideologies."[96]

Pascar's research yields a similar conclusion: "Activists for gay and plural marriage both use normalizing strategies, suggesting that mar-ginalized groups deserve equal access to rights and social acceptance based on their similarity to 'normal' (that is, heterosexual and monoga-mous) people."[97] The lure of dignity proves too strong. Possibilities for resistance compete with and often succumb to aping the "just like you" tactics that proved successful in building support for same-sex marriage. In short, advocates for poly relationships often seek traditional dignity rather than challenge it as a problematic metric of value.

Recovering Dignity: The Thirteenth Amendment as an Anti-stigma Principle

Given our criticisms of dignity as a viable constitutional principle, our critiques of Thomas's alternative rendering of the term, and our arguments about the seduction of a limited notion of dignity as respectability, we suggest that any recovery of a usable principle that would promote expansive inclusion requires a thorough reexamination of the sections of the Constitution from which a dignitary right is said to emerge. The jurisprudential line that conceptualizes dignity as respect for individual choice and the jurisprudential line that conceptualizes dignity as respectability or alignment with majoritarian norms are both grounded in the Fourteenth Amendment's due process and equal protection clauses. We turn to the Fourteenth Amendment to evaluate which meaning might follow and to the Thirteenth Amendment to suggest a more stable basis for a dignitary claim. A comprehensive analysis of whether dignity can plausibly be said to derive from the original public, legislative, and judicial readings of the Thirteenth Amendment and from more modern interpretations of that amendment is beyond our scope. Nevertheless, we offer some initial reflections on potentially grounding dignity more securely in the Constitution.[98]

Our argument rests on the supposition that the Thirteenth and Fourteenth Amendments were both, early in their judicial renderings, warped by commitments to racism and white supremacy. The legacy of that adherence to inequality has marred our contemporary readings.[99] We suggest, however, that any usable constitutional principle of dignity must recognize and account for this. The supposed limits of these amendments, which render them less useful as guards against anti-LGBTQ+ actions in public accommodation, commerce, housing, or employment, are themselves artifacts of intentionally limited, if not outright racist, readings of the amendments' original equity imperatives.[100]

These amendments, especially the Thirteenth, could (and perhaps should) be reread as an anti-stigma principle that ensures equal treatment by state authorities and equal treatment by and from our fellow citizens. To illustrate the possibility for a dignitary right that might respond to the ideas and critiques we offer, we reexamine the Supreme Court decision *Masterpiece Cakeshop v. Colorado Civil Rights Commission*.[101] As discussed in chapter 5, this ruling affirmed the dignity of LGBTQ+ identity even as it failed to recognize the validity of the equal protection claim brought by the same-sex couple. We wonder if the Thirteenth Amendment might provide for a ruling in *Masterpiece* that could more compellingly protect the same-sex couple's dignity.

Throughout *Masterpiece*, Kennedy contends that an individual's freedom of belief cannot reach so far as to permit practices that would affront the dignity of or stigmatize gays or lesbians. Kennedy's contention could find support in the constitutional text of the Fourteenth Amendment or statutory language in sections of the 1964 Civil Rights Act—particularly in Title II—which bans discrimination in public accommodations on the basis of race, color, religion, or national origin. Both texts, however, fail to achieve that objective. The Fourteenth Amendment has been read for nearly 150 years by the Supreme Court to apply only to state government actions and not to citizens' interactions; this interpretation is known as the state action doctrine.[102] The details of *Masterpiece* did not involve state action because the baker is a private company. The state was not discriminating against the couple; the baker was.

The other textual recourse for the couple—the 1964 Civil Rights Act—has relevant language in Title II, which bans discrimination in public accommodation. The Court unanimously upheld Title II as a legitimate exercise of Congress's commerce clause authority.[103] Congress could regulate person-to-person interactions in private businesses, such as restaurants, theaters, hotels, bakeries, and cafés, not because it sought to promote racial equality but because racial discrimination had a deleterious effect on economic development.[104] In other words, the Court rested its commitment to root out racial discrimination on congressional commerce clause authority rather than on Fourteenth Amendment equal protection. This decision reflected the Court's unwillingness to overturn its state action doctrine, which follows from a reading of the Fourteenth Amendment offered in the *Civil Rights Cases of 1883*. In that case, the Court evaluated the Civil Rights Act of 1875, which required that all persons in the United States be able to access "the full and equal enjoyment of the accommodations, advantages, facilities, and privileges of inns, public conveyances on land or water, theatres, and other places of public amusement; subject only to the conditions and limitations established by law, and applicable alike to citizens of every race and color, regardless of any previous conditions of servitude."[105] This provision is similar to Title II of the 1964 Civil Rights Act. However, in 1883, the Court ruled that Congress exceeded its authority under the Fourteenth Amendment to enact the 1875 law.[106] According to this decision, the Fourteenth Amendment stated that only "State action of a particular character . . . is prohibited. Individual invasion of individual rights is not the subject-matter of the amendment."[107] Consequently, a discriminatory action between individuals, not supported by government policy, was beyond Congress's purview. Consequently, if the Court were to maintain the 1964 Civil Rights Act's Title II, it would need to overturn this 1883 ruling and broaden the scope of the Fourteenth Amendment or find alternative constitutional text to uphold the statute. By resorting to the commerce clause, the Court avoided overturning its earlier decision and upsetting the doctrine of *stare decisis*, which fosters stability in constitutional interpretation.

If the state action doctrine prevents a same-sex couple from making a Fourteenth Amendment claim against a baker, can they make a claim under Title II of the 1964 Civil Rights Act? Indeed, the *Heart of Atlanta Motel, Inc. v. United States* ruling, which upheld Title II, grounds its rationale in dignity. In writing for the unanimous Court, Justice Tom C. Clark stipulates, "The Senate Commerce Committee made it quite clear that the fundamental object of Title II was to vindicate 'the deprivation of personal dignity that surely accompanies denials of equal access to public establishments.'"[108] Indeed, dignity can be affronted in a context of rights in commerce. But even if Title II can be understood as a guarantee of dignity in rights in commerce, the provision bans discrimination in commerce only on the basis of race, color, religion, or national origin. Sexual orientation and sex are not mentioned.[109]

One route for LGBTQ+ persons would be to argue that they are a suspect class and that sexual orientation is a suspect classification analogous to race, but as discussed in chapter 5, the Court has never stipulated this possibility. Consequently, neither the explicit text of Title II of the 1964 act nor the standard reading of the Fourteenth Amendment as regulating only state action would offer a textual basis to secure a dignitary right in commerce for LGBTQ+ patrons.

Is Kennedy wrong in his assertion in *Masterpiece* that the dignity of gays and lesbians cannot be trampled upon and that such dignity extends to treatment in commerce?[110] Not necessarily. Importantly, a pathway other than the commerce clause's authority to support the 1964 Civil Rights Act might have been taken, and it deserves to be revisited. Back in 1883, defenders of the 1875 Civil Rights Act also pointed to the *Thirteenth* Amendment as justification and support for Congress's authority to pass the statute. This amendment bans slavery and involuntary servitude (except as punishment for a crime). Prior to its 1883 *Civil Rights Cases* ruling, the Court held that this amendment banned slavery itself as well as what it referred to as the incidents or markers of slavery in its *Strauder v. West Virginia* decision.[111] In 1883, even the Court majority acknowledged that Congress, by terms of the Thirteenth Amendment, had the "power to pass all laws necessary and proper for abolishing all badges and incidents of slavery." It further contended "that the denial of such equal accommodations and privileges" might be seen as "a subjection to a species of servitude well within the meaning of the amendment."[112] The Thirteenth Amendment was not limited to the abolition of slavery; it included incidents of bias that might persist in the context of one's status as a formerly enslaved person or descendent of enslaved peoples. Why was this expansive understanding of the Thirteenth Amendment not pursued?

The answer perhaps has more to do with the politics surrounding the radical implications of the Union victory in the Civil War. If slavery were understood narrowly—referring only to the circumstance of owning another person—the abolition of slavery in the Thirteenth Amendment would neatly bifurcate US history into slavery and post-slavery periods. The Emancipation would seemingly be a self-contained event of abolition with no further implications of restitution required. As Pamela Brandwein and others have argued, this was the position taken by Northern Democrats in the 1860s who, often begrudgingly, supported the Thirteenth Amendment. However, many Republicans contemplated a more expansive understanding of the dangers of slavery that precipitated the Civil War—the Slave Power conspiracy that trampled basic liberties of the First Amendment—and, consequently, the policy and legal actions its abolition required.[113] For them, slavery not only was a status of bondage but also represented a culture of antebellum Southern hostility to individual civil liberties, such as free speech and assembly.[114] Therefore, eliminating slavery required more than formal legal abolition. It required a positive federal guarantee of individual civil rights. As Republican Senator Charles Sumner argued, without such a guarantee, "Emancipation will only be half done. It is our duty to see it wholly done."[115] Summarizing this perspective on the Thirteenth Amendment, legal scholar George Rutherglen writes that the Court's phrase "badges and incidents of slavery" was "used most frequently before the adoption of the Thirteenth Amendment to refer to the symbolic manifestation of political and social inferiority that was analogous, but hardly identical, to the specific legal attributes of slavery."[116] The phrase suggested an expansive understanding of what emancipation required: achieving it involved more than just formal abolition.

The Supreme Court rejected this aspiration for the Thirteenth Amendment in its *1883 Civil Rights Cases* ruling. The majority contended that both the Thirteenth and Fourteenth Amendments guaranteed civil and political rights but not *social* rights. This distinction—a guarantee of equal access to formal political and legal institutions only—is canonical in contemporary understandings of the Reconstruction and immediate post-Reconstruction Court.[117] It became a cornerstone of *Plessy v. Ferguson*'s foundation for racial segregation in public accommodations as well as for the maintenance of interracial marriage bans.[118] However, again, this was not how prominent Republicans involved in the drafting and ratification of the amendment spoke of its aims, and we contend it is racist artifice compelled by an imperative to reassert white racial dominance in the absence of any legal codification of slavery.[119]

Many congressional Republicans supported a more robust conception of equality and what emancipation would require than both their Democratic colleagues and the Supreme Court justices. This is evidenced in their response to the black codes, a set of laws passed between 1865 and 1866 that restricted the freedoms of African Americans and compelled them into a low-wage economy proximate to slavery. The Republican majority passed the Enforcement Acts of 1870 and 1871, "which brought private, racially motivated deprivations of civil, personal, and political rights within the direct reach of the federal government."[120] If the original aim of the Fourteenth Amendment was only to protect civil and political but not social or citizen-to-citizen rights, then Congress's authorization of a federal response to Southern states' restriction of social rights would be difficult. For Brandwein, the Enforcement Acts reveal that "Republicans held something more than the formal equality model."[121]

Furthermore, evidence exists that the Court's triadic division of civil, political, and social rights is contrary to the public understanding of these amendments when they were passed. Early civil litigation and state legislation during Reconstruction reveal that statutory and state constitutional bans on interracial marriage were considered impermissible perhaps after the passage of the Civil Rights Act of 1866 but certainly after the Fourteenth Amendment's passage in 1868. Various state constitutions eliminated these bans given state legislative understandings of federal authority after the Civil War.[122] The constitutionality of such bans only reemerged after judges in Indiana issued a tortured understanding of the Fourteenth Amendment in 1871, one that the Supreme Court parroted in 1873 and that helped curb the scope of the Fourteenth Amendment.[123]

Historian Peggy Pascoe notes that interracial couples defended themselves against criminal prosecution by relying on the 1866 Civil Rights Act, which declared that every citizen, regardless of race, had a right "to make and enforce contracts, to sue, be parties, and give evidence to inherit, purchase, lease, sell, hold, and convey real and personal property" and to have "full and equal benefit of all laws and proceedings for the security of person and property." She also illustrates how they turned to the Fourteenth Amendment, which elevated protections of the 1866 Civil Rights Act to a constitutional guarantee of federal security against state action that violated privileges or immunities of citizenship, equal protection, or due process.[124] Additionally, civil cases, such as those involving probate or inheritance, indicate that state judges also understood this Civil Rights Act and the amendment to negate interracial marriage bans. Pascoe points to an inheritance case in which

Texas Supreme Court justices considered that the "Civil War and Reconstruction spelled a decisive break with the past, and they, too, resigned
laws against interracial marriage to the past."[125] Judges contended that
the Fourteenth Amendment's protection of privileges or immunities of
citizenship and its guarantee of equal protection "abrogated" the state
bans on interracial marriage.[126] In Texas and Alabama, state judges
declared these bans unconstitutional, and in Louisiana, Mississippi,
and North Carolina, state judges upheld interracial marriages as valid.
Pascoe summarizes the trend: "In and outside of the South, when local
prosecutors brought these [interracial] couples to court, they discovered
that laws against interracial marriage faced significant new obstacles
including the assumption that laws against interracial marriage were an
outdated relic of slavery [eliminated by the Thirteenth Amendment], the
belief that marriage was a contractual right of free citizens [protected
by the 1866 Civil Rights Act], and the possibility that the Fourteenth
Amendment really did guarantee equal protection of the laws."[127]

State legislators maintained a similar reading; for example, Florida
lawmakers eliminated their interracial marriage ban from the state's
code in 1872, as it was considered "opposed to our Constitution and to
the legislation of Congress."[128] Between 1866 and 1873, state legislatures
in New Mexico, Louisiana, South Carolina, Washington, Mississippi,
Arkansas, Illinois, and Florida eliminated interracial marriage bans from
the statute books.[129] One commentator noted by 1870 that the interracial
marriage bans of the antebellum era "have passed into oblivion."[130]

This original judicial, legislative, and popular understanding of
post–Civil War federal authority to limit the state's capacity to restrict
social interaction was challenged by the Indiana Supreme Court in 1871
in *Gibson v. Indiana*: "We deny the power and authority of Congress to
determine who shall make contracts or the manner of enforcing them in
the several states. . . . We utterly deny the power of Congress to regulate,
control, or in any manner to interfere with the states in determining
what shall constitute crimes against the laws of the state."[131] For this
court, neither the 1866 Civil Rights Act nor the Fourteenth Amendment
changed the relationship between the federal government and the states'
authority to regulate citizens' rights.

The US Supreme Court mimicked this claim two years later when
a majority of five justices ruled in the *Slaughter-House Cases of 1873*

that the Fourteenth Amendment's privileges or immunities clause—the clause that speaks directly to the rights of citizens—in no way created a set of rights exempt from traditional state regulatory capacity. This state authority to regulate for the public good—known as police power—was maintained in the *1883 Civil Rights Cases* and relied upon in *Plessy v. Ferguson* to continue to permit state governments to regulate rights in ways that promoted white supremacy.[132] The majority in *Plessy* makes the point directly: "So far, then, as a conflict with the Fourteenth Amendment is concerned, the case reduces itself to the question whether the statute of Louisiana is a reasonable regulation. . . . In determining the question of reasonableness, it [the state legislature] is at liberty to act with reference to the established usages, customs, and traditions of the people, and with a view to the promotion of their comfort and the preservation of the public peace and good order."[133] In other words, compelling people of different races to interact socially may incite discord. This reading of the Fourteenth Amendment perpetuates the custom of stigmatizing. It ironically justifies the violence that may ensue from social integration rather than empowers Congress, as the amendment does in its last section, to pass legislation to challenge and alter these practices, policies, and institutions so that equal treatment can be realized. These limitations to the scope of the amendment solidify the foundations and infrastructure of white supremacy.

Justice John Marshall Harlan dissented from the *1883 Civil Rights Cases*. He read the Thirteenth Amendment as empowering Congress to counter those state policies *and* individuals' social practices that maintained markers of inferiority:

> That there are burdens and disabilities which constitute badges of slavery and servitude, and that the power to enforce by appropriate legislation the Thirteenth Amendment may be exerted by legislation of a direct and primary character, for the eradication, not simply of the institution, but of its badges and incidents, are propositions which ought to be deemed indisputable. . . . Such discrimination practised by corporations and individuals in the exercise of their public or quasi-public functions is a badge of servitude the imposition of which Congress may prevent under its power, by appropriate legislation, to enforce the Thirteenth Amendment.[134]

For Harlan, the Thirteenth Amendment provided Congress with author-ity to counter actions taken by government and by individual *persons* that perpetuate degradation of those associated with the once-enslaved class. He reiterated this position in *Plessy*.[135] The implications of Har-lan's dissents should not be taken too far, for we cannot forget that Harlan joined his brethren in *Pace v. Alabama*, which upheld state anti-miscegenation statutes as constitutional.[136] Nevertheless, his dissents in the *Civil Rights Cases of 1883* and *Plessy* suggest that he understood how the Thirteenth Amendment—read as banning the incidents and badges of slavery—could guard against infringements and limits on rights in commerce.

The Thirteenth Amendment—because it bans enslavement and bans actions that would stamp individuals with badges or markers of being less than equal—can be read as a radically inclusive and transforma-tive provision. Its purview is not limited to regulating state action but instead is directed toward personal interactions, such as making con-tracts for goods and services, and it stands against actions that would stigmatize, denigrate, or dehumanize. What is slavery but the denial of humanity, and what is the guarantee of dignity—in the jurisprudence as invoked by Kennedy—but a promise to protect against "institutions and relations that enable, express, or instantiate one or more of the fol-lowing inferiorizing modes of treatment: stigmatization, dehumaniza-tion, infantilization, instrumentalization, or objectification"?[137] Perhaps a guarantee of dignity—understood as an anti-stigma principle—resides in the Thirteenth Amendment?

We can reference more than Harlan's dissents for this reading of the amendment as an anti-stigma principle. His view was endorsed by seven Supreme Court justices in the 1968 decision *Jones v. Alfred H. Mayer Company*.[138] This case concerned whether Congress had authority to ban—as it did in the 1866 Civil Rights Act—covenants that prevented the sale or renting of property to African Americans. Questions about the constitutionality of a congressional statute ask under what constitutional authority Congress could pass the law being considered. With regard to the 1866 act, the relevant source of authority was the Thirteenth Amendment, in part because the Fourteenth Amendment, which guar-antees equal protection of the laws, did not exist in 1866. Speaking for the majority in *Jones*, Justice Stewart adopted Harlan's interpretation of the Thirteenth Amendment as reaching beyond the specific abolition of slavery to embracing a broader conception of regulating private action among citizens: "Surely Congress has the power under the Thirteenth Amendment rationally to determine what are the badges and incidents of slavery, and the authority to translate that determination into effective legislation. . . . At the very least, the freedom that Congress is empowered to secure under the Thirteenth Amendment includes the freedom to buy whatever a white man can buy."[139] Because the amendment bans not just slavery but also markers and badges of inferiority, it compels Congress to challenge laws and practices—public and private—that rest on a supposition of inferiority and thereby stigmatize.[140]

We now ask if an anti-stigma reading of the Thirteenth Amendment can be applied to *Masterpiece*. Race-based discrimination stands as an unparalleled stain on the Constitution's aspiration toward equal treatment. And yet the Fourteenth Amendment has, for decades, been understood to compel not only race equality but also sex equality, even as sex equality does not appear in the amendment. It is now mainstream legal thought to concede that this amendment covers claims of sex equality.[141] Can we similarly suggest that the Thirteenth Amendment be read to strike against stigma grounded in any perceived secondary status, not only racial stigma or badges of inferiority that may follow from a perceived relationship to a once-enslaved class?

But we do not need to rely solely on analogy. The Supreme Court has already ruled that the Thirteenth Amendment's prohibition on badges of inferiority can be applied beyond racial discrimination. Furthermore, such a ruling aligns with the intention of some of the amendment's framers.[142] Early judicial interpretation of the scope of the Thirteenth Amendment indicates that it "throws its protection over every one, of every race, color, and condition."[143] This phrasing might mean that the amendment only prevents all people from being held in bondage. However, later rulings suggest, following *Alfred Mayer*, that the amendment was intended "to proscribe discrimination in the making or enforcement of contracts against, or in favor, of *any* race" suggesting application beyond prohibiting formal enslavement.[144]

This extension suggests that the Thirteenth Amendment is primarily concerned with race-based stigma and not with other forms of stigma grounded in identity, such as sexuality. But in *United States v. Nelson*, a federal circuit court ruled that the Thirteenth Amendment's protections applied to other identity groups (in this case, violence against Jews).[145] Summarizing this court's rationale, legal scholar William M. Carter Jr. writes, "The court reasoned that the 'slavery' and 'involuntary servitude' prohibited by the Thirteenth Amendment's text are neither linguistically nor conceptually limited to any particular race nor, in fact, to 'race' at all."[146] If the prohibition on "badges of inferiority" can be grounded in existing precedent to mean a broad protection not limited to race—or that "the 'badges of slavery' power can be applied to remedy any form of discrimination against persons of any race or class," which seems to follow from *Nelson*—then the Thirteenth Amendment would seem to protect against disparaging treatment or stigmatization, particularly, but not exclusively, in the commercial sphere where contracts are involved (e.g., employment, purchasing of goods and services).[147]

Returning to *Masterpiece*, we must ask who is being stigmatized: the gay couple denied a wedding cake or the baker who might be compelled to bake a cake and thereby take an action that counters his beliefs. In his concurring opinion in *Masterpiece*, Justice Neil Gorsuch points to this question. He notes that the Colorado Civil Rights Commission (CCRC) permitted certain bakers to deny service to customers who sought cakes with anti-gay messages while it sanctioned Phillips, who denied service to a customer seeking a pro-gay message—that is, a cake to celebrate a same-sex marriage. Gorsuch claims that this distinction shows that the "Commission failed to act neutrally by applying a consistent legal rule" and that this further indicates that the CCRC lacked any principled basis by which to justify the differential treatment. For Gorsuch, the religious baker was being singled out and stigmatized for his beliefs.[148]

In dissent, Justice Ruth Bader Ginsburg replies that this assessment is flawed. In one situation, the baker is asked to bake a wedding cake; in the other situation, the baker is asked to bake a cake that carries a message meant to disparage a class of persons.[149] Any claim that baking a wedding cake would constitute an indignity toward or somehow disparage or stigmatize the baker must be premised on the idea that a wedding cake carries an explicit message and that a cake for a *same-sex* wedding carries a *distinct* message compared to a cake for a cross-sex wedding. As Justice Elena Kagan points out in concurrence, this position is untenable. Maintaining this distinction perpetuates the stigma that the Colorado civil rights ordinance and the Supreme Court in its marriage equality rulings (and, we have argued, the Thirteenth Amendment) seek to eradicate.

By conceptualizing the wedding cake, as Gorsuch puts it, as "a cake celebrating same-sex marriage" rather than as a cake merely celebrating a marriage, the same-sex couple is differently positioned than a cross-sex couple, and the consequent denial of service challenges their equal dignity.[150] For Kagan, "it was simply a wedding cake—one that (like other standard wedding cakes) is suitable for use at same-sex and opposite weddings alike."[151] The claim that Phillips would suffer an indignity by being compelled to bake a cake rests on a supposition that the cake for a same-sex wedding is a fundamentally different thing than a cake for a cross-sex wedding. But that supposition of difference is not permitted by the Court's previous ruling in *Obergefell* that gays and lesbians are guaranteed by the Constitution to equal dignity through marriage.[152]

If the Thirteenth Amendment can be read as an anti-stigma principle, the position that Gorsuch and Phillips seek to maintain—that there is a right to act on the belief that some people are lesser—is not tenable. We acknowledge that this reading of the Thirteenth Amendment is broad, but it may follow from original public understanding, judicial dissent, and Supreme Court precedent. Given these multiple groundings, the Court's willingness to read the First Amendment expansively to protect Phillips's expression rights and to read the Reconstruction Amendment's aspirations narrowly seems more like a legacy of racism than a neutral textual interpretation.

Conclusion

Dignity's multiple possible meanings are illuminated through a comparison of *Lawrence* and *Windsor*. In *Lawrence*, dignity would seem to guarantee a choice of how to live, even in the context of moral disapproval. In *Windsor*, Kennedy deploys dignity to mean something different. This distinction may follow from what is at stake. A marriage requires recognition and validation by the state. So in *Windsor* and in *Obergefell*, the state must take positive action rather than merely turn away as it could in *Lawrence* by permitting individuals to make the private choice to have consensual sex. In *Windsor*, when characterizing the Defense of Marriage Act, Kennedy contends that the federal government "interfere[ed] with the equal dignity of same-sex marriages, a dignity conferred by the States in the exercise of their sovereign power."[153] Here dignity is bestowed but comes with strings attached. Same-sex couples may be recognized as married so long as they respect the normative understanding of the institution and live by its expectations.

Because of dignity's unstable meanings and because of the various criticisms of the dignity jurisprudence raised in chapter 5, we have turned our attention in this chapter to questioning whether dignity, as it has thus far been deployed in the particular jurisprudential line from *Lawrence* to *Masterpiece*, can be a viable constitutional principle to arbitrate rights claims. Consequently, we have devoted this chapter to exploring three alternative notions of dignity. We began by examining Thomas's engagement with the term in his *Obergefell* dissent. For Thomas, dignity is a pre-political characteristic inherent to personhood. It cannot be altered by state action. This definition ignores the history of dignity takings, misreads the text on which it is based, and absolves the state of responsibility for any restitution or reparative justice. By conceptualizing dignity as pre-political, Thomas evades the idea we have emphasized: that dignity can function as a tool of power because its meaning is constructed by what governing authorities recognize as respectable, responsible, and in many cases, restrained. If dignity is pre-political, the deliberate and political practice of narrowly construing and deploying dignity to mean respectability remains hidden; dignity appears to have a natural meaning rather than a constructed one.[154] That naturalization renders invisible how dignity can be denied.

We next turned to CNM relationships, which might carry transgressive potential, as they challenge aspects of heteronormativity related to couplehood and monogamy. While the visibility of, infrastructure for, and advocacy supporting CNM has increased, dignity's seduction—its promise of inclusion but with conditions—often leads plural marriage advocates to minimize the transgressive possibilities of CNM. Plural marriage advocates have often followed strategies similar to those espoused by advocates for same-sex marriage, particularly embracing a "just like you" narrative, which we critiqued in our study of media representation, particularly in chapter 3.

Finally, in light of our criticisms and in hopes of not being viewed singularly as dignity skeptics, we explored whether and how we might recover dignity as a constitutional principle. A full assessment is beyond our scope. Nevertheless, we sketched a way dignity might gain more constitutional grounding as an anti-stigma principle that derives from the Thirteenth Amendment. Our reading follows from the constitutional text, original public understanding of that text, and Supreme Court precedent. By reviewing some of the congressional intent behind the Thirteenth Amendment and how it was abandoned by the early post-Reconstruction Supreme Court, we followed Pamela Brandwein's call: "The recovery of these aspects would . . . open avenues for building plausible historical justifications for federal protections of black rights, avenues that so far remained blocked."[155] In other words, excavating the meanings of freedom, emancipation, and stigmatization that were abandoned and exploring why they were abandoned could provide new understandings of what these amendments compel. Such work also highlights how cramped readings of these amendments were politically inspired positions to maintain white supremacy. It even inspires us to ask the following: If limits to equal treatment follow from a judicially imposed tradition of white supremacy antithetical to the aspirations of the Reconstruction Amendments, then should we maintain these interpretations?

If we read the Thirteenth Amendment broadly, we can illuminate its command against stigmatization. And if stigmatization is the marking of an individual or a class of individuals as lesser because of nonconformity, then challenging that stigmatization and guaranteeing dignity cannot refer only to the bounded notion of respectability, which would privilege conformity.

The move we suggest requires a deep reckoning with how entire jurisprudential lines are warped by racist imperatives to maintain white supremacy. Essentially, we urge for a reckoning with the white supremacy that warped critical judicial precedents to promote our most aspirational principles within the constitutional text. The contemporary Supreme Court, which has embraced a neoliberal conception of limited governance that refuses institutional responsibility and accountability for inequality, seems unlikely to take up this challenge.

Conclusion

Doing Dignity Differently

An Anti-stigma Approach

Throughout this book, we have critiqued how authorities have defined and deployed dignity. While the term is often conceptualized as a universal good, we have argued that the word's meaning is instead quite contextually contingent and unstable. As such, it can function as a political, legal, and cultural value with potential for exclusion. Nevertheless, we do not want to abandon dignity altogether. Indeed, we ended the previous chapter by grounding dignity in a reading of the US Constitution's Thirteenth Amendment. In this way, we follow Brittney Cooper's lead when she writes, "I actually think it's irresponsible to wreck shop in people's world without giving them the tools to rebuild. . . . The harder work is helping people find better tools to work with."[1] We must consider what possible actions follow from our critique because we do not want to reject dignity wholesale given its resonance in policy, representation, and law. As we suggested in the introduction, by thinking queerly about dignity, we are not taking away dignity's accolades; rather, we strive to do dignity differently—to imagine a better tool to build a more expansive and inclusive future.

Consequently, in this concluding chapter, we explore the actions that might follow if we refused dignity as a requirement to respect individual choice or as a command to align one's life and actions with the normative majority and embraced it as an anti-stigma principle. Such a move begins with understanding how dignity is troublingly tethered to respect and respectability. Underlying the meanings of both terms is how much dignity is a social construct; it is a value that is dependent on the recognition of others, which means that while we might espouse an ideal that all persons are born with dignity, actualization of that status depends on recognition by others. Once that contingency is clear, if our goal is to maximize dignity's inclusionary potential, then the state must have a positive responsibility to recognize and secure the dignity of all. Grappling with where that positive responsibility leads is the aim of this concluding chapter. It moves us beyond our critique of dignity as a dichotomous construction with opposing meanings—as either respect or respectability—and toward dignity as an anti-stigma imperative.

Our motivating question for this book has never been "if not dignity, then what?" Indeed, our aim has not been to offer an alternative to dignity per se; instead, we have worked to reveal the limits of how dignity is invoked and deployed in political, cultural, and legal domains and, in particular, to illustrate how it is used to exclude those persons whose actions and beliefs can be and have been denigrated as irresponsible, unrestrained, or promiscuous.

We have not advocated for replacing dignity with another concept that may avoid dignity's multiple meanings and instability. All terms—*humanity, autonomy, freedom, personhood*—are vulnerable to the manipulation, exclusion, and hierarchization that we have documented in our study of how dignity has been deployed by governing and cultural authorities. Providing a new word forecloses and delimits possibilities, for a word creates clarity because it creates boundaries and contains. But that clarity may sacrifice too much because it prevents the polyvocality that we think is needed going forward. An alternative word is not the answer, but a principle—an anti-stigma one—that can guide and motivate *multiple* possible actions may be.

When dignity conveys respectability, it has been utilized to promote stigma rather than counter it; it has been used to highlight who does not fall within the limits of normative notions of responsibility, productivity, success, and health. If we are to recover dignity to be inclusive, then we must—as we have done—acknowledge, explore, and even celebrate community-building habits, media representations, forms of legal recognition, and kinship structures that do not bolster heteronormative logics. Doing so also requires grappling with the responsibilities and accountability of political, legal, and cultural authorities in ways that challenge the neoliberal parameters of a limited state without abandoning our fundamental belief in freedom.

Consequently, our criticisms cannot be met by contending that dignity as respect should be embraced over dignity as respectability. Certainly, dignity as respect has an appeal because it aligns with notions of independence, freedom, and choice. But swapping out respectability for respect leaves dignity vulnerable to devolving into a neoliberal concept that privileges privacy above public responsibility and harbors the potential for the state to absolve itself of accountability for responding to long-standing and ongoing inequities. A requirement of respect of personal choice alone offers no way to resolve the disputes highlighted in chapters 5 and 6 between the fundamental dignity to act on one's faith and the fundamental dignity to live free from discrimination. Dignity as individual respect replaces state responsibility with competitive market principles, reducing needed action to individual choice rather than promoting efforts at structural changes. Dignity as respect neglects to recognize and reduce inequities that have produced and maintained stigmatization of those beyond the normative.[2]

If our claim is that dignity can and should convey an anti-stigma principle and if this position should avoid devolving into neoliberal promotion of individual autonomy, then we must imagine a distinct notion of freedom that embraces a robust and deliberate responsibility to human flourishing. Put differently, if the state is duty-bound to secure dignity, then it must create policies that maximize resources for individual and community opportunity.[3] Realization of inalienable rights is only possible in a society that offers *meaningful* options. Realization of dignity requires the *capacity* to act to realize one's inalienable rights.

Achieving this objective requires the work of interrogating stigma's roots and acting to destroy it at those roots. For example, as we argued in chapter 4, such action might take place at the level of the individual, like promoting visibility of stories that have often been misunderstood, disparaged, or untold. Multicultural casting is not enough. Ryan Murphy's approach to *Pose*—using his resources to bring unheard voices into the writers' room; mentoring new trans writers, actors, and directors; or getting out of the way of talent that has gone undervalued or wholly unrecognized—serves as a stronger model for action.[4] Or, as we argued in chapter 6, such action might require a reckoning with how our contemporary understandings of equal protection and due process liberties are ironically rooted in racist imperatives to preserve power inequities. If we recognize the limits we have placed on the meanings of these fundamental concepts through a jurisprudence that has been warped by white supremacy, then we might more readily recognize and realize the radical aspirations toward equity to which the Thirteenth and Fourteenth Amendments speak.

We might also consider whether state actors, who have been so involved in deploying dignity in ways that exclude LGBTQ+ communities, might take actions that are more inclusive. For example, as mentioned in chapter 5, the *Lawrence* ruling has been characterized as a form of apology. Moreover, the two dissents in *Bostock v. Clayton County, Georgia* tellingly concede that gay, lesbian, and transgender persons should be recognized as having dignity, which is a dramatic change from the dissents in *Lawrence* and *Obergefell*. This legal rhetorical shift follows a broader cultural shift made manifest in multiple municipal authorities expressing their value for LGBTQ+ citizens by encouraging the development of LGBTQ+ enclaves within city boundaries.[5] Such investments that mark and celebrate space raise the question of whether the governing authorities, which we have critiqued, can foster queer worldmaking. Ideally, we see no reason why the answer *must* be no. Nevertheless, we contend that many current examples of gayborhoods, which contain many of the contemporary bathhouses discussed in chapter 2, exemplify the critiques we have made rather than offer solutions to them.[6] That is to say, city councils have supported adorning these neighborhoods with symbols such as the rainbow flag or rainbow sidewalks, which can be read as visible markers of inclusion, equity, and community. But at a more structural level—such as the allocation of resources, including affordable housing options or investment in social services—exclusionary forces abound. What looks like queer worldmaking, relying on symbols of inclusion and pride, fails in the ways that Samuel Delany predicts when city planners and architects design for networking and discourage contact.

These efforts to mark and celebrate gayborhoods reduce to designing for networking. While sought-after visibility matters, its singular achievement can be critiqued in the way that Delany critiques the often misunderstood and overestimated benefits of networking.

While these neighborhoods have value, their potential is not fully actualized: these enclaves do not make good on their promise of equity, inclusion, and community. Ironically, despite the inclusive decorations, the values marketed in these spaces do not necessarily materialize in the lived experiences across the spectrum of queer communities.[7] State involvement can often be limited to the superficial trappings of inclusion and does not provide a fundamental intervention at the level of structure and design. Without a destabilization and reorganization of power, an interrogation of history, and a redistribution of resources, these changes in city planning and redevelopment do not address systemic inequities and fail to actualize the potential for community, equity, and inclusion of all queer people. Put differently, our critique of state support for queer worldmaking centers on its limits. This state effort can promote a visibility that looks like victory but also can foreclose the harder and necessary work of radical transformation.

We search for the kinds of actions that an anti-stigma approach to dignity might motivate. Can this anti-stigma principle inform a set of tangible actions and policies that political, legal, and cultural authorities might take to promote inclusion? One possibility is the act of apology, but not all apologies are the same: some apologies can do the work of anti-stigmatization, but others may merely reinforce the exclusionary limits to which dignity is often susceptible.

An Anti-stigma Approach for Concrete Action

On Friday, March 11, 2016, just before Nancy Reagan's funeral, Hillary Clinton praised the former first lady's advocacy for Alzheimer's research. Then, unprompted, she added, "It may be hard for your viewers to remember how difficult it was for people to talk about HIV/AIDS in the 1980s. And because of both President and Mrs. Reagan—in particular Mrs. Reagan—we started a national conversation."[8] This comment unleashed a fury of rebukes on social media. Peter Staley, a Clinton supporter and founder of ACT UP (AIDS Coalition to Unleash Power), offered an illustrative response: "Thank god I'm not a single issue voter, or she would have lost my vote with this insulting and farcical view of early AIDS history. Hillary just said that the Reagans helped start a 'national conversation' about AIDS. WTF!!!!!"[9]

Within hours, Clinton offered an apology: "While the Reagans were strong advocates for stem cell research and finding a cure for Alzheimer's disease, I misspoke about their record on HIV and AIDS. For that I'm sorry."[10] This "strange half-apology" hardly calmed the uproar, with some in LGBTQ+ communities calling it "glib" and saying it "[made] matters far worse."[11] A mocking hashtag—#HistorybyHillary—criticizing her revisionism was trending by Saturday.[12] Later that day, Clinton issued a second statement that more fully recognized the history of HIV activism in LGBTQ+ communities and offered policy proposals that would guide her potential presidential administration's aims of eradicating HIV. Clinton said her praise for the Reagans was "a mistake, plain and simple." She also recognized the action taken by the community: "To be clear the Reagans did not start a national conversation about HIV and AIDS. That distinction belongs to generations of brave lesbian, gay, bisexual, and transgender people, along with straight allies, who started not just a conversation but a movement that continues to this day. . . . When many in positions of power turned a blind eye, it was groups like ACT UP, Gay Men's Health Crisis and others that came forward to shatter the silence—because as they reminded us again and again, Silence = Death."[13] Clinton's gaffe at Reagan's funeral and her responses raise a set of questions. First, why did her original statement provoke such anger, frustration, and pain? Second, why was her first apology considered insufficient? Third, why was the second apology better? Indeed, renowned AIDS activist Larry Kramer accepted the second apology and called on others to move past the incident: "I almost cant [*sic*] believe she wrote this but am so happy that she did. Boy did she work fast to the pressure that so many of us immediately commenced. Onward!"[14]

Despite Kramer's insistence to move forward, the Clinton fiasco deserves deliberation, as it reflects a legacy of denying the dignity of LGBTQ+ persons and communities. Her original statement celebrating the Reagans perpetuated the "painful experience of non-recognition that lesbians and gay men sometimes experience in heteronormative society," and it was a manifestation of a larger phenomenon that sociologist Deborah Gould calls "social annihilation."[15] The statement's misattribution of good work to the Reagans instead of to the LGBTQ+ communities themselves seemed to reinforce the federal government's original refusal to acknowledge HIV and AIDS or whom it affected; President Reagan did not mention the disease publicly until 1987.[16]

Clinton's initial statement functions as a denial of dignity. Furthermore, the inadequacy of her first apology and the attempt at repair with her second apology make clear how dignity can be taken and the efforts by which it might be restored through deliberate actions of making an apology, taking accountability, and initiating specific reparative acts. In the original statement and in the first apology, Clinton erased the efforts of LGBTQ+ persons who had worked tirelessly to respond to the crisis. She attributed efforts and offered praise to the very individuals who are remembered as ignoring—if not exacerbating—the crisis. To respond by reducing her error to rhetorical misattribution, an instance of simply misspeaking, hardly constituted a remedy because it failed to examine the power dynamics and the raced, classed, gendered, and neoliberal assumptions that enabled her to make a flippant and insufficient first apology.

The second statement is more productive because Clinton publicly acknowledged her harmful revision of history and because she characterized the government's stunted response to the crisis as "a shameful and painful period in our country's history."[17] In other words, she placed blame and accountability on the set of institutions that must be responsible for reparative work. Additionally, she continued by specifying the reparative work needed. To correct governmental indifference, Clinton called for specific policy actions: increasing funding for HIV/AIDS research; expanding access to and cutting costs of drugs, including PrEP; and working with state governments to reform outdated HIV criminalization statutes.[18] This second apology, with its fuller recognition of the history of LGBTQ+ activism, its shaming of government for its willful ignorance, and its detailing of policy actions, advances restoration.

In her second apology, Clinton acknowledged her wrongdoing, apologized, and offered policy aims that might meet the needs of the community harmed and promote that community's flourishing and capacity to seize opportunity. Given the policies that Clinton proposes, we must ask if they meaningfully engage with queer values. Indeed, they do not. In this way, they mimic many of the efforts at inclusion without disruption that we have critiqued. These gestures that grant dignity to some—including marriage recognition, homonormative representation and multicultural casting, and increased access to PrEP—reveal their limits because they are premised upon, maintain, and reify neoliberal and heteronormative logics and fracture LGBTQ+ communities. None of them engage queer notions of space, time, kinship, intimacy, contact, and radically inclusive community. So what actions would do these things? What actions can state leaders take, if any, that would recognize queer ways of knowing and being and move beyond inviting only some within LGBTQ+ communities to be dignified if they temper their queerness?

Three other examples of apologies offer possibilities, as they each adopt an anti-stigma principle. Each demonstrates how to be accountable without eliding power inequities or histories of abuse, how to embrace difference, how to partner with wronged communities to build a better future, and how to avoid compelling marginalized communities to conform to an exclusionary notion of dignity. First, on June 22, 2016, Toronto police chief Mark Saunders apologized for the actions that catalyzed the first pride parade in Toronto: the raiding of four Toronto bathhouses in one night and the arrest of 286 patrons in February 1981. Saunders's statement recognized how the police's actions were dehumanizing: "The 35th anniversary of the 1981 raids is a time when the Toronto Police Service expresses its regrets for those very actions. It is also an occasion to acknowledge the lessons learned about the risks of treating any part of Toronto's many communities as not fully a part of society." The statement also named the need for restorative practices, which were defined by the chief as ongoing community-building work: "Policing requires building mutual trust and that means forging links with the full range of communities that make up this extraordinary city. The Toronto Police Service recognizes the lessons from that period have continuing relevance for the creation of a more inclusive city."[19]

Second, five months after Clinton's gaffe, the prime minister of Canada, Justin Trudeau, made clear his intention to issue an apology "on behalf of all Canadians to those who were imprisoned, fired from their jobs or otherwise persecuted in the past because of their sexuality."[20] The apology was part of a broader set of political reforms to which the Trudeau administration had committed in partnership with Egale, a national Canadian interest group for sexual minorities. Egale had lobbied for apologizing to all individuals arrested for homosexuality prior to its decriminalization in Canada in 1969, apologizing to all who were dismissed from public service and military service due to their sexuality, evaluating whether the government should compensate those who suffered past discrimination because of their sexuality, requiring that police officers and all other officials within justice services receive training that acknowledges the historically wrong treatment of sexual minorities, and eliminating all laws that would criminalize those who would visit a bathhouse or practice group sex.[21]

Third, in January 2017, the United Kingdom posthumously pardoned thousands of men convicted for violating that country's ban on same-sex intercourse, which was repealed in 1967.[22] Speaking in support of the new law, the UK's justice minister, Sam Gyimah, stated, "This is a truly momentous day. We can never undo the hurt caused, but we have apologised and taken action to right these wrongs. I am immensely proud that 'Turing's law' has become a reality under this government."[23] The UK's actions in this instance are similar to those taken by the New York City Council with regard to changes in jurisdiction over Hart Island. They are meant to provide some kind of restoration of dignity to the deceased by acknowledging the wrong of the stigma that permitted their criminalization while they were alive.

The apologies and commitments to policy actions in these examples are notable because they are informed by the anti-stigma approach advocated in this book. Particularly, they acknowledge long histories of wrongdoing and oppression and do not limit acknowledgment to the hurtful acts of individuals only; instead, they ground acknowledgment in structures and histories of inequality and inequity. Furthermore, they do not require restraint; they do not require that wronged communities contort themselves to align with normative majorities or abandon community-specific ways of knowing and being.

More specifically, these measures bring into stark relief why Clinton's second apology and other measures discussed throughout this book, which initially appear progressive and inclusive, fall short. First, Trudeau's and Gyimah's respective apologies were not reactive. They were not compelled under duress, and they were not issued within a competitive electoral context that might lead one to suspect their motives. Second, Clinton's policy objectives and other seemingly inclusive actions like marriage recognition or increased cultural representation tend to be premised on heteronormative notions of relationship and dignity. By contrast, the UK's commitment to expunging convictions recognizes that the basis for banning same-sex intimacy was never just. Similarly, Egale's proposed objectives, endorsed by Trudeau, do not assume the heteronormative bias that we have exposed and critiqued. Indeed, the explicit demand for elimination of laws that might impede the kind of sexual communion and kinship at the bathhouse suggests engagement with queer logics.

Doing Dignity Differently: A Polyvocal Way Forward

If dignity is to have any use value as a principle against stigmatization, then we must take seriously Tim Dean's assessment of the contemporary state of sexual politics and equal rights for LGBTQ+ persons: "The United States has taken enormous strides in recognizing lesbian and gay rights, while its view of sex has barely budged. Substantial progress in the social acceptance of homosexuality as an identity category warranting legal protection has been accompanied by—perhaps even accomplished by—the accelerating privatization and consequent repudiation of all forms of erotic expression that fall outside a narrowly prescribed band."[24] Our examination of changes in public health politics, cultural representation, and law bears out Dean's critique. The dignity often promoted in each domain refuses to acknowledge or include queer ways of thinking and doing, which would challenge heteronormative and neoliberal notions of sex, romance, privacy, responsibility, and kinship. The enormous strides thus far achieved are often premised on conformity and discursive narratives of sameness. They have been achieved by aligning with the norm. This "just like you" strategy constitutes dignity's seductive allure. It has been made manifest in some LGBTQ+ community responses to the HIV/AIDS crisis; it is a dominant theme of some increasingly mainstream cultural productions, like *Love, Simon*, even as it is beginning to be contested by others, such as *Pose*; it is evident in some strategies to gain majority public support for same-sex marriage; it is one reason plural marriage advocacy was considered a liability for the same-sex marriage movement. This seductive quality makes clear dignity's limits and its potential for harm. Dignity in this form is an ultimatum that threatens the erasure of divergent values, community, history, and queer kinship.

Promoting dignity as an anti-stigma principle rather than as meaning either respectability or respect requires actions that challenge inequity by maximizing the capacity for flourishing. Dignity as respectability is deeply exclusionary. Dignity as respect suggests mere tolerance. It gives permission to act, but it does not support that action or recognize how permission is already premised on an inequitable logic. Dignity conceptualized as an anti-stigma principle requires doing dignity differently. It can follow only if public officials and cultural authorities adopt policies and take actions that refuse to promote racial, sexual, or gendered hierarchies.[25]

For example, in public health policy, we should work to compel appropriate governing bodies not only to increase drug production and access to medications that reduce risk of HIV transmission but also to depoliticize public health policies altogether. Doing so would require a reconsideration of what constitutes sexual health and who gets to decide. Furthermore, in urban planning and policy, we must move beyond state-supported LGBTQ+ visibility and instead work to root out systemic inequities and shape this space according to queer logics and values. Importantly, this work must also be done intracommunally. Not only does this necessitate confronting the white supremacy, transphobia, and class inequalities that remain within and divide LGBTQ+ communities, but it also requires the adoption of policies that reallocate resources: investing in an economically disempowered queer community and redirecting funding toward social services, housing, healthcare, education, job training, and legal services. In media representation, we must remain critical of the limits of visibility of LGBTQ+ persons. We have highlighted how our inclusionary aspiration can be realized not only by expanding on-screen visibility but also by providing opportunities to excluded voices for content creation. Finally, with law and legal change, we should advocate not only for the state to bestow marriage to an expanding number of relationships but also for the state to recognize how marriage may not capture all the forms of valuable kinship. We should therefore ask if the state should recognize forms of relational intimacy and support beyond dyadic marriages. At the very least, similar to the Canadian and UK governments' efforts, US governing authorities should issue an unprompted apology that takes accountability for the harm inflicted and should do the necessary work to destigmatize and promote flourishing.

Whether state or cultural authorities can restore dignity to those whom they have purposefully harmed is an open question. At the very least, such restoration requires that those who committed the harm acknowledge, critique, and relinquish the power that enabled them to do so. We can say that recognition of or investment with dignity cannot be contingent on the abandonment of queer ways of knowing and being. Dignity cannot require the adoption of heteronormative, cisnormative, and white supremacist logics that build the boundaries and limits of dignity. Dignity cannot be achieved through inclusion without disruption. Dignity requires expansive and polyvocal inclusion. Dignity is not a guarantee of respect (and must not be a requirement of respectability). Dignity can and should be an active commitment to anti-stigmatization and a consequent commitment to promote flourishing. A more thoughtful strategy shaped by queer particularity is perhaps the only route forward to achieve a fuller sense of possibility, one that acknowledges, challenges, and breaks through dignity's limits. Like *queer* itself, *dignity* is an act of *doing*, not a state of being, which means we can do dignity differently. If we are committed to radically inclusive and just futures, then we should disrupt our current understandings of dignity, embrace an anti-stigma principle as a guide for empowering policy and action, and rethink what counts as LGBTQ+ progress.

ACKNOWLEDGMENTS

As we hope will become clear in the reading, this book was conceived, researched, and written in and for community. In this spirit, we wish to acknowledge all those with whom we shared space—past and present.

To our queer elders: Thank you for the fight, the vision, and the hope that has shaped us and our work.

To Steve's family—Barbara, Mark, Jarrett, David, Jennifer, Beth, Emma, and Charlotte: Thanks for your support throughout this project (and to David and Beth for providing Steve with yet another couch to crash on while working in New York City).

To Timothy's family—Mom, Stephanie, Shane, Makenzy, and Liam: Thank you for the endless support and love.

To Bernadette Atuahene: Thank you for inviting us to contribute to your extensive project on dignity takings and dignity restoration, which was the seed of this book.

To the archivists at the Lesbian, Gay, Bisexual and Transgender Community Center in Greenwich Village and to the staff of the New York Public Library: Thank you for archival research support during 2016 and 2017. And especially to The Center, thank you for helping us find joy when researching got heavy. We will never forget the mixture of laughter and tears as we were reacquainted with our collective history.

To friends, colleagues, and strangers: Thank you for extraordinarily helpful comments on various arguments presented throughout the book and for your enthusiasm for the project.

While we are sure that we are forgetting some, special thanks to the following people: Janet Mock, Julie Novkov, Connor Ewing, Yuvraj Joshi, Ryan Thoreson, Erin Daly, Ellen Andersen, Laura Beth Nielsen, Matthew Patrick Shaw, Andrew W. Kahrl, Therí Pickens, Rebecca Herzig, Charles Nero, Christina Bell, Senem Aslan, Áslaug Ásgeirsdóttir, Emily Kane, John Baughman, Jacob Longaker, Nina Hagel, Clayton Spencer, Ian Shin, Will D'Ambruoso, Darby Ray, Michael Sargent, Sonu Bedi,

Stephen Skowronek, Susan Burgess, Heath Fogg Davis, Ken I. Kersch, Jeffrey Selinger, Amin Ghaziani, dawn lonsinger, T. J. Moretti, Ivy Stabell, Dean DeFino, Miles Beckwith, Christina Carlson, James Blaszko, Adam Porter-Smith, Drew Carr, Lewis Truman Elliott, Blaine Johnston, David Kimple, and all the strangers who showed interest in our work (especially Jay and Matt from Scruff and Aaron from Grindr)

To Alex Garner: Thanks for supporting this project since 2018 and for giving us a venue at Hornet to further explore some of our arguments through four blog posts on that social media site as well as for being in conversation with us about sexual health and queer history.

To Max Gardner and Charlotte Karlsen: Thanks for the editorial and research support throughout your senior year at Bates.

To Ilene Kalish at New York University Press: Thanks for believing in our project from its earliest iteration and for shepherding it through proposal, review, and final draft with an unflaggingly critical and caring eye.

To our respective institutions: Thank you for your support throughout. This project was supported by three Bates Faculty Development Grants to Steve, one awarded in fall 2016, another awarded in fall 2018, and a third awarded in fall 2019. This project was also supported through course and other workload relief to Timothy by Iona College.

To Todd Brian Backus: Thanks from Steve for your love and support throughout the length of this project and for challenging Steve to be as queer as he theorizes!

To Jenna and Ethan Dabbs and Matt Udkovich: Thanks for providing much-needed places for Steve to stay in New York City in 2018 and 2019 and for needed distractions from this project.

To Ryan Rosario, Kris Cannon, Therí Pickens, Lewis Truman Elliott, Josh Cox, Chris Hailey, dawn lonsinger, Kendra Parker, Dana Williams, Kameelah Martin, and Shauna Morgan: Thanks from Timothy for your guidance, support, love, wisdom, and laughter.

To Johnny Taylor and Josh Manson: Thanks for helping us rethink our title and keeping it cheeky!

To Jackson (Steve's dearly departed golden retriever): Thanks for providing love and distractions throughout. We will never forget how much you loved your red bandana and how you taught us how to sigh openly and to sissify that walk.

To Zach Davies and Jonathan Mushock: Thanks for keeping our bodies snatched and for making sure that we balanced mind and body.

To our caffeine providers: Thanks to Romeo & Juliet Columbian Coffee (Hell's Kitchen, New York City) and Harlem Blues Café (Harlem, New York City) for the espresso and welcoming workspace.

And finally, thank you to the following journals, where early explorations of parts of this project were published. First, an earlier version of chapter 1 was published as "Fucking with Dignity: Public Sex, Queer Intimate Kinship, and how the AIDS Epidemic Bathhouse Closures Constituted a Dignity Taking," in *Chicago-Kent Law Review* 92, no. 3 (2017): 961–89. Second, an earlier version of chapter 5 was published as "Dynamics of Constitutional Development and the Conservative Potential of U.S. Supreme Court Gay Rights Jurisprudence, or How Neil Gorsuch Stopped Worrying and Learned to Love Same-Sex Marriage," in *Constitutional Studies* 3 (2018): 1–40. Third, some ideas on the *Masterpiece Cakeshop* decision, discussed in chapters 5 and 6, gained their earliest expression as "Masterpiece Cakeshop on Gay Rights versus Religious Liberty," in *SCOTUS 2018: Major Decisions and Developments of the US Supreme Court*, edited by David Klein and Morgan Marietta (New York: Palgrave Macmillan, 2019): 61–74.

NOTES

INTRODUCTION

1 Matt Tracy, "City to Lend Dignity to Burial Ground for People Who Died, Alone, from AIDS," GCN: Gaycitynews.com, November 15, 2019, www.gaycitynews.com. Hart Island is featured prominently in the season 2 premiere of *Pose*, "Acting Up," which is extensively discussed in chapter 4.

2 Corey Kilgannon, "Dead of AIDS and Forgotten in Potter's Field," *New York Times*, July 2, 2018.

3 Quoted in Tracy, "City to Lend Dignity."

4 Dale Carpenter, *Flagrant Conduct: The Story of Lawrence v. Texas* (New York: Norton, 2012), 259.

5 *Lawrence v. Texas*, 539 U.S. 558 (2003).

6 *United States v. Windsor*, 570 U.S. 744 (2013).

7 *Obergefell v. Hodges*, 576 U.S. 644 (2015).

8 The phrase "equal dignity" is invoked in the penultimate sentence of Kennedy's decision in *Obergefell*.

9 *Masterpiece Cakeshop v. Colorado Civil Rights Commission*, 584 U.S. ____ (2018) (slip opinion), 9, 18. Justice Neil Gorsuch spoke for the majority in the most recent *Bostock* decision, which declared that Title VII of the 1964 Civil Rights Act protected individuals from employment discrimination based on sexual orientation or gender identity. Indeed, even when dissenting in *Bostock*, both Justices Alito and Kavanaugh conceded the dignity of LGBTQ+ individuals. See *Bostock v. Clayton County, Georgia*, 590 U.S. ____ (2020) (slip opinion), 54, J. Alito dissenting; and (slip opinion), 2, J. Kavanaugh dissenting.

10 *Tales of the City*, ten episodes, aired on June 7, 2019, on Netflix.

11 Armistead Maupin's novels in this series include *Tales of the City* (1978), *More Tales of the City* (1980), *Further Tales of the City* (1982), *Babycakes* (1984), *Significant Others* (1987), *Sure of You* (1989), *Michael Tolliver Lives* (2007), *Mary Anne in Autumn* (2010), and *The Days of Anna Madrigal* (2014). The first miniseries aired on PBS in 1993; the second and third miniseries aired on Showtime in 1998 and 2000, respectively.

12 *Tales of the City*, season 1, episode 4, "The Price of Oil," directed by Silas Howard, aired on June 7, 2019, on Netflix.

13 *Tales of the City*, season 1, episode 10, "Three of Cups," directed by Kyle Patrick Alvarez, aired on June 7, 2019, on Netflix.

14 As legal scholars Yuvraj Joshi and Ryan Thoreson write, "The meaning of dignity in any given case is highly contingent and contextual, shaped by a wide variety of factors . . . [and that] lead dignity to take on certain meanings in constitutional jurisprudence" (32). Among these factors, Joshi and Thoreson include sociohistorical and legal context, constitutional law and adjudication, legal and social movements, and the particular judge. As each of these factors can be specific to country context, the meaning of dignity can be quite distinct depending on where, by whom, when, and how it is deployed. See Yuvraj Joshi and Ryan Thoreson, "Dignity in Lesbian, Gay, and Bisexual Rights Cases," presented at the Law and Society Association 2019 Annual Meeting (May 31, 2019). Paper on file with authors.

15 We suggest that particular notions of dignity become commonsensical or hegemonic in the Gramscian sense. See Antonio Gramsci, *Selections from the Prison Notebooks*, trans. Quentin Hoare and Geoffrey Nowell Smith (London: Lawrence and Wishart, 1971), 182.

16 On power imbalance in political institutions, see Terry M. Moe, "Power and Political Institutions," *Perspectives on Politics* 3 (June 2005): 215–33. On how media representation reinforces traditional norms, see Guillermo Avila-Saavedra, "Nothing Queer about Queer Television: Televised Construction of Gay Masculinities," *Media Culture Society* 31, no. 1 (2009): 5–21. On how judicial decision-making, even when pushing forward new precedent, can demonstrate status quo bias, see Robert L. Scharff and Francesco Parisi, "The Role of Status Quo Bias and Bayesian Learning in the Creation of New Legal Rights," *Journal of Law, Economics, and Policy* 25 (2006–7): 25–46; and Oona A. Hathaway, "Oath Dependence in the Law: The Course and Pattern of Legal Change in a Common Law System," *Iowa Law Review* 86 (2001): 101–65.

17 On the power of media representation to alter public opinion about LGBTQ+ rights claims and shape support for LGBTQ+ policy demands, see Jeremiah J. Garretson, *The Path to Gay Rights: How Activism and Coming Out Changed Public Opinion* (New York: New York University Press, 2018). On whether LGBTQ+ rights can be successfully pursued through litigation, see Gerald Rosenberg, *The Hollow Hope: Can Courts Bring About Social Change?*, 2nd ed. (Chicago: University of Chicago Press, 2008); Michael J. Klarman, *From the Closet to the Altar: Courts, Backlash, and the Struggle for Same-Sex Marriage* (New York: Oxford University Press, 2013); and Thomas Keck, "Beyond Backlash: Assessing the Impact of Judicial Decisions on LGBT Rights," *Law and Society Review* 43, no. 1 (2009): 151–86. On how policy reforms can both reflect and respond to popular demand for change, see John Gaventa and Rosemary McGee, eds., *Citizen Action and National Policy Reform: Making Change Happen* (New York: Zed Books, 2010); and Frank R. Baumgartner and Bryan D. Jones, *Agendas and Instability in American Politics*, 2nd ed. (Chicago: University of Chicago Press, 2009).

18 See Margot Canaday, *The Straight State: Sexuality and Citizenship in Twentieth-Century America* (Princeton: Princeton University Press, 2009); and Stephen M.

Engel, *Fragmented Citizens: The Changing Landscape of Gay and Lesbian Lives* (New York: New York University Press, 2016). On citizenship as grounded not only in a claim to rights or a requirement of communal responsibilities but more fundamentally in recognition by others, see Shane Phelan, *Sexual Strangers: Gays, Lesbians, and Dilemmas of Citizenship* (Philadelphia: Temple University Press, 2001).

19 As Young writes, "While the subject desires recognition as human, capable of activity, full of hope and possibility, she receives from the dominant culture only the judgment that she is different, marked, or inferior" (60). Iris Marion Young, *Justice and the Politics of Difference* (Princeton: Princeton University Press, 1990).

20 Martha Nussbaum, "Human Dignity and Political Entitlements," in *Human Dignity and Bioethics: Essays Commissioned by the President's Council on Bioethics* (Washington, DC: Government Printing Office, 2008), 354.

21 *Planned Parenthood of Southeastern Pennsylvania v. Casey*, 505 U.S. 833 (1992), 852.

22 *Lawrence v. Texas*, 539 U.S. 558 (2003), 567.

23 The specific text in the Declaration of Independence is "We hold these truths to be self-evident, that all men are created equal, that they are endowed by their Creator with certain unalienable Rights, that among these are Life, Liberty and the pursuit of Happiness."

24 Universal Declaration of Human Rights, Preamble.

25 Izhak England, "Human Dignity: From Antiquity to Modern Israel's Constitutional Framework," *Cardozo Law Review* 21 (2000): 1923.

26 Bernadette Atuahene, "Takings as a Sociolegal Concept: An Interdisciplinary Examination of Involuntary Property Loss," *Annual Review of Law and Social Sciences* 12 (2016): 171, 178–79.

27 *United States v. Windsor*, 570 U.S. 744 (2013), 767.

28 Ibid., 768.

29 *Obergefell v. Hodges*, 576 U.S. _____ (2015) (slip opinion), 26.

30 Ibid., 28.

31 Stephen Darwall, "Equal Dignity and Rights," in *Dignity: A History*, ed. Reny Debes (New York: Oxford University Press, 2017), 184. See also Stephen Darwall, "Two Kinds of Respect," *Ethics* 88 (1977): 36–49.

32 Yuvraj Joshi, "The Respectable Dignity of *Obergefell v. Hodges*," *California Law Review Circuit* 6 (November 2015): 119.

33 Erin Daly, *Dignity Rights: Courts, Constitutions, and the Worth of the Human Person* (Philadelphia: University of Pennsylvania Press, 2013), 13.

34 David Harvey, *A Brief History of Neoliberalism* (New York: Oxford University Press, 2005), 2.

35 Matthew Dean Hindman, *Political Advocacy and Its Interested Citizens: Neoliberalism, Postpluralism, and LGBT Organizations* (Philadelphia: University of Pennsylvania Press, 2019), 27.

36 Chriss V. Sneed, "Ga(y)tekeeping Identity, Citizenship, and Claims to Justice: 'Freedom to Serve,' 'Freedom to Marry,' and the U.S. Thirst for Good Gay

Subjects," in *Queer Activism after Marriage Equality*, ed. Joseph Nicholas DeFilippis, Michael W. Yarbrough, and Angela Jones (London: Routledge, 2019), 37.

37 See Wendy Brown, *Undoing the Demos: Neoliberalism's Stealth Revolution* (New York: Zone Books, 2015); Wendy Brown, "American Nightmare: Neoliberalism, Neoconservatism, and De-democratization," *Political Theory* 34, no. 6 (2006): 690–714; Lisa Duggan, *The Twilight of Equality? Neoliberalism, Cultural Politics, and the Attack on Democracy* (Boston: Beacon, 2003); and Antonio Vazquez-Arroyo, "Liberal Democracy and Neoliberalism: A Critical Juxtaposition," *New Political Science* 30, no. 2 (2008): 127–59.

38 Hindman, *Political Advocacy*, 37.

39 Sneed, "Ga(y)tekeeping," 39.

40 Brittney Cooper, *Eloquent Rage: A Black Feminist Discovers Her Superpower* (New York: Picador, 2019), 153.

41 Ibid.

42 The United States Supreme Court had, before 2020, focused on the rights and identities of gays, lesbians, and bisexuals and has not, by its own terms, often referenced trans or queer identities or rights. It did hear oral argument on October 8, 2019, for an anti–trans discrimination case: *R.G. & G.R. Harris Funeral Homes Inc. v. Equal Employment Opportunity Commission*, No. 18-107 (2019).

43 Neoliberalism is particularly evident in juridical conceptions of same-sex marriage. Jaye Cee Whitehead has compellingly argued that marriage is a neoliberal tool of the state: "Because marriage has the potential to reduce welfare caseloads, promoting marriage makes the state more economically efficient." Jaye Cee Whitehead, *The Nuptial Deal: Same-Sex Marriage and Neo-liberal Governance* (Chicago: University of Chicago Press, 2012), 14.

44 Laurie Ackermann, *Human Dignity: Lodestar for Equality in South Africa* (Claremont, South Africa: Jut, 2012); Bernadette Atuahene, *We Want What's Ours: Learning from South Africa's Land Restitution Program* (New York: Oxford University Press, 2014); Susanne Baer, "Dignity, Liberty, Equality: A Fundamental Rights Triangle of Constitutionalism," *University of Toronto Law Journal* 59 (2009): 417–68; Stephanie Hennette-Vauchez, "A Human Dignitas? Remnants of the Ancient Legal Concept in Contemporary Dignity Jurisprudence," *International Journal of Constitutional Law (I-CON)* 9 (2011): 32–57; Christopher McCrudden, "Human Dignity and Judicial Interpretation of Human Rights," *European Journal of International Law* 19 (2008): 655–724; Kate O'Regan, "Undoing Humiliation, Fostering Equal Citizenship: Human Dignity in South Africa's Sexual Orientation Equality Jurisprudence," *NYU Review of Law and Social Change* 37 (2013): 307–14; Neomi Rao, "On the Use and Abuse of Dignity in Constitutional Law," *Columbia Journal of European Law* 14 (Spring 2008): 201–56; Judith Resnik and Julie Chi-hye Suk, "Adding Insult to Injury: Questioning the Role of Dignity in Conceptions of Sovereignty," *Stanford Law Review* 55 (2003): 1921–62.

45 Daly, *Dignity Rights*, 5.

46 Man Yee Karen Lee, "Universal Human Dignity: Some Reflections in the Asian Context," *Asian Journal of Comparative Law* 3, no. 1 (2008): 1–33, cited in Viviana Bohorquez Monsalve and Javier Aguirre Roman, "Tensions of Human Dignity: Conceptualization and Application to International Human Rights Law," *SUR: International Journal of Human Rights* 6, no. 11 (2009): 39.

47 Ronald Dworkin, *Justice for Hedgehogs* (Cambridge, MA: Belknap Press of Harvard University Press, 2011), 13.

48 See Michael Rosen, *Dignity: Its History and Meaning* (Cambridge, MA: Harvard University Press, 2012).

49 See Henk Botha, "Human Dignity in Comparative Perspective," *Stellenbosch Law Review* 2 (2009): 171–220.

50 See Joern Eckert, "Legal Roots of Human Dignity in German Law," in *The Concept of Human Dignity in Human Rights Discourse*, ed. David Kretzmer and Eckart Klein (The Hague: Kluwer Law International, 2002); and Mirko Bagaric and James Allan, "The Vacuous Concept of Dignity," *Journal of Human Rights* 5 (2006): 257–70.

51 Gerhold K. Becker, "In Search of Humanity: Human Dignity as a Basic Moral Attitude," in *The Future of Value Inquiry*, ed. Matti Hayry and Tuija Takala (Amsterdam: Rodopi, 2001), 53.

52 John Harris, "Cloning and Human Dignity," *Cambridge Quarterly of Healthcare Ethics* 7, no. 2 (April 1998): 163.

53 Aharon Barak, *Human Dignity: The Constitutional Value and the Constitutional Right* (New York: Cambridge University Press, 2015), 9.

54 Legal scholar Leslie Meltzer Henry has documented that "after a brief period of hibernation during the Burger and Rehnquist Courts, the use of dignity is once again on the rise. . . . Dignity's increasing popularity, however, does not signal agreement about what the term means" (171, 172). Leslie Meltzer Henry, "The Jurisprudence of Dignity," *University of Pennsylvania Law Review* 160 (2011): 169–233.

55 Daly, *Dignity Rights*, 71.

56 *Cohen v. California*, 403 U.S. 15 (1971), 24.

57 *Hudson v. Michigan*, 547 U.S. 586 (2006), 594.

58 *Miranda v. Arizona*, 384 U.S. 436 (1966), 460.

59 *McKaskle v. Wiggins*, 465 U.S. 168 (1984), 176–77.

60 *Kennedy v. Louisiana*, 554 U.S. 407 (2008), 419–20.

61 *Griswold v. Connecticut*, 381 U.S. 479 (1965), 482–83.

62 *Planned Parenthood of Southeastern Pennsylvania v. Casey*, 505 U.S. 833 (1992), 851; *City of Richmond v. J.A. Croson Company*, 488 U.S. 469 (1989), 493; *J.E.B. v. Alabama ex rel. T.B.*, 511 U.S. 127 (1994), 129, 142.

63 *Rice v. Cayetano*, 528 U.S. 495 (2000), 517.

64 One exception is *Romer v. Evans*, 517 U.S. 620 (1996). The word *dignity* does not appear in this decision.

65 See Laurence Tribe, "Equal Dignity: Speaking Its Name," *Harvard Law Review Forum* 129 (2015): 16–32; and Laurence Tribe, "Equal Dignity—Heeding Its Call," *Harvard Law Review* 132 (2018): 1323–44.

66 Michael Warner, introduction to *Fear of a Queer Planet: Queer Politics and Social Theory*, ed. Michael Warner (Minneapolis: University of Minnesota Press, 1993), xix.

67 See Nancy F. Cott, *Public Vows: A History of Marriage and the Nation* (Cambridge, MA: Harvard University Press, 2000); Peggy Pascoe, *What Comes Naturally: Miscegenation Law and the Making of Race in America* (New York: Oxford University Press, 2009); and Priscilla Yamin, *American Marriage: A Political Institution* (Philadelphia: University of Pennsylvania Press, 2012).

68 See Lisa Duggan, "The New Homonormativity: The Sexual Politics of Neoliberalism," in *Materializing Democracy: Toward a Revitalized Cultural Politics*, ed. Russ Castronovo and Dana D. Nelson (Durham: Duke University Press, 2002).

69 Urvashi Vaid, "LGBTQ Politics after Marriage," edited by Joseph Nicholas DeFilippis in *Queer Activism after Marriage Equality*, ed. Joseph Nicholas DeFelippis, Michael W. Yarbrough, and Angela Jones (London: Routledge, 2018), 18, 19.

70 Michael Warner, *The Trouble with Normal: Sex, Politics, and the Ethics of Queer Life* (Cambridge, MA: Harvard University Press, 1999), 99.

71 Our use of "gays and lesbians" here is explicit. While the 2020 *Bostock* ruling indicated that the 1964 Civil Rights Act's Title VII protects transgender individuals from employment discrimination, that decision made no explicit mention of dignity. As such, the Court's explicit invocations of dignity are restricted to earlier decisions authored by Justice Kennedy, such as *Lawrence*, *Windsor*, and *Obergefell*.

72 See Laurence Tribe's praise of *Obergefell* for not staying within the tiered scrutiny paradigm: "*Obergefell* has definitively replaced . . . [the] wooden three-prong test focused on tradition, specificity, and negativity with the more holistic inquiry." Tribe, "Equal Dignity: Speaking Its Name," 16.

73 Other skeptics of dignity include Noa Ben-Asher, "Conferring Dignity: The Metamorphosis of the Legal Homosexual," *Harvard Journal of Law and Gender* 37 (2014): 243–84 (arguing that dignity may prove too constraining for a robust notion of sexual justice); and Katherine Franke, "Dignifying Rights: A Comment on Jeremy Waldron's *Dignity, Rights, and Responsibilities*," *Arizona State Law Journal* 43 (2011): 1177–1200 (contending that rights are not merely grounded in responsibilities that may follow from dignity but also that dignity creates expectations of behaving responsibly; consequently, dignity is not inherent but follows from generally accepted norms). See also Jeffrey Rosen, "The Dangers of a Constitutional 'Right to Dignity,'" *Atlantic*, April 29, 2015, www.theatlantic.com (accessed July 22, 2019) (arguing that dignity may have unintended consequences that liberals might object to even as it was used in *Obergefell* to grant what liberals had sought; this argument is pursued in chapter 5).

74 See Bernadette Atuahene, "Dignity Takings and Dignity Restoration: Creating a New Theoretical Framework for Understanding Involuntary Property Loss and the Remedies Required," *Law and Social Inquiry* 41, no. 4 (Fall 2016): 796–823.

75 For a critique of essentialist identity while acknowledging its political use value and social function, see Gayatri Chakravorty Spivak, "Can the Subaltern Speak?," in *Marxism and the Interpretation of Culture*, ed. Cary Nelson and Lawrence Grossberg (London: Macmillan, 1988): 271–313. For *queer* as a common adjective to designate a particular identity and sexual orientation, see "GLAAD Media Reference Guide—Lesbian/Gay/Bisexual Glossary of Terms," GLAAD, www.glaad .org (accessed January 3, 2020).

76 Annamarie Jagose, *Queer Theory: An Introduction* (New York: New York University Press, 1996), 131.

77 Eve Kosofsky Sedgwick, *Tendencies* (Durham: Duke University Press, 1993), 8.

78 David Halperin, *Saint Foucault: Towards a Gay Hagiography* (New York: Oxford University Press, 1995), 62.

79 Lee Edelman, *No Future: Queer Theory and the Death Drive* (New York: Columbia University Press, 2004), 17.

80 Calvin Thomas, *Ten Lessons in Theory: An Introduction to Theoretical Writing* (New York: Bloomsbury Academic, 2013), 266.

81 Nikki Sullivan, *A Critical Introduction to Queer Theory* (New York: New York University Press, 2003), 44.

82 Janet R. Jakobsen, "Queer Is? Queer Does? Normativity and Resistance," *GLQ: A Journal of Lesbian and Gay Studies* 4 (1998): 516.

83 Warner, introduction, xxvii.

84 Sullivan, *Critical Introduction*, 50.

85 See Jack Halberstam, *The Queer Art of Failure* (Durham: Duke University Press, 2011).

86 Ibid., 2–3.

87 Ibid., 2.

88 For more on phenomenological discussions about orientations and queerness, see Sara Ahmed's *Queer Phenomenology: Orientations, Objects, Others* (Durham: Duke University Press, 2006).

89 Halberstam, *Queer Art of Failure*, 9–10. See also James C. Scott, *Seeing like a State: How Certain Schemes to Improve the Human Condition Have Failed* (New Haven: Yale University Press, 1998).

90 Halberstam, *Queer Art of Failure*, 9.

91 Ibid., 10.

92 Ibid., 11.

93 Ibid., 10.

94 Ibid., 19.

95 Ibid., 25.

96 Joseph Beam, "Brother to Brother: Words from the Heart," in *In the Life: A Black Gay Anthology* (New York: Alyson Books, 1986): 230–42 (discussing constructions of "home" and "safety").

97 Edelman, *No Future*.

98 Judith Halberstam, *In a Queer Time and Place: Transgender Bodies, Subcultural Lives* (New York: New York University Press, 2005), 1–21. Please note that the

citation reflects Halberstam's self-identification at the time of publication. Other references reflect their change in legal name and pronouns to Jack Halberstam.

99 Ibid., 152–88. See also Dustin Bradley Goltz, *Queer Temporalities in Gay Male Representation: Tragedy, Normativity, and Futurity* (New York: Routledge, 2010); and José Esteban Muñoz, *Cruising Utopia: The Then and There of Queer Futurity* (New York: New York University Press, 2009).

100 For an account and analysis of interpersonal contact in public sex institutions, see Samuel R. Delany, *Times Square Red, Times Square Blue* (New York: New York University Press, 1999), which is more extensively discussed in chapters 1 and 2. For a discussion of the transgressive potential of queer sex, see Tim Dean, *Unlimited Intimacy: Reflections on the Subculture of Barebacking* (Chicago: University of Chicago Press, 2009), also discussed in chapters 1 and 2.

101 Stephen M. Engel and Timothy S. Lyle, "Fucking with Dignity: Public Sex, Queer Intimate Kinship, and How the AIDS Epidemic Bathhouse Closures Constituted a Dignity Taking," *Chicago-Kent Law Review* 92, no. 3 (2018): 961–89.

102 George Chauncey, *Why Marriage? The History Shaping Today's Debate Over Gay Equality* (New York: Basic Books, 2004), 104.

103 In an opinion piece for the *New York Times*, historian Patrick William Kelley writes, "AIDS is no longer a crisis, at least in the United States, and that is a phenomenal public-health success story." Patrick William Kelley, "The End of Safe Gay Sex?," *New York Times*, June 26, 2018, www.nytimes.com. We think this assessment ignores ongoing crises in a range of communities—for example, persons of color, trans communities, and so on. For a critique of this essay, see Daniel Villarreal, "Today, on National HIV Prevention Day, This 'New York Times' Op-Ed Got HIV Prevention All Wrong," Hornet.com, June 27, 2018, https://hornet.com.

104 See Delany, *Times Square Red*; Dean, *Unlimited Intimacy*.

105 Our goal is not to summarize the scholarship that has illustrated how increased media visibility of gay and lesbian subjects promotes a politics of respectability. Instead, we aim, first, to highlight how cultural representations can reinforce neoliberal values and confine dignity to align with those values and, second, to draw attention to those cultural representations that challenge these boundaries. With regard to the latter, we specifically draw attention to how these challenges are possible—for example, what resources need to be provided and what practices need to be undertaken if dignity's limits are to be exposed and alternatives are to be voiced and valued.

106 Becky Albertalli, *Simon vs. the Homo Sapiens Agenda* (New York: Balzer + Bray, 2015); *Love, Simon*, directed by Greg Berlanti (Los Angeles: Fox 2000 Pictures, 2018).

107 David Sims, "The Lesson Hollywood Should Learn from *Love, Simon*," *Atlantic*, March 19, 2018, www.theatlantic.com; Nellie Andreeva, "'Love, Simon' Spinoff Series 'Love, Victor' Moves from Disney+ to Hulu, Sets Launch and Opens Season Two Writers Room," *Deadline*, February 24, 2020, https://deadline.com.

108 As explored in chapter 3, the film brands itself as a progressive critique by adopting a critical question articulated in the novel—namely, "Why is straight the default?"

109 *Pose*, seasons 1 and 2, 2018 and 2019, on FX Network.

110 Bianca Betancourt, "Indya Moore Explains Why 'Pose' Continues to Be 'Revolutionary,'" *Teen Vogue*, September 11, 2019, www.teenvogue.com: "The Golden Globe–nominated series has received constant critical acclaim since its premiere in 2018 for not only having a stellar cast of almost entirely transgender actors—an unheard of casting decision for Hollywood—but also for the series' storylines about how instrumental the Black and Brown queer communities were in establishing LGBTQ+ culture today."

111 See, for example, Tribe, "Equal Dignity—Heeding Its Call"; Tribe, "Equal Dignity: Speaking Its Name"; Kenji Yoshino, "Comment: A New Birth of Freedom? *Obergefell v. Hodges*," *Harvard Law Review* 129 (2015): 149–79; and Elizabeth B. Cooper, "The Power of Dignity," *Fordham Law Review* 84 (2015): 3–22.

112 The ruling on transgender equality in the workplace is *Bostock v. Clayton County, Georgia*, 590 U.S. _____ (2020) (slip opinion). The particular case, which dealt with transgender equality and was bundled with *Bostock*, was *R.G. & G.R. Harris Funeral Homes Inc. v. Equal Employment Opportunity Commission*.

113 We share Vaid's sentiment: "The neoliberal movement has 'won' mainstreaming for middle class LGBT people, of all colors. And it has not won the same for those queer people whose lives remain constrained by economic inequality, racism, and White supremacy, a colonial US foreign policy, and a brutal economic system that cannot exist without exploitation. Real social justice, real liberation, real freedom requires a structural change, not just integration." Dignity, we add—at least as it has been invoked by normative governing authorities in law, policy, and popular culture—has been deployed as a rhetorical tool of this very kind of integration. Vaid, "LGBTQ Politics," 20.

1. FUCKING WITH DIGNITY

1 In order to break open the "state" to study it, we adopt William Novak's notion of "governance as conduct," which examines the public actions taken by those who hold political power and "highlights the nexus of political and social history, marking the point where state and civil society enter into most deep and prolonged contact." See William J. Novak, *The People's Welfare: Law and Regulation in Nineteenth-Century America* (Chapel Hill: University of North Carolina Press, 1996), 8.

2 In this chapter, we focus on how officials tended to target gay men and transgender people as particular subsets of LGBTQ+ communities. We acknowledge the critical role played by women, particularly lesbians, in confronting the challenges and building the infrastructure for community-based care responses to the HIV/AIDS crises. See Katie Hogan, *Women Take Care: Gender, Race, and the Culture of AIDS* (Ithaca, NY: Cornell University Press, 2001); and Jennifer Brier, *Infectious Ideas: U.S. Political Responses to the AIDS Crisis* (Chapel Hill: University of North Carolina Press, 2009). We also note their role in and their expertise brought to AIDS activism by the mid- to late 1980s (e.g., the 1988 protest "AIDS Activists Say

NO to Cosmo," which was the first ACT UP protest to focus on women and HIV; see the ACT UP/NY Women and AIDS Book Group, *Women, AIDS, and Activism* [Boston: South End Press, 1990]). While a common myth is that the crisis unified a fractured gay male and lesbian community (see Eric Rofes, *Reviving the Tribe: Regenerating Gay Men's Sexuality and Culture in the Ongoing Epidemic* [Binghamton, NY: Harrington Park Press, 1996]), some have pointed to how divisions remained (see Diane M. Harney, "Lesbians on the Frontline: Battling AIDS, Gays, and the Myth of Community," in *Power in the Blood: A Handbook on AIDS, Politics, and Communication*, ed. William N. Elwood [New York: Taylor and Francis, 2009], 167–79). We also acknowledge the various ways that early conceptions of HIV/AIDS were gendered and raced (with critical populations ignored) in the time period we are discussing; see Beth Schneider and Nancy Stoller, *Women Resisting AIDS: Feminist Strategies of Empowerment* (Philadelphia: Temple University Press, 1995); Nancy Goldstein and Jennifer L. Manlowe, eds., *The Gender Politics of HIV/AIDS in Women: Perspectives on the Pandemic in the United States* (New York: New York University Press, 1997); and Diane Richardson, "The Social Construction of Immunity: HIV Risk Perception and Prevention among Lesbians and Bisexual Women," *Culture, Health and Sexuality* 2, no. 1 (2000): 33–49.

3 Dennis Altman, *AIDS in the Mind of America* (New York: Doubleday, 1986); Dangerous Bedfellows, ed., *Policing Public Sex: Queer Politics and the Future of AIDS Activism* (Boston: South End Press, 1996); Martin P. Levine, Peter M. Nardi, and John H. Gagnon, eds., *In Changing Times: Gay Men and Lesbians Encounter HIV/AIDS* (Chicago: University of Chicago Press, 1997); S. Murray and K. Payne, "Medical Policy without Scientific Evidence: The Promiscuity Paradigm and AIDS," *Californian Sociologist* 11 (1988): 13–54; Randy Shilts, *And the Band Played On: Politics, People, and the AIDS Epidemic* (New York: St. Martin's Press, 1987); and William J. Woods and Diane Binson, eds., *Gay Bathhouses and Public Health Policy* (New York: Routledge, 2012).

4 Ronald Bayer, *Private Acts, Social Consequences: AIDS and the Politics of Public Health* (New Brunswick: Rutgers University Press, 1989); Eric Rofes, "Context Is Everything: Thoughts on Effective HIV Prevention and Gay Men in the United States," *Journal of Psychology and Human Sexuality* 10, nos. 3–4 (1998): 133–42; Gabriel Rotello, *Sexual Ecology: AIDS and the Destiny of Gay Men* (New York: Penguin Putnam, 1997); and Shilts, *Band Played On*.

5 See Marc Stein, *Rethinking the Gay and Lesbian Movement* (New York: Routledge, 2012), 148; and Fred Fejes, *Gay Rights and Moral Panic: The Origins of America's Debate on Homosexuality* (New York: Palgrave Macmillan, 2008).

6 See Woods and Binson, *Gay Bathhouses*.

7 See Margot Canaday, *The Straight State: Sexuality and Citizenship in Twentieth-Century America* (Princeton: Princeton University Press, 2009).

8 The word *fuck* in the chapter's title has three meanings. First, *fuck* is a synonym for "play"; we play with dignity as a theoretical concept. Our objective is to

destabilize the concept and to explore how authoritative deployment of dignity is often limited to heteronormative conceptions of safety, intimacy, and responsibility while also privileging conceptions of living that are fundamentally neoliberal, or individualized and privatized. Second, since this chapter examines how municipal authorities in New York City and San Francisco dealt with the HIV crisis in the mid-1980s by infantilizing gay men, ignoring their suffering, ignoring the communal value and queer cultural value of the bathhouse, and ignoring gay men's efforts to self-regulate bathhouses, we employ *fucking* to connote "messing with," as a hostile form of confrontation that refuses to treat others as equal. Third, we are interested in discussing how queer men can have sex with dignity in a world where political, cultural, and legal authorities have degraded the queer logics that challenge heteronormative notions of intimacy, public space, and safety.

9 Tim Dean, *Unlimited Intimacy: Reflections on the Subculture of Barebacking* (Chicago: University of Chicago Press, 2009), 35.
10 Allan Bérubé, "The History of Gay Bathhouses," in Dangerous Bedfellows, *Policing Public Sex*, 191.
11 Ibid., 190.
12 Ibid., 195.
13 George Chauncey, *Gay New York: Gender, Urban Culture, and the Making of a Gay World, 1890–1940* (New York: Basic Books, 1995), 207.
14 Ibid., 133, 224–25.
15 Bérubé, "History of Gay Bathhouses," 198.
16 Ibid., 188.
17 Ibid., 199.
18 Ira Tattelman, "Speaking to the Gay Bathhouse: Communicating in Sexually Charged Spaces," in *Private Sex/Gay Space*, ed. William Leap (New York: Columbia University Press, 1998), 73.
19 Bérubé, "History of Gay Bathhouses," 200–206.
20 Dianne Chisholm, "The Traffic in Free Love and Other Crises: Space, Pace, Sex and Shock in the City of Late Modernity," *Parallax: Journal of Metadiscursive Theory and Cultural Practices* 5, no. 3 (1999): 71.
21 Judith Halberstam, *In a Queer Time and Place: Transgender Bodies, Subcultural Lives* (New York: New York University Press, 2005). The author now identifies as Jack Halberstam.
22 Sara Ahmed, *Queer Phenomenology: Orientations, Objects, Others* (Durham: Duke University Press, 2006).
23 See Michael Warner, *Publics and Counterpublics* (New York: Zone Books, 2005), for further theorizations on performing publicness, especially chapter 5, "Sex in Public," which is cowritten with Lauren Berlant.
24 See Michael Warner's *The Trouble with Normal: Sex, Politics, and the Ethics of Queer Life* (New York: Free Press, 1999) for a more detailed account of queer oppositional logics in everyday life situations.

25 See Joseph Beam's "Brother to Brother: Words from the Heart," in *In the Life: A Black Gay Anthology* (New York: Alyson Books, 1986), 230–42, for notes about constructions of "home" and "safety" for queer men, especially Black queer men.

26 See Samuel R. Delany, *Times Square Red, Times Square Blue* (New York: New York University Press, 1999), for an account and an analysis of interpersonal contact in public sex institutions.

27 Ibid., xx.

28 Ibid., 40.

29 Ibid., 56; emphasis added.

30 Richard Tewksbury, "Bathhouse Intercourse: Structural and Behavioral Aspects of an Erotic Oasis," *Deviant Behavior* 23, no. 1 (2002): 87.

31 Adam Isaiah Green, Mike Follert, Kathy Osterlund, and Jamie Paquin, "Space, Place, and Sexual Sociality: Towards an 'Atmospheric Analysis,'" *Gender, Work and Organization* 18, no. 1 (January 2010): 13.

32 Michael Rumaker, *A Day and a Night at the Baths* (Bolinas, CA: Grey Fox Press, 1979), 13.

33 Delany, *Times Square Red*, 111; emphasis added.

34 See Lee Edelman, *No Future: Queer Theory and the Death Drive* (Durham: Duke University Press, 2004).

35 Delany, *Times Square Red*, 199.

36 Ibid.

37 Given its connection to safety (and often privacy), the state's notion of dignity would seemingly privilege what Delany calls networking as a mode of interaction over what he calls contact. This idea is explored in chapter 2.

38 Delany, *Times Square Red*, 127.

39 Dean, *Unlimited Intimacy*, 202.

40 Delany, *Times Square Red*, 193.

41 Ibid.

42 As historian Jennifer Brier notes, "The earliest gay attacks on AIDS figured the disease as the end to gay liberation." Brier, *Infectious Ideas*, 12, 13.

43 Michael Bronski, "Queers against Hate," *Boston Review*, August 8, 2016, http://bostonreview.net (accessed August 10, 2016). See Jim Down's *Stand by Me: The Forgotten History of Gay Liberation* (New York: Basic Books, 2016), which decouples the conflation of gay liberation with only sexual experimentation.

44 Richard Berkowitz, "A Catalyst for Change," *Gay Community News*, October 29, 1983, 5.

45 Shilts, *Band Played On*, 210. See also Larry Kramer, *Reports from the Holocaust: The Story of an AIDS Activist* rev. ed. (New York: St. Martin's Press, 1989).

46 Michael Callen and Richard Berkowitz, with Richard Dworkin, "We Know Who We Are: Two Gay Men Declare War on Promiscuity," *NY Native*, November 8–21, 1982.

47 Ibid.

48 Larry Kramer to Keith (Lawrence) et al., undated, the LGBT Community Center National History Archive, New York AIDS Network, Keith Lawrence Papers, record 77, box 1, folder 66.

49 Larry Kramer, *Faggots*, 1st ed. (New York: Random House, 1978), 355.

50 Charles Jurrist, "In Defense of Promiscuity: Hard Questions about Real Life," *NY Native*, December 6–19, 1982.

51 Callen and Berkowitz with Dworkin, "We Know Who We Are."

52 Ibid.

53 Ibid.

54 Handwritten notes from meeting of the Bars and Baths Subcommittee, Committee on Safer Sex, December 30, 1983, the LGBT Community Center National History Archive, New York AIDS Network, Keith Lawrence Papers, record 77, box 1, folder 66.

55 Memo from Committee on Safer Sex, January 16, 1984, the LGBT Community Center National History Archive, Joseph Sonnabend Papers, record 120, box 5, folder 55.

56 As quoted in Brier, *Infectious Ideas*, 41.

57 Memo from Committee on Safer Sex, February 27, 1984, the LGBT Community Center National History Archive, Joseph Sonnabend Papers, record 120, box 5, folder 55.

58 "Interim Report: Coalition for Sexual Responsibility," October 1985, the LGBT Community Center National History Archive, NY AIDS Network, Keith Lawrence Papers, record 77, box 1, folder 8.

59 Ibid.

60 Ibid.

61 Ibid.

62 Ibid.

63 Ibid.

64 Ibid.

65 Ibid.

66 Ibid.

67 Peg Byron and Steve C. Arvanette, "New York Shocked by Proposed Bath Ban," *NY Native*, April 9–27, 1984.

68 Steven Epstein, *Impure Science: AIDS, Activism, and the Politics of Knowledge* (Berkeley: University of California Press, 1996), 59.

69 Memo to David Axelrod, MD, Commissioner, from Peter J. Millock, General Counsel, July 25, 1983, Subject: Bathhouses, Joseph Sonnabend Papers, box 4, folder 60 (Committee on Bathhouses), LGBT Community Center National History Archive, New York City.

70 Ron Vachone, "Risks and Responsibilities of Recreational Sex: Healthful Guidelines for Gay Men," *NY Native*, April 26–May 9, 1982, 11, 30. The article invites readers to conduct a "sexual lifestyle audit" by rating their frequency of sexual

contact, the type of sexual encounter, the location of that encounter, their hygiene after the encounter, their drug use, and activities since their most recent STD test.

71 Randy Shilts, "AIDS Researches Try to Stop Bathhouse Sex," *San Francisco Chronicle*, February 4, 1984, Section A.

72 Christopher Disman, "The San Francisco Bathhouse Battles of 1984: Civil Liberties, AIDS Risk, and Shifts in Health Policy," in *Gay Bathhouses and Public Health Policy*, ed. William J. Woods and Diane Binson (New York: Routledge, 2012), 85.

73 Silverman quoted in ibid., 80 (letter to Littlejohn dated May 10, 1983).

74 Disman, "San Francisco Bathhouse Battles," 74.

75 Shilts, *Band Played On*, 448–51.

76 Silverman Press Statement, April 9, 1984, the LGBT Community Center National History Archive, Joseph Sonnabend Papers, box 4, folder 60; Shilts, *Band Played On*, 446.

77 Randy Shilts, "Feinstein Defends Use of Bathhouse 'Spies,'" *San Francisco Chronicle*, March 28, 1984.

78 Disman, "San Francisco Bathhouse Battles," 99.

79 "Human Rights Commission Opposes Bathhouse 'Sex Ban,'" *Bay Area Reporter*, August 30, 1984.

80 Disman, "San Francisco Bathhouse Battles," 106.

81 Bayer, *Private Acts*, 44.

82 Silverman quoted in Shilts, *Band Played On*, 489.

83 Disman, "San Francisco Bathhouse Battles," 112.

84 John Lindell, "Public Space for Public Sex," in *Policing Public Sex: Queer Politics and the Future of AIDS Activism*, ed. Dangerous Bedfellows et al. (Boston: South End Press, 1996), 75.

85 Edward Koch, "The Mayor Responds," *NY Native*, July 15–28, 1985.

86 Joyce Purnick, "AIDS and the State," *New York Times*, October 30, 1985.

87 Enlow, in *GMHC Newsletter*, no. 2 (1982): 12, as quoted in Samantha J. Walker, "The New York City Bathhouse Battles of 1985: Sex and Politics in the AIDS Epidemic," honors thesis, History Department of Rutgers University, April 2010.

88 Lawrence Mass, interview with Dr. Alvin Friedman-Kien, "Cancer in the Gay Community," *NY Native*, July 27–August 9, 1981.

89 Quoted in David France, "Albany Creates Bathhouse Sub-committee," *NY Native*, July 1–14, 1985.

90 Full committee membership is listed in a letter from Paul Moore Jr. to David Leven, February 8, 1985, the LGBT Community Center National History Archive, Joseph Sonnabend Papers, record 120, box 4, folder 60.

91 France, "Albany."

92 Ibid.

93 Memo from David C. Leven to the AIDS Advisory Council, Subcommittee on Bathhouses, Subject: Recommendations: April 5, 1985, the LGBT Community Center National History Archive, Joseph Sonnabend Papers, record 120, box 4, folder 60.

94 Ibid.

95 Ibid.

96 Associated Press, "Cuomo Panel Proposes Rules to Curb AIDS at Bathhouses," *New York Times*, October 10, 1985; Barry Adkins, "AIDS Advisory Council Proposes Gay Bathhouse Regulations," *NY Native*, October 21–27, 1985.

97 Quoted in Maurice Carroll, "State May Shut Bathhouses in a Drive to Combat AIDS," *New York Times*, October 25, 1985.

98 New York State Sanitary Code Section 24-2 is reproduced in Mark E. Elovitz and P. J. Edwards, "The D.O.H. Papers: Regulating Public Sex in New York City," in *Policing Public Sex: Queer Politics and the Future of AIDS Activism*, ed. Dangerous Bedfellows (Boston: South End Press, 1996), 299.

99 Quoted in Joyce Purnick, "Koch Says City Will Now Enforce New State Rules to Combat AIDS," *New York Times*, October 31, 1995.

100 Barry Adkins, "City, State, Clash over Bathhouse Controversy," *NY Native*, November 11–17, 1985.

101 Darrel Yates with Barry Adkins, "State to Regulate Gay Sex," *NY Native*, November 4–10, 1985.

102 Bruce Mailman, "The Battle for Safe Sex in the Baths," *New York Times*, December 5, 1985.

103 Joyce Purnick, "City Seeks to Close AIDS-Risk Place," *New York Times*, November 7, 1985; Barry Adkins, "Judge Orders Mine Shaft Closed," *NY Native*, November 18–24, 1985.

104 Quoted in Joyce Purnick, "City Closes Bar Frequented by Homosexuals Citing Sexual Activity Linked to AIDS," *New York Times*, November 8, 1985.

105 Ibid.

106 As Gary Mucciaroni writes, "The 'ick factor' reflects the taboo of gay sex, much of it fed by centuries of religious injunctions against sexual conduct between same-sex partners." Gary Mucciaroni, *Same Sex, Different Politics: Success and Failure in the Struggles over Gay Rights* (Chicago: University of Chicago Press, 2008), 23–24.

107 John A. Fall, "Council Passes Bathhouse Resolution," *NY Native*, December 2–8, 1985; Sarah Schulman, "Committee Resolve Close Baths," *NY Native*, December 2–8, 1985.

108 Barry Adkins, "Sencer Resigns," *NY Native*, December 16–22, 1985.

109 John A. Fall, "City Moves to Close St. Marks Baths," *NY Native*, December 16–22, 1985; John A. Fall, "St. Marks Baths Closed," *NY Native*, December 23–29, 1985; Joyce Purnick, "City Shuts Down a Bathhouse as Site of 'Unsafe Sex,'" *New York Times*, December 7, 1985.

110 Fall, "St. Marks Baths."

111 Sarah Schulman, "Koch Requests Action on Health Services and Insurance," *NY Native*, January 27–February 2, 1986.

112 Barry Adkins, "Bad News for St. Marks," *NY Native*, January 20–30, 1986; *City of New York v. New St. Mark's Baths*, 160 A.D.2d 311, 562 N.Y.S.2d 642 (New York, 1986).

113 *The City of New York et al., Plaintiffs v. The New St. Mark's Baths, etc., et al., Defendants,* 130 Misc.2d 911, 497 N.Y.S.2d 979 (New York, 1986); *The City of New York et al., Plaintiffs—respondents and David Axelrod v. The New St. Mark's Baths, et al., Defendants—Appellants, and Paul Corrigan,* 168 A.D.2d 311, 562 N.Y.S.2d 642 (New York, 1990); *City of New York, Axelrod (David, M.D.) v. New St. Mark's Baths, Corrigan (Paul),* 77 N.Y, 2d 939, 572 N.E. 2d 53, 569 N.Y.S.2d 612 (New York, 1991).

114 *City of New York v. New St. Mark's Baths,* 160 A.D.2d 311, 562 N.Y.S.2d 642 (New York, 1986).

115 Scott Bronstein, "4 New York Bathhouses Still Operate under City's Program of Inspections," *New York Times,* May 3, 1987.

2. DO YOU SWALLOW?

1 "Do You Swallow?," National Black Gay Men's Advocacy Coalition and the National Minority AIDS Council, YouTube, 2014, www.youtube.com/watch?v=Jud4mpCnqXE (accessed June 25, 2019).

2 See Samuel R. Delany, *Times Square Red, Times Square Blue* (New York: New York University Press, 1999); and Tim Dean, *Unlimited Intimacy: Reflections on the Subculture of Barebacking* (Chicago: University of Chicago Press, 2009).

3 See Julia Kristeva, *Powers of Horror: An Essay on Abjection* (New York: Columbia University Press, 1982).

4 HIV-positive individuals who have access to treatment and adhere to anti-retroviral therapy have substantially lowered their probability of developing AIDS. Nevertheless, complications from the treatment, such as organ damage related to the toxicity of medication, have emerged. See Steve G. Deeks, Sharon R. Lewin, and Diane Havlir, "The End of AIDS: HIV Infection as a Chronic Disease," *Lancet* 382, no. 9903 (November 2013): 1525–33.

5 Tim Murphy, "Sex without Fear: The New Pill That Could Revolutionize Gay Life Is Reawakening Old Arguments," *New York,* July 13, 2014, http://nymag.com (accessed October 27, 2020).

6 See Delany, *Times Square Red*; and Dean, *Unlimited Intimacy.*

7 See Matt Hennie, "AIDS Agency Calls Grindr a Diseased 'Digital Bathhouse,'" *Project Q Atlanta/Q Magazine,* October 1, 2015, www.projectq.us (accessed June 11, 2019).

8 Michael Warner, *Publics and Counterpublics* (Boston: MIT Press, 2005).

9 Eugene McCray and Jonathan H. Mermin, National Center for HIV/AIDS, Viral Hepatitis, STD, and TB Prevention, Centers for Disease Control and Prevention, *HIV and AIDS in the United States: Information from the CDC's Division of HIV/AIDS Prevention,* September 27, 2017, https://docs.wixstatic.com (accessed June 21, 2019).

10 On the "good gay" versus the "bad queer," see Chris Ashford, "Bareback Sex, Queer Legal Theory, and Evolving Socio-Legal Contexts," *Sexualities* 18, nos. 1/2 (2015): 195–209. See also Andrew Spieldenner, "PrEP Whores and HIV Prevention: The Queer Communication of HIV Pre-exposure Prophylaxis," *Journal of*

Homosexuality 63, no. 12 (2016); and Tim Dean, "Mediated Intimacies: Raw Sex, Truvada, and the Biopolitics of Chemoprophylaxis," *Sexualities* 18, nos. 1/2 (2015): 224–46.

11 Gabriela H. Breitfeller and Amar Kanekar, "Intentional HIV Transmission among Men Who Have Sex with Men: A Scoping Review," *Gay and Lesbian Issues and Psychology Review* 8, no. 2 (2012): 112–21.

12 Louise Hogarth, director, *The Gift* (Dream Out Loud Productions, 2003); Dennis Cooper, *The Sluts* (New York: Carroll and Graf, 2004; reprint 2005).

13 Leora Lev, introduction to *Enter at Your Own Risk: The Dangerous Art of Dennis Cooper*, ed. Leora Lev (Madison: Fairleigh Dickinson University Press, 2006), 21 (emphasis added).

14 Delany, *Times Square Red*, 123.

15 Ibid., 111 (emphasis added).

16 Ibid., 199.

17 Ibid., 164.

18 Ibid., xiii.

19 Ibid., 129.

20 Ibid.

21 Ibid., 139.

22 Ibid., 136.

23 Ibid., 175, 173.

24 Ibid., 193.

25 Dean, *Unlimited Intimacy*, 176.

26 Ibid., 180.

27 Ibid., 191.

28 The Clubs maintains eight locations (Club Columbus, Club Dallas, Club Fort Lauderdale, Club Houston, Club Indianapolis, Club Orlando, Club Saint Louis, and Club Aqua Miami). See The Clubs, www.theclubs.com (accessed June 13, 2019).

29 Flex Spas maintains four locations (Flex Spas Atlanta, Flex Spas Los Angeles, Flex Spas Phoenix, and Flex Hotel and Spa Cleveland). See www.flexspas.com (accessed June 13, 2019).

30 Midtowne Spa maintains three locations (Denver, Los Angeles, and Wilmington, CA). See Midtowne Spa, www.midtowne.com (accessed June 13, 2019).

31 Steamworks Baths maintains five locations (Berkeley, Chicago, Toronto, Vancouver, and Seattle). Given our focus on the United States, we only examine the main website and the websites for Berkeley, Chicago, and Seattle. See Steamworks Baths, www.steamworksbaths.com (accessed June 13, 2019).

32 Roman Holiday Health Clubs maintains two sites (Los Angeles and Van Nuys). See Roman Holiday Health Clubs, www.romanholidayhealthclubs.com (accessed June 13, 2019).

33 The Westside Club and the Eastside Club are in New York City. See The Westside Club, www.westsideclubnyc.com; and The Eastside Club, www.eastsideclubnyc.com (accessed June 13, 2019).

34 These bathhouse companies may not be corporations in the legal sense, but they do employ aesthetics and values that we might ascribe to the corporation involved in tourism: cleanliness of facilities and emphasis on consistent customer experience, as well as sleek, bright, and inviting imagery.

35 Ben Light, Jean Burgess, and Stefanie Duguay propose the "walkthrough method" as a way to study apps; see "The Walkthrough Method: An Approach to the Study of Apps," *New Media and Society* 20, no. 3 (2018): 882. We adapt this approach to study contemporary bathhouse websites and to explore geolocative apps. This method is not a full digital ethnography, as it does not involve semistructured interviews with users. Since our objective is to assess how the bathhouses and apps present themselves visually and textually to users, an ethnographic approach was not undertaken. For that kind of approach, see Jody Ahlm, "Respectable Promiscuity: Digital Cruising in an Era of Queer Liberalism," *Sexualities* 20, no. 3 (2017): 364–79; and Yoel Roth, "Locating the 'Scruff Guy': Theorizing Body and Space in Gay Geosocial Media," *International Journal of Communication* 8 (2014): 2113–33.

36 Our exploration is an "atmospheric analysis," which considers how "the physical features of the bathhouse, including its structural design, its lighting and acoustics," not only create a "passive repository or erotic oasis for sexual exploration," but also how they foster a "socializing environment that generates, builds upon and intensifies the erotic experience of the subjects." Adam Isaiah Green, Mike Follert, Kathy Osterlund, and Jamie Paquin, "Space, Place, and Sexual Sociality: Towards an 'Atmospheric Analysis,'" *Gender, Work and Organization* 17, no. 1 (January 2010): 14.

37 Delany, *Times Square Red*, 179.

38 CumUnion is a sex party hosted at bathhouses, sex clubs, and some private spaces; participants "can decide for themselves what sexual behaviors and activities are appropriate for them." See "About," CumUnion: An International Sex Party, www.cumunion.com (accessed June 1, 2020).

39 See "Club Saint Louis," The Clubs, www.theclubs.com; "Club Dallas," The Clubs, www.theclubs.com; "Club Aqua Miami," The Clubs, www.clubaquamiami.com; and "Midtowne Spa Denver," Midtowne Spa, www.midtowne.com (accessed June 14, 2019).

40 Delany, *Times Square Red*, 160.

41 Ibid., 164.

42 Steamworks Baths, www.steamworksbaths.com/chicago/ (accessed June 14, 2019).

43 Midtowne Spa, www.midtowne.com (accessed June 14, 2019).

44 The Clubs, www.theclubs.com (accessed June 14, 2019).

45 Ibid.

46 "Midtowne Spa Los Angeles," Midtowne Spa, www.midtowne.com (accessed June 14, 2019).

47 Ibid.

48 Ibid.

49 Ibid.

50 The Club Houston, www.club-houston.com (accessed June 14, 2019). On erotica linking militarism and masculinity, see John Mercer, "Homosexual Prototypes: Repetition and the Construction of the Generic in the Iconography of Gay Pornography," *Paragraph: A Journal of Modern Critical Theory* 26, nos. 1–2 (2008): 80–90.

51 See "Careers," Steamworks Baths, www.steamworksbaths.com (accessed June 14, 2019). Indeed, privileging militaristic masculinity is embedded in Steamworks's pricing structure. See additional discussion later in this chapter.

52 See "DJs," Steamworks Baths, www.steamworksbaths.com (accessed June 14, 2019). (Identical text appears on the Berkeley and Seattle sites.)

53 Ibid.

54 "Steamworks Chicago," Steamworks Baths, www.steamworksbaths.com; "Steamworks Berkeley," Steamworks Baths, www.steamworksbaths.com; and "Steamworks Seattle," Steamworks Baths, www.steamworksbaths.com (accessed June 14, 2019).

55 See "Rates," Steamworks Baths, www.steamworksbaths.com (accessed June 14, 2019).

56 Ibid.

57 Ibid.

58 "Club Tour," Steamworks Baths, www.steamworksbaths.com (accessed June 14, 2019).

59 On legal compliance and absorption of rather than transformation through interacting with difference, see Sara Ahmed, *On Being Included: Racism and Diversity in Institutional Life* (Durham: Duke University Press, 2012).

60 "Lights Out Thursday," Steamworks Baths, www.steamworksbaths.com; and "Anonymous Mondays," Steamworks Baths, www.steamworksbaths.com (accessed June 14, 2019).

61 Ibid.

62 "Frequently Asked Questions," Midtowne Spa, www.midtowne.com (accessed June 14, 2019).

63 This FAQ appears identically on all The Clubs' locations' websites, www.theclubs .com (accessed June 14, 2019).

64 "Rates," Steamworks Baths, www.steamworksbaths.com; and "Rates," Steamworks Baths, www.steamworksbaths.com (accessed June 14, 2019).

65 To be clear, five dollars of that thirteen dollars is refundable, but the option requires that folks have the available payment up front.

66 J. L. King with Karen Harris, *On the Down Low: A Journey into the Lives of "Straight" Black Men Who Sleep with Men* (New York: Penguin Random House, 2005); and J. L. King with Courtney Carreras, *Coming Up from the Down Low: The Journey to Acceptance, Healing, and Honest Love* (New York: Penguin Random House, 2007).

67 "CDC Studies Debunk Black Down Low Myths," Poz.com, October 29, 2009, www.poz.com (accessed June 19, 2019); and "Myth: HIV/AIDS Rate among Black Women Traced to 'Down Low' Black Men," NPR.org, October 28, 2009, www.npr .org (accessed June 19, 2019). The DL narrative overestimates a very small factor in HIV-infection data and distracts from the primary and secondary causes, like poverty and its relationship to healthcare, poor sexual health education, the war on drugs, under-resourced mental health programs specific to Black communi- ties, and the byproducts of mass incarceration of Black and Brown bodies. See also Ta-Nehisi Coates, "A Low-Down Crying Shame: Why the Myth of the 'On the Down Low' Brother Refuses to Die," *Slate*, March 9, 2007, https://slate.com (accessed June 24, 2019); and Jon Cohen, "A Silent Epidemic: Why Is There Such a High Percentage of HIV and AIDS among Black Women?," *Slate*, October 27, 2004, https://slate.com (accessed June 24, 2019).

68 Ibid.

69 Steamworks hosts monthly CumUnion parties. See Steamworks Baths, www .steamworksbaths.com (accessed June 14, 2019).

    The Clubs do as well. See "Club Aqua Miami," CumUnion, www.cumunion .com; and "The Club Houston," CumUnion, www.cumunion.com (accessed June 14, 2019). Midtowne Spa does not. Indeed, Midtowne maintains an explicit ban on barebacking on its premises: "Barebacking is NOT allowed in our clubs. If you are caught barebacking you will be asked to leave. Repeat offenders will be banned from all of our clubs for life." See Midtowne Spa, www.midtowne .com (accessed June 14, 2019). This policy may reflect alignment with current HIV criminalization laws in certain states. See Trevor Hoppe, *Punishing Dis- ease: HIV and the Criminalization of Sickness* (Chicago: University of Chicago Press, 2017).

70 See "New York City," CumUnion, www.cumunion.com (accessed June 14, 2019).

71 See Eros, www.erossf.com; The Zone, LA, thezone-la.net; Slammer Club, www .slammerclub.com; and 321, http://321slammer.com (accessed June 16, 2019).

72 See "About," Steamworks Baths, www.steamworksbaths.com (accessed June 16, 2019).

73 See Denver Swim Club, www.denverswimclub.com; or "Photos," Slammer Club, www.slammerclub.com (accessed June 16, 2019).

74 See "About," 321, http://321slammer.com (accessed June 16, 2019).

75 See "Slammer Admissions," Slammer Club, www.slammerclub.com; "Events," Eros, www.erossf.com; and "Membership," 321, http://321slammer.com (accessed June 16, 2019).

76 Ibid. Notably, 321 Slammer offers an incentive program like Steamworks's Fre- quent Fucker rewards.

77 See "About," Steamworks Baths, www.steamworksbaths.com; and "Events," Eros, www.erossf.com (accessed June 16, 2019).

78 See "Events," Eros, www.erossf.com; and "News," Steamworks Baths, www .steamworksbaths.com (accessed June 16, 2019). Steamworks has reached beyond the boundaries of the cities in which the baths are located; see its sponsorship of a theme night where proceeds have gone to hurricane relief in Puerto Rico.

79 Delany, *Times Square Red*, 175.

80 Ibid., 169–70.

81 Ira Tattelman, "The Meaning at the Wall: Tracing the Gay Bathhouse," in *Queers in Space: Communities, Public Spaces, Sites of Resistance*, ed. G. Ingram, A. Bouthillette, and Y. Retter (Seattle: Bay Press, 1997), 394.

82 For an examination of the idea that apps have diminished the perceived value and salience of gay bars, see Bryce J. Renniger, "Grindr Killed the Gay Bar, and Other Attempts to Blame Social Technologies for Urban Development: A Democratic Approach to Popular Technologies and Queer Sociality," *Journal of Homosexuality* 65 (2018): 1–20. For a review of scholarly literature on apps marketed to LGBTQ+ individuals, see Shangwei Wu and Janelle Ward, "The Mediation of Gay Men's Lives: A Review on Gay Dating Apps," *Sociology Compass* 12, no. 2 (February 2018): 1–11.

83 Dean, *Unlimited Intimacy*, 192.

84 C. Licoppe, C. A. Riviere, and J. Morel, "Grindr Casual Hook-Ups as Interactional Achievements," *New Media and Society*, published online before print, September 10, 2015, doi:10.1177/1461444815589702; see also C. Licoppe, C. A. Riviere, and J. Morel, "Proximity Awareness and the Privatization of Sexual Encounters with Strangers: The Case of Grindr," in *Place, Space, and Mediated Communication: Exploring Context Collapse*, ed. Carolyn Marvin and Hong Sun Ha (London: Routledge, 2017).

85 Ahlm, "Respectable Promiscuity," 365.

86 Ibid.

87 Our app database included Adam4Adam, Chappy, Daddyhunt, FAWN, GHunt, Grindr, Grizzly, Grommr, GROWLr, GRRR, GuySpy, HER, Hinge, Hole, Hornet, Jack'd, Pure, Recon, Romeo, Scissr, Scruff, Squirt, Surge, Taimi, Thurst, Tinder, Touche, Transdr, VGL, W Bear, Wapo, and Whiplr.

88 For examinations of the "public health risk" associated with hooking up utilizing apps, see C. H. Bien, J. M. Best, K. E. Muessig, C. Wei, L. Han, and J. D. Tucker, "Gay Apps for Seeking Sex Partners in China: Implications for MSM Sexual Health," *AIDS and Behavior* 19 (2015): 941–46; and M. R. Beymer, R. E. Weiss, R. K. Bolan, E. T. Rudy, L. B. Bourque, J. P. Rodriguez, and D. E. Morisky, "Sex on Demand: Geosocial Networking Phone Apps and Risk of Sexually Transmitted Infections among a Cross-Sectional Sample of Men Who Have Sex with Men in Los Angeles County," *Sexually Transmitted Infections* 90 (2014): 567–72. For analysis of how apps influence understandings of intimacy and safety, see Kathy Albury and Paul Byron, "Safe on My Phone? Same-Sex Attracted Young People's Negotiations of Intimacy, Visibility, and Risk on Digital Hook-Up Apps," *Social*

Media + Society, October–December 2016, 1–10. For an assessment of how gay men describe their use of apps, see David Gudelunas, "There's an App for That: The Uses and Gratifications of Online Social Networks for Gay Men," *Sexuality and Culture* 16 (2012): 347–65; and Brandon Miller, "'They're the Modern-Day Gay Bar': Exploring the Uses and Gratifications of Social Networks for Men Who Have Sex with Men," *Computers in Human Behavior* 51 (2015): 476–82.

89 *Pink News* notes that Grindr and Hornet are for "everyone," while Jack'd is for "POC [people of color], mainly"; Scruff is for "older, hairier, masc"; and Chappy is for "who knows." Alexis Mastoryiannis, "Gay Dating Apps: A Comprehensive Guide to Jack'd, Grindr, Hornet, Scruff, and the Rest," *Pink News*, March 5, 2018, www.pinknews.co.uk (accessed June 19, 2019). Other outlets note that Scruff is a pioneer in inclusivity. See Coffee Junkie, "Five Alternative Gay Apps to Use When Grindr Stops a Grinding :)," Chicagonow.com, January 31, 2016, www.chicagonow.com (accessed June 19, 2019).

90 Hinge, https://hinge.co (accessed August 19, 2019).

91 Ahlm, "Respectable Promiscuity," 370.

92 Grindr, www.grindr.com (accessed June 19, 2019).

93 Ibid.

94 See "Community Guidelines," Grindr, www.grindr.com (accessed June 19, 2019).

95 "Unlimited," Grindr, www.grindr.com (accessed August 19, 2019).

96 Rob Salerno, "Twenty Questions for Grindr Creator Joel Simkhai," dailyextra.com, July 27, 2011, www.dailyxtra.com (accessed June 19, 2019).

97 Other apps cater to a narrower set of communities. GROWLr: Gay Bear Social Media advertises as "More Bears in More Places . . . With over 10,000,000 members worldwide, GROWLr allows you to meet other bears from around the world" (GROWLr, www.growlrapp.com [accessed June 19, 2019]). Grommr caters to the subculture of gaining, or intentionally packing on weight (Grommr, www.grommr.com/en-US/ [accessed June 19, 2019]). Bears can also turn to W Bear, which simply calls itself the "best gay bear app," but it offers no metric or justification to support that claim (W Bear, https://wbear.lgbt [accessed June 19, 2019]).

98 Roth, "Locating the 'Scruff Guy,'" 2121.

99 On the heels of national protests demanding justice for the murder of George Floyd and critiquing state-sanctioned violence toward Black, Indigenous, and People of Color (BIPOC), corporations reacted by taking seemingly relevant actions. For example, Grindr eliminated its ethnicity filter in solidarity.

100 Hornet, https://hornet.com (accessed June, 2019).

101 "Stories," Hornet, https://hornet.com (accessed June 19, 2019). The authors published four posts on Hornet between fall 2018 and spring 2019.

102 Andre Wheeler, "Can Grindr Make Itself Less Racist?," GQ.com, September 11, 2018, www.gq.com (accessed October 27, 2020); Jon Shadel, "Grindr was the First Big Dating App for Gay Men. Now It's Falling Out of Favor," *Washington Post*, December 6, 2018, www.washingtonpost.com (accessed October 27, 2020).

103 Thurst, https://thurst.co (accessed June 19, 2019).

104 Squirt, www.squirt.org (accessed June 19, 2019).

105 Delany, *Times Square Red*, 141.

106 See Deborah Gould, *Moving Politics: Emotion and ACT UP's Fight against AIDS* (Chicago: University of Chicago Press, 2009); see also *United in Anger: A History of ACT UP*, directed by Jim Hubbard (New York: New York State Council on the Arts and the Ford Foundation, 2012).

107 Naina Khanna, "Undetectable = Untransmittable. So Why the Hell Isn't That Catching On?," HuffPost, December 1, 2017, www.huffpost.com (accessed June 21, 2019).

108 "PrEP," CDC, www.cdc.gov (accessed June 21, 2019).

109 "FDA Approves First Drug for Reducing the Risk of Sexually Acquired HIV Infection," FDA News Release, July 16, 2012, www.fda.gov (accessed August 29, 2016).

110 See Julie E. Myers, Zoe R. Edelstein, Demetre C. Daskalakis, Anisha D. Gandhi, Kavita Misra, Alexis V. Rivera, Paul M. Salcuni, Kathleen Scanlin, Chi-Chi Udeagu, and Sarah L. Braunstein, "Preexposure Prophylaxis Monitoring in New York City: A Public Health Approach," *American Journal of Public Health* 107, no. S4 (November 2018): S251–57.

111 Savas Abadsidis, "CDC Officially Admits People with HIV Who Are Undetectable Can't Transmit HIV," Plus, October 22, 2017, www.hivplusmag.com (accessed June 21, 2019).

112 See "News and Press," Gilead, www.gilead.com (accessed June 21, 2019).

113 "Payment Options for Pre-exposure Prophylaxis (PrEP)," New York State Department of Health, www.health.ny.gov (accessed June 20, 2019).

114 "How Can You Get Help Paying for TRUVADA for PrEP®?," Truvada, www.truvada.com (accessed June 20, 2019).

115 George Citroner, "Cost of HIV Prevention Drug Discouraging People from Doing PrEP Therapy," Healthline, April 4, 2020, www.healthline.com (accessed June 20, 2019).

116 Selena Simmons-Duffin, "AIDS Activists Take Aim at Gilead to Lower Price of HIV Drug PrEP," NPR.org, May 30, 2019, www.npr.org (accessed June 21, 2019).

117 Ibid.

118 Shahul H. Ebrahim, John E. Anderson, Paul Weidle, and David W. Purcell, "Race/Ethnic Disparities in HIV Testing and Knowledge about Treatment for HIV/AIDS: United States, 2001," *AIDS Patient Care and STDs* 18, no. 1 (July 2004): 27–33. On racism and the US healthcare system, see Dorothy Roberts, *Killing the Black Body: Race, Reproduction, and the Meaning of Liberty* (New York: Vintage, 1988); Deirdre Cooper Owens, *Medical Bondage: Race, Gender, and the Origins of American Gynecology* (Athens: University of Georgia Press, 2018); and, more generally, Donald A. Barr, *Health Disparities in the United States: Social Class,*

Race, Ethnicity, and Health, 2nd ed. (Baltimore: Johns Hopkins University Press, 2014). On gender and US healthcare, see Kristina Gupta, *Medical Entanglements: Rethinking Feminist Debates about Healthcare* (New Brunswick: Rutgers University Press, 2019).

119 See Thomas Lemke, *Biopolitics: An Advanced Introduction* (New York: New York University Press, 2011).

120 Dean, "Mediated Intimacies."

121 Associated Press, "Divide over HIV Prevention Drug Truvada Persists," *USA Today*, April 6, 2014, www.usatoday.com (accessed September 2, 2016).

122 See "The Questions about PrEP," PrEP Facts, http://men.prepfacts.org, where readers with the question "I don't have private health insurance and PrEP is too expensive. Can I get Truvada for PrEP at low cost or for free?" are told "Yes" and directed to various clinical trials (accessed September 3, 2016).

123 On biopower, see Michel Foucault, *Society Must Be Defended* (New York: Picador, 2003); and Nikolas Rose, *The Politics of Life Itself: Biomedicine, Power, and Subjectivity in the Twenty-First Century* (Princeton: Princeton University Press, 2006).

124 Edwin J. Bernard, "Swiss Experts Say Individuals with Undetectable Viral Load and No STI Cannot Transmit HIV During Sex," aidsmap.com, January 30, 2008, www.aidsmap.com (accessed June 21, 2019).

125 Myron S. Cohen et al., for the HPTN 052 Study Team, "Prevention of HIV-1 Infection with Early Antiretroviral Therapy," *New England Journal of Medicine* 365 (2011): 493–505.

126 Khanna, "Undetectable = Untransmittable."

127 Ibid.

128 Dean, "Mediated Intimacies," 231.

129 "Let's Stop HIV Together," Centers for Disease Control and Prevention, www.cdc.gov (accessed June 21, 2019).

130 Ibid.

131 See, generally, Hoppe, *Punishing Disease*.

132 On the criminalization of Blackness, see Michelle Alexander, *The New Jim Crow: Mass Incarceration in the Age of Colorblindness* (New York: New Press, 2012).

133 Sony Salzman, "Updated HIV Laws May Only Protect the Privileged," *Vice*, March 18, 2018, www.vice.com (accessed June 21, 2019).

134 Ibid.

135 Eli S. Rosenberg, Gregorio A. Millett, Patrick S. Sullivan, Carlos del Rio, James W. Curran, "Understanding the HIV Disparities between Black and White Men Who Have Sex with Men in the USA using the HIV Care Continuum: A Modeling Study," *Lancet* 1, no. 3 (December 2014): e112–e118.

136 In this context, hundreds of organizations have released a "Consensus Statement" contending that "reliance on viral load or compliance with medical treatment as a basis to reform HIV criminal laws poses dangerous consequences for those who lack access to care." "The Consensus Statement on HIV 'Treatment as Prevention' in Criminal Law Reform," www.hivtaspcrimlaw.org (accessed January 4, 2020).

137 George M. Johnson, "We Need to Talk about the Downside of U=U," The Body, January 27, 2020, www.thebody.com (accessed July 9, 2020).

138 David Duran, "Truvada Whores?," HuffPost, November 12, 2012 (updated February 2, 2016), www.huffpost.com (accessed June 22, 2019); Larry Kramer, "We Don't Know the Full Effects of Truvada Yet," *New York Times*, June 18, 2014, www.nytimes.com (accessed June 22, 2019); Benji Douglas, "AHF's Michael Weinstein Doubles Down on PrEP as a 'Party Drug,'" Queerty, November 3, 2016, www.queerty.com (accessed June 22, 2019).

139 For example, a 2012 CDC *Morbidity and Mortality Weekly Report* recommended, "PrEP is delivered as part of a comprehensive set of prevention services, including risk-reduction, PrEP medication adherence counseling, and ready access to condoms." "Interim Guidance for Clinicians Considering the Use of Preexposure Prophylaxis for the Prevention of HIV Infection in Heterosexually Active Adults," *MMWR* 61, no. 31 (August 10, 2012): 588.

140 Murphy, "Sex without Fear"; Donald G. McNeil Jr., "Advocating Pill, U.S. Signals Shift to Prevent AIDS," *New York Times*, May 14, 2014, www.nytimes.com (accessed June 22, 2019); on Jake Sobo's blog for the San Francisco AIDS Foundation, see https://prepfacts.org (accessed June 22, 2019).

141 See "Teenage Truvada Whore," scene 1 in *London Uncut* (2014), directed by Liam Cole of Treasure Island Media, https://timfuck.treasureislandmedia.com (accessed October 27, 2020). Note that the production date precedes the discursive shift in public health that began to link PrEP with responsible sexuality.

142 David Duran, "An Evolved Opinion on Truvada," HuffPost, March 27, 2014 (updated December 6, 2017), www.huffpost.com (accessed June 22, 2019); "Larry Kramer Has Changed His Mind about PrEP," LGBTQ Nation, December 10, 2015, www.lgbtqnation.com (accessed June 22, 2019).

143 See the 2019 CDC "Start Talking/Stop HIV" campaign, www.cdc.gov (accessed June 22, 2019).

144 See www.frontiersmedia.com for a blog series titled "My Life on PrEP" by Jake Sobo in which he discusses the dynamics of PrEP usage in a heteronormative, privatized healthcare system (accessed August 15, 2016).

145 Gregory A. Freeman, "Bug Chasers: The Men Who Long to Be HIV+," *Rolling Stone*, January 23, 2003; and Gregory A. Freeman, "In Search of Death," *Rolling Stone*, February 6, 2003. For an astute reading of Freeman and Hogarth—and the rhetorical function of the "chaser" and "giver" in contemporary culture—see Octavio Gonzalez, "Tracking the Bug-Chaser: Giving the Gift of HIV/AIDS," *Cultural Critique* 75 (Spring 2010): 82–113. Gonzalez's arguments are vital to understanding how this figure functions, and his work joins Dean's to ground our work on intentional transmission and dignity.

146 A conversation about how to do things with a virus—something Dean addresses explicitly in his text published six years after Hogarth's film—never enjoys any airtime in the documentary.

147 Cooper extends the discussion beyond intentional transmission. "Snuff scenes," for example, are not HIV specific.

148 This is one of many qualified notes of praise that decorates the book jacket of *The Sluts*.

149 Gayle Rubin, "Thinking Sex: Notes for a Radical Theory of the Politics of Sexuality," in *Pleasure and Danger: Exploring Female Sexuality*, ed. Carole S, Vance (London: Routledge, 1984): 267–319.

150 Dean, *Unlimited Intimacy*, x.

151 Ibid., 49.

152 Ibid., 88.

153 Ibid., 88–89.

154 Ibid., xii.

155 As Gonzalez argues, "The figure of the bug-chaser in contemporary American culture [is] a *rhetorical* figure above all," and "it is important to track this extremely marginal yet culturally resonant figure of the bug-chaser . . . [T]he bug-chaser is projected by a state-sponsored discursive regime and reflected in media representations." This tracking can expose representations that reinforce or contest the work of the state. Gonzalez, "Tracking the Bug-Chaser," 84–86.

156 See Max Navarre, "Fighting the Victim Label," *AIDS: Cultural Analysis/Cultural Activism*, ed. Douglas Crimp (Cambridge, MA: MIT Press, 1988): 143–46.

157 Hogarth, *The Gift*.

158 The use of the masculine pronoun is intentional; Hogarth's film focuses almost entirely on the sexual lives and practices of gay men (or presumably those who identify as cisgender). Nothing in the film suggests alternative pronoun usage, gender ambiguity, or non-normative gender expression that would merit more elastic pronoun usage.

159 Hogarth, *The Gift*.

160 Gregorio A. Millett, John L. Peterson, Richard J. Wolitski, and Ron Stall, "Greater Risk for HIV Infection of Black Men Who Have Sex with Men: A Critical Literature Review," *American Journal of Public Health* 96, no. 9 (June 2006): 1007–19.

161 Hogarth, *The Gift*.

162 Indeed, Odets's ideas completely ignore the community's efforts to regulate the bathhouses prior to the impositions of the state as discussed in chapter 1. See also Gould, *Moving Politics*.

163 Hogarth, *The Gift*.

164 Leora Lev, "Sacred Disorder of the Mind: Sublimity, Desire, Police, and Dennis Cooper's Hallucination of Words," *Enter at Your Own Risk: The Dangerous Art of Dennis Cooper*, ed. Leora Lev (Madison: Fairleigh Dickinson University Press, 2006), 203.

165 See Earl Jackson Jr., "Death Drives across Pornutopia: Dennis Cooper on the Extremities of Being," in *Enter at Your Own Risk: The Dangerous Art of Dennis Cooper*, ed. Leora Lev (Madison: Fairleigh Dickinson University Press, 2006): 151–74.

166 Robert Gluck, "Dennis Cooper (Interview)," *Enter at Your Own Risk: The Danger-ous Art of Dennis Cooper*, ed. Leora Lev (Madison: Fairleigh Dickinson University Press, 2006), 247.

167 Ibid., 245.

168 Ibid., 246.

169 For a fuller discussion of this market-ready representation, see chapter 3's discussion of *Love, Simon*.

170 Michael Worton, "(Re) Writing Gay Identity: Fiction as Theory," *Canadian Review of Comparative Literature* 21, no. 1 (March–June 1994), 19.

171 Cooper, *Sluts*, 159.

172 Ibid., 242–43.

173 Lev, "Sacred Disorder," 102.

174 Breitfeller and Kanekar, "Intentional HIV Transmission," 119.

175 Lev, "Sacred Disorder," 99.

176 Robert F. Reid-Pharr, foreword to Samuel R. Delany, *Times Square Red, Times Square Blue*, 20th anniversary edition (New York: New York University Press, 2019), xviii.

3. ISN'T STRAIGHT STILL THE DEFAULT?

1 *Love, Simon*, directed by Greg Berlanti (Los Angeles: Fox 2000 Pictures, 2018).

2 For discussion of media visibility, respectability politics, the construction of homonormativity, and the dangers of a tolerance-only approach, see Guillermo Avila-Saavedra, "Nothing Queer about Queer Television: Televised Construc-tion of Gay Masculinities," *Media Culture Society* 31, no. 1 (2009): 5–21; Steven Cohan, *Masked Men: Masculinity and the Movies in the Fifties* (Bloomington: Indiana University Press, 1997); Alexander Doty, *Making Things Perfectly Queer: Interpreting Mass Culture* (Minneapolis: University of Minnesota Press, 1993); Richard Dyer, *The Culture of Queers* (New York: Routledge, 2002); Ellis Hanson, ed., *Out Takes: Essays on Queer Theory and Film* (Durham: Duke University Press, 1999); F. Hollis Griffin, *Feeling Normal: Sexuality and Media Criticism in the Digital Age* (Bloomington: Indiana University Press, 2016); Larry Gross, *Up from Invisibility: Lesbians, Gay Men, and the Media in America* (New York: Columbia University Press, 2001); Lisa Henderson, *Love and Money: Queers, Class, and Cultural Production* (New York: New York University Press, 2013); Eve Ng, "A 'Post-gay' Era? Media Gaystreaming, Homonormativity, and the Politics of LGBT Integration," *Communication, Culture, and Critique* 6, no. 2 (June 2013): 258–83; Suzanna D. Walters, *All the Rage: The Story of Gay Visibility in America* (Chicago: University of Chicago Press, 2003); B. Ruby Rich, *New Queer Cinema: The Director's Cut* (Durham: Duke University Press, 2013); Suzanna D. Walters, *The Tolerance Trap: How God, Genes, and Good Inten-tions Are Sabotaging Gay Equality* (New York: New York University Press, 2014); Patricia White, *Uninvited: Classical Hollywood Cinema and Lesbian*

Respectability (Bloomington: Indiana University Press, 1999); and Matthew Tinkcom, *Queer Theory and Brokeback Mountain* (New York: Bloomsbury, 2017) and his *Working like a Homosexual: Camp, Capital, and Cinema* (Durham: Duke University Press, 2002). On how queerness is implicit in cinema but kept hidden from direct view, see Vito Russo, *The Celluloid Closet: Homosexuality in the Movies* (New York: Harper and Row, 1981).

3 Mainstream critical reception of *Love, Simon* considered the film to be progressive. See, for example, Michael Waters, "'Love, Simon': What Critics Are Saying," *Hollywood Reporter*, March 13, 2018. www.hollywoodreporter.com (accessed October 27, 2020). For similar assessments, see Peter Travers, "'Love, Simon' Review: Gay Teen Romance Is 'John Hughes for Woke Audiences,'" *Rolling Stone*, March 13, 2018, www.rollingstone.com. See also Richard Lawson, "*Love, Simon* Is a Charming Gay Studio Movie That Makes Me Hungry for More," *Vanity Fair*, March 13, 2018, www.vanityfair.com; see also Emily Yoshida, "*Love, Simon* Is a Sweet, Toothless, and Utterly Unstoppable Love Story," *Vulture*, March 20, 2018, www.vulture.com (all sites accessed August 19, 2019).

4 The Twitter feed can be found at "#whyisstraightthedefault," Twitter, https://twitter.com/hashtag/whyisstraightthedefault (accessed August 20, 2019). For merchandise including but not limited to stickers, T-shirts, mugs, and face masks (in the era of COVID-19) that feature key dialogue from the film, see "Love Simon," Redbubble, www.redbubble.com (accessed June 12, 2020).

5 Even as *Love, Simon* is pathbreaking as the first feature film to center a gay teenage romance, it is also part of a growing category of middlebrow LGBTQ+ representation in movies and television. For discussion and critique of this type of cultural production, see Griffin, *Feeling Normal*; Gross, *Up from Invisibility*; Henderson, *Love and Money*; Rich, *New Queer Cinema*; Walters, *All the Rage*; and Walters, *Tolerance Trap*.

6 *Call Me by Your Name*, directed by Luca Guadagnino (Crema, Italy: Frenesy Film Company, 2017); *Moonlight*, directed by Barry Jenkins (New York: A24 Films, 2016); *Carol*, directed by Todd Haynes (New York: Weinstein Company, 2016). For box office comparisons, see Sam Damshenas, "10 Iconic LGBTQ Films That Didn't Do Crazy Numbers at the Box Office," *Gay Times*, November 27, 2019, www.gaytimes.co.uk. For *Love, Simon*'s awards and accolades, see Eric Duran, "Gay Teen Romance *Love, Simon* Wins Best Kiss at MTV Movie and TV Awards," *NBC News*, June 19, 2018, www.nbcnews.com; Brendan Haley, "*Love, Simon* and Nick Robinson Won Big at the Teen Choice Awards," *Pride*, August 13, 2018, www.pride.com; and Anna Tingley, "*Queer Eye*, *Love, Simon*, and *Vida* Honored at GLAAD Media Awards," *Variety*, March 28, 2019, https://variety.com (accessed October 27, 2020).

7 Tinkcom, *Queer Theory*, 20.

8 Ibid.

9 Becky Albertalli, *Simon vs. the Homo Sapiens Agenda* (New York: Balzer + Bray, 2015).

10 Any substantive differences between *Love, Simon* and Albertalli's novel might be explained away by citing the particularities of their respective mediums: popular film and young adult fiction. But this distinction should not foreclose the critical conversations that can come from our comparative approach. Since *Love, Simon* is the first major Hollywood film to center a gay teenage romance, we must consider how financial imperatives of profit shape it. With a budget of about seventeen million, 20th Century Fox studio executives have high expectations for return on investment ("Love, Simon [2018]," IMDB, www.imdb.com [accessed June 12, 2020]).

Furthermore, for wide-release films that try to reach a broad audience, the Motion Picture Association of America (MPAA) rating system complicates financial questions. Although the MPAA rating process is voluntary, many theaters will not screen films that are unrated, and the MPAA describes itself as providing the ratings so that parents can select movies for their families ("Film Ratings," Motion Picture Association, www.motionpictures.org [accessed June 12, 2020]). As a film rated PG-13, *Love, Simon* does contain explicit sexual references and sexualized scenes, but the more "risqué" content remains limited to heterosexual experiences. For example, Simon's father accuses him of masturbating to women-identified supermodels on the internet, and Simon walks in on a developing heterosexual sex scene in a bedroom at a Halloween party. This is in stark contrast to the sexualized experiences that Albertalli gives the two developing gay characters in her novel.

When reviewing the film for the *Hollywood Reporter*, Jon Frosch makes clear the relationship between content and profitability: "It's as if Berlanti is daring audiences to find anything objectionable in what amounts to a thoroughly family-friendly queer film." If the film is to be "successful" on any widespread level, it must be relatable and inoffensive. Jon Frosch, "'Love, Simon': Film Review," *Hollywood Reporter*, February 26, 2018.

11 Treva Ellison, "The Strangeness of Progress and the Uncertainty of Blackness," in *No Tea, No Shade: New Writings in Black Queer Studies*, ed. E. Patrick Johnson (Durham: Duke University Press, 2016), 338.

12 On homonormativity, see Lisa Duggan, "The New Homonormativity: The Sexual Politics of Neoliberalism," in *Materializing Democracy: Toward a Revitalized Cultural Politics*, ed. Russ Castronovo and Dana D. Nelson (Durham: Duke University Press, 2002).

13 Roderick Ferguson, "Race-ing Homonormativity: Citizenship, Sociology, and Gay Identity," in *Black Queer Studies: A Critical Anthology*, ed. E. Patrick Johnson and Mae G. Henderson (Durham: Duke University Press, 2005), 53.

14 Ibid., 65.

15 Kaila Adia Story, "On the Cusp of Deviance: Respectability Politics and the Cultural Marketplace of Sameness," in *No Tea, No Shade: New Writings in Black Queer Studies*, ed. E. Patrick Johnson (Durham: Duke University Press, 2016), 364.

16 Alison Reed, "The Whiter the Bread, the Quicker You're Dead: Spectacular Absence and Post-Racialized Blackness in (White) Queer Theory," in *No Tea, No Shade: New Writings in Black Queer Studies*, ed. E. Patrick Johnson (Durham: Duke University Press, 2016), 49.

17 Ibid.

18 It is important to note that a spin-off ten-episode series on Hulu, *Love, Victor*, seems to address some of the criticisms of *Love, Simon*. *Love, Victor* centers a closeted Latinx teenager who attends the same high school as Simon after Simon has graduated. Victor reaches out to Simon over email and text throughout the series to seek advice on navigating questions about his sexuality. While Victor may seem quite naive about sexuality and gay identity for a nearly sixteen-year-old teenager in 2020, the character's earnestness may reflect that the show was originally developed for Disney+ and not Hulu. Nevertheless, the series is more direct than *Love, Simon* in its discussion of economic class differences among students; in its detailing of the intersections among ethnic, racial, and sexual identity; and in its promotion of intracommunal care within the LGBTQ+ communities. That the show aims to take a distinct tack is suggested in the pilot episode's first moments, when, in a voice-over narration, Victor announces, "Screw you, Simon" in the context of noting the differences in their experiences. *Love, Victor*, "Welcome to Creekwood," directed by Amy York Rubin, written by Isaac Aptaker and Elizabeth Berger, Hulu, June 17, 2020. For reviews of *Love, Victor* that not only contrast the show with *Love, Simon* but also highlight how the television series responds to criticisms of the film, see Kathryn VanArendonk, "In *Love, Victor*, a Spinoff Pushes Back against Its Origin Story," *Vulture*, June 17, 2020; or Alan Sepinwall, "'Love, Victor': A Coming-Out Story That Doubles as a Corrective," *Rolling Stone*, June 15, 2020.

19 Reed, "Whiter the Bread," 51. This notion of depoliticization aligns with Hindman's characterization of the "neoliberal citizen" as discussed in the book's introduction.

20 Roderick Ferguson, *One-Dimensional Queer* (Cambridge: Polity, 2019), 3, 8.

21 Ibid., 48.

22 Ibid., 51–52.

23 Simon's "huge-ass secret" is revealed in a voice-over that opens the 2018 film.

24 See bell hooks, *We Real Cool: Black Men and Masculinity* (New York: Routledge, 2004).

25 This criticism is brought to light, at least to some degree, in *Love, Victor* when Victor calls Simon out through the phrase "Screw you, Simon."

26 Ferguson, *One-Dimensional Queer*, 8.

27 Ibid., 1–4.

28 Berlanti, *Love, Simon*; Bleachers, "Wild Heart," *Strange Desire* (Los Angeles: Sony Legacy, 2014).

29 Berlanti, *Love, Simon.*

30 Ibid.

31 Ibid.

32 The closing shot, with the urban cityscape of Atlanta prominently captured, raises concerns of metronormativity offered by Jack Halberstam. See Halberstam, *In a Queer Time and Place: Transgender Bodies, Subcultural Lives* (New York: New York University Press, 2005), 36–37. For more, see Kath Weston, *Long Slow Burn: Sexuality and Social Science* (New York: Routledge, 1998).

33 Ferguson, *One-Dimensional Queer*, 52.

34 Sara Ahmed, *On Being Included: Racism and Diversity in Institutional Life* (Durham: Duke University Press, 2012), 13.

35 Albertalli, *Simon*, 116.

36 Ibid., 279.

37 Ibid., 37 (emphasis added).

38 Ibid., 38 (emphasis added).

39 Ibid.

40 Ibid., 58 (emphasis added).

41 Ibid., 148.

42 Ibid.

43 Ibid., 149.

44 Ibid., 78.

45 Ibid., 79.

46 Ibid., 80.

47 Ibid., 81.

48 Ibid., 258–59.

49 Berlanti, *Love, Simon.*

50 Ibid.

51 Ibid.

52 Ibid.

53 Ibid.

54 Roderick Ferguson, *Aberrations in Black: Toward a Queer of Color Critique* (Minneapolis: University of Minnesota Press, 2004), 12.

55 Kenji Yoshino, *Covering: The Hidden Assault on Our Civil Rights* (New York: Random House, 2006).

56 Story, "On the Cusp," 363.

57 Cathy Cohen, "Punks, Bulldaggers, and Welfare Queens: The Radical Potential of Queer Politics?," in *Black Queer Studies: A Critical Anthology*, ed. E. Patrick Johnson and Mae G. Henderson (Durham: Duke University Press, 2005), 44.

58 Albertalli, *Simon*, 267.

59 Ibid., 270.

60 Ibid., 277.

61 Ibid., 278.

62 Ibid., 279.

63 Ibid.
64 Ibid., 295.
65 Ibid., 163–64.
66 Ibid., 164.
67 Ibid.
68 Ibid., 98.
69 Ibid., 24.
70 Ibid., 165.
71 Ibid.
72 Berlanti, *Love, Simon.*
73 Ibid.
74 Ibid.
75 Charles Mills, *The Racial Contract* (Ithaca: Cornell University Press, 1997), 18 (emphasis in original).
76 Ibid., 19 (emphasis in original).
77 Berlanti, *Love, Simon.*
78 Ibid.
79 Ibid.
80 Ibid.
81 Reed, "Whiter the Bread," 54.
82 Ibid., 51.
83 Ibid., 57.
84 For more on what it means to "quare" (white) queer theory, see E. Patrick Johnson's "'Quare' Studies, or (Almost) Everything I Know about Queer Studies I Learned from My Grandmother," in *Black Queer Studies: A Critical Anthology*, ed. E. Patrick Johnson and Mae G. Henderson (Durham: Duke University Press, 2005), 141.
85 Albertalli, *Simon*, 32–33.
86 Ibid., 33.
87 Ibid., 121.
88 Ibid., 192.
89 Ibid., 234.
90 "Decennial Census by Decades," United States Census Bureau, www.census.gov (accessed August 22, 2019).
91 For instance, SWATS (Southwest Atlanta, too strong) was a term popularized during the mid-1990s and often referenced in hip-hop lyrics as well as in Black filmic production.
92 See Mickey Hess's *Hip Hop in America: A Regional Guide* (Santa Barbara: Greenwood, 2010).
93 For more on the development of "neoliberal urban space," see Ferguson, *One-Dimensional Queer*, particularly the chapter titled "Queerness and the One-Dimensional City." Perhaps most immediately useful is the subsection titled "Neoliberal Affirmation, Repression, and the City."
94 Albertalli, *Simon*, 147.

95 Ibid., 268.

96 Berlanti, *Love, Simon*.

97 For a critical assessment of the political strategy of "love is love" as the central message of the marriage equality movement, see Myrl Beam, "What's Love Got to Do with It?," in *Queer Activism after Marriage Equality*, ed. Joseph Nicholas DeFilippis, Michael W. Yarbrough, and Angela Jones (London: Routledge, 2018).

98 Berlanti, *Love, Simon*.

99 Reed, "Whiter the Bread," 49.

100 Ahmed, *On Being Included*, 44.

101 Ibid., 14, 33.

102 Ibid., 34.

103 Worthy of note, Ms. Albright operates as a mammy character and a sassy Black woman, capitalizing on common tropes of Blackness. See Donald Bogle, *Toms, Coons, Mulattoes, Mammies, and Bucks: An Interpretive History of Blacks in American Film* (New York: Continuum, 2003); and Patricia Hill Collins, *Black Feminist Thought: Knowledge, Consciousness, and the Politics of Empowerment*, 2nd ed. (New York: Routledge, 2000).

104 Story, "On the Cusp," 363.

105 On colorism, see Toni Morrison, *The Bluest Eye* (New York: Holt, Rinehart, and Winston, 1970); Wallace Thurman, *The Blacker the Berry: A Novel of Negro Life* (New York: Macaulay, 1929); Nella Larson, *Passing* (New York: Knopf, 1929); and Meeta Rani Jha, *The Global Beauty Industry: Colorism, Racism, and the National Body* (New York: Routledge, 2016).

106 See Robert Reid-Pharr's *Black Gay Man: Essays* (New York: New York University Press, 2001).

107 For more on the construction of Black sexuality in the West, see Brittney Cooper, *Beyond Respectability* (Urbana: University of Illinois Press, 2017); Collins, *Black Feminist Thought*; Essex Hemphill, ed., *Brother to Brother: New Writings by Black Gay Men* (Washington, DC: Redbone, 2007); and Franz Fanon, *Black Skin, White Masks* (New York: Grove, 1967).

108 On reading/shading, see our discussion of *Pose* and *Paris Is Burning* in chapter 4. On the Black buck stereotype, see Bogle, *Toms, Coons, Mulattoes*.

109 Johnson, "'Quare' Studies," 141.

110 Berlanti, *Love, Simon*.

111 See the It Gets Better Project at https://itgetsbetter.org (accessed August 20, 2019).

112 Berlanti, *Love, Simon*.

113 Whitney Houston, "I Wanna Dance with Somebody (Who Loves Me)," *Whitney* (New York: Arista Records, 1987). For cultural iconography associated with cultural signifiers of gay identity, see David M. Halperin, *How to Be Gay* (Cambridge, MA: Belknap Press of Harvard University Press, 2014).

114 On rainbow capitalism, see Yarma Velazguez Vargas, *A Queer Eye for Capitalism: The Commodification of Sexuality in American Television* (Newcastle: Cambridge Scholars, 2010).

115 For a comprehensive account of ACT UP, see Deborah Gould, *Moving Politics: Emotion and ACT UP's Fight against AIDS* (Chicago: University of Chicago Press, 2009).

116 See Joseph Beam, *In the Life: A Black Gay Anthology* (Boston: Alyson, 1986).

117 Berlanti, *Love, Simon*.

118 Albertalli, *Simon*, 188.

119 Ibid., 227.

120 Ibid., 231–32.

121 Ibid., 233.

122 Ibid., 232.

123 Interestingly, while this scene is eliminated from *Love, Simon*, a version of it is adapted for the eighth episode of *Love, Victor*. In that episode, in an attempt to learn more about queer cultures and communities, Victor ventures into New York City to meet and hang out with Simon, who now attends NYU with his boyfriend, Bram. When Victor learns that all of Simon's roommates are aware of his communications with Simon, which he assumed were private, he confronts Simon. What follows is a poignant conversation that illustrates the value of queer kinship, and intracommunal care ensues:

> SIMON: . . . Look, when you first messaged me, I was touched, really. But you know I was scared too. I know you want me to be this, like, guru who has all the answers, but the truth is I don't. And I didn't want to push you too hard or tell you the wrong thing or make your life any harder than it already was. And like you said in your first message, we're not the same. I never had a girlfriend, but Bram did. And I didn't have superreligious parents, but Justin did. Every one of my friends had a little bit to offer, a little piece of the puzzle. They weren't sitting around laughing about your life; they were in your corner listening and helping and cheering you on.
>
> VICTOR: Why would they want to help a complete stranger?
>
> SIMON: Because you're not a stranger. You're one of us. To me that's the best part about all of this—having a community, a group of friends that gave up an entire weekend to help a kid that they've never met just because they know that on some level we've all been through the same thing. Because we're family.

The scene continues with Victor and Simon joining their friends in a bar and Victor being called on stage with a drag performer. When she asks how his night has been going, Victor smiles and exclaims, "Uhh . . . it's been the best night of my life!" The bar erupts in applause. In short, Victor experiences much of the same care and happiness that comes from finding one's community and that Albertalli's Simon also experiences at the gay bar. It's a scene, a set of emotions, and a showcasing of values that Berlanti's film denies Simon and viewers alike. *Love, Victor*, "Boys' Trip," directed by

Todd Holland, written by Elizabeth Berger and Becky Albertalli, Hulu, June 17, 2020.

124 Berlanti explains his rationale for cutting the bar scenes: "It just played as it wasn't his character . . . [and] it just slowed down the narrative." Stephen Daw, "'Love, Simon' Director Greg Berlanti Talks Deleted Gay Bar Scene and Teases Potential Sequel," *Billboard*, April 3, 2018, www.billboard.com. The deleted scene, "We're Going Out," can be viewed at "'Love, Simon': 'We're Going Out' Deleted Scene, 20th Century FOX," 20th Century Studios, YouTube, www.youtube.com/watch?v=iVg9r6Kog80. The deleted scene features Colton Hayes hitting on Simon in a gay bar (which is based on a sequence in the novel).

125 The deleted scene is important in at least three ways that illustrate the film's overall refusal to present, much less engage with, queer space and queer community. First, even if the scene were included, it rejects queer excess, here presented in the form of a leather bar. The bar—a depiction of the Atlanta Eagle—is more sanitized than the actual Atlanta Eagle. The exterior aesthetic comports with the sleek, modern design of the corporatized bathhouses, such as Steamworks, discussed in chapter 2. Second, in this scene, the straight character, Nick, is foregrounded. Nick drags Simon to a bar that is, in Berlanti's narrative, appropriate or dignified: it operates with a velvet rope. Third, the film's version of queer space contains none of the ethics of care evident in the parallel scene in the novel. While Simon meets the college student Peter and dances with him in both the film and the novel, Simon does not become drunk in the film, and Peter does not care for him in the film. Instead, in the film, upon realizing that Simon and Nick are underage, the bar management kicks them out of the space.

126 Greg Berlanti interviewed by Gus Kenworthy; see Katie Muldowney, Robert Zepeda, and Pavni Mittal, "'Love, Simon' Stars, Director on the Movie's Important Impact and the Scene That Had Everyone in Tears," *ABC News*, March 16, 2018, abcnews.go.com (accessed August 20, 2019).

127 Berlanti, *Love, Simon*.

128 Ibid.

129 Ibid.

130 Adrienne Rich, "Compulsory Heterosexuality and Lesbian Existence," *Signs: Journal of Women in Culture and Society* 5, no. 4 (Summer 1980): 631–60.

131 Berlanti, *Love, Simon*.

132 Ibid.

133 Ibid.

134 Marian Meyers, introduction to *Neoliberalism and the Media*, ed. Marian Meyers (New York: Routledge, 2019), 11–12.

135 Ibid.

136 Berlanti, *Love, Simon*.

137 See Walters, *All the Rage*; Amber B. Raley and Jennifer L. Lucas, "Stereotype or Success? Prime-Time Television's Portrayals of Gay Male, Lesbian, and Bisexual Characters," *Journal of Homosexuality* 51, no. 2 (2006): 19–38; and Rodger

Streitmatter, *From Perverts to Fab Five: The Media's Changing Depiction of Gay Men and Lesbians* (New York: Routledge, 2008), especially chapter 12.

138 The character of Jack McPhee, portrayed by Kerr Smith, was introduced during the second season of *Dawson's Creek*, and he came out in an episode airing in February 1999. ". . . That Is the Question," *Dawson's Creek*, directed by Greg Prange, created by Kevin Williamson (1998–2003). Berlanti was a crucial advocate for McPhee's character and for the representation of romance between two gay high school students; the show featured the first gay kiss on primetime television on May 24, 2000. See Thea Glassman, "Inside the Thrilling, Chaotic Writers' Room of Dawson's Creek," *Vanity Fair*, January 19, 2018, www.vanityfair.com (accessed August 21, 2019).

139 Cohen, "Punks, Bulldaggers, and Welfare Queens," 21.

4. DOING THE MOST

1 *Pose*, season 1, episode 1, "Pilot," directed by Ryan Murphy, aired June 3, 2018, on FX Productions, www.fxnetworks.com (accessed June 3, 2018).

2 Roderick Ferguson, *One-Dimensional Queer* (Cambridge, MA: Polity, 2019), 16.

3 Reina Gossett, Eric A. Stanley, and Johanna Burton, eds., *Trap Door: Trans Cultural Production and the Politics of Visibility* (Cambridge: MIT Press, 2017), xviii. At the time of publication, Gossett identified as "Tourmaline."

4 Ibid., xx.

5 Ferguson, *One-Dimensional Queer*, 16.

6 Gossett, Stanley, and Burton, *Trap Door*, xv.

7 Juliana Huxtable, "Existing in the World: Blackness at the Edge of Trans Visibility / Che Gossett and Juliana Huxtable in Conversation," in *Trap Door: Trans Cultural Production and the Politics of Visibility*, ed. Reina Gossett, Eric A. Stanley, and Johanna Burton (Cambridge, MA: MIT Press, 2017), 45.

8 Che Gossett, "Existing in the World: Blackness at the Edge of Trans Visibility / Che Gossett and Juliana Huxtable in Conversation," in *Trap Door: Trans Cultural Production and the Politics of Visibility*, ed. Reina Gossett, Eric A. Stanley, and Johanna Burton (Cambridge, MA: MIT Press, 2017), 45.

9 CeCe McDonald and Miss Major Griffin-Gracy, "Cautious Living: Black Trans Women and the Politics of Documentation," in *Trap Door: Trans Cultural Production and the Politics of Visibility*, ed. Reina Gossett, Eric A. Stanley, and Johanna Burton (Cambridge, MA: MIT Press, 2017), 36.

10 Huxtable, "Existing," 44.

11 C. Riley Snorton, *Black on Both Sides: A Racial History of Trans Identity* (Minneapolis: University of Minnesota Press, 2017), x.

12 McDonald and Griffin-Gracy, "Cautious Living," 36.

13 Snorton, *Black on Both Sides*, 14.

14 *Pose*, season 1, episode 1, "Pilot," directed by Ryan Murphy, aired June 3, 2018, on FX Productions, www.fxnetworks.com (accessed June 3, 2018).

15 Janet Mock (@janetmock), 2019, Instagram video, May 7, 2019, www.instagram
.com/p/BxKoYRqgqCt/?igshid=xe5c10e8025g (accessed May 7, 2019); emphasis
added.

16 Though we anchor our reading of *Pose* in Black queer/quare studies, another productive and complementary reading could be shaped by recent threads in Black
media studies, particularly ones that explore (and even resignify) the "negative"
or "ratchet" image in popular culture. For discussions about "negativity" more
broadly, see Racquel J. Gates, *Double Negative: The Black Image and Popular
Culture* (Durham: Duke University Press, 2018). Gates challenges the ostensibly
stable binary of "positive" and "negative" images in Black cultural production, and
she discusses "the possibility of using the trope of negativity in ways that demonstrate self-awareness, agency, and even subversion" (11). Additionally, as she
explores "the productive use of negativity," Gates specifically highlights "strategic
negativity" such as excessive or ratchet performances and argues that these constructions "tak[e] advantage of their distance from the politics of respectability to
explore topics that their positive counterparts do not typically address" (34). For
more discussions focused on "ratchet," see Kristen J. Warner, "They Gon' Think
You Loud Regardless: Ratchetness, Reality Television, and Black Womanhood,"
Camera Obscura 30, no. 1 (2015): 129–53; and Therí A. Pickens, "Shoving aside the
Politics of Respectability: Black Women, Reality TV, and the Ratchet Performance," *Women and Performance* 25, no. 1 (2015): 41–58. For Warner, ratchet "is
marked by excess that is never disavowed" (130). Furthermore, "ratchetness is
performative in nature. It largely functions as something done by the individual,
an action that always demonstrates a measure of reflexivity—an awareness that
one actively puts on this hyperexcessive performance" (132). Pickens "recuperates
the derogatory term 'ratchet' as a performative strategy that secures a liberatory
space for black women" (41). Both Warner and Pickens assess how ratchet has
been used to derogate (and police) Black womanhood and how ratchet performances showcase that alternatives are possible. Finally, for specific discussions
about ratchet's relationship to Black queer folk, see Nikki Lane, *The Black Queer
Work of Ratchet: Race, Gender, Sexuality, and the (Anti) Politics of Respectability* (London: Palgrave Macmillan, 2019). As Lane argues, "Claiming, acting, or
being ratchet, involves an indirect (or direct) political orientation. To be Black
and ratchet, on purpose, means that you ascribe no value to assimilation into the
American 'way of life'" (4). She goes further to suggest that "*ratchet* also refers
to the purposeful lack of pretense for what has been defined as socially acceptable by Black and white middle-class, heteronormative logics" (8). All of this is in
the service of asking critical questions about our current moment of heightened
visibility: "What kind of Black lesbian, gay, bisexual, or trans person [is] acceptable now[?] . . . How should Black queer people act now that middle-class Black
people would now allow some of us to come to 'the table'?" (15). While *Pose* does
not use the explicit vocabulary of *ratchet*, the show does embrace the same kind of

unapologetic forms of excess that could be accused of being "negative" or "counterproductive," but as this chapter argues and as all the aforementioned scholarly work above supports, this decision to center excess can be purposeful, generative, and even liberatory.

17 In a similar way, Billy Porter, the show's leading man, has offered a common refrain in the media, specifically about his starring role as Pray Tell. He regularly describes how the industry (and the world more broadly) branded him as *too gay, too Black, too much*. As he has moved into new territory as a gender-bending fashion icon and as an actor playing an unapologetically queer, femme, Black, HIV-positive, and sexualized character on television, he notes how *Pose* is a rare moment in which he has been welcomed fully. See Malcolm Venable, "Pray Tell's Acceptance of His Feminine on *Pose* Mirrors Billy Porter's Triumphant Rise," *TV Guide*, November 29, 2019, https://tvguide.com (accessed November 29, 2019); Corey Townsend, "Billy Porter Has a Message for Those Who Were Told They Were 'Too Much,'" *The Root*, August 14, 2019, https://thegrapevine.theroot.com; and Ashleigh Lakieva Atwell, "Billy Porter Says He's Glad to Be an Idol for All the 'Little Black Sissy Boys' in His Inbox," *Blavity*, June 19, 2019, https://blavity.com (accessed June 19, 2019).

18 Tre'Vell Anderson, "Steven Canals Created *Pose*. But Still, He's Hollywood's Best-Kept Secret," *Out Magazine*, January 10, 2019, www.out.com.

19 Whitney Houston, "I Wanna Dance with Somebody (Who Loves Me)," *Whitney* (New York: Arista Records, 1987).

20 Treva Ellison, "The Labor of Werqing It: The Performance and Protest Strategies of Sir Lady Java," in *Trap Door: Trans Cultural Production and the Politics of Visibility*, ed. Reina Gossett, Eric A. Stanley, and Johanna Burton (Cambridge, MA: MIT Press, 2017), 1.

21 *Pose*, season 1, episode 1, "Pilot," directed by Ryan Murphy, aired June 3, 2018, on FX Productions, www.fxnetworks.com.

22 Brittney Cooper, *Eloquent Rage: A Black Feminist Discovers Her Superpower* (New York: Picador, 2019), 273.

23 Kaila Adia Story, "On the Cusp of Deviance: Respectability Politics and the Cultural Marketplace of Sameness," in *No Tea, No Shade: New Writings in Black Queer Studies*, ed. E. Patrick Johnson (Durham: Duke University Press, 2016), 364.

24 *Pose*, season 1, episode 1, "Pilot," directed by Ryan Murphy, aired June 3, 2018, on FX Productions, www.fxnetworks.com.

25 *Pose*, season 1, episode 8, "Mother of the Year," directed by Gwyneth Horder-Payton, aired July 22, 2018, on FX Productions, www.fxnetworks.com.

26 Ibid.

27 See William Leap and Tom Boellstorff, *Speaking in Queer Tongues: Globalization and Gay Language* (Urbana: University of Illinois Press, 2003); and E. Patrick Johnson, *No Tea, No Shade: New Writings in Black Queer Studies* (Durham: Duke University Press, 2016).

28 Just as much as the show snatches edges, the show also allows the less savory edges of ballroom culture to remain undomesticated. Another important dimension of excess is the infighting that happens on the ballroom floor. While the behavior could be coded as "dramatic," "immature," "violent," or even "banjee," *Pose* does not deny the messiness of excess or the complexity of queer community. Allowing the messiness to remain, in fact, constitutes a crucial part of the show's embrace of *doing the most*, for these moments are not only about fights. Important emotional work also happens in and through the messiness.

29 *Pose*, season 1, episode 8, "Mother of the Year," directed by Gwyneth Horder-Payton, aired July 22, 2018, on FX Productions, www.fxnetworks.com.

30 *Pose*, season 1, episode 1, "Pilot," directed by Ryan Murphy, aired June 3, 2018, on FX Productions, www.fxnetworks.com.

31 *Pose*, season 2, episode 1, "Acting Up," directed by Gwyneth Horder-Payton, aired June 11, 2019, on FX Productions, www.fxnetworks.com.

32 L. H. Stallings, *Funk the Erotic: Transaesthetics and Black Sexual Cultures* (Urbana: University of Illinois Press, 2015), 224.

33 Snorton, *Black on Both Sides*, 11.

34 *Pose*, season 2, episode 10, "In My Heels," directed by Janet Mock, aired August 20, 2019, on FX Productions, www.fxnetworks.com.

35 *Pose*, season 2, episode 3, "Butterfly/Cocoon," directed by Janet Mock, aired June 25, 2019, on FX Productions, www.fxnetworks.com.

36 We could easily add the episode titled "Blow" to this list, particularly for its rendering of ACT UP's famous condom demonstration at Jesse Helms's home.

37 *Pose*, season 2, episode 1, "Acting Up," directed by Gwyneth Horder-Payton, aired June 11, 2019, on FX Productions, www.fxnetworks.com.

38 See Michael Keene, *New York City's Hart Island: A Cemetery for Strangers* (Cheltenham: History Press, 2019).

39 See Corey Kilgannon, "Dead of AIDS and Forgotten in Potter's Field," *New York Times*, July 3, 2018.

40 *Pose*, season 2, episode 1, "Acting Up," directed by Gwyneth Horder-Payton, aired June 11, 2019, on FX Productions, www.fxnetworks.com.

41 Ibid.

42 See Deborah Gould, *Moving Politics: Emotion and ACT UP's Fight against AIDS* (Chicago: University of Chicago Press, 2009).

43 See *United in Anger: A History of ACT UP*, directed by Jim Hubbard (New York: New York State Council on the Arts and the Ford Foundation, 2012).

44 For a few critiques of and/or correctives to the white-washing of queer history and politics, see E. Patrick Johnson, *Black. Queer. Southern. Women: An Oral History* (Chapel Hill: University of North Carolina Press, 2018); Saidiya Hartman, *Wayward Lives, Beautiful Experiments: Intimate Histories of Social Upheaval* (New York: Norton, 2019); and Anita Little, "#NotOurStonewall Calls Out the White-Washing of LGBT History," *Ms. Magazine*, August 20, 2015, https://msmagazine.com.

45 While we discuss the criminal justice system later in this chapter, the creative way in which Elektra gets rid of the body and how this reflects and retells an instance in trans history occupy our attention in this section.

46 *Pose*, season 2, episode 3, "Butterfly/Cocoon," directed by Janet Mock, aired June 25, 2019, on FX Productions, www.fxnetworks.com.

47 Edward Conlon, "The Drag Queen and the Mummy," *Transition* 65 (1995): 4–24.

48 Jeanie Russel Kasindorf, "The Drag Queen Had a Mummy in Her Closet," *New York* 27, no. 18 (1994): 50.

49 *Pose*, season 2, episode 3, "Butterfly/Cocoon," directed by Janet Mock, aired June 25, 2019, on FX Productions, www.fxnetworks.com.

50 See Kimberlé Crenshaw and Andrea Ritchie, *Say Her Name: Resisting Police Brutality against Black Women* (New York: African American Policy Forum, 2015); and Joey Mogul, Andrea Ritchie, and Kay Whitlock, *Queer (In)Justice: The Criminalization of LGBT People in the United States* (Boston: Beacon, 2011).

51 For a clear picture of how central collaborations are to the shape of the show, see Ryan Murphy's comments on Hector Xtravaganza in Halle Kiefer's "Hector Xtravaganza, of the House of Xtravaganza, Has Passed Away," *Vulture*, December 30, 2018, www.vulture.com. Additionally, see Janet Mock's depiction of her early exchanges with Ryan Murphy and of how his approach (collaboration with the ball world) won her over: Janet Mock, "'Pose' Writer Janet Mock on Making History with Trans Storytelling," *Variety*, May 16, 2018, https://variety.com.

52 *Pose*, season 2, episode 1, "Acting Up," directed by Gwyneth Horder-Payton, aired June 11, 2019, on FX Productions, www.fxnetworks.com.

53 *Pose*, season 2, episode 2, "Worth It," directed by Gwyneth Horder-Payton, aired June 18, 2019, on FX Productions, www.fxnetworks.com.

54 Importantly, Elektra's all-pink Marie Antoinette stunt in "Acting Up" also pays homage to Hector Xtravaganza's all-pink Marie Antoinette production at a "Think Pink"–themed ball in 1991. As legend would have it, Xtravaganza snatched the grand prize that night—in no small part due to the all-pink pit bull that stomped the floor with the children. For visual images and community debate about that real-life ball event, see House of Xtravaganza (@houseofxtravaganza), 2019, Instagram post, June 14, 2019, www.instagram.com/p/ByrqCEMhmsx/?igshid=68xsg3828pa.

55 *Pose*, season 2, episode 2, "Worth It," directed by Gwyneth Horder-Payton, aired June 18, 2019, on FX Productions, www.fxnetworks.com.

56 Ibid.

57 For comments from actors and writers/directors about the real-life inspiration for Lulu's ballroom stunt, see Hailie Sahar (@213Sahar), 2019, Twitter post, June 19, 2019, https://twitter.com/213Sahar/status/1141385816041803777; and Janet Mock (@janetmock), 2019, Twitter post, June 18, 2019, https://twitter.com/janetmock/status/1141164806382206976.

58 *Pose*, season 2, episode 2, "Worth It," directed by Gwyneth Horder-Payton, aired June 18, 2019, on FX Productions, www.fxnetworks.com.

59 Grace Dunham, "Out of Obscurity: Trans Resistance, 1969–2016," in *Trap Door: Trans Cultural Production and the Politics of Visibility*, ed. Reina Gossett, Eric A. Stanley, and Johanna Burton (Cambridge, MA: MIT Press, 2017), 93.

60 See Constantine Chatzipapatheodoridis, "Strike a Pose, Forever: The Legacy of Vogue and Its Recontextualization in Contemporary Camp Performances," *European Journal of American Studies* 11, no. 3 (2017): 1–15.

61 *Pose*, season 1, episode 4, "The Fever," directed by aired Gwyneth Horder-Payton, June 24, 2018, on FX Productions, www.fxnetworks.com.

62 For Walter Armstrong's oral history of St. Vincent's and the HIV/AIDS epidemic in New York City, see "St. Vincent's Remembered," *Out Magazine*, August 17, 2010, www.out.com.

63 For more details on HIV/AIDS and racial disparities, see Cathy Cohen, *Boundaries of Blackness: AIDS and the Breakdown of Black Politics* (Chicago: University of Chicago Press, 1999); and Jacob Levenson, *The Secret Epidemic: The Story of AIDS and Black America* (New York: Anchor, 2005).

64 To learn more about the multidimensional experiences of the HIV/AIDS crisis, including community-building and pleasure in times of mourning and activism, see Douglas Crimp, *AIDS: Cultural Analysis/Cultural Activism* (Cambridge: MIT Press, 1988); *Melancholia and Moralism: Essays on AIDS and Queer Politics* (Cambridge: MIT Press, 2002); and Gould, *Moving Politics*. See also Tim Dean, *Unlimited Intimacy* (Chicago: University of Chicago Press, 2009); and *BPM (Beats Per Minute)*, directed by Robin Campillo (Paris: Les Films de Pierre, 2017).

65 *Pose*, season 1, episode 6, "Love Is the Message," directed by Janet Mock, aired July 8, 2018, on FX Productions, www.fxnetworks.com; *Pose*, season 2, episode 6, "Love's in Need of Love Today," directed by Tina Mabry, aired July 23, 2019, on FX Productions, www.fxnetworks.com.

66 Season 2 provides a protracted narrative arc between Blanca and her landlord, Frederica, to illustrate the history of gentrification and the fundamental erasure of Black and Brown bodies and spaces in late twentieth-century New York City. As a pointed critique of capitalistic violence and neoliberal conceptualizations of "urban development," their story line roots their characters in a specific history and provides further context to understand contemporary anxieties about displacement and increasing costs of living in New York City. See the following for conversations about space, place, and identity: Ingrid Gould Ellen and Justin Peter Steil, eds., *Debates about Housing, Segregation, and Opportunity in the Twenty-First Century* (New York: Columbia University Press, 2019); Samuel R. Delany, *Times Square Red, Times Square Blue* (New York: New York University Press, 1999); Roderick Ferguson, "Queerness and the One-Dimensional City," in *One-Dimensional Queer* (Cambridge: Polity, 2019); and Jeremiah Moss, *Vanishing New York: How a Great City Lost Its Soul* (New York: Dey Street, 2017).

67 For explorations of how normative cultures are often drawn to the othered cultures against which they define themselves and thereby consolidate their own power, see Christopher Pullen, *Straight Girls and Queer Guys: The Hetero Media*

Gaze in Film and Television (Edinburgh: Edinburgh University Press, 2016); Franz Fanon, *Black Skin, White Masks* (New York: Grove Press, 1967); Carl Van Vechten, *Nigger Heaven* (New York: Knopf, 1926); Langston Hughes, "When the Negro Was in Vogue," in *The Big Sea* (New York: Hill and Wang, 1940); and Michael Warner, *The Trouble with Normal: Sex, Politics, and the Ethics of Queer Life* (Cambridge, MA: Harvard University Press, 1999).

68 On dynamics of appropriation of queer subversion, see Phillip Brian Harper, "'The Subversive Edge': *Paris Is Burning*, Social Critique, and the Limits of Subjective Agency," *Diacritics* 24, nos. 2/3 (1994): 90–103; Marlon Riggs, "Black Macho Revisited: Reflections of a Snap! Queen," *Black American Literature Forum* 25, no. 2 (1991): 389–94; Sunaina Maira, "Henna and Hip Hop: The Politics of Cultural Production and the Work of Cultural Studies," *Journal of Asian American Studies* 3, no. 3 (2000); John Paul Brammer, "The Difference between Appreciating and Appropriating Queer Culture," *Oprah Magazine*, October 2, 2018, www.oprahmag.com; Elyssa Goodman, "The Historic, Mainstream Appropriation of Ballroom Culture," *Them*, April 25, 2018, www.them.us; and Niall Connolly, "Strike a Pose? Voguing, Ballroom and Cultural Appropriation," *The Quiet Us*, November 11, 2013, https://thequietus.com.

69 Snorton, *Black on Both Sides*, 181.

70 Ibid., 180.

71 For a few critiques of and/or correctives to the white-washing of queer history and politics, see Johnson, *Black*; Hartman, *Wayward Lives*; and Little, "#NotOurStonewall."

72 Stephen Maglott, "Tracey 'Africa' Norman," the UBUNTU Biography Project, December 15, 2017. https://ubuntubiographyproject.com.

73 Jada Yuan and Aaron Wong, "The First Black Trans Model Had Her Face on a Box of Clairol," *The Cut*, December 14, 2015, www.thecut.com.

74 Hermoine Hoby, "How Tracey Norman, America's First Black Trans Model, Returned to the Limelight," *Guardian*, August 20, 2016, www.theguardian.com; Raffaele Panizza, "Interview with Tracey Norman," *Vogue*, October 6, 2017, www.vogue.it.

75 Morgan M. Page, "One from the Vaults: Gossip, Access, and Trans History-Telling," in *Trap Door: Trans Cultural Production and the Politics of Visibility*, ed. Reina Gossett, Eric A. Stanley, and Johanna Burton (Cambridge, MA: MIT Press, 2017), 135.

76 Snorton, *Black on Both Sides*, 181.

77 See Leslie Feinberg, *Gender Warriors: Making History from Joan of Arc to Dennis Rodman* (Boston: Beacon, 1996); Snorton, *Black on Both Sides*; and Susan Stryker, *Transgender History, Second Edition: The Roots of Today's Revolution* (New York: Seal Press, 2017).

78 Huxtable, "Existing," 40.

79 PoseFX (@PoseOnFX), 2019, Twitter post, December 26, 2019, https://twitter.com/PoseOnFX. www.instagram.com/p/BxKoYRqgqCt/?igshid=xe5c1oe8025g;

PoseFX (@PoseOnFX), 2019, Instagram post, https://instagram.com/poseonfx
?igshid=1cnkz36ezq8eh; PoseFX (@PoseOnFX), 2019, Facebook post, www
.facebook.com/PoseOnFX/.

80 PoseFX (@PoseOnFX), 2019, Twitter post, "#PoseFXFact," July 9, 2019, https://
twitter.com/PoseOnFX/status/1148776611593912320; PoseFX (@PoseOnFX),
2019, Twitter post "#PoseFXFact," June 25, 2019, https://twitter.com/PoseOnFX/
status/1143714508667408386; PoseFX (@PoseOnFX), 2019, Twitter post, "#OnThis-
Day," June 16, 2019, https://twitter.com/PoseOnFX/status/1140272825066053633.

81 PoseFX (@PoseOnFX), 2019, Twitter post, "#OnThisDay," July 25, 2019, https://
twitter.com/PoseOnFX/status/1154527359489302528.

82 Blacklisted worker (@Blacklistluxury), 2019, Twitter post, "Wow! Thanks
for the lesson!," July 25, 2019, https://twitter.com/Blacklistluxury/status/
1154527713190793218; Raymonst (@raymonst), 2019, Twitter post, "the more you
know!," June 19, 2019, https://twitter.com/raymonst/status/1141455865175691264.

83 PoseFX (@PoseOnFX), 2019, Instagram post, "Pyramid," August 16, 2019, www
.instagram.com/p/B1O49h4FleT/?igshid=1pun8wlxoejgp.

84 Mel Y. Chen, "Everywhere Archives: Transgendering, Trans Asians, and the Internet,"
in *Trap Door: Trans Cultural Production and the Politics of Visibility*, ed. Reina Gossett,
Eric A. Stanley, and Johanna Burton (Cambridge, MA: MIT Press, 2017), 157.

85 See Henry Jenkins, Sam Ford, and Joshua Green, *Spreadable Media: Creating
Value and Meaning in a Networked Culture* (New York: New York University
Press, 2013); Martin Hand, *Making Digital Cultures: Access, Interactivity, and
Authenticity* (New York: Routledge, 2008).

86 Mikelle Street, "*Pose*'s 'Condom over the House' Scene Actually
Happened—Here's How," *Out Magazine*, July 31, 2019, www.out.com; Mikelle
Street, "*Pose*'s Marie Antoinette Scene Was Inspired by a Real Ballroom Moment,"
Out Magazine, June 14, 2019, www.out.com; and Stacy Lambe, "How 'Pose' Season 2
Revealed the Untold Story of Hart Island," *NewNowNext*, June 12, 2019, www
.newnownext.com.

87 Christopher Rudolph, "The Mystery of Dorian Corey, the Drag Queen Who Had
a Mummy in Her Closet," *NewNowNext*, June 25, 2019, www.newnownext.com.

88 Evan Real, "Janet Mock, Tracey 'Africa' Norman Talk Breaking Barriers, Being
a 'Heroine for Brown Trans Girls,'" *Hollywood Reporter*, May 2, 2019, www
.hollywoodreporter.com.

89 McDonald and Griffin-Gracy, "Cautious Living," 31.

90 *Love, Simon*, directed by Greg Berlanti (Los Angeles: Fox 2000 Pictures, 2018).

91 See John D'Emilio, *In a New Century: Essays on Queer History, Politics, and Community Life* (Madison: University of Wisconsin Press, 2014).

92 Page, "One from the Vaults," 135.

93 See Johnson, *No Tea*; and Jeffrey Q. McCune Jr., "'Happy at Last': Carving the
White 'Closet' Past, Creating an 'Out' Future," in *Black Sexual Economies: Race
and Sex in a Culture of Capital*, ed. Adrienne Davis and the BSE Collective
(Urbana: University of Illinois Press, 2019), 124–36.

94 Page, "One from the Vaults," 137.

95 See Rod McCollum, "The Perfect Storm Facing Black Men on HIV," *Advocate*, May 2, 2016, www.advocate.com; Daniel Reynolds, "STUDY: Half of Black Gay Men Will Test HIV-Positive," *Advocate*, February 23, 2016, www.advocate.com; Centers for Disease Control and Prevention, *HIV Surveillance Report 2017* 29 (November 2018), www.cdc.gov; Samuel Walker, Cassia Spohn, and Miriam DeLone, *The Color of Justice: Race, Ethnicity, and Crime in America* (Boston: Cengage Learning, 2018); and Michelle Alexander, *The New Jim Crow: Mass Incarceration in the Age of Colorblindness* (New York: New Press, 2012).

96 Dunham, "Out of Obscurity," 93.

97 *Pose*, season 1, episode 1, "Pilot," directed by Ryan Murphy, aired June 3, 2018, on FX Productions, www.fxnetworks.com.

98 Kirsty Robertson, *Tear Gas Epiphanies: Protest, Culture, Museums* (Montreal: McGill-Queen's University Press, 2019); Philipp Schorch and Conal McCarthy, eds., *Curatopia: Museums and the Future of Curatorship* (Manchester: Manchester University Press, 2019); B. Byron Price, "'Cutting for Sign': Museums and Western Revisionism," *Western Historical Quarterly* 24, no. 2 (May 1993): 229–34.

99 *Pose*, season 1, episode 1, "Pilot," directed by Ryan Murphy, aired June 3, 2018, on FX Productions, www.fxnetworks.com.

100 On structural roots of inequities and injustice, see James A. Tyner, *Violence in Capitalism: Devaluing Life in an Age of Responsibility* (Lincoln: University of Nebraska Press, 2016); Evan S. Lieberman and Prena Singh, "The Institutional Origins of Ethnic Violence," *Comparative Politics* 45, no. 1 (October 2012): 1–24; Miriam J. Abelson, "Institutional Contexts of Violence: Heterosexism and Cissexism in Everyday Spaces," in *Men in Place: Trans Masculinity, Race, and Sexuality in America* (Minneapolis: University of Minnesota Press, 2019), 155–92; Walker, Spohn, and DeLone, *Color of Justice*; Alexander, *New Jim Crow*; Dayna Bowen Matthew, *Just Medicine: A Cure of Racial Inequality in American Health Care* (New York: New York University Press, 2015); and Daria Roithmayr, *Reproducing Racism: How Everyday Choices Lock in White Advantage* (New York: New York University Press, 2014).

101 *Pose*, season 2, episode 4, "Never Knew Love like This Before," directed by Ryan Murphy, aired July 9, 2019, on FX Productions, www.fxnetworks.com.

102 These key illustrations join a series-long exploration of the routine, everyday violence that impacts the community through healthcare, housing, job discrimination, love and dating, governmental neglect, and exploitation in media.

103 *Pose*, season 2, episode 3, "Butterfly/Cocoon," directed by Janet Mock, aired June 25, 2019, on FX Productions, www.fxnetworks.com.

104 Ibid.

105 Ibid.

106 Ibid.

107 Ibid.

108 See Mia Fischer, *Terrorizing Gender: Transgender Visibility and the Surveillance Practices of the U.S. Security State* (Lincoln: University of Nebraska Press, 2019); Janet Mock, *Redefining Realness: My Path to Womanhood, Identity, Love, and So Much More* (New York: Atria, 2014); and Stallings, *Funk the Erotic*, particularly the chapter titled "Black Trans Narratives, Sex Work, and the Illusive Flesh."

109 *Pose*, season 2, episode 3, "Butterfly/Cocoon," directed by Janet Mock, aired June 25, 2019, on FX Productions, www.fxnetworks.com.

110 *Pose*, season 2, episode 4, "Never Knew Love like This Before," directed by Ryan Murphy, aired July 9, 2019, on FX Productions, www.fxnetworks.com.

111 Adrienne Davis and the BSE Collective, eds., *Black Sexual Economies: Race and Sex in a Culture of Capital* (Urbana: University of Illinois Press, 2019); Harvey Young, "The Black Body as Souvenir in American Lynching," *Theatre Journal* 57, no. 4 (December 2005): 639–57; Dawn Harris, "The Punished Black Body and the Public's Gaze: Demarcating Socio-Racial Structures through the Theatrics of Punishment," in *Punishing the Black Body: Marking Social and Racial Structures* (Athens: University of Georgia Press, 2017), 136–57; and Fanon, *Black Skin*.

112 Ashleigh Shackelford, "#blacktranslivesmatter: How Black Cis-Women Are Part of the Problem," *For Harriet*, October 18, 2015, www.forharriet.com; Cherno Biko, "Black Trans Lives Matter, Too," HuffPost, February 4, 2016, www.huffpost.com. For more, see #blacktranslivesmatter on Twitter and Instagram.

113 *Pose*, season 2, episode 4, "Never Knew Love like This Before," directed by Ryan Murphy, aired July 9, 2019, on FX Productions, www.fxnetworks.com.

114 Ibid.

115 Allyson Chiu, "Laverne Cox Lambastes 'Deadnaming': What Is It and Why Is It a Problem?," *Washington Post*, August 14, 2018, www.washingtonpost.com; National Center for Transgender Equality, "Issues: Antiviolence" (2019), https:// transequality.org.

116 *Pose*, season 2, episode 4, "Never Knew Love like This Before," directed by Ryan Murphy, aired July 9, 2019, on FX Productions, www.fxnetworks.com (emphasis added).

117 For more about "gay panic" or "trans panic" defenses to justify violence against LGBTQ+ people, see the "LGBTQ+ 'Panic' Defense" entry on the LGBT Bar website (lgbtbar.org). Their detailed primer provides definitions, explains how the defense is used to mitigate murder cases, details the legislative history by state in the US, and offers suggestions for resisting this legal strategy and achieving justice for slain LGBTQ+ individuals.

118 McDonald and Griffin-Gracy, "Cautious Living," 31. For more about trans amorous folks, stigma, and the consequences, see Charlie Craggs, ed., *To My Trans Sisters* (London: Jessica Kingsley, 2017); Mock, *Redefining Realness*; Janet Mock, *Surpassing Certainty: What My Twenties Taught Me* (New York: Atria, 2017); Sadhbh O'Sullivan, "'We Deserve Love Stories': Trans Women on the Highs and Lows of Dating in 2019," Refinery29, November 15, 2019, www.refinery29.com; Ashlee

Marie Preston (@AshleeMPreston), 2019, Twitter post, August 20, 2019, https://twitter.com/AshleeMPreston/status/1163884648784465921; Janet Mock (@janetmock), 2019, Twitter post, August 20, 2019, https://twitter.com/janetmock/status/1163982642359832577; and Jacob Ogles, "Man Bullied for Being Open about Trans Relationship Dies by Suicide," *Advocate*, August 21, 2019, www.advocate.com.

119 *Pose*, season 2, episode 4, "Never Knew Love like This Before," directed by Ryan Murphy, aired July 9, 2019, on FX Productions, www.fxnetworks.com. See the Trans Murder Monitoring Project for more details about the epidemic of violence against trans folks, particularly women and non-binary femmes of color.

120 Snorton, *Black on Both Sides*, 175, 180.

121 Michael Cobb, *God Hates Fags: The Rhetorics of Religious Violence* (New York: New York University Press, 2006); Janet Jakobsen and Ann Pellegrini, *Love the Sin: Sexual Regulation and the Limits of Religious Tolerance* (New York: New York University Press, 2003).

122 For more information about the Stop the Church demonstration, see Hubbard, *United in Anger*; and Gould, *Moving Politics*; *Stop the Church*, directed by Robert Hilferty (New York: Cinema Verite Documentary, 1991); or visit the ACT UP Historical Archive at actupny.org.

123 *Pose*, season 2, episode 1, "Acting Up," directed by Gwyneth Horder-Payton, aired June 11, 2019, on FX Productions, www.fxnetworks.com.

124 Ibid.

125 Ibid.

126 Ibid.

127 Ibid.

128 Ibid.

129 Ibid.

130 Theodore Kerr, "How Six NYC Activists Changed History with 'Silence=Death,'" *Village Voice*, June 20, 2017, www.villagevoice.com. See also Gould, *Moving Politics*.

131 *Pose* continues its resistance work by offering an extended critique of the violence of capitalism through interactions between Blanca and her greedy landlord, Frederica Norman. More specifically, viewers are offered a sustained critique of urban gentrification that demonstrates how entrenched economic power is and that illustrates how capitalism can sharpen the biases of racism, sexism, and transphobia. Indeed, the story line exposes the myth of equal possibility of upward mobility.

132 Dean Spade, "Models of Futurity: Roundtable Participants: Kai Lumumba Barrow, Yve Laris Cohen, and Kalaniopua Young," in *Trap Door: Trans Cultural Production and the Politics of Visibility*, ed. Reina Gossett, Eric A. Stanley, and Johanna Burton (Cambridge, MA: MIT Press, 2017), 324.

133 See Patricia Hill Collins, *Black Feminist Thought: Knowledge, Consciousness, and the Politics of Empowerment* (New York: Routledge, 1990); and Donald Bogle, *Toms, Coons, Mulattoes, Mammies, and Bucks: An Interpretive History of Blacks in American Films*, 5th ed. (New York: Bloomsbury Academic, 2016).

134 Micha Cárdenas, "Dark Shimmers: The Rhythm of Necropolitical Affect in Digital Media," in *Trap Door: Trans Cultural Production and the Politics of Visibility*, ed. Reina Gossett, Eric A. Stanley, and Johanna Burton (Cambridge, MA: MIT Press, 2017), 173.

135 For more on subversive reading strategies, see bell hooks, *Outlaw Culture: Resisting Representations* (New York: Routledge, 1994).

136 See Margaret Gibson, ed., *Queering Motherhood: Narrative and Theoretical Perspectives* (Ontario: Demeter Press, 2014); Lisa Duggan, "Queering the State," *Social Text* 39 (Summer 1994): 1–14; Tyson Pugh, *The Queer Fantasies of the American Family Sitcom* (New Brunswick: Rutgers University Press, 2018); Carla A. Pfeffer, *Queering Families: The Postmodern Partnerships of Cisgender Women and Transgender Men* (New York: Oxford University Press, 2016); and Kathryn Bond Stockton, *The Queer Child, or Growing Sideways in the Twentieth Century* (Durham: Duke University Press, 2009).

137 Cooper, *Eloquent Rage*, 243.

138 See "Pilot," "Giving and Receiving," and "Mother's Day" for the most telling illustrations.

139 See Mock, *Redefining Realness*.

140 "Mother's Day" and "Never Knew Love like This Before" are strong examples of cisgender parents struggling to love their trans kids.

141 Gossett, Stanley, and Burton, *Trap Door*, xvi.

142 See David Eng, *The Feeling of Kinship: Queer Liberalism and the Racialization of Intimacy* (Durham: Duke University Press, 2010); Kanika Batra, *Feminist Visions and Queer Futures in Postcolonial Drama: Community, Kinship, and Citizenship* (New York: Routledge, 2011); Nikki Sullivan and Sara Davidmann, "Reimag(in)ing Life Making, or Queering the Somatechnics of Reproductive Futurity," in *Critical Kinship Studies*, ed. Charlotte Krolokke, Lene Myong, Stine Willum Adrian and Tine Tjornhoj-Thomsen (New York: Rowman and Littlefield, 2016), 239–54; Delany, *Times Square Red*; and Dean, *Unlimited Intimacy*.

143 For more on ballroom community history, see Emily A. Arnold and Marlon M. Bailey, "Constructing Home and Family: How the Ballroom Community Supports African American GLBTQ Youth in the Face of HIV/AIDS," *Journal of Gay Lesbian Social Services* 21, nos. 2–3: 171–88; Lizzie Feidelson, "She Came to New York for the Vogue Ballroom Scene. She Found a Family," *New York Magazine*, May 30, 2019, www.nytimes.com; *Paris Is Burning*, directed by Jennie Livingston (Los Angeles: Off-White Productions, 1991); Joseph Cassara, *The House of Impossible Beauties: A Novel* (New York: HarperCollins, 2018); and Marlon Bailey, *Butch Queens up in Pumps: Gender, Performance, and Ballroom Culture in Detroit* (Ann Arbor: University of Michigan Press, 2013).

144 Eric Paulik, "Our Silence Will Not Protect Us: Supporting Black LGBTQ Youth," HuffPost, April 19, 2017, www.huffpost.com. For more, also see the GLSEN National School Climate Survey at glsen.org, particularly the section that details the experiences of "Black LGBTQ Students."

145 Jeannine Tang, "Contemporary Art and Critical Transgender Infrastructures," in *Trap Door: Trans Cultural Production and the Politics of Visibility*, ed. Reina Gossett, Eric A. Stanley, and Johanna Burton (Cambridge: MIT Press, 2017), 380.

146 "Pink Slip" and "Mother of the Year" depict Elektra's failed relationship with "daddy" and Blanca's rescue.

147 On the loss of elders, see Sarah Schulman, *The Gentrification of the Mind: Witness to a Lost Imagination* (Berkeley: University of California Press, 2012); Dana Rosenfeld, "The AIDS Epidemic's Lasting Impact on Gay Men," *British Academy*, February 19, 2018. www.thebritishacademy.ac.uk; Matthew Lopez, *The Inheritance* (London: Faber and Faber, 2019); and Jen Richards, "Jen Richards on Trans Media, Legacy, the Tipping Point, and Janet Mock," filmed on March 16, 2016, YouTube video, 4:59, posted March 20, 2016, www.youtube.com/watch?v= 9pYozbzJVVs.

148 *Pose*, season 2, episode 7, "Blow," directed by Jennie Livingston, aired July 30, 2019, on FX Productions, www.fxnetworks.com.

149 Ibid.

150 *Pose*, season 2, episode 10, "In My Heels," directed by Janet Mock, aired August 20, 2019, on FX Productions, www.fxnetworks.com.

151 Ibid.

152 In the pilot episode, Pray Tell tells Blanca and the newly forming House of Evangelista why they need to keep building a house from scratch. He instructs, "Houses are homes to all the little boys and girls who never had one, and they keep coming every day just as sure as the sun rises." This remark from the initial episode, set in 1987, becomes the closing epigraph for the "In My Heels" episode that closes season 2, which is set in 1991.

153 For a similar argument, see Tyner, *Violence in Capitalism*.

154 "Mother of the Year," "Acting Up," and "Blow" are examples of the dinner table as a structuring principle.

155 See "In My Heels" for the clearest demonstration of this thought process, though episodes as early as the pilot position Damon's dance talent as having communal value.

156 See "Butterfly/Cocoon" and "In My Heels" for the most revealing representations of Angel's modeling career and its impact on others.

157 *Pose*, season 1, episode 7, "Pink Slip," directed by Tina Mabry, aired July 15, 2018, on FX Productions, www.fxnetworks.com.

158 *Pose*, season 2, episode 7, "Blow," directed by Jennie Livingston, aired July 30, 2019, on FX Productions, www.fxnetworks.com; *Pose*, season 2, episode 8, "Revelations," directed by Steven Canals, aired August 6, 2019, on FX Productions, www .fxnetworks.com.

159 See "Blow" and "Revelations" for pointed examples of accountability with regard to sexual health, particularly with Ricky and Pray Tell.

160 *Pose*, season 2, episode 1, "Acting Up," directed by Gwyneth Horder-Payton, aired June 11, 2019, on FX Productions, www.fxnetworks.com.

161 On criticism of how LGBTQ+ rights progress remains exclusionary, see Roderick Ferguson, *Aberrations in Black: Toward a Queer of Color Critique* (Minneapolis: University of Minnesota Press, 2004); Ferguson, *One-Dimensional Queer*; Gossett, Stanley, and Burton, *Trap Door*; Johnson, *No Tea*; Ryan Conrad, *Against Equality: Queer Critiques of Gay Marriage* (Oakland: Against Equality Press, 2010); and Carlos Ball, *After Marriage Equality: The Future of LGBT Rights* (New York: New York University Press, 2016).

162 Berlanti, *Love, Simon.*

163 See Becky Albertalli, *Simon vs. the Homo Sapiens Agenda* (New York: Balzer + Bray, 2015).

164 See Wendy Brown, *Undoing the Demos: Neoliberalism's Stealth Revolution* (New York: Zone Books, 2015); Wendy Brown, "American Nightmare: Neoliberalism, Neoconservatism, and De-democratization," *Political Theory* 34, no. 6 (2006): 690–714; Lisa Duggan, *The Twilight of Equality? Neoliberalism, Cultural Politics, and the Attack on Democracy* (Boston: Beacon, 2003); and Antonio Vazquez-Arroyo, "Liberal Democracy and Neoliberalism: A Critical Juxtaposition," *New Political Science* 30, no. 2 (2008): 127–59.

165 Blanca showcases this clearly during the "Access" episode when she tries to claim her right to public space in a gay bar as a trans woman of color. Even though the gay community is no stranger to discrimination and stigmatization, they see Blanca as a barrier to their pursuit of progress. As a result, she is misgendered, shamed, and removed from the bar by force (and even state authority). When Blanca experiences rejection from gay cisgender guys (even a Black cisgender gay guy), the boundary-making forces of dignity become abundantly clear.

166 *Pose*, season 1, episode 5, "Mother's Day," directed by Silas Howard, aired July 1, 2018, on FX Productions, www.fxnetworks.com.

167 Ibid.

168 Ibid.

169 While the example in "Mother's Day" provides the strongest evidence of Blanca's reconceptualization of dignity, viewers can find other quieter examples of Blanca stressing the traditional boundaries that designate folks as either dignified or undignified. For instance, a conversation between Helena (the dean of dance) and Blanca in the episode titled "Giving and Receiving" reiterates Blanca's alternative understandings of dignity.

170 *Pose*, season 1, episode 2, "Access," directed by Ryan Murphy, aired June 10, 2018, on FX Productions, www.fxnetworks.com.

171 Ibid.

172 *Pose*, season 1, episode 3, "Giving and Receiving," directed by Nelson Cragg, aired June 17, 2018, on FX Productions, www.fxnetworks.com.

173 Ibid.

174 *Pose*, season 1, episode 7, "Pink Slip," directed by Tina Mabry, aired July 15, 2018, on FX Productions, www.fxnetworks.com.

175 *Pose*, season 1, episode 8, "Mother of the Year," directed by Gwyneth Horder-Payton, aired July 22, 2018, on FX Productions, www.fxnetworks.com.

176 Ibid.

177 Ibid.

178 See Blanca and Elektra's conversations in "Access" for a representation of Elektra's generational situatedness.

179 Elektra's conversations with Blanca and Candy in the first five episodes make Elektra's priorities abundantly clear. The pilot and "The Fever" join her comments in "Access" to display Elektra's ideas about success and her concerns about situating herself above the crowd.

180 *Pose*, season 1, episode 7, "Pink Slip," directed by Tina Mabry, aired July 15, 2018, on FX Productions, www.fxnetworks.com.

181 For more on the fetishization of trans women who have not had gender affirming procedures (particularly "bottom surgery"), see Mock, *Redefining Realness*; and Lady Chablis, *Hiding My Candy: The Autobiography of the Grand Empress of Savannah* (New York: Pocket Books, 1996).

182 Elektra's minor growth in "Mother's Day" and "Mother of the Year" quickly fade as her character moves into the beginning of season 2, particularly her behavior in "Acting Up" and "Worth It."

183 *Pose*, season 2, episode 3, "Butterfly/Cocoon," directed by Janet Mock, aired June 25, 2019, on FX Productions, www.fxnetworks.com.

184 Ibid.

185 *Pose*, season 2, episode 9, "Life's a Beach," directed by Gwyneth Horder-Payton, aired August 13, 2019, on FX Productions, www.fxnetworks.com; *Pose*, season 2, episode 10, "In My Heels," directed by Janet Mock, aired August 20, 2019, on FX Productions, www.fxnetworks.com.

186 Sara Ahmed, "An Affinity of Hammers," in *Trap Door: Trans Cultural Production and the Politics of Visibility*, ed. Reina Gossett, Eric A. Stanley, and Johanna Burton (Cambridge, MA: MIT Press, 2017), 221.

187 While Blanca serves as the paramount example of dignity rethought, her best friend, Pray Tell, joins her efforts. Serving as a key elder figure in the show's ballroom world, Pray Tell functions alongside Blanca's heart and example to keep the children in line. A key moment from him that exhibits his contribution to reconceptualizing dignity comes in the second episode of season 2, "Worth It." In this episode, Pray Tell welcomes the community to the Eros Ball and, in so doing, directly references dignity and what it means to him: "All right, All right, y'all. Welcome to the Eros Ball. . . . Tonight, we're celebrating passion and reveling in love and *sex*. And I'm talkin' about lust—you know, that sweet smell of new passion. And I'm talkin' about desire—and however that comes to you, I need you all to understand that you must treat yourselves with dignity because everyone in this room is deserving of love" (*Pose*, season 2, episode 2, "Worth It," directed by Gwyneth Horder-Payton, aired June 18, 2019, on FX Productions, www.fxnetworks.com). Similar to Blanca, for Pray Tell, dignity is something that

characters give themselves and something that is negotiated through the community. This works in direct contrast to the state's dignity ultimatum during this period of the HIV/AIDS crisis: clean yourselves up (restrain yourselves) or die. For Pray Tell, dignity does not involve a denial of excess or pleasure—he welcomes the community to get "nasty." For him, dignity is about protecting self and community through risk reduction with condom use.

188 Linda Xu, "From 'Transparent' to 'Pose' and Beyond: How Trans Writers Are Changing Hollywood's Script," *The Wrap*, August 23, 2018, www.thewrap.com; Robert Rorke, "'Pose' Writer Janet Mock's Trans Experience Frames the Series," *NY Post*, June 8, 2018, https://nypost.com; Mock, "'Pose' Writer."

189 Gossett, Stanley, and Burton, *Trap Door*, xviii.

190 Terry Gross, "On 'Pose,' Janet Mock Tells the Stories She Craved as a Young Trans Person," *NPR Fresh Air*, August 14, 2019, www.npr.org.

191 McDonald and Griffin-Gracy, "Cautious Living," 36.

192 Che Gossett, "Blackness and the Trouble of Trans Visibility," in *Trap Door: Trans Cultural Production and the Politics of Visibility*, ed. Reina Gossett, Eric A. Stanley, and Johanna Burton (Cambridge, MA: MIT Press, 2017), 187.

193 Katy Steinmetz, "The Transgender Tipping Point," *Time Magazine* 183, no. 22 (2014): 38–46.

194 We recognize the show's elision of transmasculine experiences and hope for more representation of transmasculine experiences in the show's future season(s).

195 Will Thorne, "'Pose' Renewed for Season 3 at FX," *Variety*, June 17, 2019, https://variety.com.

5. LIBERAL RULINGS FOR CONSERVATIVE ENDS

1 Donald Trump quoted in Eli Stokols, "Trump Says He's 'Fine' with Legalization of Same-Sex Marriage," *Politico*, November 13, 2016, www.politico.com.

2 *United States v. Windsor*, 570 U.S. 744 (2013); *Obergefell v. Hodges*, 576 U.S. _____ (2015) (slip opinion).

3 Republican Party Platforms, 2016 Republican Party Platform Online by Gerhard Peters and John T. Woolley, American Presidency Project, www.presidency.ucsb.edu (accessed January 2, 2020).

4 Neil Gorsuch quoted in Alex Bollinger, "Neil Gorsuch Said Same-Sex Marriage Is 'Absolutely Settled Law,'" lgbtqnation.com, March 22, 2017.

5 *Romer v. Evans*, 517 U.S. 620 (1996); *Lawrence v. Texas*, 539 U.S. 558 (2003). Note that *Romer* explicitly speaks of bisexuals in addition to gays and lesbians. *Lawrence*, *Windsor*, and *Obergefell* reference only gays and lesbians.

6 On changes in public support for same-sex marriage, see the first chapter of Brian F. Harrison and Melissa R. Michelson, *Listen, We Need to Talk: How to Change Attitudes about LGBT Rights* (New York: Oxford University Press, 2017). For a discussion of the mechanisms that might explain this opinion change, see Jeremiah J. Garretson, *The Path to Gay Rights: How Activism and Coming Out Changed Public Opinion* (New York: New York University Press, 2018).

7 Michele Gorman, "Schumer Urges Opposition to Gorsuch for Supreme Court," *Newsweek*, March 23, 2017.

8 Lydia Saad, "U.S. Abortion Attitudes Stable: No Consensus on Legality," Gallup .com, June 9, 2017.

9 The word *dignity* shows up at least twenty-three times in Brief for Petitioners, *James Obergefell et al. v. Richard Hodges, Director, Ohio Department of Health, et al.*, and *Britanni Henry, et al. v. Richard Hodges, Director of Ohio Department of Health, et al.*, on writ of certiorari to the United States Court of Appeals for the Sixth Circuit, No. 14-556, Susan L. Sommer, M. Currey Cook, and Omar Gonzalez-Pagan, Lambda Legal Defense and Education Fund Inc., Counsel for Henry Petitioners, James D. Esseks, Steven R. Shapiro, Joshua A. Block, Chase B. Strangio, Ria Tabacco Mar, Louise Melling, American Civil Liberties Union Foundation, Counsel for *Obergefell* Petitioners, Alphonse A. Gehardstein, Counsel of Record.

10 Even as Kennedy has used the term *dignity* in abortion rulings (see *Planned Parenthood v. Casey*, 505 U.S. 833 [1992]) and in gay rights and marriage equality readings, Yuvraj Joshi points out how the meaning of *dignity* has changed in significant ways:

> In *Casey*, "dignity" expressed respect for a woman's freedom to make choices about her pregnancy. *Casey* laid the foundation for *Lawrence v. Texas*, which similarly respected the freedom of choice of homosexual persons. Yet starting in *United States v. Windsor* and continuing in *Obergefell*, the narrative began to change. Dignity veered away from respect for the freedom to make personal and intimate choice without interference. . . . *Obergefell* shifts dignity's focus from respect for the freedom to choice toward the respectability of choices and choice makers. *Obergefell's* dignity is respectable in three ways. It depends on same-sex couples (1) choosing the heterosexual norm of marriage; (2) being and showing themselves to be worthy of marriage; and (3) being socially acceptable and accepted.

Yuvraj Joshi, "The Respectable Dignity of *Obergefell v. Hodges*," *The Circuit* 70 (2015): 117–18.

11 The judicial elaboration of dignity did not begin with the gay, lesbian, and bisexual rights jurisprudence forged by Justice Kennedy. As we discuss later in this chapter and as was mentioned in the introduction, dignity has been referenced in multiple jurisprudential traditions ranging from bodily integrity, such as the right to not be sterilized, to protections against cruel and unusual punishment. As Aharon Barak notes, "Only since the 1940s has the term 'dignity' been used frequently" in Supreme Court rulings, and while numerous justices have referenced dignity, it has been primarily relied upon by Justices Brennan and Kennedy (193). See Aharon Barak, *Human Dignity: The Constitutional Value and the Constitutional Right* (New York: Cambridge University Press, 2015), 199–208.

A right to dignity is far less developed in US jurisprudence compared to other post–World War democratic states. See Erin Daly, *Dignity Rights: Courts, Constitutions, and the Worth of the Human Person* (Philadelphia: University of Pennsylvania Press, 2013). Nevertheless, it has, through Kennedy's majority opinions in *Lawrence, Windsor, Obergefell,* and *Masterpiece,* been a dominant frame for gay, lesbian, and bisexual rights. In the first post-Kennedy LGBTQ+ rights cases, "dignity" does not appear in transcripts of oral argument (in either *Bostock v. Clayton County* or *R.G. & G.R. Harris Funeral Homes Inc. v. Equal Employment Opportunity Commission*; see www.supremecourt.gov [accessed May 6, 2020]). And the ruling in *Bostock,* which decided that employment discrimination against gay, lesbian, or transgender individuals violated the ban on sex discrimination in the 1964 Civil Rights Act, did not mention the word *dignity.* See *Bostock v. Clayton County, Georgia,* 590 U.S. _____ (2020) (slip opinion).

12 See this book's introduction for an assessment of the vagueness of the word *dignity.*

13 Jeffrey Rosen, "The Dangers of a Constitutional 'Right to Dignity,'" *Atlantic,* April 29, 2015, www.theatlantic.com (accessed July 22, 2019).

14 Leslie Meltzer Henry notes, "After a brief period of hibernation during the Burger and Rehnquist Courts, the use of dignity is once again on the rise. . . . Dignity is now more likely to appear in majority than in dissenting opinions, and as likely to be invoked by Justice Scalia as by Justice Ginsburg. Dignity's increasing popularity, however, does not signal agreement about what the term means. Instead, its importance, meaning, and function are commonly presupposed but rarely articulated." Leslie Meltzer Henry, "The Jurisprudence of Dignity," *University of Pennsylvania Law Review* 160 (2011): 171–72.

15 *Masterpiece Cakeshop v. Colorado Civil Rights Commission,* 584 U.S. ____ (2018) (slip opinion).

16 *Bostock v. Clayton County, Georgia,* 590 U.S. _____ (2020) (slip opinion). Dignity is only mentioned twice and only in dissent. Justice Alito uses the term at the end of his dissent when he acknowledges, "Today, many Americans know individuals who are gay, lesbian, or transgender and want them to be treated with the dignity, consideration, and fairness that everyone deserves." *Bostock v. Clayton County, Georgia,* 590 U.S. _____ (2020) (slip opinion), 54, J. Alito dissenting. Alito nevertheless dissents because he finds that Congress would need to alter Title VII to specify its protections for sexual orientation and gender identity; he contends the ruling constitutes judicial overreach. Justice Kavanaugh mentions the term through direct quotation of *Masterpiece*—"that gay and lesbian Americans 'cannot be treated as social outcasts or as inferior in dignity and worth.' *Masterpiece Cakeshop, Ltd. v. Colorado Civil Rights Comm'n,* 584 U. S. ____ (2018) (slip op., at 9)." *Bostock v. Clayton County, Georgia,* 590 U.S. _____ (2020) (slip opinion), 2, J. Kavanaugh

dissenting. While he claims that he fully agrees with this statement, he finds the *Bostock* ruling to be judicial overreach that violates the separation of powers.

17 Yuvraj Joshi, "Respectable Queerness," *Columbia Human Rights Law Review* 43, no. 2 (2012): 416.

18 Carl Stychin, *A Nation by Rights: National Cultures, Sexual Identity Politics, and the Discourse of Rights* (Philadelphia: Temple University Press, 1998).

19 Indeed, some scholars have contended that the twentieth-century history of gay and lesbian activism can be dichotomized between those who advocated reform and assimilation and those who advocated revolution and liberation. Seeking marriage recognition was a policy aim that fell within the former category. See Craig Rimmerman, *The Lesbian and Gay Movements: Assimilation or Liberation?*, 2nd ed. (New York: Routledge, 2014); and Marc Stein, *Rethinking the Gay and Lesbian Movement* (New York: Routledge, 2012).

20 That supporters of same-sex marriage have relied on a "just like you" or "love is love" argument and made use of *Loving v. Virginia* (1967), which struck down anti-miscegenation laws as unconstitutional, highlights how a colorblind approach to inclusion has crowded out a more critical approach, which could expose how marriage is grounded in heterosexism and patriarchal norms. As Julie Novkov cogently argues, "The more abstract, egalitarian approach of neutrally extending access to marriage to same-sex couples would simply let same-sex couples into a largely untransformed institution." Julie Novkov, "The Miscegenation/Same-Sex Marriage Analogy: What Can We Learn from Legal History," *Law and Social Inquiry* 33 (Spring 2008): 347.

21 See Carl Wittman, "A Gay Manifesto," 1970, http://library.gayhomeland.org. Queer critique positioned queerness as opposed to marriage. See Paula Ettelbrick, "Since When Is Marriage a Path to Liberation?," *Out/Look* 6 (1989): 14–16; Steven Seidman, "Identity and Politics in a 'Postmodern' Gay Culture: Some Historical and Conceptual Notes," in *Fear of a Queer Planet: Queer Politics and Social Theory*, ed. Michael Warner (Minneapolis: University of Minnesota Press, 1993): 105–42; Michael Warner, introduction to *Fear of a Queer Planet: Queer Politics and Social Theory*, ed. Michael Warner (Minneapolis: University of Minnesota Press, 1993), vii–xxxi; Lisa Duggan, "The New Homonormativity: The Sexual Politics of Neoliberalism," in *Materializing Democracy: Toward a Revitalized Cultural Politics*, ed. Russ Castronovo and Dana Nelson (Durham: Duke University Press, 2002): 175–94; and Michael Warner, *The Trouble with Normal: Sex, Politics, and the Ethics of Queer Life* (Cambridge, MA: Harvard University Press, 2000). See, generally, Mary Bernstein and Verta Taylor, "Marital Discord: Understanding the Contested Place of Marriage in the Lesbian and Gay Movement," in *The Marrying Kind? Debating Same-Sex Marriage within the Lesbian and Gay Movement* (Minneapolis: University of Minnesota Press, 2013).

22 See, generally, Joseph Nicholas DeFilippis, introduction to *Queer Activism after Marriage Equality*, ed. Joseph Nicholas DeFilippis, Michael W. Yarbrough, and Angela Jones (London: Routledge, 2018), 2.

23 Melissa Murray, "*Obergefell v. Hodges* and Nonmarriage Inequality," *California Law Review* 104 (2016): 1207–58; and Laura A. Rosenbury and Jennifer E. Rothman, "Sex in and out of Intimacy," *Emory Law Journal* 59 (2010): 809–68.

24 Joshi, "Respectable Queerness," 416.

25 See Nancy Cott, *Public Vows: A History of Marriage and the Nation* (Cambridge, MA: Harvard University Press, 2002); and Priscilla Yamin, *American Marriage: A Political Institution* (Philadelphia: University of Pennsylvania Press, 2012).

26 *Obergefell v. Hodges*, 576 U.S. ____ (2015) (slip opinion), 28.

27 Yasmin Nair, "Against Equality, against Marriage: An Introduction," in *Against Equality: Queer Revolution Not Mere Inclusion*, ed. Ryan Conrad (Edinburgh: AK Press, 2014), 18.

28 See Jaye Cee Whitehead, *The Nuptial Deal: Same-Sex Marriage and Neo-liberal Governance* (Chicago: University of Chicago Press, 2012).

29 Matthew Dean Hindman, *Political Advocacy and Its Interested Citizens: Neoliberalism, Postpluralism, and LGBT Organizations* (Philadelphia: University of Pennsylvania Press, 2019), 18.

30 See Dale Carpenter's discussion of how John Geddes Lawrence Jr. and Tyron Garner's relationship is reimagined by advocates and the justices in *Flagrant Conduct: The Story of Lawrence v. Texas* (New York: W. W. Norton, 2012).

31 See Novkov, "Miscegenation/Same-Sex Marriage." On how more substantive critique that attended to the histories and contexts of discrimination was abandoned by the Supreme Court and replaced by a colorblind and formal notion of equality, see Peggy Pascoe, "Miscegenation Law, Court Cases, and Ideologies of 'Race' in Twentieth-Century America," *Journal of American History* 83 (1996): 44–69; and Reva Siegel, "Equality Talk: Anti-subordination and Anti-classification Values in Constitutional Struggles over *Brown*," *Harvard Law Review* 117 (2004): 1470–1547.

32 Elizabeth J. Baia, "Akin to Madmen: A Queer Critique of the Gay Rights Cases," *Virginia Law Review* 104 (2018): 1043.

33 Noa Ben-Asher, "Conferring Dignity: The Metamorphosis of the Legal Homosexual," *Harvard Journal of Law and Gender* 37 (2014): 245.

34 Transcript of Oral Argument, *Obergefell*, 135 S. Ct. 2584 (No. 14-556), 4.

35 *Obergefell v. Hodges*, 576 U.S. ____ (2015) (slip opinion), 13 (emphasis added).

36 See Martha Nussbaum, *From Disgust to Humanity: Sexual Orientation and Constitutional Law* (New York: Oxford University Press, 2010).

37 Ben-Asher, "Conferring Dignity," 246.

38 *Obergefell v. Hodges*, 576 U.S. ____ (2015) (slip opinion), 3, 28.

39 Joshi, "Respectable Queerness," 122.

40 *Obergefell*, 135 S. Ct. at 2596; *United States v. Windsor*, 133 S. Ct. at 2681. Joshi, in "Respectable Queerness," makes a similar claim: "Kennedy implies that social acceptance is required for the legal protection of dignity" (123).

41 Joshi, "Respectable Dignity," 124.

42 See Bernadette Atuahene, "Dignity Takings and Dignity Restoration: Creating a New Theoretical Framework for Understanding Involuntary Property Loss and the Remedies Required," *Law and Social Inquiry* 41, no. 4 (Fall 2016): 796–823.

43 See Duggan, "New Homonormativity."

44 On how state authorities can shape the meaning of gay and lesbian identity, see Margot Canaday, *The Straight State: Sexuality and Citizenship in Twentieth-Century America* (Princeton: Princeton University Press, 2009).

45 *Obergefell v. Hodges*, 576 U.S. ____ (2015) (slip opinion), 15.

46 *Obergefell v. Hodges*, 576 U.S. ____ (2015) (slip opinion), 22, C. J. Roberts dissenting (citations omitted).

47 On the characteristics of suspect class, see *City of Cleburne v. Cleburne Living Center, Inc.*, 473 U.S. 432 (1985). For an extended conversation of this doctrine, see Sonu Bedi, *Beyond Race, Sex, and Sexual Orientation: Legal Equality without Identity* (New York: Cambridge University Press, 2013).

48 Richard H. Fallon Jr., *The Dynamic Constitution: An Introduction to American Constitutional Law and Practice*, 2nd ed. (New York: Cambridge University Press, 2013), 139–89.

49 See, generally, Siegel, "Equality Talk."

50 Joseph Lowndes, Julie Novkov, and Dorian Warren, "Race and American Political Development," in *Race and American Political Development*, ed. Joseph Lowndes, Julie Novkov, and Dorian Warren (New York: Routledge, 2008), 9.

51 See Elizabeth B. Cooper, "The Power of Dignity," *Fordham Law Review* 84, no. 1 (2015): 3–22.

52 *United States v. Windsor*, 570 U.S. 744 (2013), 793–94.

53 *Wright, et al. v State of Arkansas, et al.* (2014), 11.

54 One exception since *Romer* is *Boy Scouts of America et al. v. Dale*, 530 U.S. 640 (2000).

55 See, however, Kennedy's brief identification of gays and lesbians as having the elements of suspect class status but not applying higher scrutiny in *Obergefell*, as discussed later in this chapter.

56 See Bruce Ackerman, *We the People: The Civil Rights Revolution* (Cambridge, MA: Belknap Press of Harvard University Press, 2014); Dale Carpenter, "*Windsor* Products: Equal Protection from Animus," *The Supreme Court Review* 1 (2014): 183–86; Andrew Koppelman, "Beyond Levels of Scrutiny: *Windsor* and 'Bare Desire to Harm,'" *Case Western Review Law Review* 64, no. 3 (2014): 1045–72; Kenji Yoshino, "The Anti-humiliation Principle and Same-Sex Marriage," *Yale Law Journal* 123 (2014): 3076–3103; and Kenji Yoshino, "A New Birth of Freedom? *Obergefell v. Hodges*," *Harvard Law Review* 129 (2015): 147–79. Associating an

anti-harm principle with the motivation for *Obergefell* ignores how the decision's assumptions about what constitutes dignity—namely, adherence to heteronormative coupling—commit harm and make invisible members of LGBTQ communities. As Yuvraj Joshi has cogently argued, "*Obergefell's* reasoning inflicts its own dignitary harms. It affirms the dignity of married relationships, while dismissing the dignitary and material harms suffered by unmarried families. . . . *Obergefell* disregards the idea that different forms of loving and commitment might be entitled to equal dignity and respect" ("Respectable Dignity," 117–18). See also Ben-Asher, "Conferring Dignity."

57 Kimberlé W. Crenshaw, "Demarginalizing the Intersection of Race and Sex: A Black Feminist Critique of Antidiscrimination Doctrine, Feminist Theory and Antiracist Politics," *University of Chicago Legal Forum* 1 (1989): 151.

58 For a recent critique of suspect classification doctrine that provides a route for assessing claims of discrimination grounded in intersecting identities, see Devon W. Carbado and Kimberlé W. Crenshaw, "An Intersectional Critique of Tiers of Scrutiny: Beyond 'Either/Or' Approaches to Equal Protection," *Yale Law Journal* 129 (2019–20): 108–29.

59 Laurence H. Tribe, "Equal Dignity: Speaking Its Name," *Harvard Law Review Forum* 129 (2015): 16.

60 Emily Bazelon and Adam Liptak, "What's at Stake in the Supreme Court's Gay-Marriage Case," *New York Times Magazine*, April 28, 2015, www.nytimes.com (accessed May 6, 2020).

61 Ibid.

62 *Lawrence v. Texas*, 539 U.S. 558 (2003), 567.

63 *United States v. Windsor*, 570 U.S. 744 (2013), 800.

64 See David Harvey, *A Brief History of Neoliberalism* (New York: Oxford University Press, 2007).

65 *United States v. Carolene Products Co.*, 304 U.S. 144 (1938).

66 William N. Eskridge Jr., "Pluralism and Distrust: How Courts Can Support Democracy by Lowering the Stakes of Politics," *Yale Law Journal* 114 (April 2005): 1279–1328.

67 See Steven M. Teles, *The Rise of the Conservative Legal Movement: The Battle for Control of the Law* (Princeton: Princeton University Press, 2008); and Amanda Hollis-Brusky, *Ideas with Consequences: The Federalist Society and the Conservative Counterrevolution* (New York: Oxford University Press, 2015).

68 Stephen Skowronek, "The Reassociation of Ideas and Purposes: Racism, Liberalism, and the American Political Tradition," *American Political Science Review* 100, no. 3 (2006): 385–401. On multiple traditions, see Rogers M. Smith, "Beyond Tocqueville, Myrdal and Hartz: The Multiple Traditions in America," *American Political Science Review* 87 (September 1993): 549–66.

69 Skowronek uses the example of state self-determination as a critical illustration. A guiding principle of the US Southern slaveholding cause was transformed by an entrepreneurial President Woodrow Wilson to become a backbone of a proposed

liberal international order that would undergird the League of Nations and break up the Austro-Hungarian and Ottoman Empires, thereby enabling democracy to grow from the ashes of war.

70 Skowronek, "Reassociation of Ideas," 386.

71 Sonu Bedi, "How Constitutional Law Rationalizes Racism," *Polity* 42 (October 2010): 543; see also Adam Winkler, "Fatal in Theory and Strict in Fact: An Empirical Analysis of Strict Scrutiny in the Federal Courts," *Vanderbilt Law Review* 59 (2006): 793–871.

72 Peggy Pascoe, *What Comes Naturally: Miscegenation Law and the Making of Race in America* (New York: Oxford University Press, 2009), 287.

73 Ibid., 305.

74 Sonu Bedi, "Collapsing Suspect Class with Suspect Classification: Why Strict Scrutiny is Too Strict and Maybe Not Strict Enough," *Georgia Law Review* 47, no. 2 (2013): 301–68.

75 *City of Richmond v. J.A. Croson Company*, 488 U.S. 469 (1989).

76 Ibid., 495.

77 Ibid., 519, J. Kennedy concurring.

78 Ibid., 521, J. Scalia concurring.

79 Ibid., 522, J. Marshall dissenting.

80 Ibid., 522–23.

81 Ibid., 525.

82 Ibid., 526.

83 Ibid., 561.

84 *Adarand Constructors Inc. v. Peña*, 515 U.S. 200 (1995).

85 Ibid., 201.

86 It also resonates with Gorsuch's assertion, offered during his confirmation hearings and discussed later in this chapter, that he sees individuals as persons, not as members of particular classes or groups.

87 On creative syncretism, see Gerald Berk, Dennis Galvan, and Victoria Hattam, eds., *Political Creativity: Reconfiguring Institutional Order and Change* (Philadelphia: University of Pennsylvania Press, 2013).

88 Barak, *Human Dignity*, 12.

89 Vicki C. Jackson, "Constitutional Dialogue and Human Dignity: States and Transnational Constitutional Discourse," *Montana Law Review* 65 (2004): 17; Neomi Rao, "On the Use and Abuse of Dignity in Constitutional Law," *Columbia Journal of European Law* 14 (Spring 2008): 202; Barak, *Human Dignity*, 206.

90 Barak, *Human Dignity*, 206.

91 Adam Liptak, "'Equal Dignity': 5-4 Ruling Makes Same-Sex Marriage a Right Nationwide," *New York Times*, June 27, 2015.

92 *Obergefell v. Hodges*, 576 U.S. ____ (2015) (slip opinion), 28.

93 *United States v. Windsor*, 570 U.S. 744 (2013), 770.

94 *Romer v. Evans*, 517 U.S. 620 (1996), 624.

95 Ibid.

96 Ibid., 632.

97 Ibid.

98 Ibid., 635.

99 David L. Eng, *The Feeling of Kinship: Queer Liberalism and the Racialization of Intimacy* (Durham: Duke University Press, 2010), 17, 41.

100 *Loving* contained an equal protection component *and* a fundamental rights component. The state law banning interracial marriage under review in *Loving* violated equal protection because the law only maintained white supremacy, and the state's claim that it treated the races equally inasmuch as it banned each from marrying members of the race did not meet the standard or meaning of equal protection. As marriage constituted a fundamental right, the ban also violated a basic due process consideration.

101 *Lawrence v. Texas*, 539 U.S. 558 (2003), 574–75.

102 *Bowers v. Hardwick*, 478 U.S. 186 (1986).

103 *Lawrence v. Texas*, 539 U.S. 558 (2003), 586, J. Scalia dissenting.

104 *Lawrence v. Texas*, 539 U.S. 558 (2003), 567.

105 *United States v. Windsor*, 570 U.S. 744 (2013), 763.

106 Ibid., 768.

107 Ibid.

108 Ibid., 769.

109 Ibid., 770.

110 Ibid., 721.

111 Ibid., 722.

112 Ibid., 725–26.

113 *Obergefell v. Hodges*, 576 U.S. _____ (2015) (slip opinion), 22–23.

114 Ibid., 3.

115 Ibid., 6, 7, 10, 13, 26.

116 Department of Justice, "Statement of the Attorney General on Litigation Involving the Defense of Marriage Act," www.justice.gov (accessed June 13, 2020).

117 Department of Justice, "Attorney General Loretta E. Lynch Delivers Remarks at Press Conference Announcing Complaint against the State of North Carolina to Stop Discrimination against Transgender Individuals," May 9, 2016, www.justice .gov (accessed June 13, 2020).

118 Ibid.

119 The Obama-era rule interprets guarantees for equal treatment by sex in federal law to include sexual orientation and gender identity. Sex discrimination has long been understood by the Supreme Court and executive branch agencies to be grounded in gender stereotyping. Consequently, insofar as gay and trans individuals' challenges to gender stereotypes or discrimination against them are based in their stereotype transgression, bans on sex discrimination can be inclusive. The Trump administration rejects this reading. The director of the Office of Civil

Rights within HHS, Roger Severino, referred to the meaning of "sex" in the overly narrow way that has not comported with earlier understandings of the Court or the executive branch: "We're going back to the plain meaning of those terms, which is based on biological sex." Severino quoted in Selena Simmons-Duffin, "Transgender Health Protections Reversed by Trump Administration," NPR.org, June 12, 2020, www.npr.org (accessed June 13, 2020).

120 Severino quoted in Simmons-Duffin, "Transgender Health Protections."

121 See Keith Whittington, "Taking What They Give Us: Explaining the Court's Federalism Offensive," *Duke Law Journal* 51, no. 1 (2001): 477–520; Cornell W. Clayton and J. Mitchell Pickerill, "Guess What Happened on the Way to Revolution? Precursors to the Supreme Court's Federalism Revolution," *Publius: The Journal of Federalism* 34, no. 3 (2004): 85–114.

122 See Jack M. Balkin and Sanford Levinson, "Understanding the Constitutional Revolution," *Yale Law Journal* 87, no. 6 (2001): 1045–1109; Joseph Lowndes, Julie Novkov, and Dorian Warren, eds., *Race and American Political Development* (New York: Routledge, 2008); and Michael Avery, *We Dissent: Talking Back to the Rehnquist Court, Eight Cases That Subverted Civil Liberties and Civil Rights* (New York: New York University Press, 2009).

123 See Teles, *Rise of the Conservative*; Amanda Hollis-Brusky, "Support Structures and Constitutional Change: Teles, Southworth, and the Conservative Legal Movement," *Law and Social Inquiry* 36 (Spring 2011): 516–36; and Thomas M. Keck, "The Reagan Revolution to the Present," in *The Oxford Handbook of the U.S. Constitution*, ed. Mark Tushnet, Mark A. Graber, and Sanford Levinson (New York: Oxford University Press, 2015): 113–33.

124 Jacob Pramuk, "Neil Gorsuch: Supreme Court Has Said Same-Sex Marriage Is 'Protected by the Constitution,'" cnbc.com, March 21, 2017, www.cnbc.com.

125 See also Reginald C. Oh, "A Critical Linguistic Analysis of Equal Protection Doctrine: Are Whites a Suspect Class?," *Temple Political and Civil Rights Law Review* 13 (Spring 2004): 583–610.

126 *Stenberg v. Carhart*, 530 U.S. 914 (2000).

127 Ibid., 962, J. Kennedy dissenting.

128 *Gonzales v. Carhart*, 550 U.S. 124 (2007).

129 Ibid., 157.

130 David D. Meyer, "*Gonzales v. Carhart* and the Hazards of Muddled Scrutiny," *Journal of Law and Policy* 17, no. 1 (2008): 59.

131 *Gonzales v. Carhart*, 127 S. Ct. 1610, 1635 (2007).

132 Joanna Grossman and Linda McClain, "*Gonzales v. Carhart*: How the Supreme Court's Validation of the Federal Partial-Birth Abortion Ban Act Affects Women's Constitutional Liberty and Equality: Part Two in a Two-Part Series," *Findlaw*, May 7, 2007, https://supreme.findlaw.com.

133 *J.E.B. v. Alabama ex rel. T.B.*, 511 U.S. 127 (1994), 152.

134 *Rice v. Cayetano*, 528 U.S. 495 (2000), 962.

135 *Parents Involved in Community Schools v. Seattle School District No. 1*, 551 U.S. 701 (2007), 797.

136 As Kenji Yoshino notes, to designate a suspect class may put the Court into an uncomfortable position of "picking favorites among groups." By resorting to dignity, the Court avoids this challenge. Kenji Yoshino, *Covering: The Hidden Assault on Our Civil Rights* (New York: Random House, 2006), 188.

137 See Frank Colucci, *Justice Kennedy's Jurisprudence: The Full and Necessary Meaning of Liberty* (Lawrence: University Press of Kansas, 2009); Anne Jelliff, "Catholic Values, Human Dignity, and the Moral Law in the United States Supreme Court: Justice Anthony Kennedy's Approach to the Constitution," *Albany Law Review* 76, no. 1 (2012): 335–65; and Samuel Moyn, "The Secret History of Constitutional Dignity," *Yale Human Rights and Development Journal* 17, no. 1 (2014): 39–73.

138 See Lee Epstein and Jeffrey Segal, *Advice and Consent: The Politics of Judicial Appointments* (New York: Oxford University Press, 2005).

139 This passage in *Bowers* is a quotation of an earlier statement by Justice Stevens offered in *Fitzgerald v. Porter Memorial Hospital* (cert. denied), 425 U.S. 916 (1976); and *Bowers v. Hardwick*, 478 U.S. 186 (1986), 215.

140 Reporting on that rule by Simmons-Duffin summarized its broad impact: "The Trump rule makes changes to gender-based discrimination protections beyond Section 1557 of the ACA; it affects regulations pertaining to access to health insurance, for example, including cost-sharing, health plan marketing and benefits. The rule could also mean that those seeking an abortion could be denied care if performing the procedure violates the provider's moral or religious beliefs." Simmons-Duffin, "Transgender Health Protections."

141 *Bostock v. Clayton County, Georgia*, 590 U.S. _____ (2020) (slip opinion), 2.

142 *Hurley v. Irish American* Gay, Lesbian, and Bisexual Group of Boston, 515 U.S. 557 (1995) (ruling that a private organization could exclude a group from participating in a parade under the First Amendment, as the parade constitutes expressive conduct); and *Boy Scouts of America et al. v. Dale*, 530 U.S. 640 (2000) (ruling that a private organization could exclude a gay person from membership under the First Amendment given that the exclusion falls within its expressive association).

143 *Masterpiece Cakeshop v. Colorado Civil Rights Commission*, 584 U.S. _____ (2018) (slip opinion).

144 Ibid., 1–2.

145 Ibid., 9.

146 *Obergefell v. Hodges*, 576 U.S. _____ (2015) (slip opinion), 27.

147 *Masterpiece Cakeshop v. Colorado Civil Rights Commission*, 584 U.S. _____ (2018) (slip opinion), 9.

148 Ibid.

149 Ibid., 10.

150 Ibid., 12.

151 Bazelon and Liptak, "What's at Stake."

152 In this way, Kennedy's argument parallels ideas offered by Rogers Smith. In Smith's estimation, a resolution of the dispute in *Masterpiece* for the same-sex couple would endorse a particular version of the American experiment (that which values equality and progressive inclusion) at the expense of another version of that experiment (that which values liberty). Of course, this celebration of pluralism leads to the denigration of the dignity of one side of the conflict depending on how the substantive resolution is reached. Perhaps recognizing this quandary, Smith falls back on principles of pluralism that speak more to the processes of argumentation than to the outcomes of argument: "I believe that if Americans see themselves as a people defined by the project of securing the Declaration of Independence's rights and liberties, ultimately for all persons, of all colors, everywhere, they can find a sense of shared moral purpose that may enable them to work through their differences." This statement defers the question at stake, instead expressing faith in democratic deliberation that might also allow for avoidance under the guise of policy experimentation. Smith marks out the parameters of pluralism but ultimately provides no sense of how the pluralist conversation or argument must or should be resolved. Kennedy performs similarly in *Masterpiece*. See Rogers Smith, "To Secure the Blessings of Liberty: Sharing Stories of American Civic Purposes," *Cultivating Virtuous Citizenship: A Law and Liberty Symposium*, April 3, 2018, https://old.lawliberty.org (accessed May 6, 2020).

153 Ibid., 12–13.

154 Ibid., 13.

155 See William N. Eskridge Jr., "Noah's Curse: How Religion Often Conflates Status, Belief, and Conduct to Resist Antidiscrimination Norms," *Georgia Law Review* 45, no. 3 (Spring 2011): 657–720; and James M. Oleske Jr., "The Evolution of Accommodation: Comparing the Unequal Treatment of Religious Objections to Interracial and Same-Sex Marriages," *Harvard Civil Rights-Civil Liberties Law Review* 50, no. 1 (Winter 2015): 99–152.

156 On dignity as inherent in the Christian or Kantian traditions, see Andrea Sangiovanni, *Humanity without Dignity: Moral Equality, Respect, and Human Rights* (Cambridge, MA: Harvard University Press, 2017), 27–60.

157 *Masterpiece Cakeshop v. Colorado Civil Rights Commission*, 584 U.S. ____ (2018) (slip opinion), 18.

158 Adam Liptak, "Civil Rights Law Protects Gay and Transgender Workers, Supreme Court Rules," *New York Times*, June 15, 2020, www.nytimes.com (accessed June 15, 2020). *Bostock* only spoke to discrimination in employment. It did not speak to discrimination in public accommodation (the issue at stake in *Masterpiece*). One way to think about *Bostock* is this: you can no longer be fired by a bakery for being LGBTQ+, but that bakery may still deny you the ability to purchase a cake.

159 *Bostock* was combined with *Altitude Express, Inc., et al. v. Zarda* 590 U.S. ____ (2020) and *R.G. & G.R. Harris Funeral Homes Inc. v. Equal Employment Opportunity Commission* 590 U.S. ____ (2020).

160 *Bostock v. Clayton County, Georgia*, 590 U.S. _____ (2020) (slip opinion), 32
(citations omitted).

161 Neither route that Gorsuch laid out is fully convincing. Constitutional requirements, as higher law, negate statutory stipulations. Nevertheless, a case of
employment discrimination may invoke a Fourteenth Amendment claim to equal
protection, and when a First Amendment position conflicts with a Fourteenth
Amendment one, it's not obvious which should prevail, although the former may
if strict scrutiny (applied to a fundamental right to religious belief) trumps intermediate scrutiny (perhaps applied to discrimination on the basis of sexual orientation and/or gender identity). Even less clear is why RFRA should be considered
more of a super-statute than the 1964 Civil Rights Act.

162 Tim Dean, *Unlimited Intimacy: Reflections on the Subculture of Barebacking* (Chicago: University of Chicago Press, 2009), 197.

163 *Parents Involved in Community Schools v. Seattle School District No. 1*, 551 U.S. 701
(2007).

164 Lowndes, Novkov, and Warren, *Race*, 10. Roberts ends his decision for the
majority in *Parents Involved* with the statement, "The way to stop discrimination
on the basis of race is to stop discriminating on the basis of race." *Parents Involved
in Community Schools v. Seattle School District No. 1*, 551 U.S. 701 [2007], 749–50.

165 Lowndes, Novkov, and Warren, *Race*, 10.

166 Importantly, *Bostock* resolves the matter of discrimination of employment, but
that decision came after Kennedy departed the Court, and the majority decision
by Gorsuch is not premised on dignity.

6. IS DIGNITY A DEAD END?

1 *Lawrence v. Texas*, 539 U.S. 558 (2003); *United States v. Windsor*, 570 U.S. 744
(2013); *Obergefell v. Hodges*, 576 U.S. _____ (2015) (slip opinion); *Masterpiece Cakeshop v. Colorado Civil Rights Commission*, 584 U.S. _____ (2018) (slip opinion).

2 See Yuvraj Joshi, "The Respectable Dignity of *Obergefell v. Hodges*," *California Law
Review Circuit* 6 (2015): 117–25, for a discussion of the dual meaning of dignity as
either respect or respectability in this jurisprudential line.

3 *Obergefell v. Hodges*, 576 U.S. _____ (2015) (slip opinion), 2, J. Thomas dissenting.

4 Polyamory is a form of consensual non-monogamy with either cross-sex or
same-sex participants. By CNM, we mean those relationships involving multiple
partners who have consented to emotional and/or sexual non-exclusivity. See
T. D. Conley, A. C. Moors, J. L. Matsick, et al., "The Fewer the Merrier? Assessing
Stigma Surrounding Consensually Non-monogamous Romantic Relationships,"
Analyses of Social Issues and Public Policy 13, no. 1 (2013): 1–30.

5 See Mark Goldfeder, *Legalizing Plural Marriage: The Next Frontier in Family Law*
(Waltham: Brandeis University Press, 2017), 1–2; Ronald C. Den Otter, *In Defense
of Plural Marriage* (New York: Cambridge University Press, 2015); Deborah
Anapol, *Polyamory in the Twenty-First Century: Love and Intimacy with Multiple
Partners* (Latham, MD: Rowman and Littlefield, 2010); and D. Marisa Black,

"Beyond Child Brides: Polygamy, Polyamory, Unique Familial Constructions, and the Law," *Journal of Law and Family Studies* 8 (2006): 498.

6 See Joshi, "Respectable Dignity."

7 *Lawrence v. Texas*, 539 U.S. 558 (2003), 579, 568.

8 Joshi, "Respectable Dignity," 118.

9 Connor M. Ewing, "Dignity and America's Multiple Constitutional Tradition," presented at the Law and Society Association 2019 conference, Washington, DC, May 2019. Paper on file with authors.

10 *United States v. Windsor*, 570 U.S. 744 (2013), 770.

11 Ibid., 766, 772.

12 Ibid., 772.

13 Ibid., 792.

14 Ewing, "Dignity," 13.

15 *Obergefell v. Hodges*, 576 U.S. _____ (2015) (slip opinion), 3.

16 Ibid.

17 Ibid., 4.

18 Ibid., 28.

19 Ibid., 13.

20 Ibid., 28.

21 Ibid.

22 Ibid., 14.

23 Quoted in Joyce Purnick, "City Closes Bar Frequented by Homosexuals Citing Sexual Activity Linked to AIDS," *New York Times*, November 8, 1985.

24 One might wonder whether Justice Kennedy has ever watched an episode of *The Golden Girls* or *Sex and the City*, which both celebrate kinship and family forms beyond romantic love and marriage.

25 Ewing suggests that whereas *Windsor* posits a positive capacity for the state to grant dignity, *Obergefell* retreats to a more limited conception of state power and dignity as innate. Ewing, "Dignity," 17.

26 Clifford Rosky, "Same-Sex Marriage Litigation and Children's Right to Be Queer," *GLQ: A Journal of Lesbian and Gay Studies* 22, no. 4 (2016): 542.

27 In both cases, governments (the federal government in *Windsor* and the state government in *Obergefell*) are denying recognition of marriage to same-sex couples.

28 Indeed, Thomas's notion of dignity as innate would seem to, at least in part, meet some of the objections raised by Noa Ben-Asher, "Conferring Dignity: The Metamorphosis of the Legal Homosexual," *Harvard Journal of Law and Gender* 37 (2014): 243–84, which is discussed in chapter 5.

29 *Obergefell v. Hodges*, 576 U.S. _____ (2015) (slip opinion), 10, C. J. Roberts dissenting.

30 See, generally, Alexander M. Bickel, *The Least Dangerous Branch: The Supreme Court at the Bar of Politics*, 2nd ed. (New Haven: Yale University Press, 1986); and John Hart Ely, *Democracy and Distrust: A Theory of Judicial Review* (Cambridge, MA: Harvard University Press, 1980). But what are the metrics of judicial overreach? For example, by the time of *Obergefell*, majorities of the US public were in

favor of same-sex marriage, and a majority of states had recognized it, so was the Court's ruling activist? See Stephen M. Engel, *Fragmented Citizens: The Changing Landscape of Gay and Lesbian Lives* (New York: New York University Press, 2016), particularly chapters 6 and 7.

31 See Christopher R. Leslie, "Dissenting from History: The False Narratives of the *Obergefell* Dissents," *Indiana Law Journal* 92, no. 3 (Summer 2017): 1027–30.

32 See Steven M. Teles, *The Rise of the Conservative Legal Movement: The Battle for Control of the Law* (Princeton: Princeton University Press, 2008); and Stephen Skowronek, *The Politics Presidents Make: Leadership from John Adams to Bill Clinton* (Cambridge, MA: Belknap Press of Harvard University Press, 1997), chapter 8.

33 *Obergefell v. Hodges*, 576 U.S. ____ (2015), 2, J. Thomas dissenting. This critique echoes Thomas's long-standing criticism of substantive due process. See, for example, Thomas's concurrence in *MacDonald v. City of Chicago*, 561 U.S. 742 (2010).

34 See Bickel, *Least Dangerous Branch*. See also Mark Graber, "The Nonmajoritarian Difficulty: Legislative Deference to the Judiciary," *Studies in American Political Development* 7 (Spring 1993): 35–73.

35 On why substantive due process is controversial, see Richard H. Fallon Jr., *The Dynamic Constitution: An Introduction to American Constitutional Law and Practice*, 2nd ed. (New York: Cambridge University Press, 2013), 111–17, 207–14. For discussion of how *Obergefell* falls within the substantive due process doctrine and a critique of the dissenter's position, see Leslie, "Dissenting from History," 1031–35. See also Bradley C. S. Watson, "Reclaiming the Rule of Law after *Obergefell*," *National Review*, July 9, 2015, www.nationalreview.com (accessed July 22, 2019).

36 The distinction between negative and positive liberty arises in Isaiah Berlin's "Two Conceptions of Liberty" (1958), which defines negative freedom as the right to be left alone and positive freedom as the right to self-determination. See Isaiah Berlin, *The Proper Study of Mankind*, ed. Henry Hardy and Roger Hausheer (New York: Farrar, Straus, and Giroux, 1997). See also Frank B. Cross, "The Error of Positive Rights," *UCLA Law Review* 48 (2001): 857–924. For a fuller discussion of the positive freedom tradition in US constitutional tradition, see Emily Zackin, *Looking for Rights in All the Wrong Places: Why State Constitutions Contain America's Positive Rights* (Princeton: Princeton University Press, 2013).

37 *Obergefell v. Hodges*, 576 U.S. ____ (2015) (slip opinion), 6, J. Thomas dissenting.

38 The use of *persons* here instead of *citizens* is deliberate, as due process protections apply to persons more broadly and beyond the narrower category of citizens.

39 See Engel, *Fragmented Citizens*.

40 See Douglas NeJaime, "Marriage Equality and the New Parenthood," *Harvard Law Review* 129 (2016): 1185–1266; Evan Wolfson, *Why Marriage Matters: America, Equality and Gay People's Right to Marry* (New York: Simon and Schuster 2004); and Courtney G. Joslin, "Travel Insurance: Protecting Lesbian and Gay Parent Families Across State Lines," *Harvard Law and Policy Review* 4 (2010): 31–48.

41 *Obergefell v. Hodges*, 576 U.S. ____ (2015) (slip opinion), 10, J. Thomas dissenting.

42 Engel, in *Fragmented Citizens*, refers to the status of gays and lesbians in the United States as "fragmented citizenship" to describe how that status is contingent on time, location, and the governing authority with which they are interacting. On challenges faced by same-sex couples particularly related to parenting, see Carlos A. Ball, *The Right to Be Parents: LGBT Families and the Transformation of Parenthood* (New York: New York University Press, 2012). And for an incisive analysis of how race intersects with sexuality such that same-sex, particularly lesbian, families remain invisible to cultural and political authorities and thus the challenges faced by these families both within their communities and in their relationship to regulatory and legal power, see Mignon R. Moore, *Invisible Families: Gay Identities, Relationships, and Motherhood among Black Women* (Berkeley: University of California Press, 2011).

43 Leslie, "Dissenting from History," 1009.

44 Ibid., 1035–56.

45 *Obergefell v. Hodges*, 576 U.S. ____ (2015) (slip opinion), 17, J. Thomas dissenting.

46 Ibid., 16, J. Thomas dissenting. As Ewing has aptly summarized, Thomas's dissent boils down to the claim that "because dignity is innate, it cannot be conferred by government; as a corollary, dignity cannot be withdrawn by government." Ewing, "Dignity," 6.

47 *Obergefell v. Hodges*, 576 U.S. ____ (2015) (slip opinion), 17, J. Thomas dissenting.

48 Bernadette Atuahene, *We Want What's Ours: Learning from South Africa's Land Restitution Program* (New York: Oxford University Press, 2014), 3. See also Andrew W. Kahrl, "Unconscionable: Tax Delinquency Sales as a Form of Dignity Taking," *Chicago-Kent Law Review* 92, no. 1 (2017): 905–35; and Matthew Patrick Shaw, "Creating the Urban Educational Desert through School Closures and Dignity Taking," *Chicago-Kent Law Review* 92, no. 1 (2017): 1087–1113.

49 See Jamil Smith, "Clarence Thomas's Disgraceful Definition of Human Dignity," *New Republic*, June 26, 2015, https://newrepublic.com (accessed July 12, 2019); See also Alison Griswold, "Read the Most Brutal Paragraph from Clarence Thomas' Same-Sex Marriage Dissent," *Slate*, June 26, 2015, https://slate.com (accessed July 12, 2019); and Lev Raphael, "Clarence Thomas's Judicial Cruelty," HuffPost, June 28, 2015, www.huffpost.com (accessed July 12, 2019). George Takei penned a direct rebuttal of Thomas's position. George Takei, "George Takei to Clarence Thomas: Denying Our Rights Denies Our Dignity," MSNBC.com, July 1, 2015, www.msnbc.com (accessed July 12, 2019).

50 Atuahene, *We Want What's Ours*, 4.

51 Leslie, "Dissenting from History," 1057.

52 *Lawrence v. Texas*, 539 U.S. 558 (2003), 589–90.

53 Ibid., 604–5.

54 *Obergefell v. Hodges*, 576 U.S. ____ (2015) (slip opinion), 20–21, C. J. Roberts dissenting.

55 *Obergefell v. Hodges*, 576 U.S. ____ (2015) (slip opinion), 27 (emphasis added).

56 See Andrew March, "What Lies beyond Same-Sex Marriage? Marriage, Reproductive Freedom and Future Persons in Liberal Public Justification," *Journal of
   Applied Philosophy* 27, no. 1 (2010): 39–58; and Andrew March, "Is There a Right to
   Polygamy? Marriage, Equality, and Subsidizing Families in Liberal Public Justification," *Journal of Moral Philosophy* 8 (2011): 346–72.

57 Laurence H. Tribe, *American Constitutional Law*, 2nd ed. (New York: Foundation Press, 1988), 521–28; Sanford Levinson, "The Meaning of Marriage: Thinking
   about Polygamy," *San Diego Law Review* 42 (2005): 1049–58.

58 Nussbaum argues that polygamy (one man with more than one woman) may
   be acceptable if women can also marry more than one man (polyandry). See Martha C. Nussbaum, *Women and Human Development: The Capabilities Approach*
   (New York: Cambridge University Press, 2000), 230.

59 Sarah Song, *Justice, Gender, and the Politics of Multiculturalism* (New York: Cambridge University Press, 2007), 162.

60 Den Otter, *In Defense*, 19 (emphasis added).

61 Goldfeder, *Legalizing Plural Marriage*, 7.

62 Ibid.

63 Den Otter, *In Defense*, 19–28.

64 Sonu Bedi, *Beyond Race, Sex, and Sexual Orientation: Legal Equality without
   Identity* (New York: Cambridge University Press, 2013), 224.

65 Den Otter, *In Defense*, 21–22.

66 Michael Sandel, *Justice: What's the Right Thing to Do?* (New York: Macmillan,
   2010), 257.

67 Tamara Metz, *Untying the Knot: Marriage, the State, and the Case for Their
   Divorce* (Princeton: Princeton University Press, 2010), 89.

68 *Maynard v. Hill*, 125 U.S. 190 (1888), 213 (emphasis added).

69 For example, Michel Foucault conceptualized urban gay bathhouses in similar
   terms, as "laboratories of sexual experimentation" where "the idea is to make use
   of every part of the body as a sex-instrument." Michel Foucault, "Sexual Choice,
   Sexual Act," in *Foucault Live. Interviews 1961–1984* (New York: Semiotext(e),
   1996), 330, 331. Gayle Rubin's canonical work has argued that heteronormativity is
   a systematized privileging not only of heterosexuality but also of monogamy, pri-
   vacy, couplehood, and marriage. Gayle Rubin, "Thinking Sex: Notes for a Radical
   Theory of the Politics of Sexuality," in *Pleasure and Danger*, ed. C. S. Vance
   (London: Pandora, 1992), 267–319. On heteronormativity as hegemony, see Anna
   Marie Smith, *New Right Discourse: On Race and Sexuality* (New York: Cambridge
   University Press, 1994); and Anna Marie Smith, *Laclau and Mouffe: The Radical
   Democratic Imaginary* (London: Routledge, 1998).

70 Yet realization of any transgressive potential for poly relationships requires not
   only the possibilities of "freedom of choice" as espoused by Foucault but also
   critical attention to power relations within poly relationships that include raced,
   gendered, classed, and body-image concerns. See Christian Klesse, *The Spectre of*

Promiscuity: Gay Male and Bisexual Non-monogamies and Polyamories (Hampshire, England: Ashgate, 2007), 16–17.

71 Ibid., especially 148–51. On gay, lesbian, or queer erotics as having the potential to resist heteronormativity in the ways proposed by Foucault, see Mark Blasius, *Gay and Lesbian Politics: Sexuality and the Emergence of a New Ethic* (Philadelphia: Temple University Press, 1994); and Michael Warner, *The Trouble with Normal: Sex, Politics, and the Ethics of Queer Life* (New York: Free Press, 1999).

72 Nathan Rambukkana, *Fraught Intimacies: Non/Monogamy in the Public Sphere* (Vancouver: UBC Press, 2015), 6.

73 For a listing of representations of non-monogamy in film, on television, in print, in digital space, and in academic scholarship, see Rambukkana, *Fraught Intimacies*, 6–8. See also Den Otter, *In Defense*, 14–16.

74 See Gillian Calder and Lori G. Beaman, eds., *Polygamy's Rights and Wrongs: Perspectives on Harm, Family and Law* (Vancouver: UBC Press, 2014); Jin Haritaworn, Chin-ju Lin, and Christian Kless, eds., *Sexualities: Special Issue on Polyamory* 9, no. 5 (2006); Christian Klesse, "Polyamory: Intimate Practice, Identity, or Sexual Orientation," *Sexualities* 12, nos. 1/2 (2014): 81–99; and Elisabeth Sheff, "Polyamorous Families, Same-Sex Marriage, and the Slippery Slope," *Journal of Contemporary Ethnography* 40, no. 5 (2011): 487–520. For an excellent review of scholarship on multipartner relationships, see Christian Klesse, "Theorizing Multi-partner Relationships and Sexualities—Recent Work on Non-monogamy and Polyamory," *Sexualities* 21, no. 7 (2018): 1109–24.

75 For example, Scruff allows users to mark their relationship status as single, dating, in a relationship, partnered, engaged, married, open relationship, polyamorous relationship, and widowed.

76 For example, monthly social gatherings are hosted in Brooklyn by the group Tableaux. Olivia Goldhill, "Polyamorous Sex Is the Most Quietly Revolutionary Political Weapon in the United States," *Quartz*, December 20, 2018, https://qz.com (accessed August 12, 2019).

77 Mimi Schippers, "The Monogamous Couple, Gender Hegemony, and Polyamory," in *Gender Reckonings: New Social Theory and Research*, ed. James W. Messerschmidt, Patricia Yancey Martin, Michael A. Messner, and Raewyn Connell (New York: New York University Press, 2018), 319.

78 Anaguedes1, "'Sense8': Why Kala and Wolfgang's Ending Matters," Hypable, June 12, 2018, www.hypable.com (accessed August 16, 2019).

79 At the same time, this critic also noted that the series *You Me Her* "shows a traditionally male fantasy: being in a relationship with two women" and therefore praises *Sense8* for representing the more transgressive formulation of one woman with two men.

80 Lital Pascar, "From Homonormativity to Polynormativity: Representing Consensual Non-monogamy," in *Queer Families and Relationships after Marriage*

Equality, ed. Michael W. Yarbrough, Angela Jones, and Joseph Nicholas DeFilippis (New York: Routledge, 2019), 93–107 (particularly 95–98).

81 Lea Seguin, "The Good, the Bad, and the Ugly: Lay Attitudes and Perceptions of Polyamory," *Sexualities* 22, no. 4 (2019): 684.

82 Importantly, Pascar highlights that these portrayals are often racialized. See Pascar, "Homonormativity to Polynormativity," 95–98.

83 Jaime M. Gher, "Polygamy and Same-Sex Marriage—Allies or Adversaries within the Same-Sex Marriage Movement," *William and Mary Journal of Race, Gender, and Social Justice* 14, no. 3 (2008): 559–603.

84 Kaila Adia Story, "On the Cusp of Deviance: Respectability Politics and the Cultural Marketplace of Sameness," in *No Tea, No Shade: New Writings in Black Queer Studies*, ed. E. Patrick Johnson (Durham: Duke University Press, 2016), 373.

85 Ibid., 99. On an empirical analysis of the importance of coming out to the shaping of majority public opinion on gay and lesbian rights, see Jeremiah J. Garretson, *The Path to Gay Rights: How Activism and Coming Out Changed Public Opinion* (New York: New York University Press, 2018).

86 Pascar, "Homonormativity to Polynormativity," 99.

87 Ibid., 100.

88 Goldhill, "Polyamorous Sex."

89 M. J. Nöel, "Progressive Polyamory: Considering Issues of Diversity," *Sexualities* 9, no. 5 (2006): 602–20; H. L. Sklar, "Meet the Swingers," *SELF*, March 2010, www.self.com. But more recent analysis suggests this depiction may be an artifact of sampling techniques that render diversity within this community invisible. See Jennifer D. Rubin, Amy C. Moors, Jes L. Mastick, Ali Ziegler, and Terri Conley, "On the Margins: Considering Diversity among Consensually Non-monogamous Relationships," *Journal für Psychologie* 22, no. 1 (2014): 19–37.

90 Myrl Beam, "What's Love Got to Do with It?," in *Queer Activism after Marriage Equality*, ed. Joseph Nicholas DeFilippis, Michael W. Yarbrough, and Angela Jones (London: Routledge, 2018), 55, 54 (emphasis added).

91 Ibid., 55.

92 Pascar, "Homonormativity to Polynormativity," 101.

93 Christian Klesse, "Polyamory and Its 'Others': Contesting the Terms of Non-monogamy," *Sexualities* 9, no. 5 (2006): 566.

94 Klesse, *Spectre of Promiscuity*, 114.

95 Some discourse seeking to normalize polyamory relies on a neoliberal conception of personal choice. Schippers notes, "In the how-to poly literature and in mainstream treatments of polyamory, for instance, there is a neoliberal emphasis on polyamory as an individual choice and as a matter of taste or relationship orientation." But Schippers also notes how poly relationships could also "transform gender, race, and class relations or how it might lead to rethinking intimacy more generally." Schippers, "Monogamous Couple," 325. See also Rambukkana, *Fraught Intimacies*.

96 Klesse, *Spectre of Promiscuity*, 114.

97 Pascar, "Homonormativity to Polynormativity," 105.

98 We build on scholarship that has pushed to understand the Thirteenth Amendment as not only banning slavery but banning treatment premised on any badge of inferiority. See Douglas L. Colbert, "Liberating the Thirteenth Amendment," *Harvard Civil Rights-Civil Liberties Law Review* 30 (1995): 1–56, which suggests that the amendment's ban on such "badges" can be extended to apply "to citizens from any race or class who have [been] branded with a badge of inferiority" (1). See also William M. Carter Jr., "A Thirteenth Amendment Framework for Combating Racial Profiling," *Harvard Civil Rights-Civil Liberties Law Review* 39 (2004): 17–94, which views racial profiling as a Thirteenth Amendment violation, since the practice is premised on the stigmatization of African Americans as more likely to commit crimes. For an application of the Thirteenth Amendment to anti-LGBTQ+ discrimination, see David P. Tedhams, "The Reincarnation of 'Jim Crow:' A Thirteenth Amendment Analysis of Colorado's Amendment 2," *Temple Political and Civil Rights Law Review* 4 (1994–95): 133–65.

99 While the Supreme Court played a role in curbing the reach of the Thirteenth and Fourteenth Amendments, other forces, such as an economic depression that depleted resources for federal civil rights enforcement as well as a resurgent Democratic Congress also undermined Reconstruction's potential. See Pamela Brandwein, *Rethinking the Judicial Settlement of Reconstruction* (New York: Cambridge University Press, 2014).

100 See Pamela Brandwein, *Reconstructing Constitution: The Supreme Court and the Production of Historical Truth* (Durham: Duke University Press, 1999).

101 *Masterpiece Cakeshop v. Colorado Civil Rights Commission*, 584 U.S. _____ (2018).

102 *The Civil Rights Cases*, 109 U.S. 3 (*1883*). For a discussion of the state action doctrine, see Fallon, *Dynamic Constitution*, 336–39.

103 *Heart of Atlanta Motel, Inc. v. United States*, 379 U.S. 241 (1964).

104 See *Katzenbach v. McClung*, 379 U.S. 294 (1964); and *Daniel v. Paul*, 395 U.S. 298 (1969); the Court summarizes the content and limits of its commerce clause jurisprudence in *United States v. Alfonso D. Lopez, Jr.*, 514 U.S. 549 (1995).

105 *Civil Rights Act of 1875* (18 Stat. 335–337).

106 *The Civil Rights Cases*, 109 U.S. 3 (*1883*).

107 Ibid., 12.

108 *Heart of Atlanta Motel, Inc. v. United States*, 379 U.S. 241 (1964), 251.

109 Importantly, Title VII of the 1964 Civil Rights Act bans discrimination in employment on the basis of sex. So while sexual orientation is not mentioned in any section of the act, such discrimination could violate that act if it is viewed as a form of sex discrimination. Since sex discrimination is unconstitutional if grounded in gender stereotypes that inhibit equal opportunity (see *Craig v. Boren*, 429 U.S. 190 [1976]), then discrimination on the basis of sexual orientation could be grounded in the idea that LGBTQ+ individuals violate the stereotypical behaviors assigned to their gender or perceived gender identity.

The Equal Employment Opportunity Commission endorsed this reading of Title VII in *Macy v. Department of Justice*, EEOC Appeal No. 0120120821 (April 20, 2012) and in *David Baldwin v. Department of Transportation*, EEOC Appeal No. 120133080 (July 15, 2015). The Supreme Court reached the same conclusion in *Bostock v. Clayton County*, 590 U.S. _____ (2020). Importantly, Title VII contains the word *sex*, which Title II does not. This difference suggests that the *Bostock* ruling might not help resolve a claim of sexual orientation or gender discrimination in public accommodations.

110 Indeed, this position is often voiced in contemporary legal journalism. For example, in critiquing a 2019 Arizona State Supreme Court ruling that protected a small business from being compelled to provide wedding invitations to same-sex couples, Jeffrey Toobin writes, "The owners of Brush & Nib are free to believe anything they want. What they should not be allowed to do is to use those beliefs to run a business that is open to the general public but closed to gay people." And he defends this position by referencing Justice Clark's argument centered on dignity in *Heart of Atlanta*. See Jeffrey Toobin, "The Right Wing's War on the L.G.B.T.Q. Community," *New Yorker*, September 19, 2019.

111 As the Court ruled, "The very fact that colored people are singled out . . . is practically a brand upon them, affixed by the law, an assertion of their inferiority, and a stimulant to that race prejudice which is an impediment to securing to individuals of the race that equal justice which the law aims to secure to all others." *Strauder v. West Virginia*, 100 U.S. 303 (1880), 309.

112 *The Civil Rights Cases*, 109 U.S. 3 (1883), 109.

113 Republicans, during the years that immediately preceded the Civil War, often framed Southern slave-holders, the entire South, or the Democratic Party as a Slave Power conspiracy, which threatened the liberties granted by the First Amendment and the Constitution more broadly. On the difference conceptions and scope of the Slave Power conspiracy, see Michael Pfau, *The Political Style of Conspiracy: Chase, Sumner, and Lincoln* (Lansing: Michigan State University Press, 2003).

114 See Brandwein, *Reconstructing Constitution*, 42–60. See also George Rutherglen, "The Badges and Incidents of Slavery and the Power of Congress to Enforce the Thirteenth Amendment," in *Promises of Liberty: The History and Contemporary Relevance of the Thirteenth Amendment*, ed. Alexander Tsesis (New York: Columbia University Press, 2010).

115 *Congressional Globe*, 39th Congress, First Session 2394 (Phelps, May 4) quoted in Brandwein, *Reconstructing Constitution*, 48. Brandwein details why and how this vision of emancipation was abandoned by Congress, but it is also evident in the dissents offered in the first Supreme Court decision to interpret the meaning of the Thirteenth and Fourteenth Amendments, *The Slaughter-House Cases of 1873*. For example, Justice Stephen Johnson Field spoke to the vast array of rights that would follow from these amendments and that were to be protected by the federal government against state infringement (*Slaughter-House Cases*, 83 U.S. 36 [1873],

102). And Justice Swayne spoke to how these amendments should be understood as a new regard for national power to protect individuals from state attempts to curb rights: "They are, in this respect, at the opposite pole from the first eleven" (*Slaughter-House Cases*, 83 U.S. 36 [1873], 126).

116 George Rutherglen, "State Action, Private Action, and the Thirteenth Amendment," *Virginia Law Review* 94, no. 6 (October 2008): 1368.

117 See Mark Tushnet, "The Politics of Equality in Constitutional Law: The Equal Protection Clause, Dr. Du Bois, and Charles Hamilton Houston," *Journal of American History* 74, no. 3 (1987): 884–903.

118 *Plessy v. Ferguson*, 163 U.S. 537 (1896): "If the civil and political rights of both races be equal, one cannot be inferior to the other civilly or politically. If one race be inferior to the other socially, the Constitution of the United States cannot put them upon the same plane" (552–53).

119 For another argument that highlights how racism undergirds the state action doctrine, see Francisco M. Ugarte, "Reconstruction Redux: Rehnquist, Morrison, and the Civil Rights Cases," *Harvard Civil Rights-Civil Liberties Law Review* 41, no. 2 (Summer 2006): 481–508.

120 Brandwein, *Reconstructing Constitution*, 48.

121 Ibid.

122 For a comprehensive history of Reconstruction, see Eric Foner, *Reconstruction: America's Unfinished Revolution, 1863–1877* (New York: Harper and Row, 1988).

123 *State v. Gibson*, 36 Ind. 389 (1871); *The Slaughter-House Cases*, 83 U.S. 36 (1873).

124 An Act to Protect All Persons in the United States in Their Civil Rights, and Furnish the Means of Their Vindication, ch. 31, 14 Stat. 27, 27 (1866); U.S. Constitution, Amendment 14, sec. 1 (adopted 1868); see Peggy Pascoe, *What Comes Naturally: Miscegenation Law and the Making of Race in America* (New York: Oxford University Press, 2009), 33.

125 Pascoe, *What Comes Naturally*, 39.

126 *Bonds v. Foster*, 36 Tex. 68, 69 (1872).

127 Pascoe, *What Comes Naturally*, 39.

128 Footnote q in Allen H. Bush, *A Digest of the Statute Law of Florida of a General and Public Character, in Force up to the First Day of January, 1872* (Tallahassee, FL: C. H. Walton, 1872), 578, quoted in Pascoe, *What Comes Naturally*, 41.

129 Pascoe, *What Comes Naturally*, 40.

130 James Schouler, *A Treatise on The Law of Domestic Relations*, 6th ed. (Boston: Little Brown, 1870), 29.

131 *State v. Gibson*, 36 Ind. 389 (1871), 402.

132 On police power, see William J. Novak, *The People's Welfare: Law and Regulation in Nineteenth-Century America* (Chapel Hill: University of North Carolina Press, 1993).

133 *Plessy v. Ferguson*, 163 U.S. 537 (1896), 551.

134 *The Civil Rights Cases*, 109 U.S. 3 (1883), 35, J. Harlan dissenting.

135 Speaking against the Louisiana statute that required whites to use separate train cars than other races, Harlan held the Thirteenth Amendment to be a declaration against stigmatization, which "not only struck down the institution of slavery as previously existing in the United States, but . . . prevents the imposition of any burdens or disabilities that constitute badges of slavery or servitude" (*Plessy v. Ferguson*, 163 U.S. 537 [1896], 555).

136 *Pace v. Alabama*, 106 U.S. 583 (1883). See, generally, Julie Novkov, *Racial Union: Law, Intimacy, and the White State in Alabama, 1865–1954* (Ann Arbor: University of Michigan Press, 2009).

137 Andrea Sangiovanni, *Humanity without Dignity: Moral Equality, Respect, and Human Rights* (Cambridge, MA: Harvard University Press, 2017), 4.

138 *Jones v. Alfred H. Mayer Co.*, 392 U.S. 409 (1968).

139 Ibid., 441, 443.

140 William M. Carter Jr. has argued that the full potential of the Thirteenth Amendment has not been realized and that the language of the amendment goes beyond protecting African Americans, even as his expansive reading still centers on race. William M. Carter Jr., "The Thirteenth Amendment, Interest Convergence, and the Badges and Incidents of Slavery," *Maryland Law Review* 71 (2011): 21–39.

141 Reva B. Siegel, "Constitutional Culture, Social Movement Conflict, and Constitutional Change: The Case of the de facto ERA," *California Law Review* 94, no. 5 (October 2006): 1323–1419. On interpreting the Constitution as guaranteeing sex equality through an intratextual reading of the Nineteenth and Fourteenth Amendments, see Akhil Reed Amar, "The Supreme Court, 1999 Term—Foreword: The Document and the Doctrine," *Harvard Law Review* 114 (2000): 26–134; see also Vicki C. Jackson, "Holistic Interpretation: Fitzpatrick v. Bitzer and Our Bifurcated Constitution," *Stanford Law Review* 53, no. 5 (2001): 1259–1310. One argument is that the Nineteenth Amendment, which grants suffrage to women, alters the meaning of the Fourteenth Amendment to include sex equality. See Steven G. Calabresi and Julia Rickert, "Originalism and Sex Discrimination," *Texas Law Review* 90, no. 1 (2011): 1–101.

142 See William M. Carter Jr., "Race, Rights, and the Thirteenth Amendment: Defining the Badges and Incidents of Slavery," *U.C. Davis Law Review* 40, no. 4 (April 2007): 1357.

143 *United States v. Rhodes*, 27 F. Cas. 785, 793 (1866).

144 *McDonald v. Santa Fe Transportation Co.*, 427 U.S. 273 (1976), 295 (emphasis added).

145 277 F.3d 164 (2nd Cir. 2002), *cert. denied* 537 U.S. 835 (2002).

146 Carter, "Race," 1363. Carter argues that this position is "problematic" inasmuch as it completely severs the amendment from its context of a particular concern with African slavery.

147 Ibid., 1365. Importantly, Carter disagrees with the Court's broad interpretation, writing, "The fact that the Amendment prohibits the actual enslavement of any

person does not compel the conclusion that any person of any race or class can suffer a badge or incident of slavery."

148 *Masterpiece Cakeshop v. Colorado Civil Rights Commission*, 584 U.S. ___ (2018) (slip opinion), 5, J. Gorsuch concurring.

149 Ibid., 6, J. Ginsburg dissenting.

150 *Masterpiece Cakeshop v. Colorado Civil Rights Commission*, 584 U.S. ___ (2018) (slip opinion), 3, J. Gorsuch concurring.

151 *Masterpiece Cakeshop v. Colorado Civil Rights Commission*, 584 U.S. ___ (2018) (slip opinion), 3, J. Kagan concurring.

152 Of course, the deep irony of this rationale is that it reinforces the troubling logic of sameness that we have explored and critiqued throughout this book—namely, that for same-sex couples to be protected (i.e., for their equal access to wedding cakes to be assured), any difference cannot be acknowledged much less celebrated. Equal protection, in this rendering, demands sameness.

153 *United States v. Windsor*, 570 U.S. 744 (2013), 764.

154 For example, Pascoe's *What Comes Naturally*, an account of bans on interracial sex and marriage in the United States, uncovers how socially constructed notions of white supremacy are naturalized over time so that they become commonsensical.

We suggest that Justice Thomas's attempt to construct dignity as a natural right rather than a socially constructed concept similarly naturalizes hierarchies of value, thereby masking how dignity can be deployed as an exercise of power.

155 Brandwein, *Reconstructing Constitution*, 7.

CONCLUSION

1 Brittney Cooper, *Eloquent Rage: A Black Feminist Discovers Her Superpower* (New York: Picador, 2018), 273.

2 Dignity as respect is vulnerable to the problems associated with a thin liberal pluralism, or the notion that the state should be as minimal as possible in order to promote the maximum amount of individual choice. For defenses of liberal neutrality, see Matthew Clayton, *Justice and Legitimacy in Upbringing* (New York: Oxford University Press, 2006); Steven Lecce, *Against Perfectionism: Defending Liberal Neutrality* (Toronto: Toronto University Press, 2008); and Jonathan Quong, *Liberalism without Perfection* (New York: Oxford University Press, 2011). Summarizing the challenge but appeal of liberal neutrality, Andrew Koppelman writes, "Neutrality is unsustainable when it is formulated this abstractly, but it is nonetheless a valuable political ideal. One of the many ways that government can go wrong is to take a position on some question that it would, all things considered, be better for it to abstain from deciding." Andrew Koppelman, "The Fluidity of Neutrality," *Review of Politics* 66, no. 4 (2004): 633.

3 Indeed, Joseph Raz has shown that a robust responsibility to support flourishing can, perhaps paradoxically, be derived as a core principle of negative

freedom—namely, the autonomy of the self. Raz defines *autonomy* as the capacity for self-realization, and thus freedom demands the provision of meaningful options. His idea of positive freedom—the capacity to create and control one's own life—is essential for the realization of autonomy. Consequently, negative freedom is valuable only insofar as it supports this self-creation. If the state is considered duty-bound to promote the good life conceived merely as individual autonomy, then the state must provide the resources for individual opportunity. Autonomy and, by extension, freedom are only possible in a society that offers meaningful options. See Joseph Raz, *The Morality of Freedom* (New York: Oxford University Press, 1988). For a similar notion of freedom as realized through supports to accessible opportunity, see James Fishkin, *Bottlenecks: A New Theory of Equal Opportunity* (New York: Oxford University Press, 2016).

4 As Steven Canals said in an interview marking the premiere of *Pose's* second season, "My feeling was, I just don't buy into the rhetoric [that] there is no LGBTQ talent or, specifically, there's no trans talent out there. There is, and I'm proud to now be able to use my show as a model to say, 'You're just not looking hard enough.' Clearly, you aren't, because we've got a bunch of folks here!" Steven Canals quoted in Pat King, "Ryan Murphy, Steven Canals and Janet Mock on the Bold Second Season of 'Pose,'" *Metro*, June 11, 2019, www.metro.us (accessed August 5, 2019). And Janet Mock notes how Ryan Murphy encouraged her to become the first trans woman to direct a television episode and served as a mentor:

> As a woman, a black person and a trans individual, I carry the gift and burden of multiple communities in an industry where those communities rarely hold power or control. I've had to carve out a path where there was none. "Who better to tell this story than you?" Ryan asked when I questioned his offer. "You wrote it, and you lived it. No one is more qualified." Ryan didn't only give me a shot and words of encouragement; he invited me to shadow him and director Gwyneth Horder-Payton. He was a phone call away when I started prep, he stood nearby as I completed my first few days of shooting, and he stepped away when the doubt finally subsided and gave way to greater confidence—a confidence that I can now impart to others directing for the first time.

Janet Mock, "'Pose' Writer-Producer: What I Learned from My First Directing Experience," *Hollywood Reporter*, June 7, 2019, www.hollywoodreporter.com (accessed August 5, 2019).

5 See, for example, Kelson Northeimer, "The Making (and Marketing) of the Modern Gayborhood," *Hidden City: Exploring Philadelphia's Urban Landscape*, May 12, 2017, https://hiddencityphila.org (accessed June 22, 2020); and Sarah Friedmann, "Examining the Past, Present, and Future of Chicago's First Gay Neighborhood," Daily Beast, July 25, 2019, www.thedailybeast.com (accessed June 22, 2020).

6   For example, Steamworks Chicago is located in "Boystown," the historic gaybor-
    hood of the East Lakeview neighborhood. The neighborhood is demarcated by
    rainbow pylons along Halsted Street. For a discussion of this area, see Amin
    Ghaziani, *There Goes the Gayborhood?* (Princeton: Princeton University Press,
    2015); and Jason Orne, *Boystown: Sex and Community in Chicago* (Chicago: Uni-
    versity of Chicago Press, 2017).

7   See Theodore Greene, "Queer Street Families: Place-Making and Community
    among LGBT Youth of Color in Iconic Gay Neighborhoods," in *Queer Families
    and Relationships after Marriage Equality*, ed. Michael Yarbrough, Angela
    Jones, and Joseph Nicholas DeFilippis (New York: Routledge, 2019): 168–81.

8   Clinton quoted in Abbey Phillip and Anne Gearan, "Hillary Clinton Apologizes
    for Praising Nancy Reagan's Response to HIV/AIDS," *Washington Post*, March 11,
    2016, www.washingtonpost.com (accessed August 1, 2016).

9   Peter Staley quoted in Mathew Rodriguez, "Ronald and Nancy Reagan Ignored
    the AIDS Crisis and You Know It, Hillary Clinton," Mic.com, March 11, 2016,
    https://mic.com (accessed August 1, 2016).

10 Clinton quoted in Phillip and Gearan, "Hillary Clinton Apologizes."

11 David Atkins, "How Clinton's Reagan-AIDS Gaffe Helps Explain Why Populism
    Is Rising," *Washington Monthly*, March 12, 2016, http://washingtonmonthly.com
    (accessed August 1, 2016); Kevin Naff, "Hillary's Painful Mistake," *Washington
    Blade*, March 14, 2016, www.washingtonblade.com (accessed August 1, 2016).

12 James West, "'I Made a Mistake, Plain and Simple': Clinton Issues Longer Apology
    for Praising Nancy Reagan's AIDS Record," *Mother Jones*, March 12, 2016, www
    .motherjones.com (assessed August 1, 2016).

13 Hillary Clinton, "On the Fight against HIV and AIDS—and on the People Who
    Really Started the Conversation," *Medium*, March 12, 2016, https://medium.com
    (accessed August 1, 2016).

14 Larry Kramer quoted in "If Larry Kramer Can Accept Hillary Clinton's Apology,
    So Can I," *Randy Report* (blog), March 13, 2016, www.got-blogger.com (accessed
    August 1, 2016).

15 Deborah Gould, *Moving Politics: Emotion and ACT UP's Fight against AIDS* (Chi-
    cago: University of Chicago Press, 2009), 58.

16 Jennifer Brier, *Infectious Ideas: U.S. Political Responses to the AIDS Crisis* (Chapel
    Hill: University of North Carolina Press, 2009), 7.

17 Clinton, "On the Fight."

18 Ibid.

19 Saunders quoted in "Toronto Police Chief Mark Saunders Apologizes for 1981 Gay
    Bathhouse Raids," *CBC News*, June 22, 2016, www.cbc.ca (accessed September 3,
    2016).

20 John Ibbitson, "Justin Trudeau to Apologize for Historic Persecution of Gay
    Canadians," *Globe and Mail*, August 11, 2016, www.theglobeandmail.com
    (accessed September 3, 2016).

21 Ibid.

22 Individuals convicted before the Sexual Offenses Act of 1967 lifted the ban already had a procedure in place by which they could have their convictions expunged.

23 Sam Gyimah quoted in Owen Bowcott, "UK Issues Posthumous Pardons for Thousands of Gay Men," *Guardian*, January 31, 2017, www.theguardian.com (last accessed November 10, 2019). "Turing" refers to Alan Turing, the famed British mathematician who broke the German Enigma Code during World War II but was later convicted for the "gross indecency" of same-sex intimacy and subsequently committed suicide.

24 Tim Dean, "Mediated Intimacies: Raw Sex, Truvada, and the Biopolitics of Chemoprophylaxis," *Sexualities* 18, nos. 1/2 (2015): 226.

25 Gayle Rubin, "Thinking Sex: Notes for a Radical Theory of the Politics of Sexuality," in *Pleasure and Danger: Exploring Female Sexuality*, ed. Carole S. Vance (London: Pandora, 1992), 283.

INDEX

Foucault, Michel, 381n69

Fourteenth Amendment, 11, 226, 246, 248, 251, 264, 269, 287, 289–90, 302, 377n161; interpretations of, 231, 236, 239, 255, 269, 276, 283–86, 292; protections of, 5; racism and, 22; reach of, 384n99

Fourth Amendment, 11

Freeman, Gregory, 101

Friedman-Kien, Alvin, 54, 55

Fundamentalist Church of Jesus Christ of Latter-Day Saints, 279

Gay Activists Alliance, 35

gayborhoods, 302–3, 390n6

Gay Men's Health Crisis (GMHC), 44, 45, 55, 304

gay pride, 33, 34, 158

geolocative social media apps, 20, 24, 64, 81–92, 114–15, 336n97; non-monogamy and, 279, 382n75

Gibson v. Indiana, 289

Gift, The (Hogarth), 66, 101–2, 104, 105–9, 110–11, 113–14

Gilead Sciences Inc., 93–94

Ginsburg, Ruth Bader, 293–94

GMHC. *See* Gay Men's Health Crisis

Goldhill, Olivia, 281

Gonzales v. Carhart, 250

"good gay," 65, 227

Goodridge v. Public Health, 277

Gorsuch, Neil, 223, 226, 248, 252–53, 257, 258, 293, 294, 372n86

Gossett, Che, 174, 218–19

Gossett, Reina, 172–74

Green, Adam Isaiah, 37

Griffin-Gracy, Miss Major, 174, 196

Grindr, 64, 83–88, 89, 91

Gun-Cock (Higginson), 104

Gyimah, Sam, 307

HAART. *See* highly active anti-retroviral therapy

Halberstam, Jack, *The Queer Art of Failure*, 14–16

Hallward-Driemeier, Douglas, 229

Halperin, David, 13

Harlan, John Marshall, 238, 290–92, 387n135

Hart Island, New York City, New York, 1, 184–85, 307

Harvey, David, 7

healthcare, 93–94, 115; access to, 338n136; limited access to, 247, 252, 375n140

Heart of Atlanta Motel, Inc. v. United States, 285

Helms, Jesse, 207

Henry, Leslie Meltzer, 319n54, 367n14

HER app, 89

heteronormativity, 7, 16–17, 122, 129, 133, 134, 162, 172; boundaries and, 31; challenges to, 295; couplehood and, 264; dignity and, 265; family and, 212; gaze and, 169; homonormativity and, 124; ideal of, and same-sex marriage, 11–12; liberation from, 34; logics of, 35, 173, 300, 310; marriage and, 227–28; neoliberal, 66; non-monogamy excluded from, 278; privacy and, 59; productivity standards and, 39; resistance to, 278; standards, threatening of, 18; transgression of, 61, 278

heterosexism, 149

HHS. *See* Department of Health and Human Services

Higginson, James, *Gun-Cock*, 104

highly active anti-retroviral therapy (HAART), 92

Hindman, Matthew, 7, 8, 228

history-building, 183–84

HIV: bathhouses and, 30; criminalization of, 97; discovery of, 52; intentional transmission of, 20, 64, 65–66, 100–114, 115; as manageable, 65, 94, 114; transmission risk reduction, 64–65

ABOUT THE AUTHORS

Stephen M. Engel (he/him/his) is Professor of Politics at Bates College in Maine and an Affiliated Scholar of the American Bar Foundation. He teaches courses in US constitutional law, American political development, and LGBTQ+ politics. He is the author of multiple books, including *Fragmented Citizens: The Changing Landscape of Gay and Lesbian Lives* and *American Politicians Confront the Court: Opposition Politics and Changing Responses to Judicial Power*.

Timothy S. Lyle (they/them) is Assistant Professor of English at Iona College. They specialize in contemporary African American literature and culture, focusing on the intersections of race, gender, sexuality, and disability. They have published work on Tyler Perry in *Callaloo* and *Continuum*; on Janet Mock in the *College Language Association Journal*, *Callaloo*, and *MELUS*; and on HIV/AIDS narratives in *African American Review* and the *Journal of West Indian Literature*.